Dark Nights of the Soul:

Reflections on Faith and the Depressed Brain,
2nd Ed.

*With Dedication, Foreword, Acknowledgements, and bonus essay
"The One Thing: The 5,000 Most Important Words I Have Ever
Written (So Far)"*

By
David Anderson, MTS, ThM, MLIS

Independently published

www.davidandersontheauthor.com

Independently published
David Anderson, MTS., ThM, MLIS
www.davidandersontheauthor.com

Book Layout © 2017 BookDesignTemplates.com

Dark Nights of the Soul: Reflections on Faith and the Depressed Brain/ David Anderson. – 2nd ed.
ISBN 978-1-7343703-0-0

To Dr. B.J. Seymour, d. 2010

… to put off your old self, which belongs to your former manner of
life and is corrupt through deceitful desires, and to be renewed in the
spirit of your minds.
—Ephesians 4:22–23 ESV

For the being who has conquered the mind, that being's mind is the
best of friends; but for one whose mind is uncontrolled, that very mind
acts as the worst of enemies.
—Bhagavad Gita 6:6

CONTENTS

Foreword: On Chemical Imbalances and Winning Awards

I'm very excited to say the original ebook version of this volume won first place, category nonfiction, in the 2019 Self-Published Ebook Awards from *Writer's Digest*. This version you have now (whether ebook or paperback) has the same content and more.

The length of the original version was about 25,000 words. That's fine for an ebook, but it needed more to be viable for print. That gave me the opportunity to add this foreword, acknowledgments, and a dedication to my favorite college professor, without whom I might have no real faith to speak of today. And the format of the references needed to be corrected.

It still needed more, so at the end, there is a bonus essay called "The One Thing: The 5,000 Most Important Words I Have Ever Written (So Far)."

However, this foreword is not just about patting myself on the back or additional material not in the original version. Recently, it has come to my attention that one of the theories on which this book is based is controversial. When I was diagnosed with clinical depression, the psychologist explained what it means this way. My brain doesn't get enough natural antidepressants like serotonin, dopamine, and norepinephrine, so it needs help, the same way a diabetic does not produce insulin naturally. The theory of "chemical imbalance" has guided my recovery to a great extent.

Among some experts, however, this theory is falling out of favor. Because of that, I need to explain why I still believe my depression came, at least in part, from a chemical imbalance.

From what I understand, here are the main reasons why some experts reject a person's biology and chemical imbalance as causes of depression:

- It leaves out or minimizes the impact of traumatic experience and modern lifestyle on depression.

- Medication for chemical imbalances in the brain has a high failure rate.

- Genetic causes cannot explain the epidemic of depression we have seen in the last thirty years or so.

I feel like this is an unnecessary war between two philosophies. We could call it nature versus nurture. Nature includes genetics and brain chemistry. Nurture includes traumatic life experiences and some aspects of modern lifestyle that appear to contribute to depression. The experts on the nature side say the nurture side is wrong because they ignore how nature can predispose someone to depression. The nurture side says the nature side is wrong because only nurture can explain the rapid upsurge in rates of depression in modern times.

Why does either side have to be wrong? We accept that many aspects of health and personality are the product of *both* nature and nurture. *Why can't we accept the causes of depression could be a combination of genetics, brain chemistry, traumatic experiences, and lifestyle?*

I'm no expert, but I have done a lot of research trying to understand the nature of my depression. I am still convinced it came from a chemical imbalance in my brain that I was born with. That is not true for everyone, and I never claim it is. But here are the reasons I believe *my* depression was at least in part genetic.

- There is a strong history of depression in my family.

- I didn't have any great traumatic life experience as a child or adult, but I still struggled with depression all my life.

- Medication worked for me.

To further distinguish between nature and nurture, I talk about clinical versus situational depression. Situational depression usually has a clear trigger: the death of a loved one, an important relationship ended, a significant loss like a home or a job, surviving violence and abuse, a debilitating physical illness, and so on. Clinical depression, on the other hand, does not have any clear trigger and needs to be professionally diagnosed. This is the type believed to be caused by a chemical imbalance in the brain and likely to be a product of genetics.

If, like me, you struggle with depression, even when you don't see any clear reason for it, I urge you to get tested. Once I knew I had clinical depression, the path to recovery became much clearer. And more than anything, it forced me to acknowledge I needed treatment.

Other reasons some people oppose the theory of chemical imbalance are more emotional or social than medical. They say talking about depression as a brain disorder makes them more pessimistic about their chances of recovery, and it makes others less sympathetic. A difference in brain chemistry, some people think, marks you as "other" or less than human.

It is certainly not my intention to make people pessimistic about their chances of recovery. When I was diagnosed, at first it was devastating. But a good psychologist can not only diagnose you but also help you work out a treatment plan, like mine did. We talked medication and counseling. He recommended a pastoral counselor, because I knew I needed someone who could address the issues of faith that made me feel more depressed. With medication, I noticed a difference immediately. I had more resilience to deal with the ups and downs of life. It does not work for everyone, but it worked for me.

What if medication had not worked? I don't know how I would have felt. But I understand how if you've been told your depression is genetic or based in brain chemistry, *and* medication does not work, that can be terribly discouraging. Whether it works for you or not, your strategy for recovery should *never* be medication only. Medication might help you cope with the feelings that can overwhelm you, but you still need to deal with the thoughts, emotions, and life experiences that weigh you down.

Those who criticize the psychiatric and similar professions say they only talk about medication and counseling. You have to understand that is how they are trained. For you as a patient, the path from depression to happiness often begins with medication and counseling, but real recovery goes beyond that. If those things did not work, you might have got the wrong medication or the wrong counselor for you. And these are not the only options available. Most people who truly recover have more than one or two tools in their therapy plan. Medication and counseling can be a beginning, but they are not the end. That's why I include a chapter called "Tools for Depression" that has twenty-two scientifically proven ways to alleviate depression and promote happiness.

As for others being less sympathetic when they hear you have a mental illness, a brain disorder, or a chemical imbalance, I think that is changing. I certainly hope it is. Many celebrities are speaking openly about how they were diagnosed with depression, anxiety, bipolar disorder, panic attacks, PTSD, OCD, and so on. Princes William and Harry have become great advocates for mental health worldwide. And if Duane "the Rock" Johnson says he struggles with depression, are you going to call him a wimp or a freak? I may have a brain disorder, but at least I'm not a fool. Like other celebrities, they are coming forward to take away the stigma that comes with these labels, and I for one applaud them.

To anyone who sees us as "other" because we have a mental illness, whether it is the result of genetics or trauma, our brains might work differently from yours. That does not mean we are inhuman. It does not make it okay to bully us. We don't need you to coddle us. All we ask for is access to effective treatment, the same pursuit of happiness we all have a right to, and a little understanding.

David Anderson
January 4, 2020

Acknowledgments

I need to thank those who showed me recovery from depression is possible. My mother and sister, who urged me to get tested. The neuropsychiatrist (I'm actually not sure what his title is. I just know he was a trained mental health expert) who diagnosed me, eased me through the initial shock, and helped set up my first treatment plan. The counselor who first took me on. The pastors who showed me the Bible really is about justice, righteousness, and loving your neighbor as yourself: David Bailey, Nibs Stroupe, and Allen Fisher especially. My father who has been amazingly supportive of my education (all those degrees after my name) and my writing endeavors. My Aunt Dottie, who has prayed for me probably more than anyone else alive.

And there are countless more. The many church members whose friendship helped me through more dark nights of the soul than I could tell you. My extended family of 1) aunts, uncles, and cousins I look forward to seeing every year at our two family reunions, and 2) in-laws through both my sister's and my own marriages, who have grown our family exponentially.

A special thanks to Fran, the love of my life. The healing that made it possible for me to write about recovery and happiness began when she agreed to meet me for coffee and a critique session.

When I decided to self-publish this book, I knew I would need help. Thanks to Chandler Bolt and the Self-Publishing School community for their coaching and support through the process, and to everyone on my launch team for helping to spread the word about this project.

Should I thank God? Since the ebook won an award from *Writer's Digest* (as I mentioned in the Foreword), I guess it's mandatory. So yes, I thank God for that. But even without any awards, you gave me the gift of communing with you through writing. That is all the reason I need to thank you from the bottom of my heart.

And, of course, I must thank *Writer's Digest* for choosing this as the winner in the nonfiction category for self-published ebooks. As a child, I dreamed of appearing in *Sports Illustrated*. As an adult, I realized my talents were much more literary than athletic. So today, winning my category in a *Writer's Digest* contest is a dream come true on the same level as *Sports Illustrated* to the child I once was.

Wrestling with Divine and Human Beings

On August 19, 2015, I started a blog called "Fawns of Naphtali." It started as a Bible study blog and morphed into a blog about faith and recovery from depression. I worked on it for about two years, posting once a week. It didn't get many visitors. Maybe it's because I broke the first rule of getting found on the web: *Use a name and URL that people are actually searching for*. Not too many people say, "Hey Google, find me that Fawns of Naphtali site."

But I thought the name was appropriate. Fawns of Naphtali comes from Jacob's blessing to his son Naphtali (Genesis 49:21). The Hebrew text can be translated two ways:

> *Naphtali is a doe let loose that bears lovely fawns (NRSV).*

> *Naphtali is a doe let loose, He gives beautiful words (NASB).*

Jacob says his son bears lovely fawns, and that appears to be an expression for creating beautiful words. But beautiful words don't come easy. The name Naphtali means "My wrestling" (Gen 30:8). My words come from wrestling with divine and human beings (Gen 32:25-28), and I like to think they are lovely fawns, even if it is wishful thinking.

Even though my blog did not reach many people, I still think there must be others who wonder why they are depressed despite their faith. So I've gathered together the posts that explore the relationship between faith and depression. In order to put those blog posts into a book, I have edited some for clarity, grammar, and consistency, and to answer some questions my editor and beta readers had. I included posting dates for most of them. I also removed photos, because the formatting doesn't always work in an eBook and makes print books more expensive.

I've found there are some kinds of faith that are good for recovery and healing, and some that are bad. If you're looking for an "I overcame depression through Jesus" book, this is not it. This is about real experience, not a phony testimonial or religious clichés. And yet I have found that faith and happiness are possible, even for me—and you—if you understand the nature of the depressed brain.

Here are the four principles that guide my recovery.

1. God is for your recovery and healing, not against it.

2. God will not kick you when you're down.

3. Some kinds of faith are good for recovery, and some are bad. Make sure you know the difference.

4. With the right help—spiritually, psychologically, emotionally, and perhaps medically—you can live a happy and fulfilling life. You just need to learn how to stop your depressed brain from sabotaging it.

I would love to promise that if you follow my principles, you will never be depressed again. But I've been given too many false promises, and you probably have, too. That is why I have principles for recovery, not steps (with apologies to AA, because I love their program). Principles are not solutions. They are simply rules for living that will get you moving toward recovery. I can't promise you anything, but I can tell you these principles (even before I knew how to put them into words) have seen me through more than a few dark nights of the soul.

Now here's a look at what's ahead.

###

The chapters titled "Depressed Christian," Parts 1 and 2, address specific issues of depression in the life of a Christian. Some depression is normal, and some is a sign you need help. I explain the distinction between situational depression and clinical depression. I'll tell you how I found out I had the latter. The chapters also include some guidelines, with specific examples, for separating good information from bad. You will see I have some very strong opinions on that issue. Those opinions come from years of experience, so you won't have to learn the hard way, like I did.

"The Voice ... That No One Wants to Hear" is about the voice that speaks in the clinically depressed brain. It will say things like, *You're pathetic. You're a loser. You screw up everything. No one wants you. God hates you. God has rejected you. God must have cursed you. There is no God. You'd be better off dead. Just kill yourself already.* I'll show you how my experience with antidepressant (AD) medication taught me that voice is a liar.

"Why Faith Matters in Recovery" started when I tried to offer encouragement to someone who was depressed, and I happened to mention God. His response was, in effect, "There is no God. Everyone knows it. They're just afraid to admit it." I did not try to prove God exists. I doubt that's even possible. Instead, I talked about why accepting and trusting in a higher power—whatever that means to you—is important for recovery.

"Roots of Depression," Parts 1 & 2, are reflections on gardening as a metaphor for recovery.

In "Tools for Depression," I list twenty-two scientifically proven ways to alleviate the effects of depression. Some of them will surprise you. And surely, you can find a few tools on this list that will help you.

The next two chapters are about Chris Cornell's suicide in 2017. All suicide is tragic, and it is a real danger for anyone living with depression. Cornell's, in particular, raised so many issues and memories for me that I needed two blog posts to work through them. He is an example of how depression, anxiety disorder, or mental illness of any kind, can strike anyone, no matter how rich and famous you are or how happy you appear in public.

"Mark 4:40—Where Is Your Faith?" was originally a devotion for my local American Christian Fiction Writers (ACFW) chapter. It comes from the story where Jesus calms a storm for his disciples. A verse that once made me feel condemned now offers me comfort and courage.

"The War on Thanksgiving" was at first a response to the hysteria over the so-called "war on Christmas." That led to reflections on the need to make space for gratitude in recovery. Forgetting to be thankful for what you have is sure to make depression worse.

I have heard rates of depression and suicide go up during the holidays. Because of that, I added two chapters called "The Holiday

Blues," and "The Longest Night Service." In the first, I talk about reasons why people sometimes feel more depressed and anxious during the holidays and offer suggestions for coping. The other is about Longest Night services that some churches offer to help people acknowledge feelings of depression, grief, and loneliness that traditional holiday services do not offer.

The chapter titled "Total Eclipse of the Soul" was inspired by the eclipse of August 21, 2017. An eclipse is the only time you can see the sun, moon, and stars together. That got me thinking about the account of creation in Genesis 1, how frightening an eclipse must have been to prehistoric peoples, and dark nights of the soul. It seemed appropriate to end with that because it was my most hopeful chapter.

Finally, I added a conclusion and three Appendices. Appendix A lists common symptoms and causes of depression. Appendix B lists some resources for finding a counselor. And Appendix C lists a few Bible verses to go with my principles of recovery.

For a bonus, this edition includes a personal essay titled "The One Thing: The 5,000 Most Important Words I Have Ever Written (So Far)."

###

Note: Bible quotations are taken from the New Revised Standard Version unless otherwise noted.

CHAPTER ONE

Depressed Christian, Part 1

Posted July 26, 2016

There are a lot of misconceptions about depression that prevent people who suffer from getting the help they need. In my own experience, religion sometimes brought healing and comfort when nothing else would, and sometimes it made my depression worse in ways nothing else could. And so I say I am in recovery from two things: depression and bad faith.

The first misconception is thinking depression is only an emotional state. Typically, people say they're depressed when they are *very* sad. So depression in this sense is extreme sadness. Anyone can feel depressed after the death of a family member or friend, loss of a job, divorce or breakup, or some tragic event in their lives. This is *situational depression.*

But depression in the sense I'm talking about is not that kind of sadness. It is a medical condition. It is not something that happens because of life. It is an ongoing condition of the brain. This is *clinical depression.*

The Depressed Brain

Did you know that your brain processes more than 100,000 chemical reactions every second?[1] Obviously, that is too much to describe in detail here. For most purposes, you just need to know that an important part of this activity involves the production of chemicals like serotonin and dopamine. I will refer to them generally as "happy chemicals." You have happy chemicals and stress chemicals. The brain processes them, but most of them are actually produced in the gut. This is why people with depression or anxiety often have gastro-intestinal (GI) illnesses as well.

Regardless of where they come from, when your brain does not get normal levels of happy chemicals, the stress chemicals affect your mood. You live in a constant, underlying, and invisible state of depression—*even when there is no reason for you to be sad.* This kind of depression is a medical condition, not an emotional state where you can just "cheer up" or pray your way out of it.

I did not know any of this until I was professionally tested. The psychiatrist summed up the results like this: "You tested high for depression in every possible way."

It was one of those moments when I knew my life would never be the same. How I viewed myself, life, the world, God, and everything changed forever with that one sentence. I only felt mildly depressed, and I still tested high in every possible way? I never thought it could be that bad. Yet, as the psychiatrist explained it, I saw how it was not only possible. It explained a lot about my whole life.

Clinical depression is not about how you feel at any given moment. It means you need help in creating a healthy level of happy chemicals. Without that help, I walked around numb, moody, temperamental, irritable, and looking angry even when I was not. I isolated myself and either dreaded or loathed social interaction. I thought all kinds of bad thoughts about myself, friends, enemies, family, strangers, the world, God, and life itself. I suffered from anxieties for no good reason. I thought no one understood me, so there was no point in talking to anyone.

Of course, I did not feel that way 24/7. It would have been easier to recognize if I did. I had ups and downs just like everyone, or so I thought. My emotional/mood spectrum felt normal to me because it

---

[1] "How Many Chemical Reactions Occur in the Brain Every Second,"
Answers, Answers Corporation, accessed July 26, 2016,
http://www.answers.com/Q/How_many_chemical_reactions_occur_in_the_hu man_brain_every_second.

was the only thing I had ever known. This is what it's like to live with clinical depression and not know it.

If any of this sounds familiar, especially if you can't identify any good reason for your sadness, irritability, apathy, or hopelessness, you may be one of the millions of people living with undiagnosed depression of some kind. How do you know for sure? Since it is a medical condition, it needs to be diagnosed by a medical or psychiatric professional (See Appendix B). But if people close to you think you are depressed, even when you don't, you should seriously consider getting tested. I only got tested because my mother and sister urged me. If they hadn't, I would still be undiagnosed, still moody and depressed, and still thinking it was normal.

Bad Faith

Clinical depression is not about feeling sad or anxious. It's about living with a brain that does not get enough happy chemicals. It is very important you understand this, because when religion gets mixed up in depression without understanding what it really is, it creates more problems than it solves. An article on Beliefnet said it well: "As we consider the causes of depression, those of us in the church must face the ways we might be responsible for creating it."[2]

I've experienced some of those ways that church/religion/faith—whatever you want to call spiritual life and practice—can be responsible for creating it or making it a lot worse. I thank God from the depths of my soul that He led me out of that and into a church, faith, and spiritual practice that helps my recovery and healing, rather than beats me down for not having "enough faith," whatever that means. Because the only thing worse than living for ten years (in my case) in a faith or religion that will only acknowledge "spiritual" causes of depression is living in that kind of faith for ten years ... and one day.

A New Mission

What I say next, I don't say lightly. I'm not the type of person who goes around saying, "God told me this. God told me that. God has called me to do this." So many times I have heard people say things

---

[2] "Christians: Take Depression Seriously," Beliefnet, July 26, 2016, https://www.beliefnet.com/wellness/health/emotional-health/christians-take-depression-seriously.aspx.

like that and thought, *I bet if I could hear God as well as you claim to, right now I'd hear God saying, "Leave Me out of this!"*

It's not that I believe God does not talk to people. I believe God talks to us all the time, but hearing God is tricky. I've learned from hard experience that I don't hear nearly as well as I would like to. Probably because it's being filtered through a clinically depressed brain.

With that disclaimer, I'm going to go out on a limb and say I believe God is calling me to help others who are in the same position I was. People who know they are depressed and are trying to be happy. People who don't know it but have a sense that something is wrong with them. People who think it's normal because they have lived with depression all their lives. And especially, depressed people who have been hurt by religion. I believe I am in a position to help point you to what is helpful—and away from most of what is hurtful. I don't think I will ever say I am healed of depression. In Alcoholics Anonymous, they call themselves *recovering* alcoholics, not recovered.

Just recently, I have been able to look at my life today and realize I have come a long way on this road of recovery, though I have by no means come to the end. This journey has been a quest for happiness, purpose, and meaning in spite of a brain that is tilted toward depression, and God has been with me through it all. There are some lessons I have had to learn the hard way. I hope to spare you some of that drama. The greatest happiness, purpose, and meaning comes from helping others, so I pray this will in some way help you.

Grace and Peace to you.

CHAPTER TWO

Depressed Christian, Part 2

Posted September 2, 2016

The Internet has a lot of good information and a lot of bad. If you are a Christian struggling with depression, you might search on the Internet for help. You want something that not only helps with depression but addresses the extra dimensions that faith adds to it. For example, I came across one person who said, when a psychiatrist told him he would need medication, he felt "like a failure."[3]

I knew what he meant. He felt like a failure because, for Christians, it's so easy to get the idea that you shouldn't need help for depression beyond talking to someone, praying, living a faithful life, and obeying the Word. "I can do all things through Christ who strengthens me" (Phil. 4:13), so Jesus and faith in Him should be all you need.

That might be what you're telling yourself, and it might be what your church tells you. I heard it from preachers on TV and motivational speakers. But you've done all that, and you're still depressed. It must be your fault, right? Wrong!

The causes of depression are not just spiritual, and they are not a failure of faith. You need to address more than just spiritual issues. You need to understand there are physical and psychological reasons for it. And most of all, you need to arm yourself with accurate knowledge so you know how to find the right kind of help.

---

[3] Mark Mounts, "It Can't Be Depression: I'm A Christian," Christian Living, Grace Communion International, accessed September 2, 2016, https://www.gci.org/articles/it-cant-be-depression-im-a-christian/.

Separating the Wheat from the Chaff

To see what's out there, I searched "depressed christian" on Pchsearch (Google is not offering the chance to win $5,000/week for life. Who knows? I might win. And, as unchristian as it might sound, I think some financial security would help my depression to some degree. I'll probably need to say more about that another time).

As usual, with the Internet, the results were relevant but very unequal in quality. They ranged from wonderfully helpful to downright awful, with varying degrees in between. I have ranked my first page results using the customary 5-Star scale and included notes below about the reasons for the ranking. This is just a first step. The goal here is to use specific examples to help you separate good information from bad.

The Articles with a 5-Star Rating Meet These 4 Criteria:

1. The author has experience helping people with depression and uses sound research.

2. The author understands the unique ways a person's Christian faith affects their experience of depression—how it can either help or hinder recovery.

3. The author addresses physiological causes of depression. Religious people will always recognize spiritual causes. That is part of the equation, but, just as with physical illness, you cannot properly treat it if you don't acknowledge the physical causes.

4. The author clearly distinguishes between clinical/major depression (and similar types that are caused by deficiencies or imbalances in brain chemistry) and situational depression, a normal (and often healthy) response of sadness and grief after some tragic life event or loss.

And of course, the scale goes down from there. Drum roll, please

...

Setting the Bar for Everyone (5 Stars)

Brandon W. Peach, "5 Things Christians Should Know about Depression and Anxiety," *Relevant*.

✻✻✻✻✻

This article not only meets the standards I laid out but also does a great job in identifying the most common pitfalls for people seeking help from a well-meaning but ill-informed church.

The "five things" are:

1. "Depression isn't what the church makes it out to be." It's not a failure of faith, disobeying the Word, or a character defect. It's a mental illness.

2. "Mental illness is not a sin." Treating mental illness as an unconfessed, unrepented sin just makes us feel more alienated.

3. "The Bible doesn't provide any 'easy answers.'" You are not going to be cured by a Bible verse and exhortations to "obey God," but some people in the church will expect you to.

4. "Anxiety and depression don't often look like we think." As depressed people, we often get good at hiding our symptoms, we may not have admitted it to ourselves, and the symptoms are not always easy to recognize. The best the church can do is take away the shame associated with mental illness, so it will be easier to seek help when we're ready.

5. "Strong churches don't 'fix' depression." Most churches, no matter how well-intentioned, are ill-equipped to handle severe or clinical depression. They may even act in ways that make it worse. Church can provide a loving, supportive community, but it cannot take the place of a medical or psychiatric professional.

###

Mark Mounts, "It Can't Be Depression. I'm a Christian." Grace Commission International.

✶✶✶✶✶

If you have felt shame or failure over depression because you are a Christian, imagine how that is magnified if you are a pastor or priest. That was this author's situation.

It explains in detail, without getting too technical, how the chemistry of depression affects the brain. Remember how I explained a depressed brain does not produce normal levels of "happy chemicals"? When you experience stress or trauma, it affects the chemistry of your brain. Studies have shown clinical depression makes it more difficult for us to recover from those events, because our chemical imbalances shrink a part of the brain that affects mood.

It includes a sidebar with the American Psychiatric Association's (APA) definition of a "major depressive episode," which is very technical. (See Appendix A for a list in layman's terms). But you don't need to be an APA-certified counselor to understand the rest of the article.

Good (4 Stars)

"Christians: Take Depression Seriously," Beliefnet.

✶✶✶✶

The colon is very important in this title. With the colon, it's an imperative, as in, "Hey Christians. Take depression seriously." Without it, you have "Christians take depression seriously," as if it were a statement of fact. Unfortunately, not all Christians take depression seriously. As the article says, "Those who try to dissuade religious people from getting medical help for clinical depression, claiming that faith alone is the cure, can do devastating harm."

I'm giving it four stars instead of five because 1) It talks about situational depression vs. clinical depression but does not distinguish them as clearly as the two 5-star articles, and

2) This sentence is confusing: "Psychoanalysis can dig out of the subconscious such ugly realities so that they can be dealt with the effects negated."

... so they can be dealt with the effects negated? What is dealt with? What is negated? Are the ugly realities dealt with or negated? This is why grammar and proofreading matter.

Still, though, the information is good. The author uses real life and Biblical examples that illustrate vividly how important it is to take depression seriously and get proper treatment.

Karen Morgan, "Depression in the Christian Family" (part 4 of 5 of a series on depression)."

✳✳✳✳

This article is part of a series on depression. Both this article and the series have very good advice. However, it comes from Focus on the Family. I have heard Dr. James Dobson, the ministry's founder, tell parents to reject their LGBTQ children until they agree to live "according to the Word of God."

This is exactly the kind of rejection that causes LGBTQ teenagers as a group to have a higher rate of depression and suicide than their straight peers. Therefore, I cannot recommend this without a caveat of saying if you are LGBTQ, then aside from this article and series, stay away from Focus on the Family and Dr. Dobson. If not for that, it and the series would get five stars.

If you can separate out that baggage and judge the article on its own merits, then you should read it. It tells the story of Earle and his experience with severe depression that led him to seek counseling, medication, and even go on disability for a few months. He describes the issues honestly and in a way a depressed Christian will understand. This quote from Earle says it all:

> *For a long time, I thought if I just kept focused on God's Word, I'd find relief. But the depression just got worse.*
>
> *Spiritually, I couldn't feel God's presence. I couldn't understand why He didn't heal me. Reading the Bible didn't help. I couldn't even pray. Others had to pray for me. Only after I'd received some counseling and started taking anti-depressant medication did I start to feel better.*

Another reason I like this article is indicated in the title. Earle's depression affected his entire family. And that's something many people don't think about. Depression doesn't just affect the depressed person. It causes you to behave in ways that people around you don't know how to handle, no matter how much they love you. Hopefully, realizing that will prompt you to get the help you need.

###

Stephanie Husk, M.S.W., "Do Real Christians Get Depressed?"

✴✴✴✴

On my first impression, I gave it three stars. However, as I've looked over it again, I decided to upgrade it to four. For the most part, there is good advice here—for situational depression, and clinical depression as well. It might appear to point to sin, i.e., personal failure, as the cause of depression, but it's actually more nuanced than that. Take this statement for example (I de-italicized some parts to make the meaning clearer):

> *... problems in our brain's chemistry or in our body's functions are ultimately a spiritual problem ... since all of creation is affected by sin.* However, this does not mean that depression is necessarily a result of individual spiritual shortcomings. It also does not mean that a person shouldn't seek out healthy relief wherever it may be found. *Every good and perfect gift comes from above. Solutions to prolonged depression are no less spiritual if they come in the form of changed diet, exercise, cognitive counseling, or medication.*

The "sin" talked about here should probably have a capital "S," because it is much bigger than your or anyone else's individual sins. It is much bigger than the social sins of a community, institution, or nation. It is even bigger than the sin of all humanity, as in "all have sinned and fallen short of the glory of God" (Rom. 3:23). It is a condition of brokenness, decay, and mortality that afflicts not only humanity but all of creation (Rom. 8:22-23). *In this sense*, I think it is healthy to acknowledge Sin (with a capital S) as a cause of depression.

We are all broken in some way. For some of us, that manifests in a brain prone to depression or other mental illness. But preaching that says you are depressed because you are not obeying the Word, you are not praying enough, you don't have enough faith, or anything along those lines does more harm than good. When you have clinical depression, the primary cause is physical, not spiritual.

Fair (3 Stars)

"How to Cope with Depression as a Christian," wikiHow.

✳✳✳

It gives seven steps to cope with depression. Most of the advice is good, but I'm downgrading it to three stars for two reasons: 1) The writing is wordy and makes for awkward reading. 2) Some of the "related articles" were not appropriate to this subject. Particularly, one says "How to convert a Muslim to Christianity."

Maybe if you click the article today, the related articles will be better. If so, you can tell me to repent in sackcloth and ashes. I just don't think it's right to talk about converting people to your religion when they are seeking help for depression.

My experience of engaging religion and spirituality with a clinically depressed mind is Christian. How depression affects the experience of Islam, Judaism, or any other religion is something I'd like to explore with people who are more qualified than I.

Now, if a Muslim is interested in what being a Christian means to me, I'm happy to share it. And if anything about my experience helps them with depression, to God be the glory. But I know how I would feel if someone said to me, "You must convert to Islam in order to be saved," or, "Only Muhammad can heal your depression." I won't be the one who does that to someone whose faith is different from mine.

"What Does the Bible Say about Depression? How Can Christians Overcome Depression?" Got Questions.org.

✳✳✳

This article distinguishes between situational and clinical depression, which is very important. The description of clinical depression is pretty good, but it needs some editing, as in the following with my comments in parentheses:

- "It may not be caused by unfortunate life circumstances ...." (Change *may not* to *is not*. We are talking about clinical depression now, not situational),

- "… nor can the symptoms be alleviated by one's own will" (True. A five-star statement).
- "Contrary to what some in the Christian community believe, clinical depression is not always caused by sin" (Delete *always*. Clinical depression *by definition* means the cause is physical, not spiritual).
- "They should make sure that they are staying in the Word, even when they do not feel like it. Emotions can lead us astray, but God's Word stands firm and unchanging." (This is an example where, yes, it's true, but it's important to put it in the right context. And I have to ask, what do you mean by "staying in the Word"? That can mean different things to different people).
- "Although being depressed is not a sin, one is still accountable for the response to the affliction, including getting the professional help that is needed" (Stress the last part of this sentence. Without that, I would reject this advice. For someone in major depression, *you are accountable for your response* is like *you should have more faith*—whatever that means. The thing to understand if your depression is as bad as Earle's (review of Morgan, "Christian Family," above) is you are accountable in as much as you cannot get out of this darkness on your own, but you can get professional help).

One statement was dead on, though: "… in some cases, seeing a doctor for depression is no different than seeing a doctor for an injury."

Amen and amen! If you remember nothing else from this article, remember this. Seeing a doctor (or psychiatrist or therapist) for depression is no different than seeing a doctor for an injury.

In Between (2 ½ Stars)

"Christian Testimonies about Depression and Suicide," About.com: Christianity.

✳✳1/2

Forty-seven stories of people who found peace to "overcome" depression. Why the quotes? I am always skeptical when people say they are cured or have overcome depression, as if depression has been banished to the Outer Darkness, wailing and gnashing its teeth, never to return. If so, it probably wasn't clinical depression but situational. They don't give specifics about how they were cured beyond "Jesus is the answer."

There was a time when I would have given this five stars. "Jesus is the answer," I would say as the solution to any problem. Well, that did not always work for me, so how can I expect it to work for Muslims, Jews, or even all Christians? I cannot promote that (or anything) as the one and only answer for depression anymore.

But the stories might give hope to some people.

Bad (2 Stars)

"What Should a Christian Do if Overwhelmed with Depression?" Christian Answers.

✷✷

Although it acknowledges some kinds of depression are caused by chemical imbalances and may require medication and/or professional help, it puts the stress on spiritual causes: sin, not following the Word, not believing the Bible, etc.

It says, "Aim to work on the causes of your depression, not just the symptoms," which is what I advocate as well. But working on the real causes requires professional help, not a few Bible verses and a sermon.

Super-Bad (1 Star)

"Overcoming Depression," CBN.

✷

Causes named: physical (for example, not taking care of yourself, illness, medication), losses and other hurts, sin (not the capital-S kind but yours).

There is not one mention of clinical, bipolar, or any form of depression which is primarily caused by chemical imbalances. Here are some examples:

- "The Bible says that Jesus 'bore our griefs' on the cross (Isaiah 53:4 NAS). He feels our pain as strongly as we do and will carry it for us. Give your hurt to Him." (As I said about an article above, this can be helpful *in the right context*. But what do you do next? His answer is …)

- "Then resolve not to dwell on it again." (The worst thing to say to someone with clinical depression. Right up there with, *Stop sinning. Snap out of it. Pray the depression away. All the answers are in the Bible. You've got to have more faith.* Recovery is one day at a time. If you can resolve never to dwell on depressing thoughts again, great. I couldn't. But I did find that, with help, I could resolve to focus on something else right now.)

Faith, prayer, and Bible study can all be powerful tools for situational depression. But if you are Christian and seeking help for depression, I know you have already done these things, and they were not enough. And most importantly, *it's not your fault that they weren't enough.* Refer to Earle's story above in the "Christian Family" entry.

A Black Hole (0 Stars)

Melissa Barnhart, "Christian Counselor: Depression Demands Living By Faith, Not By Sight."

0

A Christian counselor is interviewed for advice about depression. At first, I gave the article one star; but then I realized it does not even deserve that because it comes from a licensed professional. It's all about "spiritual causes" of depression, and not a word about the biological causes. Christian or not, a licensed neuropsychologist really should know better.

So what's the opposite of a star? A black hole.

###

That is a sampling of the advice that is out there. As I said above, the intention with this article is to help you separate good sources of information from bad. Some of the "bad" advice can be true and helpful in the right context, as I mentioned a couple of times. What is the right context? That would take a long time to answer. The best I can offer now is it goes back to the four criteria I used to rate these articles. If you have a type of depression that has physical or biological causes, you need more than a "spiritual" answer. Just like if I break my arm, I will pray. But I will also get to a doctor as soon as I can.

In coping with depression, I used and still use spiritual sources of comfort. However, I did not get better until I was properly diagnosed and able to address the physical causes as well as the spiritual. That is why I am so adamant about not reducing everything down to "sin" or "failure to obey the Word." As Mark Mounts, one of our 5-star sources, said,

> *We all accept the fact that our bodies wear out and run down and are susceptible to disease. We can even accept the fact that our brains can be ravaged by diseases such as Alzheimer's. But some Christians will not accept the fact that clinical depression also has specific biological causes. They'd rather categorize depression as a "bad attitude" or "lack of faith."[4]*

As far as I am concerned, that is the worst thing you can do to someone with depression. If it messes with your theology that I won't say all the answers are in Jesus or the Bible, I'm sorry. But I know what kind of religion/faith/spirituality (whatever you want to call it) helped me and what kind made everything worse. And to paraphrase Paul, I will not submit again to bad faith just to accommodate your dogma.

Grace and Peace to you.

P.S. www.webmd.com is a treasure trove of information. It does not address the faith-related issues of depression, but you can find information on the medical side that is comprehensive, easy to understand, and reviewed by doctors.

---

[4] Mounts, "It Can't Be Depression."

CHAPTER THREE

The Voice … That No One Wants to Hear

Posted October 28, 2016

Do you have a voice in your head? If you have clinical depression, you probably do. A lot of people claim they don't. In fact, they think hearing voices is a sign of mental illness. Personally, I don't believe them. I think everyone has a voice or even voices in their heads. And those who say they don't are either lying or in denial. Then again, I've already admitted to having a mental illness, so maybe I'm the wrong person to ask.

I don't know how the voices in normal brains talk. However, if you have clinical depression, that voice in your head is your worst enemy. It's the opposite of a motivational speaker. It tries to convince you you're worthless and no good to anyone. If you pray or try to live by faith, the Voice tries to convince you the reason your life sucks is God is against you, not for you. "God hates me. God has given up on me, and I don't blame Him. I'm like the tree that bore no fruit, so God has cut me off. I'm cursed. And there is no God anyway, so why do I care?"

If you know that voice, let me tell you something it doesn't want you to know. That voice is a liar. This is not something I believe. I *know* it. Let me tell you how.

Medication and the Voice in My Head

Taking medication for depression is still controversial for some people of faith. When a psychiatrist first recommended it for me, I had some reservations. However, he had just told me I tested high for depression in every possible way, so I took his advice. Sometimes I have wondered if it was really working, especially at times when I have been sad, moody, anxious, just fill in the blank with any negative emotion.

I can still say, though, that medication does make a difference for me. I know because a couple of times I have changed medications. When you change from one antidepressant (AD) medication to another, you first have to wean yourself off of your current med. That usually lasts two to four weeks. Then you can start the new one. It can take several days for the new medication to start taking effect. During that transition, those depressed thoughts you had forgotten about can come back, along with other possible side effects.

The first time I switched medications, I had suicidal thoughts. I can't say it was the first time (for suicidal thoughts, I mean), but it was more frequent and intense than ever. *Is the new med not working?* I wondered.

My doctor said it was a low dose and suggested trying a "medium" dose. Within a few days, the suicidal thoughts stopped. That medium dose worked for me. But without talking to my doctor, I might have thought it was the wrong medication.

The second time I switched meds was more recent. Bad thoughts came but in a different way. Instead of feeling depressed in the way we usually think of (deep and persistent sadness, suicidal thoughts, etc.), it came in a way I had forgotten about: anger. I was angry much of the day. Angry at family and friends over past slights that my balanced brain had forgiven long ago. Angry at people for the downward spiral the world seems to be in. Unreasonably angry. But when the new medicine kicked in, I was back to being happy. And I am proud to say I did not take my anger out on anyone.

The Decision

Why did I not act out my anger or my suicidal thoughts during those times? Before I started transitioning medications, I made a crucial decision. Until I know if the new med is good for me and until I get my brain normalized again with either the new or return to the old, *I will not believe that voice in my head.*

I got the idea from the movie *A Beautiful Mind*. Russell Crowe plays Nobel Prize-winning mathematician John Forbes Nash, Jr., who was found to be paranoid schizophrenic. He had more than just a voice in his head. He had full-on hallucinations of three people telling him all kinds of conspiracies. When he was diagnosed and got medication, the hallucinations disappeared. However, he was having difficulty with the side effects. He told his wife and doctor he wanted to go off the medication.

But those imaginary people will come back.

Yes, but this time he will know they are not real, and he will absolutely refuse to believe them. It was not easy. Those hallucinations had a life of their own. They tried really hard to convince him to listen to them. But he remained resolute. *You are not real. I won't listen to you. I won't believe anything you say.*

Because of past experience with depression, I knew I needed to reject, ignore, and otherwise neutralize those thoughts temporarily. Let's review what happened in these two instances.

1. I stopped one AD medication.

2. The Voice in my head that fuels my depression went from being a surly kitten to a roaring tiger.

3. When the new AD medication kicked in, the Voice calmed down, the bad thoughts sunk back to a manageable level, and happy thoughts returned.

What is going on? I've talked about the chemical imbalances that exist in a clinically depressed brain. It is a medical condition where your brain does not get normal levels of "happy chemicals," so the "stress chemicals" overwhelm it. Medication helps your brain produce and absorb more happy chemicals. When your brain chemistry is balanced, your emotional state can get back to normal—in a good way.

The Revelation

That last experience changing meds really drove something home for me. The Voice in my head did not bother me when I was on meds. But when I was in that transition phase, the Voice came back with a vengeance. Now that I am on meds again, the Voice is gone. And that's when it hit me like a revelation of Biblical proportions:

That voice in my head is the product of a chemically imbalanced brain.

If you have that Voice, too, let that sink in. That Voice in your head that tells you, "I'm no good. I'll never get anything right. I'm a burden to everyone who loves me," or even worse, "No one loves me. I might as well kill myself." Or maybe you have that angry voice, like I experienced. And you believe it, don't you? It is the product of a chemically imbalanced brain.

The problem is not so much the voice itself but that we believe it so readily. In thinking about this, I was amazed at how anything we hear inside our head, we just believe it. We don't question it; we don't evaluate it. We just accept whatever it says, even when it has no basis in reality.

"Everyone hates me."

Oh really? There are 7.5 billion people in the world, and every single one of them hates you? Unless you're Hitler, that's not possible. Maybe you just meant everyone in your school or in your town. But still, how many people is that, a few hundred? A few thousand? A few hundred thousand or a few million if it's a major city? How could every one of them hate you? Simple logic should tell you that's not even possible. But you believe it. Why? Because it comes from your head, so it must be true, right? Wrong!

That Voice Is a Liar

Are you telling me I'm lying to myself?

That's exactly what I'm telling you! That voice in your head is the product of a chemically imbalanced brain.

My angry voice said things to me like, "They always disrespect me. They never listen to me. They're idiots. They don't care about me, so screw 'em all." (That's as politely as I can say it). And again, it was the product of a chemically imbalanced brain.

And bottom line: Don't believe a chemically imbalanced brain, even if it's your own. You're just as likely to get the truth from a Magic 8-Ball. If it is telling the truth, that's purely by accident.

{Don't ask me. I'm a ball.}

I suppose this begs the question, If you can't believe your own mind, what can you believe? How do you know what the truth is? There is no simple answer to that, and anyone who tells you there is is setting you up for failure. But I will reiterate the four principles I gave you in the introduction.

1. God is for your recovery and healing, not against it.

2. God will not kick you when you're down.

3. Some kinds of faith are good for recovery, and some are bad. Make sure you know the difference.

4. With the right help—spiritually, psychologically, emotionally, and perhaps medically—you can live a happy and fulfilling life. You just need to learn how to stop your depressed brain from sabotaging it.

That's all the truth you need for now.

Grace and Peace to You.

Why Faith Matters in Recovery

Posted November 9, 2016

A couple of months ago, I got an email notification that someone liked one of my posts. It happens sometimes. (Why do you look skeptical?)

Because we're both on WordPress, the email gave links to a few of his posts. I clicked one where he talked about reading his official diagnosis from his therapist, and it got him down. I knew what he meant. When I got tested for depression, the therapist was very helpful after the fact. But the report was one of the most depressing things I had ever read.

If you are considering getting tested for depression, I do want to encourage you to do it (See Appendix B). It was very enlightening for me. But I'll give you the same advice I wish I could have given this person: do not read the report unless you absolutely have to. Keep a copy of it in your file cabinet in case you need it to claim disability, *but do not read it yourself.*

In his case, it was too late, though. So I told him whatever it said that got him down, ignore it. That report is filled with jargon that was meant for other health professionals, not for laymen like us. Only two parts of the report will help you: the diagnosis (clinical depression, bipolar, whatever), and the recommended treatment. Nothing else in the report will be helpful to you. In fact, it may do more harm than good.

He said, "Amen to this. Focusing on the treatment is much more productive. Of course, being depressed, my mind enjoys wandering to the negative. Fighting it, one day at a time. Thanks for your perspective!"

That might have been the end of our exchange, but it sounded like he needed a little more encouragement, so I responded, "That's how it is with the depressed brain. Our vision tends to be dark, so we need to find light wherever we can. One thing I like about my religious tradition is it says our purpose is to glorify God and to enjoy God forever. God is for our joy and our recovery. So keep turning toward the light."

I didn't think I was forcing my religion on him. First, I acknowledged a depressed brain does gravitate toward darkness. I know the same way he does, from experience. So I was just offering a bit of light I've found. And in case I didn't make this clear, when I share with you something that's helped me, I'm not trying to convert you. All I'm saying is this helped me. If it helps you, great. If it doesn't, find something that does.

This was his response, and I'll warn you there is some rough language in it:

> *I'm glad you find strength in your religion. However, we are all a product of our circumstances. There is no god. And I think a part of us knows that this is true. There are about two billion Christians who believe to be blessed to the have true faith. Now replace 'Christians' with 'Muslims.' The truth is, none of us know what the f*ck we are doing. All of us are just desperate for meaning.*

Apparently, it was not received the way I intended. Of course, I wanted to smooth things over, so I said, "Whatever you believe or don't believe is fine. I don't subscribe to any idea of one and only one way or one and only one truth. Even with my faith, I have felt lost at times. As you say, we are all desperate for meaning, so I just want to encourage you to find your source (or sources) of light and meaning."

Is There a God? I Mean, Really?

The reason I'm sharing this is I think he expressed something a lot of people are thinking. Even if they don't believe with assurance that there is no god, like a genuine atheist, they do sometimes wonder, *Is there a God? I mean really? How do I know?*

To address this, I want to break down what he said:

1. There is no God.

2. A part of us knows this is true, but most people are just afraid to admit it.

3. All Christians believe they have the true faith. So do Muslims. [Implied: which one is right?]

4. None of us knows what we are doing.

5. We are all just desperate for meaning.

I'm not sure how numbers 4 and 5 are supposed to prove there is no God. To me, they just sound like a description of the human condition and point out the need for a good recovery program. So what about numbers 1-3?

There is no God, and everyone really knows it. They're just afraid to admit it.

He might really believe this. If someone honestly believes there is no God, I have no quarrel with that. However, I know these are the kind of thoughts a depressed brain will tell you. The depressed brain will speak with the authority of ultimate truth, and it will be easy to believe. It's like Poe's "Raven."

Quoth the Raven, Nevermore!

The narrator in the poem is depressed. A raven flies into his house. The raven can speak, but only one word: nevermore. The narrator asks questions that need positive answers, and he's asking a bird that can only say, "Nevermore." You see the problem there? No matter what he asks, the bird's answer will always be, "Nevermore."

The love of my life has died. Will I ever be happy again? *Nevermore.*

Is there a God? *Nevermore.*

Will the Cubs win the World Series? *Nevermore.*

On that last question, what if an overzealous Cubs fan who lived to see his team win the World Series asked the Raven that question two weeks ago and, because of the bird's answer, killed himself (See posted date above)?

That's crazy, you say. *No one would kill themselves over their sports team.* Have you seen sports fans?

But you see the irony. Just two weeks ago, it could have appeared to be true. But the bird isn't speaking "the truth." It does not even know how to give positive answers. It's the same with the depressed brain. It says things like, "You're worthless. No one loves you. There is no God, and everyone knows it. They just don't have the guts to admit it," because, like the Raven, that's all it knows how to say. So never take your depressed brain to be the ultimate truth. You are just as likely to get "the truth" from a Magic 8-Ball.

{My sources say, "Nevermore"}.

One of the most important things I heard when I was at a low point in my life was, Don't believe your feelings [or thoughts] when you're depressed. Your feelings will tell you God does not love you. God has abandoned you. You are all alone in this world. But God's word says I will never leave you nor forsake you. God so loved the world (that includes you) that God gave God's only begotten Son. While we were yet sinners (i.e., worthless), Christ died for us. That is true no matter what you feel. Feelings will change according to circumstances, but God's word is always true in any circumstance.

If you are not a Christian or don't read the Bible, you may not think that applies to you, but please keep reading. I promise there is something here for you regardless of what you believe.

When the depressed thoughts come, it's so easy to believe them. I don't know why. Maybe it's because it comes from our own mind, so we automatically assume it's the truth. Our own mind wouldn't lie to us, right? Wrong! It lies to us all the time (See Chapter, "The Voice..."). And when it assaults you with dark thoughts like these, you are in a battle like what Paul described in 2 Corinthians 10:4-5.

(For the weapons of our warfare are not carnal, but mighty through God to the pulling down of strong holds;) Casting down imaginations, and every high thing that exalteth itself against the knowledge of God, and bringing into captivity every thought to the obedience of Christ (KJV).

The depressed brain conjures up imaginations and high things that will remove all hope and light from your vision if you let it. In order to stop the dark imaginations from taking over your mind and your life, you need to have the tools and weapons to fight against them. When De-elevator attacks you (I've started calling the depressed voice in my head De-elevator, from Prince's song, "Let's Go Crazy"), you need to fight back. Ephesians 6:13-18 is the famous passage about the Whole Armor of God: Faith, Salvation, Truth, Peace, the Word of God. These are powerful armor and weapons in the fight.

These are examples from my own faith. But regardless of what you believe, you've got to find something, some power and authority and truth that is greater than your own thoughts and feelings. And whatever your greater truth is, it must be rooted in love, or it will fail. That is the only saying of my religion I hold to be absolute truth. *God is love* (1 Jn 4:8).

Which God?

But you say, "Which God? The Christian God? The Muslim God? The Jewish God? Some Pagan God? How does anyone know what the true God is?"

When it comes to recovery, that is the wrong question to ask.

As a Christian, Presbyterian to be specific, I would love it if everyone believed in the same God I do. But that's not going to happen. History has shown over and over that you cannot force everyone in any society to believe the same way. Any religion can resonate with some people, but there has never been a religion that resonates with everyone. In order to live together, we all have to make room for people who come from a belief system or culture that's different from our own. And we can do that as long as we remember to treat each other the way we want to be treated.

This is one reason I recommend getting familiar with Alcoholics Anonymous's 12 Steps. I can't name off all the Steps, but I always remember the first three.

1. Admit that you are an alcoholic [an addict, depressed, or whatever you seek to recover from].

2. Believe in a higher power.

3. Submit your life to your higher power.[5]

I like that term *higher power*, because your higher power does not have to come from any particular religion. It does not even have to be a "god" in the traditional sense. Some forms of Buddhism, for exam-

---

[5] "The Twelve Steps."

ple, have no formal belief in God. But any Buddhist I've met still believes in a power greater than him or herself. My advice, if you have a problem with "God," is the same as A.A.'s: Be open to the possibility of a higher power, even if you don't know what it is yet.[6]

The reason for a higher power is if you could recover under your own power, you would have done it by now. But your own thinking and your own power got you where you are. It's like you found yourself in a pit, and someone handed you a shovel and said, "Dig your way out." You dug and dug and instead of getting out, you got further and further down the hole. Now you realize no amount of digging is going to get you out of this pit. In fact, digging is only making it worse.

You look up, and you are in too deep to climb out. Your only way out is to find a higher power, i.e., someone at the top of the pit to throw you a rope so you can climb, and maybe to help pull you up if you are too weak to climb all the way. For me, that person at the top is God Almighty, maker of heaven and earth, and the rope is the way of all-inclusive love that Jesus taught.

So who or what is that higher power for you? Once you've identified that, you'll be able to see the rope He/She/It/They have thrown down to you and start to climb out.

Grace and Peace to you.

---

[6] Bill W., *Twelve Steps and Twelve Traditions* (A.A. World Services, Inc.: New York, 2012), 27-28, https://www.aa.org/assets/en_US/en_step2.pdf.

CHAPTER FIVE

Roots of Depression, Part 1

Note: This was originally a three-part series,
but I edited it down to two, so it would read better.

I was working in the yard, which always seems to involve more work than I think it will initially. There have been these vines interweaving in the links of the chain-link fence. I decided to un-weave them. Of course, it's not enough to free the vines from the fence. I had to pull the vines up out of the ground, so they could not grow back.

Pulling up the vines revealed their roots. Pulling up those roots revealed more roots, and then more roots and more roots. There were long roots, short roots, thin roots, thick roots. The long, thicker roots did not go down vertically but rather horizontally, so I could grab one in the middle and pull it up like a cable. It would come out of the ground, and I could follow it to the right and the left. The ground above it gave way easily, and other roots snapped and broke as I disrupted the interweaving, intertwining network of roots beneath that foot of ground between the driveway and the chain-link fence.

As I was working on these roots, I realized getting rid of these weeds and vines and the roots beneath them is similar to recovery. You start off with something easily visible: sadness, moodiness, a quick temper, or whatever. You pull on that, but those visible weeds are connected to roots underground. You go after those roots, and you find there is a whole lot more going on beneath the surface than you ever imagined. As I pondered this, here's what I noticed:

You Think Each Weed or Vine Has Only One Root, but There Are Way More Roots Than Weeds

It took maybe twenty minutes at most to remove the vines. I found a few weeds and pulled them up in minutes. But I was pulling up roots probably for three or four hours. Just when I thought I was close to finishing, I'd pull one little root, and it would reveal a whole new network.

Whatever the roots of your depression, once you start digging them up, you will find they are far deeper and more extensive than you expected.

The Roots Are Interconnected

Small roots lead to big roots, and big roots are joined with a lot of small roots. Along the branches of the roots are these tiny tendrils that make them stick to the ground and other nearby roots. When you pull up one, it's bound to break up some of the ties to another. So each one you remove makes it easier to remove another. You remove one of those long cable-like roots, and you have disrupted many smaller ones. With their connections snapped, they come out easier.

As you make progress in your recovery, you will find that improvement in one area spills over into other areas.

There Are Entire Communities Living around Those Roots

Every root I pulled made earthworms, tiny centipedes, termites, and scores of other bugs scramble for safety. I imagine if somehow they knew this was coming and could communicate with me, they would try to trick me into letting those roots stay where they are. Who could blame them? They were just minding their own business, doing what worms and bugs do, and here I come uprooting their entire neighborhood—literally.

This is how depression takes on a life of its own. You may have noticed that in your recovery, you are often your own worst enemy. You want to be well. You want to be happy. You want to do something with your life that feels worthwhile. But something inside you keeps wanting to sabotage that. That's the bugs and worms that have made their homes around the roots and don't want you disturbing them. They will try to convince you those roots are fine where they are. Don't bother working on your recovery. You'll only make things worse. It won't do any good anyway.

Tell those voices this is your recovery. The roots are coming up, and they can either adjust to it or move to someone else's yard.

You're Not Going to Get Them All First Time around, so You'll Need to Keep Watching

Some roots I could remove completely. Some broke off before I could get them all out. There are still roots under there, most of them shorter and damaged, but they tend to grow back. This is why recovery is an ongoing process.

If you've been working on recovery and made progress, remember not to get complacent. That yard may look clear now. Even beneath the surface, you may find it clear of roots. But new weeds can always come in. Some of them may lie dormant, waiting for the right time to reappear. Some of those roots that broke off will grow back. Life won't let you off the hook completely. Develop skills and strategies to stop them from taking over your yard. Be ready for them. Be ready to remove those same roots again, or maybe new roots that have found their way into that clearing you created. Recovery is a lifelong process, but your mental health and pursuit of happiness are worth it.

Grace and Peace to you.

Roots of Depression, Part 2

In Part 1, I talked about some of my gardening experience and how it relates to recovery from depression. I thought I was done with that topic for a while, but I see some more possible application. Before I continue, I'd like to tell you a little background on how I ended up being the caretaker for this yard.

My grandparents passed away last year (2015). I moved into their house, where they had lived for over thirty years. The last three to four years of their lives, they were not in good health. They needed round-the-clock care. Of course, they couldn't take care of the yard the way they wanted to. Now that it's my home, I feel a responsibility to take care of this land where I live. And I hope this doesn't sound new age-y or "woo-woo," but I feel like, by reclaiming their yard, I am in some way keeping their presence alive here.

Okay, so there's a little bit of my sentimentality. Now here are my gardening/recovery tips.

Get Your Tools

In the yard, I don't do much work to remove weeds. Just spread some type of Weed-and-Feed. Grass and weeds sometimes pop up in the sidewalk or driveway. A shot of Roundup is good enough for that. I'm not going to use Roundup on the whole yard. That is way too destructive. Just a few weeds here or there away from the yard or other plants.

But when you get around the trees or into the flower beds, you don't want any kind of chemicals there. Weeds in those areas require a more hands-on approach, which means you need the right tools: gloves, hand spade, Garden Weasel(R) Cultivator and Weed Popper, hedge clippers, and pruner.

I wear gloves for all yard work because some of these weeds have thorns. I need some protection to get a good grip and pull them out. Also, even though I've remembered the "Leaves of three, Leave it be" rule, sometimes I still get these welts like insect bites or poison ivy, so I'm wearing long sleeves to work anywhere in the yard.

Some weeds are too entrenched to pull out. You can get the weed, but too much of the root is left behind. The Garden Weasel(R) Weed Popper comes in handy for that. You place it so the little blades go into the ground on both sides of the weed, twist it around a full 360 degrees, and it pulls up the weed and root with it. It can even get ordinary dandelions pretty well. But I've seen these bigger weeds that are like dandelions crossbred with thistle. A friend called them dandelions on steroids.

For this, I need another standing weed remover but bigger. The Garden Weasel(R) Cultivator works well on them. You can get the whole plant out, and it pulls up the root as well. It's made for cultivating ground, but it's okay to repurpose your tools. It works similar to the Weed Popper. You get these spikes into the ground, twist, and pull up the weed.

When you pull up one of these big weeds, it leaves a hole, and that brings me to my next lesson.

Do Not Leave a Hole Unfilled, Because an Empty Space Will Be Filled One Way or Another

Since weeds grow faster than anything else, they will fill any emptiness if left unattended. Not to mention, this Garden Weasel leaves a hole big enough for someone to step in, twist their ankle, and sue you. I try to leave as much of the original dirt and as little of the root as possible. But nature abhors a vacuum. Just like weeds will come back to an empty space, self-defeating thoughts will return to a depressed brain if you don't watch out.

Soil Is Neutral

It will grow almost anything you plant if it has the right nutrient content and is in the right climate. You can't blame the soil for your weeds, so it's up to you to keep the soil cleared of undesirables while planting and tending the right seeds.

It's Not Just about Removing Weeds; It's about Clearing Space for What You Want in Your Garden

I've probably pulled up more grass than weeds in the flower beds. The type of grass in my yard has a very extensive, intricate, intertwining root system, which is good for crowding out weeds in the yard, but I don't want it getting mixed with the flower's roots.

It requires some pulling, digging, and breaking up grassroots along with the weeds and their roots. It's a lot more involved than I expected, but I think flowers and trees need a clearly delineated space.

There's a big rose bush on the east end of the yard and azalea bushes around the house. They had looked a little sickly the last few years. As I examined the bushes, it was easy to see why. Some vines grew up and wrapped around the branches, choking the life out of them. And there were other plants, like budding acorns, growing right underneath. Sometimes, they looked like they had been grafted into the azaleas and roses. I cleared them out a few months ago and removed most of the dead branches. This spring (2016), those bushes produced more flowers than they had in years.

Some bushes had grown so much, though, that they were crowding out their neighbors. For example, I had pink azaleas growing into and blending in with white azaleas. The pink was threatening to take over the white. So I decided it was time to trim the hedges. I pulled out the hedge clippers and pruners and went to work.

It sounds a little backward. I had done all this work to remove weeds and thorns so the azaleas and roses could thrive, and they thrived so much I'm actually cutting back on their growth. But gardening isn't about letting the desirable plants grow indiscriminately. It's about setting parameters, so all the desirable plants are free to grow and thrive and contribute to the variety of the garden as a whole.

Know When to Say, "That's Enough for Today."

I worked in the flowerbeds most of the morning and had lunch. I knew I had made progress, but there was more to be done. My body was telling me not to go back out, but I didn't listen. I was just going to work on this one patch of weeds, but I continued to work through most of the afternoon. Two days later, I'm still sore.

When my grandfather was still strong enough to work in the yard, we used to joke about how he was "addicted to weed," because once he got started pulling weeds, he could be out all day if someone didn't call him in. *Let me tell you, that condition is hereditary.* You may intend to work on one very specific patch of ground this time, but then there are a few more weeds here, a few more there. Now the flowerbed looks unbalanced. If you just take care of that patch, it will look better. Okay, another patch and you'll almost be through. Just one more patch ... you get the idea.

Like reclaiming a yard, garden, or flowerbed after years of neglect, recovery is not going to happen all in one day. If you've made progress and are encouraged to continue, but it was draining—physically or emotionally—or you have other responsibilities to attend to, you have a life, leave the yard for now. It will still be there tomorrow. Give yourself permission to say, "That's enough for today," and then, for the rest of the day, take care of anything else that needs your attention. Or maybe get some well-earned rest.

Final Words

I intended this "roots of depression" metaphor to be a parable about recovery. By their nature, parables leave room for you to interpret them out of your own experience. You may have seen some parallels in your own garden of recovery. If not, you may make connections later.

Here is my interpretation, if it helps. In general, I see the work of recovery as three things: 1) planting the seeds of your best self and best life, 2) promoting the growth of those seeds in healthy ways, and 3) removing the vines, weeds, and roots that crowd out and even choke to death the good seeds in the garden of your life—metaphorically speaking, of course.

As in gardening, I have found the following true in recovery:

1. Getting it right takes time and work.

2. There is a natural tendency for weeds to overtake and choke out the beautiful parts of your garden.

3. All plants have roots. To really get the weeds out, you have to pull and dig up the roots. That can get messy.

4. No one tool can do every job, so keep a variety of tools on hand.

5. As you remove the weeds, fill in the empty places with good soil and the right kind of seeds.

6. Under the right conditions, the seeds of recovery—love, joy, peace, faith, hope, vision, purpose, belonging, and confidence—will grow and bloom. The conditions are as simple as soil, water, and sunlight.

7. With the right tools and a little consistent effort, the weeds are no match for you.

Grace and Peace to you.

CHAPTER SEVEN

Tools for Depression

Posted December 1, 2016

One of my lessons from gardening was that with the right tools, the weeds are no match for you. Now, I want to list some of the tools you can use to remove the "weeds of depression" from the garden of your soul. This is just a list. I'm not going in-depth here. I want to name as many tools as I can for you, because you will need many tools to keep your "weeds" under control. Real life gardening and yard work have been good for me not only in living out metaphors for recovery. It gives me three forms of therapy at once: exercise, sunlight, and soil. Here is every tool I can think of.

Soil—Ever heard of *Mycobacterium vaccae*? It is a type of bacteria found in soil. Medical studies have shown when it gets into your system, it has antidepressant properties. If you enjoy gardening, this is probably one reason why. And not a bad reason to start if you haven't done it before.

Medication—If you have some form of clinical depression, your brain needs help producing "happy chemicals." Medication is the most direct way to do that, but using it raises objections for some people. Understanding my depression was a medical issue helped me be at peace with it spiritually. However, its use continues to be controversial, even among doctors and mental health experts. I would recommend trying other items on this list and other natural treatments before resorting to medication.

Counseling—It was very disorienting when I found out I had clinical depression. If you've been diagnosed, you will most likely need professional counseling to help get re-oriented. If incorporating faith in your recovery is important to you, you might want to look for a pastoral counselor (see Appendix B). But studies suggest Cognitive Behavior Therapy might be most effective for clinical depression.

Tell that voice in your head to shut up!—You know the one I'm talking about (See "The Voice ... That No One Wants to Hear"). If you're depressed, the voice in your head tells you you're a loser and gives you all the reasons why. It is quick-tempered and brings back old anger, even for things you and the other person have already made up for. What I finally realize is that voice is not real. It is the product of a chemically imbalanced brain. So drown it out with something positive and uplifting, like ...

Music—Music affects the brain in ways we are only beginning to understand. You might have a particular song that lifts your mood. If happy and upbeat music cheers you up, go ahead. When I hear Queen's "Seven Seas of Rye," I have to stop whatever I'm doing and sing along.

Does it have to be happy music? Not necessarily. Sad music can make you feel less alone in sadness. A lot of people feel better if they hear songs like "Everybody Hurts" by R.E.M. Musical taste is individual, so just play whatever works for you.

Diet & Exercise—I don't want to sound like a certain actor who suggested all you need to cure depression (post-partum in that case) is diet and exercise.[7] However, you should make it part of your recovery. Certain nutritional deficiencies can exacerbate depression. Also, people who live around the Mediterranean have very low rates of depression. It might be because of the beach or the sun, but another theory is that the Mediterranean diet might boost your natural antidepressants.

As for exercise, you've heard of the "runner's high"? That's your brain producing happy chemicals in response to exercise. I don't

---

[7] Peoplestaff, "Tom Cruise Criticizes Brooke Shields' Use of Antidepressants for Post-Partum Depression," People.com, May 25, 2005, https://people.com/parents/tom_cruise_crit/.

run because I have flat feet. However, there are other kinds of exercise that can give you the same effect: swimming, bicycling, rowing, etc. Try to find something you enjoy, so you can stick with it.

Laughter—You've heard the saying "Laughter is the best medicine." It's hard to be sad or angry while you're laughing. So watching a funny movie is more than entertainment. It's therapy. Solomon agrees. *A cheerful heart is a good medicine* (Proverbs 17:22a).

Sunlight—Seasonal Affective Disorder (SAD) is a type of depression specifically linked to lack of exposure to sunlight. Even if you don't have SAD, a little more sunshine (with sunscreen) might help lift your mood.

Meditation—Many studies have shown meditation affects the brain in very healthy ways. It promotes calmness, reduces stress and anxiety, and increases your sense of well-being. Over time, it has even been shown to change the structure of the brain, so the benefits become more permanent.

Prayer—This does not necessarily make me *feel* better, but it has been absolutely crucial for coping with stress and with life in general. Some people of faith, however, tend to think prayer should be the only thing you need to cure depression. Prayer is a great tool—but not the only tool—for recovery.

Favorite activities—This might be the best advice I ever got for coping with depression: Find something you love to do, and do it (from Kevin Gates, rapper). For him, it's rapping and making music. So any day he is not on tour, he is in the studio. It's not just his job. It's his therapy. Writing is the same for me. It's therapy because I love doing it. Do you have anything like that you love to do? Make sure you do it every day, even if it's just for a few minutes.

Forgiveness—You cannot recover if you are weighed down with anger, grudges, and resentment. If the wounds are fresh, it may take time. But make forgiveness the goal, even if it looks unforgivable right now.

Gratitude—The more you occupy your mind with anything, positive or negative, the more you will embody it. If you focus on what you are grateful for, you will find more reasons to be grateful. Maybe this is why Paul said to the Philippians,

Do not worry about anything, but in everything by prayer and supplication with thanksgiving let your requests be made known to God. And the peace of God, which surpasses all understanding will guard your hearts and your minds in Christ Jesus (Phil 4:6-7).

Set a timer—This is a trick I read in an interview with Christopher Reeve. If you remember, he had a horse-riding accident that left him quadriplegic. In public, it looked like he never let it get him down. One of his tricks was each morning he would set a timer for twenty minutes. During that time he could cry, rant, and rave about how unfair this is, how much it sucks, and when the timer went off, *stop right there!* Time to stop feeling sorry for yourself and get back to living.

Posture—Will changing your posture really change your mood? There is a mind-body connection. If you are hunched over, arms crossed, looking down, you look depressed and most likely feel depressed, too. Straighten your back. Lift your head. Look forward. Open your arms. You'll not only look confident but most likely feel more confident as well.

The Twelve-Step Model—I'm not an alcoholic, but I have found the AA model of recovery helpful in a number of ways. Its compassionate approach is conducive to healing. It teaches you to take responsibility without beating yourself up. You never say you are "recovered," but you are recovering. It teaches you to recognize the triggers of addiction (or depression), so you can avoid them. It gives you tools to choose happiness over addiction. It invokes the help of a higher power, but what that means is left open to you. And it incorporates the power of a supportive community, which is my next tool.

Community—I believe we were made to live in loving community, at home, at work, and in public life. The more places you have it, the better. I remember hearing of a news article with the title,

"Loneliness: The Number One Disease in America." I did not read the article, but the title alone is enough to get the point. Depression, especially, is exacerbated by loneliness.

The best cure for loneliness is loving, supportive community. I experience that in my family—including oodles of extended family—and in my church. Even if I did not believe the tenets of the church, I would still go because of the relationships I have there.

Whatever a loving community means to you, seek it out. It is the one place where I have always found this scripture to be true: Give, and it will be given unto you. A good measure, pressed down, shaken together, running over, will be put into your lap; for the measure you give will be the measure you get back (Luke 6:38).

Human touch—Studies have proven what I think most of us know in our hearts. Affectionate touching, from holding hands, to an arm around the shoulder, to snuggling, to hugging, to sex (when it is a genuine expression of love) reduces stress and anxiety and increases feelings of connection and well-being, all of which go a long way to alleviating depression.

But keep in mind, this is only true if the touching is desired by *both* people. Some people don't like to be touched (so they say). And not all forms of touching are appropriate in all situations. If you want to incorporate touching to help your recovery, be appropriate, and make sure the person on the receiving end welcomes it.

Nature (Ecotherapy)—Exposure to nature is good for mental health. An article on Vice.com gives some easy to understand info on the research in this area. A recent study at Harvard University published in April (2016) is among the latest of many to confirm this. A member of the research team summed up the findings up this way: "[T]here's a direct cognitive benefit and restorative quality of being in nature, that we've evolved in nature to enjoy being in nature."[8]

This does not mean you have to move out to the backwoods and reject civilization, a la Thoreau. Simply incorporate time with nature into your routine.

- Visit a park

---

[8] Lucy Jones, "How Nature Benefits Your Mental Health," Vice, May 24, 2016, https://tonic.vice.com/en_us/article/av37kp/how-nature-benefits-your-mental-health.

- Notice what's in your backyard

- Plant a tree

- Enjoy a local green space

- Take a break at your favorite lake, river, arbor, or any natural attraction.

If none of this is available in or near your city, maybe you need to petition the authorities to add some. Any municipality should at least be able to plant trees along a street or open a park.

Transcranial Magnetic Stimulation (TMS)—This is a new technology of using magnets to stimulate serotonin and epinephrine production in the brain. Like anti-depressant medication, the purpose is to get your brain producing more "happy chemicals." But with TMS, the treatment is concentrated in the areas of the brain where you need help rather than all over the body. I like the idea of it, but it's expensive and requires daily in-office treatments for five to six weeks.

Cannabidiol (CBD) Oil—*The Early Show* on CBS ran a story on CBD oil's possible use helping NFL players deal with pain, and it might even help with brain injuries.[9] It comes from the cannabis plant, but it does not have the psychoactive properties of THC. Doctors are saying it could have many medicinal uses including anti-seizure, cancer treatment, and anti-anxiety. Could it be an effective treatment for anxiety and depression? It works through the same mechanisms as AD medication, but it appears to have fewer side effects.

If you are taking AD medication, going off it can be rough, even if it's to replace it with something else. Natural and prescription AD medications usually do not work well when taken together. You should consult your physician before taking on this or any new treatment.

I'm not sure if the research is complete yet, so for me the jury is still out. However, it looks like it could be promising not only for depression and anxiety but for many other health issues.

---

[9] "Could Marijuana Compound CBD Help NFL Players With Pain?" *The Early Show*, CBS Interactive, Inc., November 30, 2016, television.

###

These are the tools I have found so far. Hopefully, it was enough to give you some ideas of what you can do for your depression. You don't have to use all of them, of course. Just see if there are any you could add to your toolbox.

Grace and Peace to you

CHAPTER EIGHT

Chris Cornell's Black Hole Sun

Posted May 21, 2017

As rock fans know, on May 18, Soundgarden's Chris Cornell was found dead in his hotel room in Detroit. It was officially ruled a suicide by hanging. It was probably related to Ativan,[10] a prescription drug mostly used to treat anxiety disorders. I know he had a history of depression and drug addiction. That combination often ends in tragedy.

Still, I have a hard time understanding it, because I saw him on CBS's *Saturday Morning Show* last month,[11] and it looked like everything was going well for him. He wrote the theme song for the movie *The Promise*. The song was so beautifully poignant, I really wanted to see the movie after that. My girlfriend and I both loved it. We had never heard of the Turkish genocide campaign against the Armenians, so we learned some important history. Cornell made us both want to see it.

He was touring with Soundgarden and excited about the new music they were making. He was proud of the music he wrote for the movie. He sounded optimistic, and it seemed like he had every reason to be

---

[10] Gil Kaufman, "Chris Cornell's Death: Mental Health Experts Talk Depression, Suicide & Ativan," Billboard, May 19, 2017, https://www.billboard.com/articles/news/7801027/chris-cornell-death-mental-health-experts-depression-suicide-ativan.

[11] "Soundgarden's Chris Cornell on Writing for Movies," *CBS This Morning*, CBS News. CBS Interactive, April 22, 2017, television.

happy with his life now. He did not look like he had any reason to want to die. That's why the news came as such a shock. And yet I know that is what depression can do to you.

He called his wife just before. He told her he had taken "extra Ativan." I have let you know about my use of antidepressant drugs. In my case, they have helped tremendously, but they don't work for everyone. Sometimes, they can make the condition worse, so you have to work closely with your physician or psychiatrist if you decide to try it. While Ativan is an anti-anxiety medication rather than antidepressant, any kind of psychotropic drug affects everyone differently. It is possible that too much of it took his mind to a place we cannot understand, where hanging himself made perfect sense. The fact that an anti-anxiety drug was prescribed for him shows he was having some struggles.

When Your Sun Is a Black Hole

I've seen it before, especially in people who struggle with both depression and drug addiction. They get treatment, they get clean and sober, and they look happy. They show no signs of being suicidal. They get their career and family life back on track. You think they've turned their lives around, then *bam*! The news hits you like a 2″ x 4″. You saw them just a few days or weeks ago, and you wonder why you didn't see any signs.

Since my girlfriend knows I have a history with depression, she couldn't help wondering about me. I reassured her that I'm not just pretending to be happy. I really am, thanks in large part to her. But that's what happens to the people left behind. It makes them second-guess themselves and you, especially if they know you have struggled with depression, anxiety, and/or drugs in the past. You look happy, but how do they know? And so with her worried about me, I gave my word I would never do that to her. Was that enough? I hope so, because it really was the only assurance I could offer.

I would not do that to her, or my mother, or sister, or father, or niece or nephew, or brother-in-law, or all the relatives I see almost every year in our family reunions, or my friends at church. When I think of Cornell, I feel at a loss. Such a great talent. Such a great voice. Such great music he made. He had a wife and children who loved him. If I was shocked, sad, and baffled, how must they feel?

Higher Truth

I don't care who you are; you have people in your life who love you and care about you. Suicide will leave them devastated and agonizing about where *they* went wrong. Even if it's just one person who cares, think how they will feel if you go through with it. Even if no person on earth loves you, God does. If you don't believe in God, God still believes in you.

I'm still not sure what purpose God made me for. But in my lowest points in life, what stopped me from suicide was I didn't want to hurt my family, and I didn't want to die without fulfilling God's purpose for me. I just kept trudging through the darkness, not knowing if I was going in the right direction, with nothing but the hope that someday, somehow, I would find out my reason for living. And now, I'm finally starting to see that as a possibility.

Some of those things I went through for so long when I was really in the depths of depression, I wouldn't wish on anyone. I would never want to go back there. But the fact that I can see the light now proves I did the right thing to keep living when that was all I knew how to do. And if I can use that experience to help one person who is lost, who doesn't see any possibility for happiness in this life, if I can convince you to never give up on life because one day, you will find your way as I did, then everything I went through was worth it.

Keep living. Seek your purpose, and you will find it. You can have a happy and fulfilling life. You just need to learn how to stop your depressed brain from sabotaging it.

Grace and Peace to you.

CHAPTER NINE

Fell on Black Days

Posted May 27, 2017

Chris Cornell was laid to rest in Seattle today. I know I've already written one post, and I don't want to look like I'm rehashing the same subject. It's just that so much about the circumstances in which he died touches on my own experiences with depression and hard lessons I've learned through them that one post was not enough.

Depression and Grunge Music

The Seattle Grunge that exploded onto the music scene in the early '90s sounded like it came from a city where it rained nine months out of the year: dark, depressed, moody, brooding, and riddled with distortion and druggy haze but also brilliantly creative and original. If I asked who were the Big Four of Grunge, I think anyone would say, Nirvana, Pearl Jam, Alice in Chains, and Cornell's Soundgarden. We had already lost Kurt Cobain and Layne Staley. In a 2014 interview for *Rolling Stone*, Cornell said this about them and other area musicians he knew.

The tragedy was much more than the fact that I would never see him again—it was that I would never hear him again. There's this projection I had with Andy, Kurt, Jeff Buckley and other friends of mine that died of looking into the future at all these

> *amazing things they're going to do. I'll never be able to predict what that is. All this music that will come out that will challenge me and inspire me—that sort of romantic, dramatic version of the perspective. When that goes away, for me in particular, it was a really hard thing. And it continues to be a hard thing....*
>
> *So part of my memory of every record, and certainly Superunknown, there's an eeriness in there, a kind of unresolvable sadness or indescribable longing that I've never really tried to isolate and define and fully understand. But it's always there. It's like a haunted thing.*[12]

And now those same words apply to Cornell himself. Of the Big Four, three have now lost lead singers to depression and/or drug addiction. The two often go hand in hand. I never got on drugs myself, but I am convinced a lot of drug use associated with these bands was really self-medicating undiagnosed depression.

Where Do "Black Days" Come From?

In that same interview, Chris Cornell opened up about his depression. On the inspiration behind the song "Fell on Black Days," he said,

> *No matter how happy you are, you can wake up one day without any specific thing occurring to bring you into a darker place, and you'll just be in a darker place anyway. To me, that was always a terrifying thought, because that's something that— as far as I know—we don't necessarily have control over. So that was the song I wanted to write. It just took a while.*[13]

Cornell accurately described the experience of millions of people living with depression. You look around at your life, you think you should be happy, and you're not. You're depressed, and you have no reason to be. If you can't be happy when everything in life is going well, how can you ever be happy? Maybe you think there's no point in

---

[12] "Soundgarden's Chris Cornell on Superunknown, Depression, and Kurt Cobain." Rolling Stone. Edited and posted May 19, 2017. https://www.rollingstone.com/music/music-features/soundgardens-chris-cornell-on-superunknown-depression-and-kurt-cobain-119623/.
[13] Ibid.

going on. Or maybe you sabotage your career or your relationships, so at least then you have a reason to be depressed. It doesn't make sense to you, but I'm here to tell you there's a reason for it.

Depression can either be clinical or situational. If there is nothing in your situation that can explain your depression, then it must be clinical. There are a number of possibilities, but the most common is that you have a chemically imbalanced brain. I've talked before about the depressed voice in my head (See Chapter, "The Voice..."). When I was off my medication, the depressed voice came back with a vengeance. But as I took my new medication, the voice went away. What this means is that voice in your head that tells you, *you're worthless, you're a waste of space, you're a burden, you'll never be happy so why not end it all, no one loves you, God has forsaken you, blah blah blah*–that is the voice of a chemically imbalanced brain.

This is nothing to be ashamed of. Some people are born with a heart murmur. You were born with something like a "brain murmur." It's not your fault, any more than the person with the heart condition. Clinical depression, like all mental illness, needs to be treated like a medical condition, not a failure of character.

My Diagnosis

I did not always know this. Seventeen years ago, I was diagnosed with clinical depression. Before that, there had been times I knew I was depressed. But I always thought it was temporary. There were times I thought I was happy. But even then, people sometimes asked why I was sad, or even worse, why I was angry. It's frustrating when people don't believe you when you say you're happy. When I found out about clinical depression, this finally made sense. I might have felt happy, but chemically, my brain was still depressed. There was this underlying sadness people sometimes picked up.

It did not feel like depression, I guess, because it was normal to me. It was the way I had always felt. When I heard a psychologist say, *You tested high for depression in every possible way*, I don't think anyone had ever said anything about me that shocked me more.

It was totally surreal. It was something I never would have thought of myself in a million years. I thought, *it can't really be that bad*, and yet I knew it was true. Like I said, even at times when I felt happy, people around me thought I was sad or upset. No matter how I felt– happy, sad, good, bad, apathetic, optimistic, or hopeless–every moment of my life, I had been living with a brain tilted toward depression.

Do Not Believe Every Spirit

If I could have been there with Cornell, I would have pleaded, "Whatever you're thinking, don't do it. These thoughts you're having are not real. I know they feel real to you. They sound like the Gospel truth. But they are not. These thoughts are just chemical imbalances in your brain. Whatever you do, don't let these chemically induced voices make life-and-death decisions for you. Don't believe these voices in your head. Fight them. Treat them like the enemy, because they want to kill you. Don't let them. God will help you if you call on Him. God can help you fight these thoughts and imaginations that exalt themselves against the knowledge that you are a child of God with unique gifts to give the world. Music is part of it, but there is much more ahead. Even if you have never believed that before, dare to believe that just this once."

Don't believe anyone who says Chris Cornell died because of drugs. He died because he had a mental illness, an anxiety disorder of some kind. He was under the influence of a drug, but he had a prescription for it. He did the right thing by seeking professional help for his condition. And so it breaks my heart that the very thing that saved my life ended up killing him.

Medications like Ativan can help some people with anxiety disorders, just like Zoloft and Trintellix helped me with depression. Unfortunately, they don't help everyone. In fact, for some people, it may make them more depressed, more anxious, and more suicidal. If that is happening to you, don't make life-and-death decisions from your chemically imbalanced brain. At least, wait until you tell your doctor the medication is making it worse, and come up with another plan.

Suicide is a permanent solution to a temporary problem. Wouldn't it be tragic if you killed yourself before you found out the solution was as simple as changing your medication?

Grace and Peace to you.

P.S. The National Suicide Prevention Lifeline is always open. 800-273-TALK (800-273-8255).

###

Update: There were a few facts I did not know at the time I posted this. Toxicology reports showed Cornell had six prescription drugs in his system.[14] A couple of months before his death, he admitted to a friend he had relapsed.[15] One can only imagine with all of that in his system what was going on in his mind.

I still stand by my statement that we did not lose Cornell to drugs. We lost him to mental illness. The drugs in his system were *prescription* drugs. According to his widow, it most likely started with pain from a torn shoulder. He got a prescription for painkillers, which is already dangerous for a recovering addict.[16]

I can easily imagine when that did not work, he took more, then got a prescription for another drug, then another, including Ativan, which also should not be given to recovering addicts.[17] Addiction never really leaves you, even if you have been clean and sober for years. That is why Alcoholics Anonymous says recovery is one day at a time.

If he could have made it through one more day, so he could look for a better doctor, get support from family and friends, get into a recovery program, maybe...I don't know. We can never know what goes on in someone else's head. That is why so often after suicide, friends and family are left seeing signs *in hindsight.*

If you are one of those left behind after a suicide, I can tell you this. It is normal to feel guilty. It is normal to think you should have seen it coming. That is because it is easy to connect the dots after it happens. But before then, it is only speculation. You've probably been told "you can't blame yourself." You might be sick of hearing it, so I'll just say, you're not alone.

I have not had thoughts of suicide since one time about fifteen years ago when I switched antidepressants. My mind went crazy. There is no telling what kind of thoughts you'll have when your brain is chemically imbalanced. If you are thinking about suicide, remember: Do not let your chemically imbalanced brain make any life or death decisions for you.

---

14 TMZ Staff. "Chris Cornell's Toxicology Report Reveals Prescriptions Drugs." TMZ, June 2, 2017. https://www.tmz.com/2017/06/02/chris-cornell-toxicology-report-overdose-drugs-suicide/.

15 "Chris Cornell's Widow Opens Up about Her Husband's Addiction before His Suicide," *ABC News*, February 22, 2018, television.

16 Ibid.

17 Brett Buchanan, "Dr. Drew Reveals What He Thinks Led to Chris Cornell's Death," Alternative Nation, May 21, 2017, http://www.alternativenation.net/dr-drew-reveals-thinks-led-chris-cornells-death/.

Finally, I will say this. When it is that desperate, I don't know how anyone makes it out of that darkness without trust in God, a loving, supportive community, and a strong program for recovery. If you haven't done it yet, the wisest thing is to start on those three things now.

Do you know who/what your higher power is? Have you found a loving, supportive community, even if it's just one or two friends you can share your struggles with? Do you have a good model of recovery to follow? Don't wait until despair overwhelms you. Get started now, so when those voices in your head try to kill you, you have something to fight back with.

Grace and peace to you.
January 10, 2019

Mark 4:40–Where Is Your Faith?

Posted January 25, 2018

This was originally a devotion I wrote for a meeting of the American Christian Fiction Writers (ACFW). A verse that once made me feel like a failure now gives me hope and confidence.

He Said to Them, "Why Are You Afraid? Have You No Faith?" (Mark 4:40)

I'm reading from the Revised Standard Version. This verse comes from the story of Jesus calming the storm on the sea of Galilee (Mark 4:35-41). With so many translations available now, some words might be different, but this is basically how most of them read this verse. Occasionally, though, you find someone who wants their translation to stand apart, like one that says, *Jesus reprimanded the disciples: "Why are you such cowards? Don't you have any faith at all?" (The Message).*

As a writer, I look at that and say, "Wow, that's powerful dialogue. It's got some punch to it." But as a follower of Jesus, I have to be honest, I don't respond well to that kind of tone. It just reminds me of so many times when I was wracked with guilt for not having enough faith, which led to me thinking I was a coward, and, of course, God does not bless cowards, which was why God wasn't blessing me.

A couple of weeks ago, Fran and I went to a baby shower at a friend's church. The preacher was very good. She preached from this text; yes, she was a woman, and with an accent that sounded Australian. Not what you expect to find in the boondocks of upstate South Carolina. Anyway, the version she read from said it this way: *"Why are you afraid? Where is your faith?"*

I haven't been able to find this translation. I guess I will have to go back to that church and see what they use as their pew Bibles. In her message, she pointed out Jesus was not condemning or reprimanding the disciples, despite *The Message*'s translation. He was not berating them, saying, "Why are you such cowards? Don't you have any faith at all?" He did not even get angry at them for waking him up. Because if you remember, Jesus was in the bottom of the boat asleep, and they had to wake him up, saying, "Don't you care if we perish?"

First, he calmed the storm, so they could hear him clearly. And then, the question was, "Where is your faith?" In other words, have you forgotten your faith? Have you forgotten who I am? And in the midst of the storm, it is so easy to forget.

Forgetting

I felt so good when I finally finished the manuscript for my novel. When I shopped it around to agents and editors, however, they weren't exactly thrilled. And the most common and frustrating objection I kept hearing was they didn't want multiple points of view. It's too confusing.

Are you kidding me? I know there are bestsellers with multiple points of view. Some of my favorite authors use multiple points of view. How can you tell me multiple POV makes my novel unpublishable?

But they countered by telling me those who use it are already bestsellers, and I'm not an established bestselling author.

I seriously considered reworking it to tell the story with two point of view characters, which they said would be acceptable. Maybe I could, but I don't believe it would be as good a story if I did. And only one point of view character for the whole novel? Forget it.

Don't You Care If I Perish?

So I turn to God like, "Why didn't you tell me? How was I supposed to know they wouldn't publish multiple points of view?"

I wrestled for weeks and months with what to do. Should I keep looking for that one publisher who's willing to take a chance on me? Should I try to make a better query letter and book proposal? Or should I go through the daunting task of self-publishing it? Eventually, a conversation like this unfolded in my mind.

Do you believe God gave you this story? Yes.
Do you believe God would give you an unpublishable story? No? No. NO!

God did not give me this story, knowing how long it would take, writing and rewriting every scene until I had it to where I thought it was good enough to publish, and had that confirmed from critique groups and friends and family, just to find out, "Sorry, the publishing industry has changed. No one is buying novels with multiple points of view anymore." Agents and editors know a lot, but they don't know everything.

So now what are you going to do?

There must be a path to publication, and God knows what that is. I will seek, and I will find it.

Storms in the Life of a Creative

If you believe God has given you a gift of creativity, at some point, you have to share that gift with the world. No matter how you decide to do that, there will be storms ahead. You may think you will never be as good as that writer you admire so much. You may get so many rejections that it will cause you to question every decision you've made in life. You may start a blog and, after two years, still have fewer followers than your shirt size and wonder what you're doing wrong. You may hear God calling you to make this your career, and, six months later, you're not even being paid enough to make rent or mortgage payments. And I could go on, but I don't want you to lose sight of the hope offered in this story.

In these storms, do you hear Jesus saying, "Why are you afraid? Where is your faith?" To me, that is a gentle reminder that God did not send me out in this boat to drown in the storm halfway to the other side. It simply comes down to what everything in life seems to come down to: God saying, "Do you trust me?"

Now, hear these words from Isaiah.

> *When you pass through the waters, I will be with you; and through the rivers, they shall not overwhelm you; when you walk through fire you shall not be burned, and the flame shall not consume you (Is 43:2).*

Grace and Peace to you.

The War on Thanksgiving

Posted December 1, 2016

Sometime in December, probably multiple times, I expect to hear about the "war on Christmas," because someone said Happy Holidays instead of Merry Christmas. Has anyone noticed there has been an ongoing war on Thanksgiving?

I remember when stores would wait until after Thanksgiving to play Christmas music and put up Christmas decorations. Black Friday marked the beginning of the Christmas shopping season. Now, it's the day after Halloween. This year, on November 1, I was in a discount grocery store. It was sunny and almost 80 degrees outside, not even a hint of snowflakes, and I heard "Sleigh Bells" through the store speakers. I wanted to shout, "This is just wrong, people! It's still more than three weeks until Thanksgiving!"

And a few years ago, stores started opening on Thanksgiving day. Really? You can't wait until Black Friday for your big sale?

Good or Bad for Business?

A *USA Today* article showed the state of the debate from the business side. On one hand, there is the question about whether it makes business sense. Instead of resulting in more sales and profits, the numbers suggest Thanksgiving Day sales dilute the sales and purchases of Black Friday. So you are open on this holiday, but overall you are not making any more money. On the other hand, some believe being closed on Thanksgiving will soon be outdated. Most stores used to be closed on Sunday. Now shopping and running errands on Sunday is normal. Will the same thing happen with Thanksgiving?

"As long as shoppers want to make purchases on Thanksgiving, stores will continue to accommodate them," one professor said.[18]

Either way, however, it comes down to a business decision. Retailers need to maximize the Christmas shopping season any way they can. If you don't make it at Christmas, you don't make it. I understand that. But do you have to make your employees sacrifice a major holiday and the last chance to spend meaningful time with their families before the Christmas rush?

Why Am I Talking about This on a Blog about Faith and Depression?

Because gratitude and giving thanks are powerful antidotes to depression and perhaps the most important (and underrated) acts of faith. Think about a time when you were truly grateful from the bottom of your heart. When gratitude overwhelmed you. Were you depressed then? Did it even occur to you that you could possibly be depressed at that moment? That's what I mean about it being a powerful antidote. You can't be depressed when you are truly thankful.

We have a day set aside to give thanks for our blessings and the blessings of this nation: the fourth Thursday of every November. And every year we ignore it, trivialize it, and treat it as a speed bump in our rush to get started shopping for Christmas. Black Friday is threatening to take over Thanksgiving altogether. Taking even one day out of the shopping season to stop, remember our blessings, share them with our families, and be thankful is treated as a waste of time, and even worse, a waste of money.

Isn't that a perfect metaphor for our lives? We rush and rush to acquire more stuff and buy the love of our families and never stop to be grateful for what we already have. Sounds like the perfect recipe for depression.

So this year I am going to support Thanksgiving by doing my Christmas shopping only at stores that close on Thanksgiving Day. And I will wait until after Christmas before I shop any stores that were open on Thanksgiving. The only way this will change is if consumers

---

[18] Josh Hafner, "To Open or Not? Inside Stores' Thanksgiving Dilemma," USA Today, October 19, 2016, https://www.usatoday.com/story/money/nation-now/2016/10/19/open-not-retailers-wage-battle-thanksgiving/92380280/

prove to these companies that it really makes no business sense to try to make people shop when we should be giving thanks.

> *If the only prayer you ever say in your entire life is thank you, it will be enough.*
>
> *-Meister Eckhart (1260-1328)*

Grace and peace to you.

CHAPTER ELEVEN

The Holiday Blues

Posted November 30, 2018

'Tis the season when you hear "Joy To The World" and "The Most Wonderful Time Of The Year" everywhere you go. We think of the holidays as a joyful time, where we get to enjoy our families, food, and gifts. Yet for some, the holidays are a time of stress, sadness, and loneliness.

Why are the holidays a depressing time for some people? Experts cite a number of reasons.

- **Stress**. The parties, the get-togethers, the shopping, the decorating, yes, it's all fun, but it's stressful, too. Normal irritations can become magnified during the holidays.

- **Pressure to be happy**. When you see people around you happily saying "Merry Christmas" or "Happy Holidays," and stores are playing holiday music to get people in a shopping mood, you feel out of place if you cannot get into "the holiday spirit."

- **Unrealistic expectations**. Comparisons often lead to depression. If you are comparing this holiday to ones in the past, you'll feel disappointed if this year does not measure up. If your neighbors are cheerful and appear to have it together better than you do, remember at home behind closed doors, they are probably as stressed as you are.

- **Doing too much**. If just the thought of holidays brings stress and anxiety, it's probably because you have done too much in the past. Maybe it's time to scale back.

- **Neglecting self-care**. If you meditate and exercise, you might be tempted to put that on hold because you feel pressed for time. You might not be getting enough sleep or taking time during the day to decompress.

- **Family strife**. Spending time with family is the most important part of the holidays for most people. However, there might be some family you'd rather avoid.

- **Overindulging**. If you have depression, WebMD recommends you avoid food and drink that makes your blood sugar spike. This includes most of the holiday treats we love. Sugar highs and the inevitable crashes afterward are not a recipe for holiday cheer. And of course, overindulging in alcohol will not help.

- **Isolation**. Being apart from those you love never feels good. But during the holidays, you miss them even more. For those who have just moved to a new city, especially if they are single, they may not have made any friends where they are. They feel alone because they have no one to celebrate with.

- **Grieving**. The first holiday after the loss of your spouse or parents or children can be rough. If most of your best holiday memories are with someone who can no longer be with you, the loss you feel will most likely be magnified during the holidays.

- **Seasonal Affective Disorder (SAD)**. This is a condition where people become more depressed as the days get shorter. The holiday season, from Thanksgiving to New Year's, is timed perfectly for SAD.

- **Post-holiday letdown**. You manage to get your fill of holiday cheer in spite of the stress, and then it's over. Until next year at least. As stressful as it was, some people miss the activity, the busyness, the holiday cheer, and the people who have gone back home.

- **Overspending**. Some people use "retail therapy" to cope with depression, and the holidays present every temptation to overspend. Buying those expensive gifts is a big hit with those you give to. Then the credit card bills arrive.

What You Can Do

1. **Set expectations low.** The lower your expectations, the less you can be disappointed. Don't expect everything to be perfect, and you won't have a meltdown when it's not.

2. **Plan ahead and prioritize.** Make a list of all the things you expect to do for the holidays, then prioritize. Schedule time for the most important things. If you don't have time for everything on the list, some lower priority items have to go. Do you have to go to every party you're invited to? Can someone else host the family Christmas party this year? Can you enlist friends and family to help with the preparations? Say no to a few things that are not high on the priority list. Most people will not be nearly as disappointed as you think.

3. **Set a budget.** Know how much money you have to spend on each person before you start shopping. Don't pressure yourself to buy the best and most expensive version. If you don't trust yourself, bring a friend who will make you stick to your budget. The best gifts don't have to cost anything. I honestly believe if I gave my wife a "coupon" for a free massage, she would like that better than a diamond necklace. Remember they want your presence more than your presents.

4. **Maintain healthy habits.** Enjoy your treats, but remember to eat healthy, get enough sleep, and avoid overindulging. Keep up your exercise and meditation routines. If you don't meditate, you should start. A few minutes of meditation can do wonders for stress. Whatever you normally do to de-stress, don't forget to do it during the holidays.

5. **Manage family encounters.** If you dread getting together with some family members, here are some options, listed in increasing severity.

a) *Set aside differences.* Don't get baited into those same old debates. If you argue with the same person every year, you already know what they are going to say. Resolve before you go in you will not waste any more time trying to set them straight. If they start, just say Merry Christmas and talk to someone else. If there is some past slight you are still sore about, what better time to forgive than the holidays?

b) *Seek out the positive people.* Instead of fretting over that relative who is always critical, think of the people you enjoy, and seek them out. If you are busy with them, that means less time with negative people. You can ask the person arranging the seating to place you next to someone more supportive. Better to say, "Can you sit me next to this cousin?" than "Don't sit me next to Aunt Martha."

c) *Make an early exit.* You can always make an appearance, and make sure those who need to see you do so. After a decent amount of time, you can say you have to go because of another commitment.

d) *Avoid certain people altogether.* It is better for your mental health to forgive than to hold grudges. But if the pain is too raw, or if you know they are going to make you miserable, then don't go to the party or to their house.

6. **Volunteer.** Nothing is more in keeping with the season than helping someone in need. Volunteer at a homeless shelter, soup kitchen, or other community service. Helping others feels good and is often the best antidote for depression. You might even want to make it a new tradition.

7. **Attend Community, Religious, or Social Events.** Religious services have always been a part of my holiday tradition. With or without my family, I like being a part of them. If that is not your thing, look for other community and social events open to the public. They present low pressure opportunities to do something with friends or meet new people who share your interests.

8. **Call friends and family.** One year my sister was working as a missionary in Mexico. We celebrated Christmas as usual—me, my parents, and grandparents. In the afternoon, we used my iPad to call my sister on Skype. My grandparents were thrilled not only to talk to her but also to see her. It is easy these days to set up video chat online. Skype is still available, though WhatsApp and Viber seem to be more popular now. If you have an iPhone, Facetime is included. Bottom line, for your loved ones who are miles away, if you have a cell phone, tablet, or computer, you can contact them.

9. **Journal your feelings.** I started keeping a journal in college. I journaled about things that happened to me and how I felt about them. During bouts of depression, it was a lifeline for me. Which is why if you read my journals, you would probably think I was a basket case. But studies have shown that journaling your feelings, especially during times of grief or depression, helps people feel less depressed and less anxious. Darlene Mininni, author of *The Emotional Toolkit*, suggests writing for 15 minutes three or four days in a row to start. If you don't know what to write, you can prompt yourself by writing and answering questions like, "Why does this upset me?" or "What do I want to happen now?"[19]

10. **Get counseling.** If you can't shake feelings of sadness, loneliness, or anxiety, it might be time to seek professional help. I've listed some websites where you can search for a counselor in your area (Appendix B).

11. **Remember to be grateful.** The holiday season starts with Thanksgiving. That's a hint. Begin each day with just a minute or two to think of three things you are grateful for, and the rest of your day is likely to go better.

12. **Plan a post-holiday get-together.** This is a way to ease any post-holiday letdown. Set a date to get together with a friend in mid or late January. This will give you something to look forward to after the holidays.

---

[19] Cited in Denise Mann, "Depression during the Holidays," WebMD, November 8, 2007. https://www.webmd.com/depression/features/emotional-survival-guide-for-holidays#1.

###

In the chapter called "The War on Thanksgiving," I said this. "We rush and rush to acquire more stuff and buy the love of our families and never stop to be grateful for what we already have. Sounds like the perfect recipe for depression."

The point I was trying to make is not to let commercialization take over the real meaning of the holidays. Sure, I buy gifts for whoever I'm spending Christmas with. I enjoy getting presents, but I also enjoy seeing their faces when they open a gift I gave them, especially when my niece and nephew are there. They are still young enough to approach Christmas morning with unbridled joy. Isn't that what we really want from the holidays? To give and receive joy?

So whatever you do, whether it's decorating, baking, making the holiday dinners, trimming the tree, eating with family and friends, shopping for gifts, making gifts, volunteering, attending religious services, whatever your traditions are, or if you think it's time to start a new tradition, do it with the intent of spreading joy. That is the surest way I know to have a happy Thanksgiving, happy Chanukah, merry Christmas, happy Kwanzaa, happy Boxing Day, happy New Year, and Epiphany/Dia de los Reyes. And a happy Festivus for the rest of us.

Grace and peace to you.

CHAPTER TWELVE

Longest Night Service

Posted December 2, 2018

We celebrate Christmas on December 25, but that is not when Jesus was most likely born. The Gospel of Luke says, "And in the same region there were shepherds out in the field, keeping watch over their flock by night" (Luke 2:8).

If Luke is correct, this would place his birth between February and April, when the ewes give birth to their lambs. This is when shepherds had to watch them all night, to be ready to assist the laboring sheep. This begs the question, why do we celebrate on December 25?

In about 312 AD, Constantine became emperor of Rome. He credited a key victory over his rival to a vision of the cross. He wanted to make an official holiday for Jesus's birth. Mithras, a Persian deity, was also popular in the empire. His devotees celebrated his birthday on December 25. Constantine thought celebrating Jesus's birth on the same day would help unify the people.

It also corresponded with the winter solstice and the Unconquered Sun celebration. Back then, as today, people noticed the days getting shorter until the winter solstice, the longest night of the year. It was as if the sun was weakening over months, maybe dying. Just when hope was at its lowest, the sun would gather its strength, and the days started getting longer again. The sun was still unconquered.

The Longest Night of the Year

Some churches have taken this idea of the longest night and made services around that theme. The idea is to give people who are depressed, lonely, and grieving during the holidays a chance to acknowledge those feelings. In my own denomination (Presbyterian Church USA), only about 25% of congregations offer this type of service. I have never been to one. Here is what I've learned so far.

- They may be called Blue Christmas or Longest Night services. I think the Longest Night is a more appropriate name. As one pastor said, "When you hear, 'Come to the Blue Christmas service,' you might think it is a service where you will get depressed."[20] That is not the impression they want to give.

- In some churches, the Advent candles of hope, peace, joy, and love, are extinguished. For the Longest Night, they are replaced by hopelessness, fear, grief, and loneliness. This is not to depress people but to give them a chance to acknowledge these feelings.

- Some churches have parish nurses plan and participate in the services.

Even though many acknowledge the need for a service like this during the holidays, attendance is often low. When one associate pastor of a congregation with 1,500 members proposed the idea, the members overwhelmingly approved it. But at the service itself, only twenty-five attended. Despite putting more effort into publicizing it and explaining the purpose, next year was the same. When asked why, people said they were not depressed, so they did not think this service was for them.[21]

This is less than two percent of the congregation. The percentage of people living with depression is much greater than that. This points to a larger problem, not only in the church, but also in society as a whole. It is still difficult for many people to acknowledge depression and the feelings associated with it, especially during the holidays. As one pastor said, "People are really unwilling to self-identify as grieving. People seem to prefer to think of themselves as independent and

---

[20] Eric Dunigan, "Blue Christmas: 'Tis The Season—For Depression," *Presbyterians Today,* Oct. 26, 2018, https://www.presbyterianmission.org/story/pt-1118-bluexmas/.
[21] Ibid.

self-reliant and all those 'boot strappy' words that are part of our American ideal."[22]

Another said, "We as a culture tend to overlook the people who are grieving, who are lonely, especially at this time of year."[23]

In light of this, some churches found they had a better response when they focused on healing for others. Most people are more willing to come on behalf of a friend or family member who has experienced loss than for themselves.

Christmas on the Longest Night

Even though it is not historically accurate, Christmas on or near the longest night of the year fits spiritually. On Christmas, we celebrate the eternal Word of God becoming flesh and dwelling among us in the person of Jesus of Nazareth. In him was the same light that was with God in the beginning. And like the unconquered sun, even though the light may be hidden, it has always been and will always be there. *The light shines in darkness, and the darkness did not overcome it* (John 1:5).

In his flesh, Jesus experienced all the hopelessness, fear, grief, and loneliness you or I ever have. We believe he is present to walk with us through our darkness and pain until we see the light again. Knowing this has not canceled out the light represented in Advent, Christmas, and Easter services for me. It has made them meaningful at a deeper level.

One pastor said it very well. "The Incarnation is a reason for celebration that God loved us so much that God sent Jesus to be with us, but it is also a reason for celebration that Jesus came to walk with us through the pains of life as well. I wish we could better hold these two messages together."[24]

Grace and peace to you.

---

[22] Ibid.
[23] Ibid.
[24] Ibid.

CHAPTER THIRTEEN

Total Eclipse of the Soul

Posted September 12, 2017

I bet when Bonnie Tyler recorded "Total Eclipse of the Heart," she had no idea it would be one of the biggest hits of 1983. Even more so, I bet she had no idea that thirty-four years later, it would become number one *again*, and everyone would be talking about it. Or that a cruise ship would hire her to sing it as they sailed into the path of a solar eclipse.[25] I didn't make it to that cruise, but I was one of the lucky ones who only had to step into my backyard to see the eclipse. I didn't really want to get caught up in eclipse-mania, but when a wonder of the heavens is observable right where you live, you know you will never forgive yourself if you miss it.

The sun is the very model of consistency and dependability. The earth keeps spinning on its axis, and the sun holds its position (relatively), so every part of the globe experiences daytime and nighttime. Sunrise and sunset happen at totally predictable times each and every day. You can literally set your watch and calendar by it. It shines on everyone on the face of the earth ... except during an eclipse.

Thanks to the website www.eclipse2017.org, I found out the eclipse I watched started at 1:09:15 PM. I saw totality for 2 minutes, 35 seconds, starting at 2:37:57 PM. And "total" is important. The dif-

---

[25] Chris Graham, "Bonnie Tyler Sings 'Total Eclipse of the Heart' on Cruise Ship to Celebrate Solar Eclipse," *Telegraph*, August, 21, 2017, https://www.telegraph.co.uk/news/2017/08/21/bonnie-tyler-perform-total-eclipse-heart-solar-eclipse/.

ference between 99% and 100% is never more striking than when you are watching an eclipse.

It amazes me how today, scientists can calculate exactly where the path of totality will travel, and based on your location, tell you exactly when the eclipse will begin, exactly when and for how long you will see totality, and exactly when it will end, down to a fraction of a second.

But what if you were living at a time before that kind of mathematical precision? What if you were a caveman, and you saw a total eclipse for the first time? You know it's supposed to be daytime, and then all of a sudden it's night. You look up, and it looks like the sun has been swallowed by the moon, which now has this fiery halo all around it. (I know you're not supposed to look directly at an eclipse without those special glasses, but stay with me on this). Day has turned to night. Nocturnal birds are waking up. Crickets and cicadas are chirping. *What's happening???*

But after about two and a half minutes, the sun returns, and you've learned an important lesson. The sun can be hidden, but it is always where it should be in the sky.

Fourth Day vs. First Day

In Genesis Chapter 1, the sun, moon, and stars were created on the fourth day of creation. I thought about this, because the only time you can see the sun, moon, and stars all together is during a total eclipse. Unfortunately, when it turned dark, the automatic streetlights in my neighborhood turned on. The ambient light hid all but a handful of stars. Still, it was enough to make me marvel that for the first time in my life, I could see all the heavenly bodies represented at once. It made me appreciate that fourth day of creation in a new way.

Also in Genesis, light was created *before* the sun, moon, and stars. Light was created on the first day, but then God waited three more days to create the heavenly bodies that shine their light on earth. I'm not arguing for a literal six-day creation here, but I do believe the author of that particular passage did this deliberately. Whether the author was Moses (as tradition says) or the unknown author called the Elohist (as scholars say), by separating the creation of light from the familiar lights in the sky, he wanted to tell us something much more profound than how old the heavens and earth are, or in how many days it all came together. And were they actually the 24-hour days we know, or were they 1,000 years as the Psalmist said, a thousand years are a day to God (Psalm 90:4)? Or were they billions of years, as evidence now indicates the universe is approximately 13.8 billion years old?

I find all this fascinating to think about. But at the end of the day, I don't know, and I don't care. What the author was trying to tell us is this. It is not the sun, moon, and stars that are the source of light. It is God, who made all of them.

Most people at that time worshiped the sun, moon, and stars as gods. In that context, Genesis says those bodies we see in the sky give light for only one reason. God said it, and it was so. And so they are not gods. They are natural phenomena that operate under the sovereignty of God. God is light and the source of all light. God's light pre-existed and is independent of the light we see with our eyes.

But sometimes God's light may be blocked from our vision, like the moon hides the sun during an eclipse. Many saints of old said they experienced something called "The Dark Night of the Soul." I've experienced a few times in life when God's clear light of day suddenly turned to night. And they lasted a lot longer than the roughly two and a half minutes I experienced under a total eclipse. If Bonnie Tyler's song was called "Total Eclipse Of The Soul," would you have known what she meant? I would.

Maybe you have experienced some of your own dark nights of the soul. Maybe you are going through one now. If so, one bit of good news I can offer is you are not alone. Name any biblical hero (and in some cases, I use "hero" loosely), and I guarantee you the Bible includes accounts of their dark nights of the soul. God's light was hidden, and it was as strange for them as that caveman I mentioned who saw day turn to night. All the caveman had to do was wait, and the sun would reappear. God, however, does not move as predictably as the sun, moon, and stars. No one can give you a timetable for when your dark night will end, but it will end.

The moon appears to swallow and devour the sun, but really the sun is still there all along. In the same way, no matter how long God's light remains hidden from you, it is always there. Neither life nor death, nor angels, nor principalities, nor things present, nor things to come can destroy it (Romans 8:38-39). They can only hide it for a time.

When the moon moves, as it always will, the light you see will most likely look different than before. Don't worry. That is a good thing. Our dark nights of the soul remove the illusions and delusions we once held so dear, so that we can see the true light more clearly.

Grace and peace to you.

Conclusion

This is my first book on the relationship between faith and depression. I could have said a lot more, and I probably will in future books. As I said in the introduction, these chapters were originally posts on a blog. A few things have changed between the original postings and writing this book. Most importantly, the girlfriend I mentioned in the Chris Cornell chapters is now my wife. Before we met, I was in another dark night of the soul, and I could not see any way out. Being able to write about recovery from depression was possible because of her. Since we are married now, I moved into her home and sold my grandparents' house.

Regarding my four principles for recovery, you might be wondering where they came from. Let's review them.

1. God is for your recovery and healing, not against it.

2. God will not kick you when you're down.

3. Some kinds of faith are good for recovery, and some are bad. Make sure you know the difference.

4. With the right help—spiritually, psychologically, emotionally, and perhaps medically—you can live a happy and fulfilling life. You just need to learn how to stop your depressed brain from sabotaging it.

Before continuing here, I recommend reading Appendix C, so you know the Bible verses I'm referring to. Then after reading the conclusion, read those scriptures again. See if there is any difference in how you read them before and after.

Principles one and two are closely related. The scriptures referenced in both come from passages called "the Songs of the Suffering Servant." All four songs appear in Deutero-Isaiah, which refers to chapters 40-55 of Isaiah. (Did I mention I'm a Bible Geek?) Most of "First Isaiah" (chapters 1-39) was written to the Jews in the 8th Century BC. Deutero-Isaiah was written to the Jews who were in exile but close to being allowed to return to their homeland (ca. 540 BC). They had just been through the darkest night of the soul in their history (after their slavery in Egypt), and they were about to come out of it.

In that context, we hear about the "suffering servant," a mysterious figure whose suffering brings about redemption and healing for the nations. Jews understand the servant to be the Jewish people or the nation of Israel as a whole. Christians understand the servant to be Jesus. I think either interpretation is legitimate. However, as a Christian in recovery from depression, I naturally think of Jesus first. I hope my Jewish friends understand.

Principle 1: God Is for Your Recovery and Healing, Not against It.

Isaiah 53:3-6 describes the vicarious suffering of the servant and the redemption it brings in detail. If you think about the suffering Jesus went through and the redemption it brought, you see the lengths God is willing to go to make relationship with God possible for us. A God who makes his righteous servant suffer like this for our healing certainly is for our recovery, not against it. This is why I feel confident in affirming what one article said, "Every good and perfect gift comes from above. Solutions to prolonged depression are no less spiritual if they come in the form of changed diet, exercise, cognitive counseling, or medication."[26]

Principle 2: God Will Not Kick You When You're Down.

Isaiah 42:2-3 is a beautiful portrait of God's gentleness toward our vulnerability. That was a side of God I missed for a long time. When I was down, I heard a voice telling me all the ways God was disappointed in me. I thought it was God, but it wasn't. *God does not kick*

---

[26] Stephanie Husk, "Do Real Christians Get Depressed?" Crosswalk, April 11, 2013. https://www.crosswalk.com/faith/spiritual-life/do-real-christians-get-depressed.html.

us when we're already down. That voice came from internalizing bad religious teachings. If you feel like turning to God is making your depression worse, you probably have been taught bad religion, like I was. Instead of turning away from God, I recommend getting to know the God who promised not to break a bruised reed or quench a dimly burning candle.

Principle 3: Some Kinds of Faith Are Good for Recovery, and Some Are Bad. Make Sure You Know the Difference.

This was my reason for writing the blog that led to this book. I hope I have given you enough to discern better the difference between faith that is good for recovery and faith that is bad. Jesus said you will know the good and bad ones by their fruits (Matthew 7:15-20). This is why Galatians 5:22-23 is one of my favorite scriptures: *By contrast, the fruit of the Spirit is love, joy, peace, patience, kindness, generosity, faithfulness, gentleness, and self-control. There is no law against such things.*

If you don't find the fruit of the Spirit in your religious experience, it might be time to leave for another.

Principle 4: With the Right Help—Spiritually, Psychologically, Emotionally, and Perhaps Medically—You Can Live a Happy and Fulfilling Life. You Just Need to Learn How to Stop Your Depressed Brain from Sabotaging It.

I wrote a lot about the voice in my head. Through writing in my journal and blog, I became aware that voice is the product of a chemically imbalanced brain. *Your clinically depressed brain will sabotage your recovery and happiness if you believe what it says.* Learn to recognize its voice. Don't believe it. Be prepared to fight, because it will not give up easily. I am fortunate that I have been able to quiet that voice with medication. But whatever I've done, I have sought to follow this advice from Paul: *... work out your own salvation [i.e., recovery] with fear and trembling; for it is God who is at work in you, enabling you both to will and to work for his good pleasure* (Philippians 2:12b-13).

In this book, I have given you a taste of what those four principles look like in action. As a whole, I saw this book as a movement from darkness to light. I hope that was your experience. I could not have taken you on that journey before now. But psychologically, emotionally, and spiritually, I am in a better place than I have ever been. My healing really began when I met my wife. I don't know any secret or magic prayer or faith confession that brought her to me. All I know is

I lived long enough for it to happen. But she is all the proof I need that God is with me.

Now that I've shared my journey with you, I hope you can at least see recovery is possible. What you do with this is up to you.

Grace and peace to you.
David Anderson
January 3, 2019

Appendix A: Symptoms and Causes of Depression

Symptoms

A depressed mood includes sadness, apathy, inability to feel pleasure, and/or irritability. Anxiety can be a sign of either depression or an anxiety disorder. The American Psychiatric Association (APA) gives the following description:

"Depression symptoms can vary from mild to severe and can include:

- Feeling sad or having a depressed mood

- Loss of interest or pleasure in activities once enjoyed

- Changes in appetite—weight loss or gain unrelated to dieting

- Trouble sleeping or sleeping too much

- Loss of energy or increased fatigue

- Increase in purposeless physical activity (e.g., hand-wringing or pacing) or slowed movements and speech (observable by others)

- Feeling worthless or guilty

- Difficulty thinking, concentrating, or making decisions

- Thoughts of death or suicide.

"Symptoms must last at least two weeks for a diagnosis of depression. … Also, medical conditions (e.g., thyroid problems, a brain tumor, or vitamin deficiency) can mimic symptoms of depression, so it is important to rule out general medical causes."[27]

If you have several of these symptoms over two weeks or more, but they are not debilitating, you may still have some form of depression. It is a good idea to ask your doctor if you should be tested for depression.

---

[27] "What Is Depression?" Depression. American Psychiatric Association (APA), January 2017. https://www.psychiatry.org/patients-families/depression/what-is-depression.

Causes

WikiHow's article "Cope with Depression as a Christian" lists these common causes of depression.

1. Brain chemistry is out of balance (clinical depression)

2. Endocrine system is out of balance in either gender

3. Postpartum chemistry is overloaded (known as Postpartum Depression)

4. An undiagnosed medical condition exists such as fibromyalgia, high blood pressure, low thyroid, chronic fatigue syndrome, or a host of other conditions

5. Trauma, death in the family, divorce, murder of loved one, car accident, abuse, or other life difficulties

6. Genetic predisposition

7. Unrecognized problem of bitterness, anger, hate, jealousy, condemnation, and other sins affecting emotional balance.[28]

I hesitated to include the last one. It's true that bitterness, anger, hate, jealousy, and condemnation of yourself or others often lead to depression. As I've said earlier, though, I hate it when people call depression a sin or say you are depressed because you sinned. This is because that does not take the biological causes into account. However, sin is something people of faith worry about, so it needs to be addressed.

I know that sins real and imagined can cripple you with guilt, which will also lead to depression. But I've seen many people think they know what sin is but really don't. That's why I said sins real and imagined. Some "sins" I used to feel guilty about I now consider either not sins or just part of being human.

Today, I understand sin to be this: any way we fail to love our neighbor as ourselves. If you have hurt someone, that is a sin, and you should feel guilty. But don't stop there. Let that guilt motivate you to repent and make amends to that person. That is the ninth step of AA's steps of recovery as well: "[Make] direct amends to such people [you

---

[28] "Cope," wikiHow.

have harmed] wherever possible, except when to do so would injure them or others."[29]

Beyond that, I offer this from the Apostles Paul and John:

> *"All have sinned and fall short of the glory of God" (Romans 3:23).*

So if you know you sinned, you are not alone.

> *"If we confess our sins, he who is faithful and just will forgive us our sins and cleanse us from all unrighteousness" (1 Jn 1:9).*

Confess it to God and be willing to make amends. If you do that, God promises to forgive you. If you can make amends to the person without injuring them or others, do it. If not, pray and wait for an opportunity.

---

[29] "The Twelve Steps."

Appendix B: To Find a Counselor

Online Counseling. www.betterhelp.com/start/

A guide for finding a therapist. www.webmd.com/mental-health/features/how-to-find-therapist#1

A guide for getting tested for depression. www.webmd.com/depression/guide/understanding-depression-treatment#1

Pastoral or Christian Counseling
www.christiancounselordirectory.com/default.aspx

Finding a Mental Health Counselor near You

Psychology Today. www.psychologytoday.com/us/therapists

Better Help. www.betterhelp.com/advice/therapy/how-do-i-find-a-therapist-near-me/

Network Therapy. www.networktherapy.com/directory/

National Suicide Prevention Lifeline 800-273-TALK (800-273-8255).

Appendix C: Scripture References for the Four Principles

First Principle: God is for your recovery and healing, not against it.

Isaiah 53:3-6 He was despised and rejected by men; a man of sorrows, and acquainted with grief; *and as one from whom men hide their faces he was despised, and we esteemed him not. Surely he has borne our griefs and carried our sorrows; yet we esteemed him stricken, smitten by God, and afflicted. But he was wounded for our transgressions; he was crushed for our iniquities; upon him was the chastisement that brought us peace, and with his stripes we are healed. All we like sheep have gone astray; we have turned—every one—to his own way; and the LORD has laid on him the iniquity of us all (ESV, emphasis mine; also Mat 8:17; Acts 8:32-33).*

Second Principle: God will not kick you when you're down.

Isaiah 42:2-3 He will not cry or lift up his voice, or make it heard in the street; a bruised reed he will not break, and a dimly burning wick he will not quench; he will faithfully bring forth justice (emphasis mine; also Mat 12:20).

Third Principle: Some kinds of faith are good for recovery, and some are bad. Make sure you know the difference.

1 John 4:1 Beloved, do not believe every spirit, but test the spirits to see whether they are from God; for many false prophets have gone out into the world.

Matthew 7:15-20 Beware of false prophets, who come to you in sheep's clothing but inwardly are ravenous wolves. You will know them by their fruits. Are grapes gathered from thorns, or figs from thistles? In the same way, every good tree bears good fruit, but the bad tree bears bad fruit. A good tree cannot bear bad fruit, nor can a bad tree bear good fruit. Every tree that does not bear good fruit is cut down and thrown into the fire. Thus you will know them by their fruits.

Galatians 5:22-23 By contrast, the fruit of the Spirit is love, joy, peace, patience, kindness, generosity, faithfulness, gentleness, and self-control. There is no law against such things.

Fourth Principle: With the right help you can live
a happy and fulfilling life.
You just need to learn how to stop your
depressed brain from sabotaging it.

Philippians 2:12-13 Therefore, my beloved, just as you have always obeyed me, not only in my presence, but much more now in my absence, work out your own salvation with fear and trembling; for it is God who is at work in you, enabling you both to will and to work for his good pleasure.

James 1:17 Every good and perfect gift is from above, coming down from the Father of the heavenly lights, who does not change like shifting shadows. (NIV)

Luke 1:37 For nothing will be impossible with God.

References

"Alcoholic Anonymous 12 Steps: 12 Steps of AA Explained." The Alcoholism Guide. Accessed November 9, 2016. https://www.the-alcoholism-guide.org/alcoholic-anonymous-12-steps.html.

Barnhart, Melissa. "Christian Counselor: Depression Demands Living by Faith, Not by Sight." *Christian Post*, April 11, 2013. https://www.christianpost.com/news/christian-counselor-depression-demands-living-by-faith-not-by-sight-93701/.

"The Brain-Gut Connection." Johns Hopkins Medicine. Accessed March 14, 2019. https://www.hopkinsmedicine.org/health/healthy_aging/healthy_body/the-brain-gut-connection.

Buchanan, Brett. "Dr. Drew Reveals What He Thinks Led to Chris Cornell's Death." Alternative Nation, May 21, 2017. http://www.alternativenation.net/dr-drew-reveals-thinks-led-chris-cornells-death/.

"CBD Oil for Anxiety: Is Cannabidiol an Effective Treatment?" Mental Health Daily, February 9, 2018. https://mentalhealthdaily.com/2016/02/24/cbd-oil-for-anxiety-is-cannabidiol-an-effective-treatment/.

"Chris Cornell's Widow Opens Up about Her Husband's Addiction before His Suicide." *ABC Nightline*. ABC News Network, February 22, 2018.

"Christian Testimonies about Depression and Suicide." Christianity. About.com. Accessed September 2, 2016. https://christianity.about.com/od/depressionandsuicide.

"Christians: Take Depression Seriously." Beliefnet, September 1, 2016. https://www.beliefnet.com/wellness/health/emotional-health/christians-take-depression-seriously.aspx.

"Could Marijuana Compound CBD Help NFL Players with Pain?" *The Early Show*. CBS Interactive, Inc., November 30, 2016.

Dengler, Phil. "Stores Closed on Thanksgiving Day 2018."
BestBlackFriday.com (blog), November 20, 2018.
https://bestblackfriday.com/blog/stores-closed-on-thanksgiving-
day-2018.

Dunigan, Eric. "Blue Christmas: 'Tis the Season—for Depression."
Presbyterians Today. Presbyterian Mission Agency, October 26,
2018.
https://www.presbyterianmission.org/story/pt-1118-bluexmas/.

"Foods to Avoid If You Have Anxiety or Depression." WebMD, October 10, 2017. https://www.webmd.com/depression/ss/slideshow-
avoid-foods-anxiety-depression.

Goldberg, Joseph. "Holiday Depression and Stress." WebMD, February 22, 2018. https://www.webmd.com/depression/holiday-
depression-stress#1.

Graham, Chris. "Bonnie Tyler Sings 'Total Eclipse of the Heart' on
Cruise Ship to Celebrate Solar Eclipse." *Telegraph*, August 21,
2017. https://www.telegraph.co.uk/news/2017/08/21/bonnie-tyler-
perform-total-eclipse-heart-solar-eclipse/.

Grow, Kory. "Soundgarden's Chris Cornell on 'Superunknown,'
Depression, Kurt Cobain." *Rolling Stone*, May 19, 2017.
https://www.rollingstone.com/music/music-features/soundgardens-
chris-cornell-on-superunknown-depression-and-kurt-cobain-
119623.

Hafner, Josh. "To Open or Not? Inside Stores' Thanksgiving
Dilemma." *USA Today*, October 19, 2016.
https://www.usatoday.com/story/money/nation-
now/2016/10/19/open-not-retailers-wage-battle-
thanksgiving/92380280/.

Hart, Archibald D. "Depression." Focus on the Family, February 1,
1999.
https://www.focusonthefamily.com/lifechallenges/emotional-
health/depression/depression.

"How Many Chemical Reactions Occur in the Human Brain Every
Second." Answers. Answers Corporation. Accessed July 26, 2016.

http://www.answers.com/Q/How_many_chemical_reactions_occur_in_the_human_brain_every_second.

"How to Cope with Depression as a Christian." WikiHow, January 2, 2016. https://www.wikihow.com/Cope-With-Depression-As-a-Christian.

Husk, Stephanie. "Do Real Christians Get Depressed?" Crosswalk.com. Salem Web Network, April 11, 2013. https://www.crosswalk.com/faith/spiritual-life/do-real-christians-get-depressed.html.

Jones, Lucy. "How Nature Benefits Your Mental Health." Vice, May 24, 2016. https://tonic.vice.com/en_us/article/av37kp/how-nature-benefits-your-mental-health.

Kaufman, Gil. "Chris Cornell's Death: Mental Health Experts Talk Depression, Suicide & Ativan." *Billboard*, May 19, 2017. https://www.billboard.com/articles/news/7801027/chris-cornell-death-mental-health-experts-depression-suicide-ativan.

Kerr, Michael. "Holiday Depression: Statistics & How to Deal." Healthline. Healthline Media, February 8, 2017. https://www.healthline.com/health/depression/holidays#1.

Mann, Denise. "Depression during the Holidays." WebMD, November 8, 2007. https://www.wcbmd.com/depression/features/emotional-survival-guide-for-holidays#1.

Mininni, Darlene. *The Emotional Toolkit: How to Cope with What Life Throws at You*. London: Piatkus, 2006.

Morgan, Karen. "Depression in the Christian Family." Focus on the Family, February 1, 2004. https://www.focusonthefamily.com/lifechallenges/emotional-health/depression/depression-in-the-christian-family.

Mounts, Mark. "It Can't Be Depression ... I'm a Christian." Grace Communion International. Accessed September 2, 2016. https://www.gci.org/articles/it-cant-be-depression-im-a-christian/.

Paddock, Catherine. "Soil Bacteria Work in Similar Way to Antidepressants." *Medical News Today.*
MediLexicon International, April 2, 2007.
https://www.medicalnewstoday.com/articles/66840.php.

Peach, Brandon W. "5 Things Christians Should Know about Depression and Anxiety." *Relevant,* February 20, 2014.
https://relevantmagazine.com/god/church/5-things-christiansshould-know-about-depression-and-anxiety.

Peoplestaff. "Tom Cruise Criticizes Brooke Shields' Use of AntiDepressants during Her Post-Partum Depression." People.com,
May 25, 2005. https://people.com/parents/tom_cruise_crit/.

"Soundgarden's Chris Cornell on Writing Music for Movies." *CBS This Morning Saturday.* CBS Interactive, April 22, 2017.

"Tips for Coping with Holiday Stress." Mayo Clinic. Mayo Foundation for Medical Education and Research, September 16, 2017.
https://www.mayoclinic.org/healthy-lifestyle/stressmanagement/in-depth/stress/art-20047544.

TMZ Staff. "Chris Cornell's Toxicology Report Reveals Prescriptions Drugs." TMZ, June 2, 2017.
https://www.tmz.com/2017/06/02/chris-cornell-toxicology-reportoverdose-drugs-suicide/.

"The Twelve Steps of Alcoholics Anonymous." Alcoholics Anonymous World Services, Inc., 1981.
https://www.aa.org/assets/en_US/smf-121_en.pdf.

W., Bill. *Twelve Steps and Twelve Traditions.* New York: Alcoholics Anonymous World Services, 2017.

"What Does the Bible Say about Depression? How Can a Christian Overcome Depression?" GotQuestions.org, May 16, 2009.
https://www.gotquestions.org/depression-Christian.html.

"What Is Depression?" Depression. American Psychiatric Association (APA), January 2017. https://www.psychiatry.org/patientsfamilies/depression/what-is-depression.

"What Should a Christian Do If Overwhelmed with Depression?" ChristianAnswers.Net. Accessed September 2, 2016. https://christiananswers.net/q-acb/acb-f001.html.

"When TMS Works for Depression, Patients Talk about Their Experience," YouTube video, 3:49. A copy of "Magnets to Treat Depression." Melissa's Healthworks. Houston, TX: Fox 26 News. Uploaded by Daniela White, February 13, 2014. https://youtu.be/UX8vJ2ucV7U.

About the Author

If you don't mind leaving an honest review, please go to this book's page on Amazon or wherever you buy books online.

David Anderson is a multi-passionate writer of fiction and nonfiction. He won honorable mention in the Writer's Digest Annual Contest, 2018. He has published articles in *Theological Librarianship* magazine, *Anderson* magazine, and the *Independent-Mail*. He is a member of American Christian Fiction Writers (ACFW), and of the Foothills Writers Guild, where he won the Juanita Garrison Prize for unpublished fiction.

He has two master's degrees in theology from Duke Divinity School and a Master of Library and Information Science from the University of South Carolina.

He is happily married to Fran Strickland Anderson. When he's not writing at home, you can find him in coffee shops, bookstores, and trying to tame the wilderness that is his and Fran's yard.

He is available to speak on topics of faith, spirituality, and depression. Just send an email to david@davidandersontheauthor.com with "speaker request" in the subject line.

You can sign up for updates at his author page, www.davidandersontheauthor.com.

Just look for the email sign up on the Sidebar. You will be notified when new content becomes available like blog posts, podcasts, book release information, and more.

A Bonus

What is the Bible all about? If I told you I had the answer, would you be interested? It may sound presumptuous, but I really think I've found it. I'm including an essay explaining what that is and why I believe it. It was not part of this book originally. Consider it a bonus.

I'm calling it "the 5,000 most important words I have ever written (so far)." It's not about depression (directly, I mean). But once I figured this out, both my spiritual and mental health improved tremendously. It's something I can't possibly keep to myself. Maybe it will help you in some way.

The 5,000 Most Important Words I Have Ever Written (So Far)

There's a question that's been vexing me for years—decades really. Jesus said he did not come to abolish the Law and the Prophets,[30] but to fulfill them. But sometimes he appeared to break a commandment or two. How could he do that and fulfill the Law and the Prophets?

In wrestling for this answer, I believe I have found not only the answer for that, but the key to the entire Bible. Get this one thing right, and you will get the entire Bible right. Get this one thing wrong, and you'll get the entire Bible wrong. That's a bold claim, I know. So I'll give it to you, and you can tell me whether I made good on it.

Not to Abolish but to Fulfill

The passage that got me started was a part of the Sermon on the Mount, probably Jesus's most famous sermon.

> *"Do not think that I have come to abolish the law or the prophets; I have come not to abolish but to fulfill. For truly I tell you, until heaven and earth pass away, not one letter, not one stroke of a letter, will pass from the law until all is accomplished. Therefore, whoever breaks one of the least of these command-*

---

[30] When referring to "the Law" or "the Prophets" as a specific body of scripture in the Jewish canon, I capitalize them. Most Bible translations do not.

> *ments, and teaches others to do the same, will be called least in the kingdom of heaven; but whoever does them and teaches them will be called great in the kingdom of heaven." (Mat 5:17-19 NRSV)*

You see there? *Whoever breaks one of the least of these commandments, and teaches others to do the same, will be called least in the kingdom of heaven.* Jewish tradition counts 613 commandments in the Law of Moses. Here, Jesus says you must obey every one, down to the least. And yet he did break commandments. The most obvious regarded working on the Sabbath. He had this annoying habit of healing people on any day of the week, including the Sabbath.

Christians usually argue that Jesus challenged not the commandment itself but traditions of men (John 7:23; Mark 2:24-27). It was religious leaders who created the traditions that said you can't heal on the Sabbath. That is not the same as the Law of Moses. Let's see if they're right. The commandment says,

> *Remember the sabbath day, and keep it holy. Six days you shall labor and do all your work. But the seventh day is a sabbath to the LORD your God; you shall not do any work—you, your son or your daughter, your male or female slave, your livestock, or the alien resident in your towns.*
>
> *For in six days the LORD made heaven and earth, the sea, and all that is in them, but rested the seventh day; therefore the LORD blessed the sabbath day and consecrated it. (Ex 20:8-11 NRS)*

The commandment only says *you shall not do any work* on the Sabbath. But what exactly is work? For example, how far can you walk? Even if you're not working, you will probably have to walk some. And how do you eat on the Sabbath if you can't work? What if someone is injured on the Sabbath? Can you treat them?

These were a few questions that came up. The religious leaders discussed these over time and tried to interpret the commandments as faithfully as possible. That is why they developed traditions to know what to do in these situations. The Law and the Prophets give some examples of what not to do on the Sabbath. But they give no definitive answer to the question, "What exactly is work?" So to say these are just traditions of men, and not the Law of Moses, is only half right.

Such traditions were necessary because some situations were not covered in the Law.

Otherwise, if your justification is, "This is not in the Law of Moses, but rather human traditions," does that mean everyone is free to interpret "work" however they like? They needed these traditions to avoid that kind of chaos.

Is This Work?

Furthermore, the Gospel of John presents a case where Jesus clearly violated the Sabbath and taught others to do so. A paralyzed man was waiting by a pool called Beth-zatha, because whenever an angel troubled the waters, the first one in the pool got healed. When Jesus asked if he wanted to be whole, he explained that because he had no one to lower him in the pool, someone always got in before him. He probably hoped Jesus would volunteer to lower him in the pool next time the waters were troubled. But Jesus did one better than that.

> *Jesus said to him, "Stand up, take your mat and walk."*
>
> *At once the man was made well, and he took up his mat and began to walk. Now that day was a sabbath.*
>
> *So the [Jewish authorities] said to the man who had been cured, "It is the sabbath; it is not lawful for you to carry your mat."*
>
> *But he answered them, "The man who made me well said to me, 'Take up your mat and walk.'" (John 5:8-11 NRS)*

Jesus not only broke the commandment about not working on the Sabbath; he taught the man to do the same by ordering him to carry his mat. That may sound trivial, but wasn't it Jesus who said, *"Whoever breaks one of the least of these commandments, and teaches others to do the same, will be called least in the kingdom of heaven"* (Mat 5:19)?

Most of us would say healing the man should make up for breaking the Sabbath. But for someone who says you must obey every commandment down to the least, down to every letter and every stroke of a letter, shouldn't he err on the side of obedience rather than disobedience?

Righteousness That Exceeds the Scribes and the Pharisees

And if you're not confused enough yet, now I'm going back to Matthew, chapter 5. In verse 20, Jesus really ups the ante.

> *"For I tell you, unless your righteousness exceeds that of the scribes and Pharisees, you will never enter the kingdom of heaven."*

Until he said this, the scribes and Pharisees probably thought they were in good shape. They dedicated their whole lives to studying the scriptures, identifying each and every commandment, all 613 of them, parsing each one, interpreting it line by line, word by word, letter by letter, down to every stroke of a letter. That was their specialty. They would have been saying, "Every commandment, down to the least one, down to every stroke of every letter. That's right, Jesus."

But then he tells everyone even the scribes and Pharisees are not righteous enough for the kingdom of Heaven. The ordinary Jews in the audience—remember, his audience would have been almost completely Jewish—would think this is impossible. No one was better qualified for obeying every commandment down to the least than the scribes and the Pharisees. So if their righteousness had to exceed that of the scribes and Pharisees, there was no hope for anyone. If the most observant Jews do not obey every commandment and teach others to do so, how could anyone be righteous enough?

It looks impossible, but Jesus will soon show them how it is possible and actually much, much simpler than they think. Later in the same sermon, he says,

> *"In everything do to others as you would have them do to you; for this is the law and the prophets" (Mat 7:12).*

Remember, he said he came not to abolish the Law and the Prophets but to fulfill them. How do you fulfill the Law and the Prophets? How can your righteousness exceed that of the scribes and the Pharisees? He just told you. Not in 613 commandments but in one sentence: *In everything do to others as you would have them do to you.*

With all the attention the scribes and Pharisees spent in focusing on each and every one of the 613 commandments, line by line, word by word, letter by letter, down to every stroke of a letter, they were forgetting the entire purpose of the Law. The Law and every commandment in it was given with the goal that God's people would live by that one rule Jesus gave: "In everything do to others as you would have them do to you." That is why this is commonly called the Golden Rule. If you follow this rule, you will fulfill the Law and the Prophets.

Which Commandment Is the Greatest?

There is another instance where Jesus boils down all of the Law and the Prophets to its greatest simplicity. Staying in Matthew, this is from chapter 22:34-40.

> *When the Pharisees heard that he had silenced the Sadducees, they gathered together, and one of them, a lawyer, asked him a question to test him. "Teacher, which commandment in the law is the greatest?"*
>
> *He said to him, "'You shall love the Lord your God with all your heart, and with all your soul, and with all your mind.' This is the greatest and first commandment. And a second is like it: 'You shall love your neighbor as yourself.' On these two commandments hang all the law and the prophets."*

You shall love the Lord your God with all your heart, and with all your soul, and with all your mind. That's one. And *you shall love your neighbor as yourself.* That's two. *On these two commandments hang all the Law and the Prophets.* There's that phrase again.

With all the negative press the Pharisees get, it's interesting that Jesus probably learned this from a Pharisee named Hillel. He told of a man who asked one rabbi, "Can you teach me the Law while I stand on one foot?" The rabbi said it was impossible. Well, if there are 613 commandments in the Law, of course it's impossible.

But the man went to another rabbi and asked him the same question. This rabbi said, "You shall love the Lord your God with all your heart, and with all your soul, and with all your mind; and you shall love your neighbor as yourself. The rest is commentary. You can put your foot down."

Jesus echoed this not only in the commandments he named but also when he said, "On these two commandments hang all of the Law and the Prophets." In other words, the rest is commentary. These are the two commandments you need to know, because all the other 611 commandments are *commentary* on *how* to love God and love your neighbor. That is why Jesus, along with Hillel, could say all of the Law and the Prophets hang on these two commandments.

Who Is My Neighbor?

The first great commandment was to love God. Long before Hillel, Joshua reminded the Jews of this after they entered the promised land.

> *"Take good care to observe the commandment and instruction that Moses the servant of the LORD commanded you, to love the LORD your God, to walk in all his ways, to keep his commandments, and to hold fast to him, and to serve him with all your heart and with all your soul." (Jos 22:5 NRS; see also Deut 10:12-13; 11:1; 30:16; Luke 6:46; John 14:15; 1 Jn 5:2-3; 2 Jn 1:6).*

This recalls the language of the Shema. *Love the LORD your God ... and serve him with all your heart and soul.* The same word says *to walk in all his ways*, which is synonymous with *keeping his commandments.*

We know the scribes and Pharisees loved God. They showed it by carefully studying and scrutinizing the scriptures. As they studied and interpreted, they taught it to the people. They sought to obey each of the commandments and taught others to do the same. Because that is how you show you love God, by obeying God's commandments.

But did they love their neighbor? An incident from the Gospel of Luke sheds light on this question.

> *Just then a lawyer stood up to test Jesus. "Teacher," he said, "what must I do to inherit eternal life?"*
>
> *He said to him, "What is written in the law? What do you read there?"*
>
> *He answered, "You shall love the Lord your God with all your heart, and with all your soul, and with all your strength, and with all your mind; and your neighbor as yourself."*
>
> *And he said to him, "You have given the right answer; do this, and you will live." (10:25-28)*

Again, a lawyer asks him a question to test him. In Matthew, the question was "What is the most important commandment?" Here the question is "What must I do to inherit eternal life?" The answer to both questions is the same. Love God with all your heart, soul, strength, and mind, and love your neighbor as yourself. To inherit eternal life, you must keep the Law and the Prophets. Every Jew knew that. How do you keep the Law and the Prophets? Love God and love your neighbor. Do this and you will live, Jesus tells him. But like many lawyers, he doesn't believe the answer can be that simple.

> *But wanting to justify himself, he asked Jesus, "And who is my neighbor?" (10:29)*

Here it would be really tempting to say, "Lawyers. Always looking for a loophole." The commandment is simple enough, "Love your neighbor as yourself." And of course, a lawyer looks for a way to justify himself for not doing that. But don't we all do the same? Don't we want to know who we are obligated and not obligated to love? *Who is my neighbor? Can't be that jerk over there, can it?*

One of my professors in seminary gave this great illustration on how you can take this reasoning to its logical absurdity. A friend from graduate school was coming to visit him. Leviticus 19:18 says you shall love your neighbor as yourself. Deuteronomy 10:19 says you shall love the stranger. This guy was not his neighbor. He lived in Texas. He was not a stranger. They went to graduate school together. Therefore, he could cheat him.

Hopefully, you're laughing at that. That is what "wanting to justify yourself" looks like. But haven't there been times in all of our lives when we wanted to justify ourselves for not loving our neighbor?

Jesus's answer to him is one of those moments where, even if I were not a Christian, I would have to concede that Jesus was one of the most brilliant teachers of ethics in all of human history.

> *Jesus replied, "A man was going down from Jerusalem to Jericho, and fell into the hands of robbers, who stripped him, beat him, and went away, leaving him half dead. Now by chance a priest was going down that road; and when he saw him, he passed by on the other side. So likewise a Levite, when he came to the place and saw him, passed by on the other side.*

> *"But a Samaritan while traveling came near him; and when he saw him, he was moved with pity. He went to him and bandaged his wounds, having poured oil and wine on them. Then he put him on his own animal, brought him to an inn, and took care of him. The next day he took out two denarii, gave them to the innkeeper, and said, 'Take care of him; and when I come back, I will repay you whatever more you spend.'*
>
> *"Which of these three, do you think, was a neighbor to the man who fell into the hands of the robbers?" (10:30-36)*

We call this the Parable of the Good Samaritan. Most commentators point out that of the three potential heroes in this story, the Samaritan was the least likely the lawyer—or any Jew for that matter—could imagine. Jews and Samaritans hated each other. Their feud went back centuries. To Jews in Jesus's time, a good Samaritan was like a unicorn. There was no such thing.

It would be like in America today saying the good Arab, the good immigrant, or the good illegal alien. *They couldn't possibly be good. They couldn't possibly be my neighbor, could they?* So the fact that Jesus made the Samaritan the hero was revolutionary to begin with.

But what Jesus did was even more radical than that. Notice how he asked the question: "Which of these three, do you think, was a neighbor to the man who fell into the hands of robbers?"

He took the question out of the realm of "Who am I obligated to love?" and instead asked the question as, "Who do you consider your neighbor when *you* are the one beaten, robbed, thrown into a ditch, and left for dead?" When you think in those terms, the answer to who is my neighbor is obvious, even for the lawyer. Which brings us to the conclusion.

> *He said, "The one who showed him mercy."*
>
> *Jesus said to him, "Go and do likewise." (10:37)*

The neighbor was the one who had mercy; in other words, the one who did for others what he would have wanted, even if he was an illegal alien—I mean, a Samaritan. See, the lawyer already knew the answer. He just needed to get out of his lawyer mode of trying to justify himself.

So how do you fulfill the Law and the Prophets? Love your neighbor as yourself. How do you love your neighbor as yourself? In everything, do to others as you would have them do to you.

Love God with All Your Heart, Soul, Strength, and Mind

The first great commandment, according to Jesus and Hillel, is to love God with all your heart, soul, strength, and mind. This comes from one of the standard Jewish prayers called the Shema.

> *Hear, O Israel: The LORD is our God, the LORD alone. You shall love the LORD your God with all your heart, and with all your soul, and with all your might. (Deut 6:4-5 NRS)*

Since Jesus called this the first commandment, you would think he would name it first any time he talked about the second commandment (Mat 22:38-39). But watch this exchange between him and an unidentified man in Matthew 19.

> *Then someone came to him and said, "Teacher, what good deed must I do to have eternal life?"*
>
> *And he said to him, "Why do you ask me about what is good? There is only one who is good. If you wish to enter into life, keep the commandments."*
>
> *He said to him, "Which ones?" (Mat 19:16-18a)*

Which ones? All of them! Didn't Jesus already say that in Matthew 5:17-20? Continuing from the second half of verse 18,

> *And Jesus said, "You shall not murder; You shall not commit adultery; You shall not steal; You shall not bear false witness; Honor your father and mother; also, You shall love your neighbor as yourself." (Mat 19:18b-19)*

I was wondering when Jesus would address the Ten Commandments (Ex 20:2-17; Deu 5:6-21). People have noticed for millennia that in what we call the Ten Commandments, the first four are about loving God, and the next six are about loving your neighbor. When

Jesus names the Ten Commandments to this man, he only mentions the ones that talk about loving your neighbor. What about loving God? Let's keep reading.

> *The young man said to him, "I have kept all these; what do I still lack?" (19:20)*

I can see what he still lacks. He hasn't mentioned loving God. Go ahead. Tell him, Jesus.

> *Jesus said to him, "If you wish to be perfect, go, sell your possessions, and give the money to the poor, and you will have treasure in heaven; then come, follow me."*
>
> *When the young man heard this word, he went away grieving, for he had many possessions. (Mat 19:21-22)*

What? There were two great commandments. Jesus covered the second one, but he didn't even mention the first. Not only that, Jesus's Golden Rule covers loving your neighbor, but not loving God. Why? And "sell all your possessions and give the money to the poor"? That wasn't one of the commandments. Not one of the two. Not one of the ten. Not even one of the 613. Why is he telling him that instead of telling him to love God? Sure, he should give to the poor. The Jews were told to do that multiple times in the Old Testament. That falls under the second commandment.

In case you're worried, Jesus did not tell everyone who sought to follow him to sell *everything* and give the money to the poor (*whew!*). In the Gospel of Luke, when Zacchaeus, a tax collector, said he would give half his money to the poor and repay everyone he defrauded, that was good enough for Jesus (Luke 19:1-10). Maybe this man would have taken the same deal. So why did he tell this man to give *everything* to the poor? That particular question is one I still can't answer.

What I want you to see, though, is Jesus never mentioned loving God as the way to receive eternal life, at least not in this case. He talked about loving your neighbor as yourself and giving to the poor. The Golden Rule implies it's really not two commandments but rather one, "Love your neighbor as yourself," that is necessary to fulfill the Law and the Prophets. The rich man we just encountered kept the commandments (Mat 19:20). But he failed to enter eternal life. Jesus asked him to sell all he had and give the money to the poor, and he walked away grieving, because he loved his possessions more than his neighbor.

Paul said this in his letter to the Romans.

> *Owe no one anything, except to love one another; for the one who loves another has fulfilled the law. The commandments, "You shall not commit adultery; You shall not murder; You shall not steal; You shall not covet"; and any other commandment, are summed up in this word, "Love your neighbor as yourself."*
>
> *Love does no wrong to a neighbor; therefore, love is the fulfilling of the law. (Rom 13:8-10 NRS)*

Like Jesus, Paul lists from the Ten Commandments the ones about loving your neighbor. And also in his letter to the Galatians, he says,

> *For the whole law is summed up in a single commandment, "You shall love your neighbor as yourself." (5:14)*

James says it this way:

> *You do well if you really fulfill the royal law according to the scripture, "You shall love your neighbor as yourself." (2:8)*

They do not mention loving God either. Why? To the Jews, loving God meant obeying God's commandments, all 613 of them. So perhaps the answer will come by asking the question, "What does it mean to keep God's commandments?"

To Jesus, the way to obey the commandments is to love your neighbor as yourself. Ergo, that is the way to love God. That is why in Matthew he told the lawyer the second command is *like* the first (22:39), not just similar but equal to. He is introducing a new idea. Love God by loving your neighbor as yourself.

The Golden Rule and the Day of Judgment

The best illustration of this in my mind comes from Matthew 25. This is Jesus's description of the final judgment.

> *Then the king will say to those at his right hand, "Come, you that are blessed by my Father, inherit the kingdom prepared for you from the foundation of the world; for I was hungry and you gave me food, I was thirsty and you gave me something to drink, I was a stranger and you welcomed me, I was naked and you gave me clothing, I was sick and you took care of me, I was in prison and you visited me."*
>
> *Then the righteous will answer him, "Lord, when was it that we saw you hungry and gave you food, or thirsty and gave you something to drink? And when was it that we saw you a stranger and welcomed you, or naked and gave you clothing? And when was it that we saw you sick or in prison and visited you?" (25:34-39)*

The next verse is something I think every Christian should memorize, like Jews memorize the Shema.

> *And the king will answer them, "Truly I tell you, just as you did it to one of the least of these who are [my brothers and sisters], you did it to me." (25:40)*

That phrase *the least of these who are my brothers and sisters* is difficult to understand. What did he mean by that? We could look at verses like this to try to interpret it.

> *"Whoever welcomes you welcomes me, and whoever welcomes me welcomes the one who sent me ... and whoever gives even a cup of cold water to one of these little ones in the name of a disciple truly I tell you, none of these will lose their reward." (Mat 10:40, 42)*

One of these little ones. That sounds a lot like "the least of these." And giving a cup of cold water ties in with the judgment day scene. But he specified giving it *in the name of a disciple.* Is he saying giving water to one who is thirsty only counts if they are Christian? It almost sounds like that. But I think approaching the question this way makes us like the lawyer who asked, "Who is my neighbor?" So I'm going to take a different approach.

Jesus also said,

"For whoever does the will of my Father in heaven is my brother and sister and mother." (Mat 12:50)

Who are his "brothers and sisters" referred to in 25:40? Those who do the will of his Father in heaven. What is the will of his Father in heaven? Follow the Golden Rule. How do we know that is the will of his Father in heaven? Because Jesus said that is the Law and the Prophets. All of scripture is fulfilled in that one sentence.

Love Is a Verb

Love the way Jesus taught is not about feelings. It's about actions. *Do unto others*, not just feel sorry for them. What actions did "the righteous" do? They gave to people who lacked basic necessities: food, water, clothing, shelter, health care, hospitality, and friendship. When they treated others, especially the poor and needy, the way they wanted to be treated if the situation were reversed, as far as Jesus was concerned, they did it for him, even though they didn't know it.

Here's how John says it.

"How does God's love abide in anyone who has the world's goods and sees a brother or sister in need and yet refuses help? Little children, let us love, not in word or speech, but in truth and action." (1 Jn 3:17-18 NRS)

Little children is similar to "the least of these," and "one of these little ones" (cf. Mat 10:42; 25:40). But now, like Jesus did with the lawyer who asked, "Who is my neighbor," John turned that around to say that "little children" are not "the least of these" whom we are obligated to love. We are little children who are called to *love, not in word or speech, but in truth and action.*

The Day of Judgment Continued

Now, back to Judgment Day, Matthew 25. Brace yourselves, because this is heavy.

Then he will say to those at his left hand, "You that are accursed, depart from me into the eternal fire prepared for the devil and his angels; for I was hungry and you gave me no food, I was thirsty and you gave me nothing to drink, I was a stranger

> *and you did not welcome me, naked and you did not give me clothing, sick and in prison and you did not visit me."*
>
> *Then they also will answer, "Lord, when was it that we saw you hungry or thirsty or a stranger or naked or sick or in prison, and did not take care of you?"*
>
> *Then he will answer them, "Truly I tell you, just as you did not do it to one of the least of these, you did not do it to me."*
>
> *And these will go away into eternal punishment, but the righteous into eternal life. (Mat 25:41-46)*

Just as you did not do it to one of the least of these, you did not do it to me. And notice these were Christians. They called him "Lord." Even so, when they failed to help others in need, as far as Jesus was concerned, they failed to do it to him. Could it be that eternal life depends on doing to others as we want done to us, like he told the lawyer?

John said it this way.

> *Those who say, "I love God," and hate their brothers or sisters, are liars; for those who do not love a brother or sister whom they have seen, cannot love God whom they have not seen. (1 Jn 4:20 NRS)*

John says "brother or sister" instead of "neighbor." However, the whole body of scripture—the Law, the Prophets, the other Old Testament writings, and the New Testament—says the same principle applies to your neighbor as well. You say you love God. You say you love Jesus. But you hate your neighbor. You do not help those who lack basic necessities. You cannot say you love God whom you have not seen if you don't love your neighbor whom you have seen.

The One Thing

The question I started with was how Jesus could disobey some commandments and still fulfill the Law. The answer, it turned out, was simple. All the commandments are fulfilled when you obey the two great commandments: Love God, and love your neighbor. But typically we've viewed that statement as a hierarchy in this order:

1. Love God with all your heart, soul, strength, and mind.
2. Love your neighbor as yourself.
3. All the other 611 commandments in the Law of Moses.

First love God. Then love your neighbor. Then work on all the other commandments.

But that is not how Jesus taught it. In the Golden Rule, the Parable of the Good Samaritan, his interactions with two lawyers and a rich man, and his depiction of the final judgment, he made the commandment to love your neighbor as yourself the same as the commandment to love God. This was confirmed by several of his disciples. Not love God, *then* love your neighbor. Love God *by* loving your neighbor. So Jesus's hierarchy of commandments is

1. Love God by loving your neighbor as yourself.
2. There is no 2. There is only 1.

That is why Jesus could heal on the Sabbath and still fulfill the Law. If he had made the paralyzed man wait one more day to avoid working on the Sabbath, he would have obeyed the commandment. But he would not have fulfilled the Law. Because what would you want done to you? Would you want to wait one more day? Is that really what the Sabbath is about? To do harm rather than do good (Mark 3:4)? If you see someone drowning, do you try to rescue him or her? Or do you stand on the shore shouting, "The sign says no swimming!"

This is the one thing you must get right, or you will never get the Bible right. And the Good News is if you do that, God reckons it as righteousness (Mat 25:37), which is the same as keeping all 613 commandments.

Standing on One Foot

Jesus and Hillel showed us how to teach the Law of Moses while standing on one foot. We saw two lawyers who knew the answer but did not know what it meant. Or maybe they knew, but they needed someone to remind them, just like we do. So to give you something fairly easy to remember, I will review how the Two Great Commandments, the other 611, and the Golden Rule all work together to fulfill the Law and the Prophets. It will take a little bit longer than Hillel and Jesus, but I think, if you can stand normally, you can learn this while you stand on foot. Ready?

How do you love God? By obeying all of God's commandments.
How do you obey all of God's commandments? By loving your
neighbor as yourself.
How do you love your neighbor? In everything, do to others as you
would have them do to you.
This is the Law and the Prophets.

You can put your foot down. Now, go and do likewise.

NOW IT'S YOUR TURN

81% of people say they have a book inside them, but only 1% actually get a book written and published. The vast majority of people who want to write a book probably just find the whole process too daunting. "I'm bad at writing. I don't have time. I don't know where to start. Even if I get it written, how will I get it published?"

Self-Publishing School helped me, and they can help you. With tools and experience across a variety niches and professions, Self-Publishing School has everything you need to take your book to the finish line.

DON'T WAIT. Say "YES" to yourself: Get that book out of your head and into the world. The QR Code will take you to a free webinar.

Or go to www.self-publishingschool.com/apply to sign up.

Tell them I referred you, and you'll receive for a $250 discount. (As of the printing of this book. I don't know how long that offer is good).

For other resources, go to
www.davidandersontheauthor.com/recommended/self-publishing

Made in the USA
Monee, IL
07 July 2026

56551648R00079

Proceedings of the 2012 International Conference on Detection and Classification of Underwater Targets

Proceedings of the 2012 International
Conference on Detection and Classification
of Underwater Targets

Edited by

Isabelle Quidu, Vincent Myers and Benoit Zerr

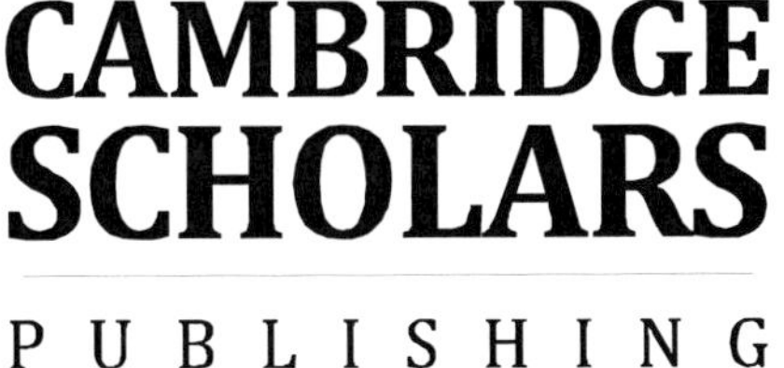

Proceedings of the 2012 International Conference on Detection and Classification
of Underwater Targets
Edited by Isabelle Quidu, Vincent Myers and Benoit Zerr

This book first published 2014

Cambridge Scholars Publishing

12 Back Chapman Street, Newcastle upon Tyne, NE6 2XX, UK

British Library Cataloguing in Publication Data
A catalogue record for this book is available from the British Library

ISBN (10): 1-4438-5709-2, ISBN (13): 978-1-4438-5709-3

TABLE OF CONTENTS

Session III: ATR Classification
Chaired by: Scott Reed, SeeByte Ltd

Session IV: Survey and MCM Operations
Chaired by Michel Couillard, Centre for Maritime Research
and Experimentation

FOREWORD

The International Conference on Underwater Remote Sensing (ICoURS) was held from 8-11 October 2012 at the Le Quartz Conference Centre in Brest, France as part of Sea Tech Week. It was composed of three symposia: Quantitative Monitoring of the Underwater Environment (MOQESM), Advances in Seafloor Mapping, and Detection and Classification of Underwater Targets (DCUT), and the last one being the subject of these proceedings. DCUT took place on 9-10 October and was organized by the Ocean Sensing and Mapping Team of ENSTA Bretagne and was, in spirit, the 3rd conference on what can broadly be described as Automatic Target Recognition (ATR) for underwater applications: The first was CAD/CAC 2001 organized by Defence R&D Canada and held in Halifax, Nova Scotia, Canada; and the second was the International Conference on Detection and Classification of Underwater Targets, organized by Heriot-Watt University and held in Edinburgh, Scotland.

It was noted during the Plenary Session by keynote speaker Dr. John Fawcett that during the 11 years that have passed since the original CAD/CAC 2001 conference, progress in the fields of pattern recognition, machine learning, image and signal processing, as well as the advent of high-resolution sensors such as synthetic aperture sonars have led to significant improvements in underwater ATR technology. Perhaps more salient, however, is the now ubiquitous presence of Autonomous Underwater Vehicles (AUV), making high-performing, computationally-efficient ATR no longer simply an aid for human operators, but rather a necessary technology to enable the use of unmanned systems. In addition, the applications of this technology has started to move out of military applied research programs, typically the naval mine countermeasures (MCM) community, and is being applied in civilian applications such as pipeline inspection and environmental monitoring. For this reason, the papers of these proceedings will also be of interest to researchers working the area of remote sensing (for instance, with Synthetic Aperture Radar) as well as medical imaging and robotic perception.

The increasingly interdisciplinary nature of this field is evident by the papers that were presented during DCUT: From traditional acoustics/sonar to non-acoustic methods such as ground penetrating radar, magnetic gradiometry and video; application of machine learning, pattern recognition, image processing, optimization, anomaly detection, acoustic modelling and data fusion; as well as applications such as environmental characterization and change detection.

These proceedings contain 20 papers whose abstracts were reviewed by at least two reviewers. We would like to thank all of the reviewers in the Scientific Committee listed immediately below for providing their time and effort to ensure the quality of the articles in this conference. Also included are abstracts of four papers from the Poster Session. We would sincerely like to thank Annick Billon-Coat for her help in organizing this conference, as well as the staff at the Le Quartz conference centre and Brest Métropole Océane for their support.

The discussions and collaborations that ensue from these conferences are key to moving the field forward. With a relatively small community, it is important that we come together occasionally in a specialized forum in order to share ideas, show some fresh results and obtain feedback on our work. We look forward to seeing you all again, along with some new faces, during the next incarnation of the DCUT conference, wherever and whenever it may be.

Vincent Myers, Isabelle Quidu and Benoit Zerr
Brest, France, October 2012

Scientific Committee

Maude AMATE (DGA), Toulon, France

Didier BILLON (Thales Underwater Systems), Brest, France

Didier CHARLOT (IxBlue), Brest, France

Gerald DOBECK (NSWC), Panama City, Florida, USA

Yves DUPONT (Belgian Navy), Belgium

John FAWCETT (DRDC), Halifax, Canada

Johannes GROEN (Atlas Electronik), Bremen, Germany

Ursula HÖLSCHER-HÖBING (Atlas Electronik), Bremen, Germany

Dieter KRAUS (University of Applied Sciences), Bremen, Germany

Øivind MIDTGAARD (FFI), Kjeller, Norway

Yvan PETILLOT (Heriot-Watt University), Edinburgh, Scotland

Benoît QUESSON (TNO), The Hague, The Netherlands

Scott REED (SeeByte), Edinburgh, Scotland

David WILLIAMS (CMRE), La Spezia, Italy

PLENARY SESSION

PREFACE

AUTOMATIC TARGET RECOGNITION METHODS FOR SIDESCAN SONAR IMAGES: THE ADVANCES AND THE CHALLENGES

JOHN A. FAWCETT

Abstract

Over approximately the last decade Defence R&D Canada – Atlantic, Canada (also known as DRDC Atlantic) has been involved with research into Automated Target Recognition (ATR) algorithms for sidescan sonar imagery. In this paper, some of the past and present DRDC Atlantic work in ATR will be discussed with some illustrative experimental results. Related work by other authors is also discussed.

Keywords: Sidescan Sonar, Automatic Target Recognition, Detection, Classification.

1. Introduction

In 2001 Defence R&D Canada – Atlantic hosted the conference CAD/CAC 2001 in Halifax as an initial start into a research program for the development of automated sidescan sonar detection and classification methods in support of the Canadian Remote Minehunting System project. Now, eleven years later, there has been much progress in image-processing and pattern recognition algorithms. Synthetic aperture sonars (SAS) have significantly improved the resolution of the images of the seabed. The use of autonomous underwater vehicles (AUVs) for sonar surveys has become very common and there has been interest in making AUVs more intelligent and adaptable during a mission. For example, after an initial standard survey, an AUV could revisit a list of Automatic Target Recognition (ATR) contacts for another sonar look [1] or during the survey the AUV could perform a multi-aspect run at each potential target [12, 23]. However, such concepts rely upon accurate and robust ATR processing. The development of reliable and computationally-efficient ATR methods is more relevant than ever in minehunting.

(a)   (b)

Figure 1: The semi-submersible remote minehunting vehicle DORADO (a) out of the water (b) underway

For several years, the Mine Counter-Measures group (now Mine Warfare group) at DRDC Atlantic, in collaboration with Canadian industry, was involved with the development of the remote minehunting vehicle DORADO and its associated sensors and software. This vehicle is shown in Fig. 1(a) out of the water. On the bottom of the Aurora towfish, the Klein 5500 sidescan sonar can be seen. The actively controlled towfish can be winched out to depth. The sonar data is transmitted back, in near real-time, to a mother ship at distances of up to 12 km away from the DORADO. The vehicle is shown underway in the water in Fig.1(b). The data is displayed as a waterfall on this ship and an operator and/or background ATR algorithms analyze the data for mine-sized contacts. Much of the DRDC Atlantic data used for research over the last decade was collected from various trials using this system.

In the following sections, the ATR processing stream is broken down into three basic steps: (1) normalization of sonar data (2) simple and rapid automated detection and (3) more detailed analysis of small images (mugshots or snippets extracted from the second step). This breakdown is historically the approach taken at DRDC Atlantic but the divisions are somewhat arbitrary. For example, some newer methods of automated detection/classification [34, 38] combine, to some extent, steps (2) and (3).

2. Normalization

Typically, recorded sonar data shows systematic amplitude variations with respect to range (travel time) and the sonar's beampattern. The large scale amplitude variations can be reduced by computing a local background mean amplitude and dividing through by this value. For the Klein 5500 data, we typically compute, on a per file and per side basis, an average empirical amplitude/cross-range curve and normalize the data by this curve. For some sonar data, more complicated vertical beampattern effects are observed in the data and need to be accounted for. Dobeck [39, 40] has described sophisticated normalization algorithms. In these papers, he also emphasizes that by reducing the system amplitude variations the subsequent false alarm rate in the automated detection phase can be significantly reduced.

There are also environmental features in the data which will cause significant false alarms for many automated detectors; in particular, sand ripples cause a sequence of highlights and shadows in the sonar data which can resemble a minelike structure. In [40, 41], Fourier- and wavelet-based methods are described to reduce the effect of ripples on the sonar image. In [42], Williams mitigates the effects of ripples during the detection phase by considering the distribution of elliptical descriptors of the shadow regions and eliminating those regions which are consistent with ripples (with some additional criteria to mitigate against "losing" targets). In Fig. 2(a) we show an unnormalized sonar image (Marine Sonic) from a Remus AUV. A surface echo has already been suppressed from the original image by predicting its position in the image and replacing abnormally high values with a local median value. The coloured lines (cyan and green) indicate some predicted grazing angle curves on the seabed as the altitude of the AUV varies (the red lines indicate along-track regions of turns). By integrating the amplitudes along these curves, across-track normalization curves can be computed. The resulting normalized image is shown in Fig. 2(b). Figs. 2(c) and 2(d) show the results of a simplistic segmentation of the image into 5 values representing the range of deep shadow to high highlight; first using the normalized image (Fig. 2(c)) and secondly (Fig. 2(d)) combining the segmentation of Fig. 2(c) with a segmentation [2] after filtering the image using the method of Dobeck [40]. The results of Fig.2(d) show that much of the shadow due to the sand ripples has been eliminated. More details of this processing are described in [2].

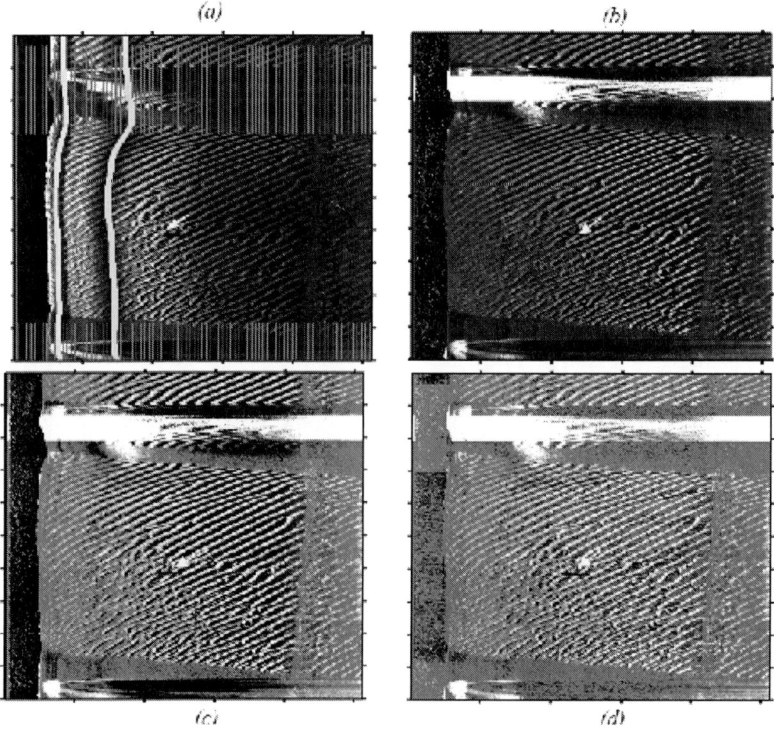

Figure 2: A Marine Sonic sonar file showing some different phases of normalization: (a) unnormalized data with representative grazing angle curves (b) normalized data (c) rebinned into shadow-highlight values and (d) rebinning in combination with Fourier filtering. The yellow arrow indicates a mine-like object. Data Source: NURC.

3. Automatic Target Detection

Given a normalized, filtered sonar image, the DRDC Atlantic detection process consists of cross-correlating the image (or a transformation of the image) with various filters. One which we have used for several years is based upon the work of [3]. As mentioned above, the sonar image is roughly segmented into 5 basic values based upon the median value or on percentiles of the pixel values. A two-dimensional filter consisting of +1 for highlight and -1 for shadow is then cross-correlated with the data and regions exceeding a threshold are taken to be detection regions. The predicted shadow length for a target of fixed height should increase linearly with range. This is difficult to implement with FFT-based cross-correlations and, in the past, we used 3 different sized (in terms of shadow extent) filters to address this issue. The implementation we use in a structured C++ development does utilize a continuously growing shadow. There are also a variety of other filter possibilities. We have found that the local Lacunarity [4] (defined as variance of pixel values/squared mean value) can, for some environments, be a very good detection feature. Here too, this feature can be computed by using sliding windows to compute the local means and mean squared values. In Fig. 3(a) we show a sonar image (from the NURC AUV/synthetic aperture sonar vehicle, MUSCLE) (unnormalized), in Fig. 3(b) the match-filtered output, in Fig. 3(c) the Lacunarity output, and in Fig. 3(d) the detections (yellow) based upon a match-filtered threshold and those which exceed the threshold for the match filter and also another threshold for Lacunarity (cyan). Here the seabed has patches of the seagrass Posidonia. This produces "natural" pairs of highlight and shadow which can cause detector false alarms. There is a dummy target which can be observed as a high output for both the match-filter and the Lacunarity images.

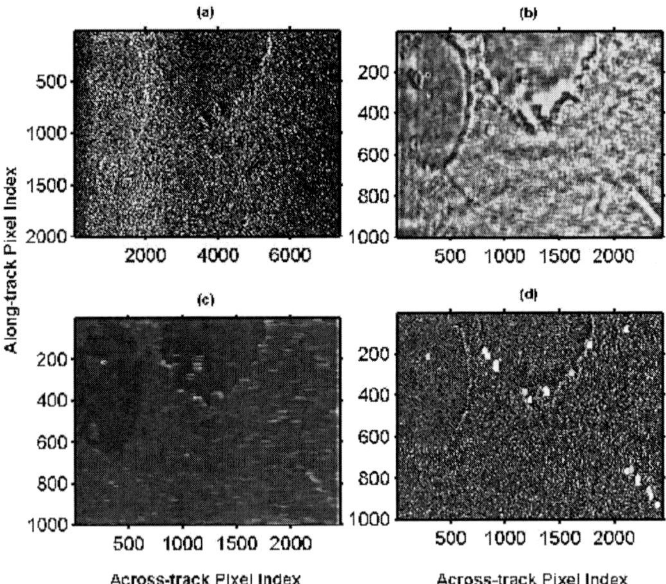

Figure 3: (a) unnormalized NURC MUSCLE data tile (b) matched-filter output (c) Lacunarity output (d) resulting detections from a matched-filter threshold (yellow boxes) – also satisfying a threshold on Lacunarity (cyan). The output images (b),(c) and (d) are computed on a reduced version of the image of (a). Data Source: NURC.

Williams [42] uses a moving window to find regions of shadow and then considers those shadow regions with an associated highlight or echo region. In general, one can compute a number of features for a detection region: various filter outputs and local statistical values, and the detection process (or a secondary detection process) can be improved by looking for combinations of features which improve the detection/false alarm ratio [2, 5, 6]. The method of Williams [42] is a simple example of a cascade: (1) a simple detection method (*e.g.*, existence of shadow) is used to eliminate much of the sonar image from consideration and then a second detection method (*e.g.*, the existence of an associated echo) is applied to those regions of the image which remain after step (1). In general, one can use a cascade of several detectors to sequentially eliminate regions of the image for further consideration. At each successive level of the cascade, the detection test used may be more complex (*e.g.* may involve more features), but this is offset by the fact that the number of image regions to process at the higher levels is smaller. Sawas et al [34] and Petillot el al. [38] used a trained Haar Cascade detection method to obtain very good detection performances. This type of detection method was first developed in the face-recognition community [7, 8] and various training and testing methods are available in the openCV [9] library. In Fig. 4 we show the results from a face detection method available in the openCV library which uses an existing trained Haar cascade for face detection. We have also used the openCV software to train our own cascade for sonar images (MUSCLE data from NURC) and utilize the same face detection algorithm (with some adjustments of the parameters). A sonar image with the resulting detections is shown in Fig. 5.

Figure 4: Two Canadian scientists and a French scientist relaxing on a trial with their faces detected by the openCV face detection routine.

Whether one wishes to use this type of detection method or not, a very powerful concept utilized in this application is that of the integral image and the rapid computation of rectangular-based features. The integral image is computed from the image $I(i,j)$ by computing its two-dimensional cumulative sum. Then the summed value of the image over a specified rectangle can be expressed as the sums and differences of the 4 corner points. If we wish to consider two adjacent rectangles, one positive and one negative, this can be expressed as 6 operations. In fact, the sliding window output from a number of different combinations of adjacent rectangles or nested rectangles can be very efficiently computed from the integral image. In addition, this concept has been extended to include rotated rectangular features [8]. This method can be applied to our simple matched-filter or Lacunarity detectors (in this case, also computing an image of squared pixel values). The increase of the shadow length with the across-track pixel index is very simply included with this approach. Once a detector, a fused set of detectors, or a cascade of detectors has determined a detection point, then a small image about this point (mugshot) is extracted. The resulting set of small images is then passed to the next stage of analysis – classification.

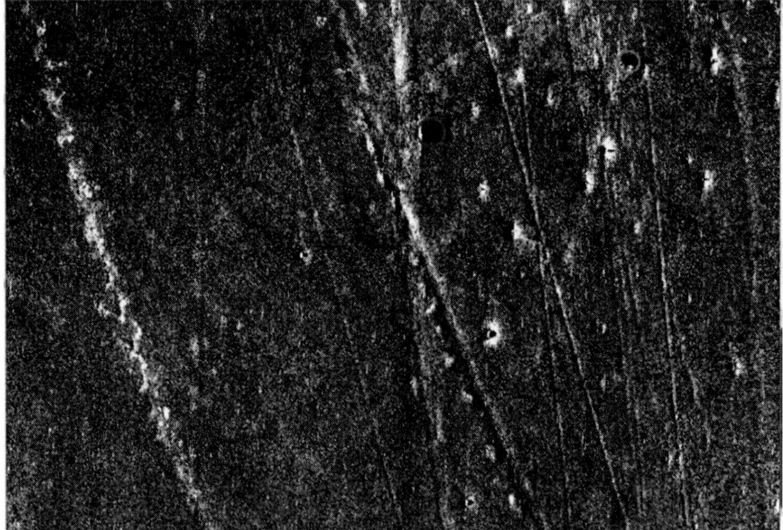

Figure 5: A sonar image with a fairly complex seabed and two detected objects (no false alarms) using a trained Haar-Cascade classifier. Data Source: NURC.

4. Classification

The boundary between classification and detection is not well-defined. In the classification phase, it is often desired to classify the mugshots resulting from the detection phase as a possible generic mine type: *e.g.*, cylinder, sphere, truncated cone, etc… However, since the detection phase has usually yielded many false alarms, it is important to eliminate more of these. We have tended to think of the detection phase of ATR as being computationally efficient, but not being particularly sophisticated. The classification phase utilizes more sophisticated methods which require more computation time (*e.g.*, feature computation, support vector machine classification and template-matching). The face-detection methods described in Section 3 are trained with a large set of data (positives and negatives) and the training time can be long. However, in the detection phase they are very computationally efficient. These methods blur the boundary somewhat between the detection and classification phases.

There are two main approaches in sonar image classification. One is shadow- and highlight-feature based. In this approach, the mugshot is first segmented into shadow and highlight regions. This is normally a fairly sophisticated segmentation approach. That is, instead of using simple hard image thresholds to define shadow and highlight, these algorithms consider the pixel values and also the neighbouring values in order to obtain accurate representations of the shadow and highlight regions. Some of these algorithms are an iterative threshold and connectivity method [10], Markov Random Fields [11], Statistical Snakes [11], and Fourier Descriptors [13]. Although the concept of shadow and highlight segmentation is straightforward, it can be surprisingly difficult to develop robust methods for complex seabed types. Once the segmentation has been performed (and the appropriate regions associated with the detected object) various features based upon these regions can be computed. These features are often geometrical or statistical in nature: for example, the estimated height of the object from the shadow length (and known range/altitude of detection), the length of the object, the ratio of the convex area/area of the shadow, the standard deviation of the shadow profile, the eccentricity of the shadow, the orientations of the shadow and highlight regions, the width of the highlight region, etc. A full description of some of the features we have used at DRDC Atlantic can be found in [14]. In [15] the height profile of an object (estimated from the shadow length) was considered as the feature vector. There are also choices of features which are invariant to scaling and rotation [16]. In Fig.6 we show a screen capture of the display from the DRDC Atlantic Sonar Image Processing

System (SIPS) showing the results for an automatic segmentation of shadow and highlight and some computed feature values. These feature values can subsequently be used for training and testing classifiers.

Given a set of features, a classifier can be trained using labelled mugshots. This can be a binary-classifier or a multi-class classifier. There are many possible choices for a classifier. We have often used a kernel-regression method [17] with an exponential kernel based at each training point. For multiple classes, our method is equivalent to solving multiple binary problems (i.e, 1 if a specific target type and -1 if not). In this approach, we also specifically consider clutter to be a class and train with it. This type of approach works well, as long as the preliminary shadow/highlight segmentation and computed features are good.

Sonar images of mine-like objects are collected during sea trials with dummy mine shapes deployed on the seabed. There are often only a few (*e.g.* 9) deployed at a site and these are repeatedly imaged at different ranges and aspects to yield a few hundred images. The danger in training and testing with such a data set is that, despite the changing sonar position, it is often the same object (and surrounding seabed) being imaged. In the Citadel trial [14, 18], targets and a rock were deployed at 2 sites. The rocks were mine sized but were taken to represent the clutter class. They were different at the 2 sites. In Table 1 we show the averaged confusion matrices from a set of training/testing runs. First, the confusion matrix data for a classifier tested using data from Site 2 when trained with Site 1 data is shown. Below these classification rates, the results for training and testing with just the Site 1 data are shown. In this second case, the classifier was able to distinguish the rock from the targets about 83% of the time at Site 1. However, when the classifier trained with Site 1 data was used at Site 2, the rock at Site 2 is most often confused with the truncated cone shape. Thus the "clutter" sample at Site 1 was not sufficiently diverse to provide good clutter discrimination at Site 2. The classification results for the other dummy target types at Site 2 are good, with the classification of the cylindrical shape being somewhat poorer. This example illustrates a fundamental concern for ATR using trained classification: its ability to perform well in a new environment.

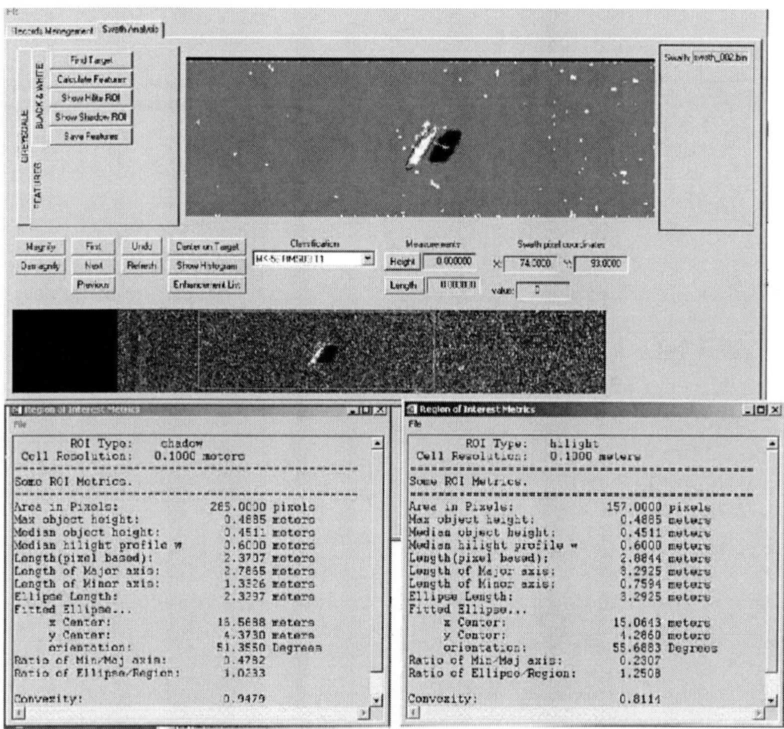

Figure 6: The segmentation and feature computation tool from DRDC Atlantic SIPS database viewer.

Table 1: The confusion matrices resulting from using (1) a classifier trained with Citadel Site 1 data and tested with Site 2 data and below (2) a classifier trained with Citadel Site 1 data and tested with Site 1 data.

	Rock	T. Cone	Wedge	Cyl
Rock	**0.26**	0.53	0.17	0.03
	0.83	0.08	0.06	0.03
T. Cone	0.08	**0.82**	0.09	0.02
	0.05	**0.92**	0.03	0.00
Wedge	0.00	0.01	**0.99**	0.00
	0.01	0.04	**0.93**	0.02
Cyl	0.15	0.03	0.06	**0.76**
	0.05	0.03	0.03	**0.89**

The other type of classification approach is to work more directly with the mugshots' pixel values. There are pros and cons to this approach. The advantages are that it avoids the preliminary shadow/background/highlight segmentation. There are often seabed or target features which can cause problems for shadow/highlight segmentation. Also, the image-based approaches do not rely on explicitly defined features. On the other hand, they may be sensitive to the range of the mugshot detection (because of the increasing shadow length), normalization effects, the size of the mugshot, etc... Some of these problems can be mitigated. For example, careful image normalization and consistent placement of the objects within the mugshots can help classification performance. One can consider the use of expansion functions such as Zernicke polynomials [16, 19, 20] which are range/aspect independent.

Once again, as with the previously-described Haar Cascade methods for detection, the image-based classification methods follow closely some of the approaches used in facial recognition. In fact, as shown in [34, 38] one can train the Haar Cascade method for specific mine types. An approach which has been enjoying popularity in the last few years is template matching [21, 22, 24, 25, 26, 27] and this is certainly an approach which is used, in general, in the object detection community. Various algorithms can be found, for example, in the openCV library. The idea is to construct for the range (the sonar range corresponding to the across-track pixel of the detection) of the mugshot detection a set of ray-trace model templates (*i.e.,* a basic highlight/shadow structures) encompassing the various possible target types and a discrete set of aspects. In our implementation, a library of precomputed templates at a discrete set of ranges is used. However, one can compute the templates "on the fly" with a ray-tracing subroutine. In many of the template approaches, the templates are then cross-correlated with the mugshot (or a rebinned version of it). The maximum value of the output-filtered image (the cross-correlation is typically performed by moving the template about the image in some neighbourhood of the detection centre) is computed for each template and the maximum of these values is taken to indicate the best target and aspect match. If this value is not sufficiently high, then the object may be deemed to be clutter. There are a variety of different cross-correlation measures which can be used. Reference [26] discusses various template-matching measures. For example, one can simply use the true cross-correlation value (as defined for normxcorr2 in the MATLAB image processing toolbox based upon the method of [37])

$$C(u,v) = \frac{\sum_{x,y} (I(x,y) - \bar{I}_{u,v})(t(x-u,y-v) - \bar{t})}{(\sum_{x,y} (I(x,y) - \bar{I}_{u,v})^2)^{1/2} N_T} \tag{1}$$

Here the template t is centred at (u,v) and x,y vary over the portion of the image contained within the template.

A template $t(x,y)$ is moved about the image and a local image mean $\bar{I}_{u,v}$ and normalization of I within the region of the template is computed. We have used N_T in Eq.(1) to denote the L_2 norm of the template. It is interesting to note that the computation of the image mean and standard deviation within the the moving template window is most efficiently accomplished using the method of integral images [37]. A simpler expression for Eq.(1) results when the mugshot and template's mean values are taken to be zero [26] (we typically first remap the mugshot and template into positive and negative values for relative highlight and shadow regions),

$$C_1(u,v) = \frac{\sum_{x,y} (I(x,y)t(x-u,y-v)}{N_T N_I} \tag{2}$$

where N_T is the L_2 norm of the template and N_I is the L_2 norm of the image within the extent of the template. In Fig. 7(a) we show a cylinder lying in a sand ripple field (NURC MUSCLE data). The template yielding the best match is shown in Fig. 7(b). As can be seen, the match is very reasonable. In Fig. 7(c) the variation of the maximum value of $C_1(u,v)$ is shown as a function of the hypothesized templates and it can be seen that there is a significant relative peak in the neighbourhood of the correct match. Although this particular result is encouraging, there can be problems with the method. Even in this example, the actual value of the output is fairly low – approximately 0.28. This is due to the fact that there is a fair amount of speckle in the shadow regions and in our remapping of the original image into [-1 1], much of the shadow region is defined as background. This means that if we had set a simple threshold to reject clutter, this target may have been lost. Also, although we do not show it here, there was a rock in this dataset which was quite mine-like and simply using the correlation value to discriminate this particular object is not reliable. Of course, images from multiple sonar aspects could help this situation. Also, simply using a single correlation value as a means of classification may not be optimal. There is more information in the entire correlation curve (*e.g.* Fig. 7(c) which is not used and one can also consider the curves from other correlation measures. We have [21, 27] considered using various sets of template features for classification.

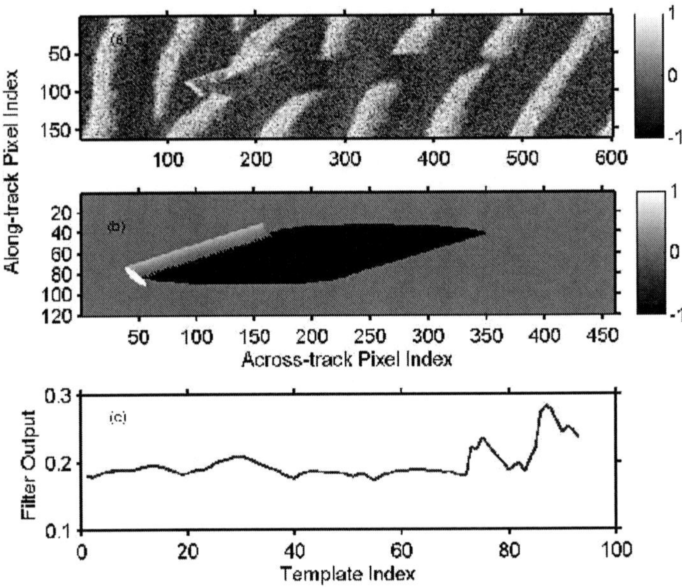

Figure 7: Template matching Eq.(2): (a) the input mugshot (a normalized, remapped version) (b) the best matching template and (c) the variation of the correlation score with template index. Data Source: NURC.

In [18, 28] we considered expressing a collection of mughots in terms of their principal component representation. That is, each mugshot can be rearranged as a one-dimensional vector of pixel values. This set of vectors has a set of principal components. Linear combinations of the first 50 or so of these principal component vectors can often yield very good approximations to the image vectors. Of course, each of the Principal Component vectors can be reshaped into a two-dimensional image or template. The Principal Component coefficients for the mugshots can be considered as classification features. Linear combinations of these features can be found which optimally discriminate between target classes and/or clutter. This is analogous to the concepts of eigen- and Fisher-faces [29] in facial recognition. In Fig. 8 we show some results taken from [28]. Here the sonar images for rock, truncated cone and small cylinder classes were simulated for a fixed range using a ray-trace model. The dimensions of these objects were varied randomly within specified limits. Some example images are shown in Fig. 8(a). A portion of the images were used to determine the best discriminating pixel features or templates which are shown in Figs. 8(b) and 8(c). The images from the testing set can then be projected onto those templates resulting in the clustering shown in Fig. 8d. Another image-based approach was used in [30]. Here, the authors used a convolutional restricted Boltzmann machine to "learn" discriminating features and the outputs from the top layer of this machine are then used by a support vector machine for classification.

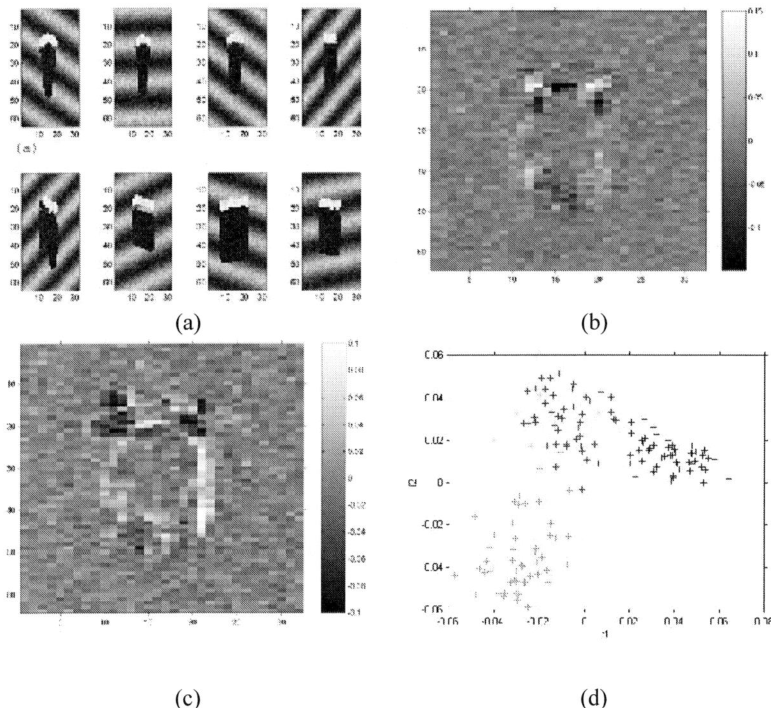

Figure 8: (a) some simulated images – truncated cone, small cylinder, rock (b) first discriminating template (c) second discriminating template (d) resulting clustering of the testing set images. In (a),(b), and (c) the horizontal indices are the across-track pixel indices and the vertical indices are the along-track indices. In (d) the axes are the two discriminating feature values. This figure is taken from [28].

We have considered only a fraction of the available image classification techniques which can be applied to the problem of automated detection and classification of mine-like objects in sidescan sonar imagery. Much of the ATR problem is concerned with rejecting false alarms. In the case that an AUV will revisit a contact at a different aspect(s), either immediately or in a later re-survey, the number of contacts must be reasonable. However, there may be seabed regions, such as boulder fields, where it will always be difficult to reduce the number of false alarms. Another issue with existing ATR methods is that they often rely on *a priori* knowledge of the objects of interest. The more specific this knowledge, the less robust the method may be. One approach which addresses these issues is change detection [31, 32]. In this approach, a very high percentage of the false alarms which would be present on a single survey are effectively eliminated because they are present on a previous survey. It is only the differences between the images which are of interest. In addition, there is no reliance on *a priori* information to find the regions of change. It is important in this approach that the 2 surveys be accurately co-located so that any differences are meaningful. This can be done by estimating relative local translations and rotations between the sonar images from the data sets themselves. Of course, this approach assumes that one is able to carry out repeated sonar surveys of a region.

It may also be possible to improve target/clutter discrimination by considering lower sonar frequencies and wider bandwidths. The ATR approaches described in this paper are based upon the analysis of features extracted from an image. The sidescan and/or SAS frequencies are usually high and any elastic/structural scattering characteristics of a target are not exploited. Man-made objects often have distinctive scattering characteristics which distinguish them from, for example, rocks. The successful use of lower frequency/large bandwidth sonars to detect/classify different types or targets has been shown in [33, 35, 36]. A hybrid system using high-frequency sonar imagery combined with lower-frequency wideband spectral information could be an effective system for lower false alarm rates.

5. Summary

Automatic Target Recognition for sidescan or synthetic aperture sonar imagery is a complex area of scientific research. It combines the disciplines of sonar sensors, image and statistical processing, fusion theory, pattern recognition and more. It plays a fundamental role in expanding the autonomous behaviour of AUVs. Despite the advances in sonar performance and algorithms, there remain fundamental problems in making ATR robust for a wide variety of seabed environments and minimizing the number of false alarms without missing the real objects of interest.

Acknowledgements

I would like to thank my colleagues over the years at DRDC Atlantic for their help and collaboration in the results shown in this paper. I have also benefited from very helpful collaborations with NATO and TTCP colleagues. Some of the data shown in this paper is courtesy of NURC.

References

[1] M. Couillard, J. Fawcett, and M. Davison, "Optimizing constrained search patterns for remote mine-hunting vehicles," *IEEE Journal of Oceanic Engineering*, vol. 37, pp. 75–84, Jan. 2012.

[2] J. Fawcett, "Automatic target recognition for an autonomous underwater vehicle (AUV) sidescan sonar in complex environments," in *Proceedings of the Fourth International Conference and Exhibition on Underwater Acoustic Measurements: Technologies and Results*, (Kos, Greece), pp. 123–130, June 2011.

[3] G. Dobeck, J. Hyland, and L. Smedley, "Automated detection/classification of seamines in sonar imagery," in *Proceedings of SPIE*, vol. 3079, pp. 90–110, 1997.

[4] R. Kessel, "Using sonar speckle to identify regions of interest and for mine detection," in *Detection and remediation techniques for mines and minelike targets, Proceedings of SPIE*, vol. 4742, pp. 440–451, 2002.

[5] C. Ciany, W. Zurawski, and G. Dobeck, "Application of fusion algorithms for computer-aided detection and classification of bottom mines to shallow water test data," in *Detection and remediation techniques for mines and minelike targets, Proceedings of SPIE*, vol. 4742, pp. 412–418, 2002.

[6] V. Myers and Ø. Midtgaard, "Fusion of contacts in synthetic aperture sonar imagery using performance estimates," in *International Conference on Detection and Classification of Underwater Targets, Proceedings of the Institue of Acoustics*, (Heriot-Watt University, U.K.), Sept. 2007.

[7] P. Viola and M. Jones, "Rapid object detection using a boosted cascade of simple features," *IEEE CVPR*, 2001.

[8] R. Lienhart and J. Maydt, "An extended set of Haar-like features for rapid object detection," *IEEE ICIP 2002*, pp. 900–903, 2002.

[9] Open Source Computer Vision OpenCV 2.3, http://opencv.willowgarage.com/wiki/, Access date:(January 2012).

[10] V. Myers, "Image segmentation using iteration and fuzzy logic," in *Proceedings of CAD/CAC 2001*, (Halifax, Canada), 2001.

[11] S. Reed, Y. Petillot, and J. Bell, "An automatic approach to the detection and extraction of mine features in sidescan sonar," *IEEE Journal of Oceanic Engineering*, vol. 28, pp. 90–105, Jan. 2003.

[12] B. Zerr, J. Fawcett, and D.Hopkin, "Adaptive algorithm for sea mine classification," in *Proceedings of the Third International Conference and Exhibition on Underwater Acoustic Measurements: Technologies and Results*, (Nafplion, Greece), pp. 319–326, June 2009.

[13] I. Quidu, J. Malkass, G. Burel, and P. Vilbe, "Mine classification based on raw sonar data: An approach combining fourier descriptors, statistical models and genetic algorithms," in *Proceeedings of OCEANS 2000 MTS/IEEE Conference*, vol. 1, (Providence, U.S.A.), pp. 285–290, 2000.

[14] J.Fawcett, V. Myers, D. Hopkin, A. Crawford, M. Couillard, and B. Zerr, "Multiaspect classification of sidescan sonar images: Four different approaches to fusing single-aspect information," *IEEE Journal of Oceanic Engineering*, vol. 35, pp. 863–876, Oct. 2010.

[15] B. Zerr, B. Stage, and A. Guerrero, "Automatic target classification using multiple sidescan sonar images of different orientations," *SACLANTCEN SM-309*, 1997.

[16] I. Quidu, "Classification multi-vues d'un objet immergé à partir d'images sonar et de son ombre portée sur le fond," *Doctoral Thesis, L'Université de Bretagne Occidentale*, 2001.

[17] J. Shawe-Taylor and N. Cristianini, *Kernel Methods for Pattern Analysis*. Cambridge University Press, 2004.

[18] J.Fawcett, M. Couillard, D. Hopkin, A. Crawford, V. Myers, and B. Zerr, "Computer-aided detection and classification of sidescan sonar images for the Citadel trial," in *International Conference on Detection and Classification of Underwater Targets, Proceedings of the Institue of Acoustics*, (Heriot-Watt University, U.K.), Sept. 2007.

[19] A.Khotanzad and Y. Hong, "Invariant image reconstruction by Zernike moments," *IEEE Transactions on Pattern Analysis and Machine Intelligence*, vol. 12, pp. 489–497, May 1990.

[20] G. Tao, M. Azimi-Sadjadi, and A. Nevis, "Underwater target indentification using GVF snake and Zernike moments," in *Proceeedings of OCEANS 2002 MTS/IEEE Conference*, vol. 3, pp. 1535–1541, 2002.

[21] J. Fawcett, "Computer-aided detection and classification of minelike objects using template-based features," in *Proceeedings of OCEANS 2003 MTS/IEEE Conference*, vol. 3, pp. 1395–1401, 2003.

[22] S.Reed, Y.Petillot, and J.Bell, "Automated approach to classification of minelike objects in sidescan sonar using highlight and shadow information," *IEE Proc-Radar Sonar Navig.*, vol. 151, pp. 48–56, 2004.

[23] V. Myers and D. Williams, "Adaptive multiview target classification in synthetic aperture sonar images using a partially observable markov decision process," *IEEE Journal of Oceanic Engineering*, pp. 45–55, Jan. 2012.

[24] V. Myers and J. Fawcett, "A template matching procedure for automatic target recognition in synthetic aperture sonar imagery," *IEEE Signal Processing Letters*, vol. 17, pp. 683–686, 2010.

[25] H. Midelfart, J. Groen, and Ø. Midtgaard, "Template matching methods for object classification in synthetic aperture sonar images," in *Proceedings of the Third International Conference and Exhibition on Underwater Acoustic Measurements: Technologies and Results*, (Nafplion, Greece), June 2009.

[26] H. Midelfart and Ø. Midtgaard, "Robust template matching for object classification," in *Proceedings of the Fourth International Conference and*

Exhibition on Underwater Acoustic Measurements: Technologies and Results, (Kos, Greece), June 2011.

[27] J. Fawcett and V. Myers, "Computer-aided classification for a database of images of minelike objects," *DRDC Atlantic TM 2004-272*, 2005.

[28] J. Fawcett, "Image-based classification of sidescan sonar detections," in *Proceedings of CAD/CAC 2001*, (Halifax, Canada), 2001.

[29] P. Belhumeur, J. Hespanha, and D. Kriegman, "Eigenfaces vs. Fisherfaces: Recognition using class specific linear projection," *IEEE Transactions on Pattern Analysis and Machine Intelligence*, vol. 19, pp. 711–720, 1997.

[30] P. Hollesen, W.Connors, and T.Trappenberg, "Comparison of learned versus engineered features for classification of raw sonar images," in *Canadian AI'11 Proceedings of the 24th Candian conference on Advances in artificial intelligence*, pp. 174–185, Springer-Verlag, 2011.

[31] S. Daniel, F. LeLeannec, C. Roux, B. Soliman, and E.Maillard, "Side-scan sonar image matching," *IEEE Journal of Oceanic Engineering*, vol. 23, pp. 245–259, 1998.

[32] Ø. Midtgaard, R. Hansen, T. Saebo, V. Myers, J. Dubberley, and I. Quidu, "Change detection using synthetic aperture sonar: Preliminary results from the Larvik trial," in *Proceeedings of OCEANS 2011 Conference*, (Waikoloa, U.S.A), 2011.

[33] A. Tesei, J. Fawcett, and R.Lim, "Physics-based detection of man-made elastic objects buried in high-density-cluttered areas of saturated sediments," *Applied Acoustics*, vol. 69, pp. 422–437, 2008.

[34] J. Sawas, Y. Petillot, and Y. Pailhas, "Cascade of boosted classifiers for rapid detection of underwater objects," in *Proceedings of ECUA 2010*, (Istanbul, Turkey), 2010.

[35] J. A. Bucaro, B. II. Houston, M. Saniga, L. R. Dragonette, T. Yoder, S. Dey, L. Kraus, and L. Carin, "Broadband acoustic scattering measurements of underwater unexploded ordnance (uxo)," *Journal of the Acoustical Society of America*, vol. 123, pp. 738–746, 2008.

[36] Y. Pailhas, C. Capus, K. Brown, and P. Moore, "Analysis and classification of broadband echoes using bio-inspired dolphin pulses," *Journal of the Acoustical Society of America*, vol. 127, pp. 3809–3820, 2010.

[37] J. Lewis, "Fast normalized cross-correlation." Industrial Light & Magic.

[38] Y. Petillot, Y. Pailhas, J. Sawas, N. Valeyrie, and J. Bell, "Target recognition in synthetic aperture sonar and high-resolution side scan sonar using auvs," in *Proceedings of International Conference: Synthetic Aperture Sonar and Synthetic Aperture Radar, Institute of Acoustics Proceedings*, (Lerici, Italy), Sept. 2010.

[39] G. Dobeck, "Image normalization using the serpentine forward-backward filter: Application to high-resolution sonar imagery and its impact on mine detection and classification," in *Proceedings of SPIE*, vol. 5794, pp. 381–391, 2005.

[40] G. Dobeck, "Adaptive large-scale clutter removal from imagery with application to high-resolution sonar imagery," in *Detection and Sensing of Mines, Explosive Objects, and Obscured Targets XV, Proc. of SPIE*, vol. 7664, 2010.

[41] J. Nelson and N. Kingsbury, "Fractal dimension based sand ripple suppression for mine hunting with sidescan sonar," in *Proceedings of International Conference: Synthetic Aperture Sonar and Synthetic Aperture Radar, Institute of Acoustics Proceedings*, (Lerici, Italy), Sept. 2010.

[42] D. Williams, "On adaptive underwater object detection," in *Proceedings of IEEE/RSJ Interntaional Conference on Intelligent Robots and Systems (IROS)*, (San Francisco, U.S.A), pp. 4741–4748, Sept. 2011.

Session I

Target Recognition

Chaired by John Fawcett
Defence R&D Canada

CHAPTER ONE

AUTOMATIC TARGET RECOGNITION
FOR IMPROVED UNMANNED UNDERWATER
VEHICLE NAVIGATION:
EXPERIMENTAL RESULTS

JOHN DUBBERLEY AND BRIAN BOURGEOIS

Abstract

In this paper we will explore the results of a navigation sea trial to determine if automatic target recognition (ATR) in an 875 kHz Edgetech 2200-S sidescan sonar improves the navigation solution for the REMUS 600 unmanned, underwater vehicle (UUV). The navigation and sidescan data were collected in August of 2011 near Victoria, Canada for a navigation test of the REMUS 600 receiving positioning information from a high-precision acoustic positioning system (HiPAP). Preliminary investigation of the sidescan imagery revealed several boulders suitable for use as navigational fixed points. An ATR was applied to the imagery data, targets were found and the target positions were fed back into the Navigation Laboratory (NavLab) without the beacon data. This created a new navigation solution that could be compared to the HiPAP-enabled navigation solution as ground truth. From these navigation solutions, the ATR's contribution to improving the UUV navigation can be analysed.

Keywords: Navigation, Unmanned Underwater Vehicle, Automatic Target Recognition.

1. Introduction

Surface vessel navigation has greatly improved over time due to the improvements in both the number and positional accuracy of external fixed navigational points. These combinations have improved from instrumentless views of the stars, to instrumented celestial navigation, to LORAN fixed points [1] and finally to GPS [2]. Underwater navigation has always been more difficult than surface navigation primarily because of the lack of this external feedback into the navigation solution. In the past, this has been adjusted for by closely tracking the change in vehicle attitude and speed from the last known navigation fix and by periodically surfacing to acquire a new navigation fix. Here we will use multiple views of objects on the seafloor as supplemental external fixed points. We will also introduce a method for calculating the positioning error of these fixes.

To illustrate this method for navigation improvement, data from a recent sea trial off shore from Victoria, Canada will be processed to find the fixed objects present in multiple locations in the imagery. The trial was conducted using a REMUS 600 AUV imaging the seafloor with the 875 kHz Edgetech 2200-S sidescan sonar. Given the geological history of the area [3], several rocks deposited on the seafloor were available for use as navigation fixes in the mission that had the best track overlap for testing these navigation fixes.

2. Navigation method

The method is as follows: Navlab [4] assimilates the last surface GPS fix along with an instrument reading on the UUV to produce an estimated navigation solution for the UUV mission. When the mission completes and the UUV resurfaces, the navigation solution is recomputed using surface GPS fixes at the end of the mission. Post-mission seafloor objects are detected using ATRs, but at this point correlated with human assistance. Position errors are calculated and the object with the lowest calculated fix error is placed into the inertial guidance system input at each location that the object was viewed. Navlab then recalculates the navigation solution. The next lowest position error object is processed and so on, until all observed objects have been inserted into the navigation solution. The resulting navigation solution is then plotted along with the navigation error at each imaging pulse.

The Navigation Processing Suite (NavP) is the navigation tool developed for the HUGIN vehicle by the Norweigian Defence Research Establishment [5]. It coordinates the vehicle clocks on all internal systems to within one millisecond of GPS times, integrates acceleration and rotational information from the inertial measurement unit (IMU) [6], receives data from the Doppler velocity logger (DVL), and calculates sound speed from the conductivity temperature density profiler (CTD). Post mission the data gathered by NavP is reprocessed and analyzed using the Matlab graphical software NavLab. In the data analysis, erroneous and noisy measurements are removed or repaired, improving the overall navigation solution. The suite and instrumentation are precise enough for creating coherence-matched synthetic aperture sonar images [7]; however over time, without external navigation fixes, Abbe errors accumulate, degrading the navigation solution as the vehicle dead reckons [8].

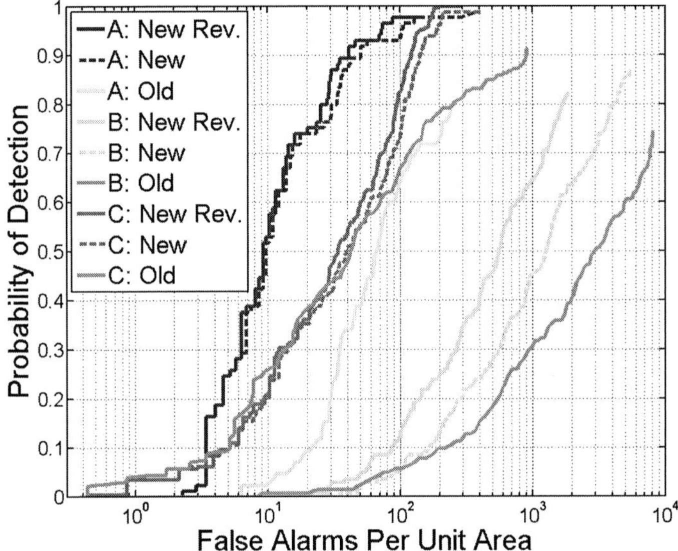

Figure 1. Observed ROC curves from versions of the detector over A) soft mud B) boulders and sand ripples C) flat sand. This is Figure 16 in [10]. Here, we are using the "New" detector.

Previously, the authors have used an ATR to detect bottom objects in sidescan imagery using automatic change detection and classification (ACDC) [9]. ACDC primarily keys on shadow identification through a negative energy detector, and then validates the detection by determining the presence of a correctly sized object highlight corresponding to the detected shadow. Here we are using a similar type of detector, described in [10] as the "New" detector. The advantage of this detector is greater processing speed due to its application of the image integral technique. The integral image rapidly integrates intensity over an image area with just four memory calls, one addition, and two subtractions. In comparison, the new detector has improved ROC curves over ACDC on this data set. However, even with the improvements, there are still significant false alarms when the 80% probability of detection is used to find enough target objects, as can be seen from the graph in [10] shown in Fig. 1. Because of the presence of false targets, a human operator assists in checking if the found object is real and if the reacquisitions are the same object using EPMA's North Up tool, as in Fig. 2.

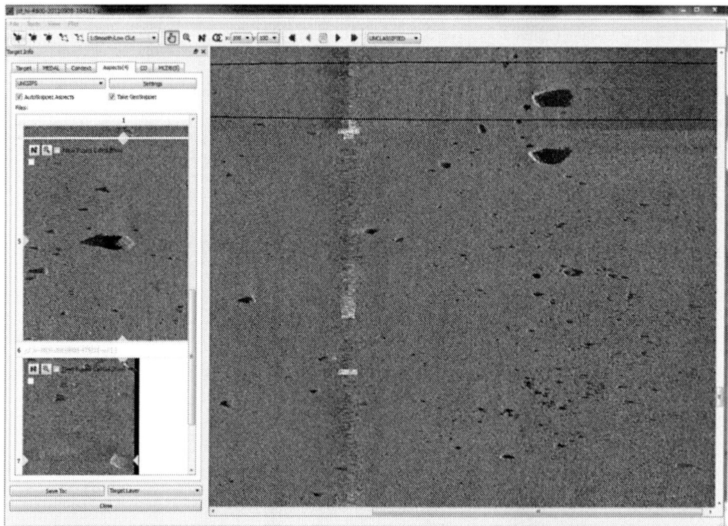

Figure 2: Original detection of the object, Rock 1, inside the black bands on right panel. The left panels are other detections of the object for manual matching.

The total position error uncertainty at a selected feature in the imagery, $F_{\Delta p}$, can be expressed as:

$$F_{\Delta p} = \sqrt{T_{\Delta p}^{2} + P_{\Delta p}^{2} + UUV_{\Delta p}^{2}}\,, \tag{1}$$

where $T_{\Delta p}$ is the target selection position uncertainty, $P_{\Delta p}$ is the sonar pointing position uncertainty, and $UUV_{\Delta p}$ is the uncertainty of the position of the UUV's navigation reference point.

Target selection position uncertainty arises due to the selection of a single pixel within an observed object that will be used to define its position. Uncertainty is introduced since different perspectives on the same object can have different appearances, making it difficult to choose the same position on the object for each independent observation of the object. This uncertainly varies with the size of targets, and for these objects one third the object size will be used as the target selection position uncertainty.

Sonar pointing position uncertainty arises from errors in the estimation of the object's position relative to the UUV. Sources of error contributing to this include: angular alignment errors between the sonar head and the vehicles reference frame; position offsets from the sonar head and vehicle reference frame; heading, pitch, roll, altitude sensor errors; incomplete sound speed profile information; and timing errors. After system calibration, this uncertainty could be estimated experimentally by calculating the circular error observed from running a star pattern over a known object. Here, since such a calibration was not done, we will estimate using average angular change in the rotational errors near the object sensing time projected out to l_o, the distance to the object detected. The sound speed error will be estimated as 2 m/s times the travel time in seconds, Δ_{tt}. Timing errors between instruments have been measured to less than one millisecond, and therefore will be ignored for this analysis. Together $P_{\Delta p}$ is represented here as:

$$P_{\Delta p} = \sqrt{(\sin(\Delta_{head})\cdot l_o)^2 + (\sin(\Delta_{pitch})\cdot l_o)^2 + (\sin(\Delta_{roll})\cdot l_o)^2 + 2\cdot\Delta_{tt}} \qquad (2)$$

Uncertainty of the position of the UUVs navigation reference point, $UUV_{\Delta p}$, is the best current estimate of the UUV position error at the time the object was detected. Sources of error include time since last navigation fix, quality of the navigation fixes, instrument drift, clock drift, variations in the ocean environment, and previous assimilated object navigation fixes. For a Kalman filter navigation system such as NavLab, the Kalman estimated position error at the ping time can be used for this uncertainty.

Once $F_{\Delta p}$ has been calculated for all bottom objects, the observation with the lowest position error estimate is chosen as the first reference error. Usually, that will be the object closest to the beginning or ending of the mission. At all other instances where the reference object is observed, a navigation fix projected from the object to the UUV location with a position error, E_{ob}, which is the L_2 norm of the reference error, plus the observation pointing error:

$$E_{ob} = \sqrt{F_{\Delta p}{}^2 + P_{\Delta ob}{}^2} \qquad (3)$$

At this point NavLab is re-run, creating the next iteration of UUV reference point uncertainties. $F_{\Delta p}$ is calculated for all the remaining objects and the lowest position error uncertainty is chosen as the second reference error. Navigation fixes related to the second reference object are applied and the process is repeated until all objects have been represented and the final navigation solution has been calculated by NavLab.

3. Data set

The data set was collected August of 2011 near Victoria, Canada as part of a vehicle acceptance test for the REMUS 600 vehicles produced for the Naval Oceanographic Office. The test encompassed 25 missions to determine navigational error, bathymetric data quality and target positional accuracy. Emphasis was placed on the output of the in 875 kHz Edgetech 2200-S sidescan sonar which was operated on a 75 meter range scale with a nominal vehicle altitude of ten meters.

For this paper, we will concentrate on the four hour length mission 15. The vehicle operated on dead reckoning navigation but was closely tracked by a small surface vessel equipped with HiPaP [11]. The UUV path associated with this mission is visible in Fig. 3. This mission was chosen for analysis because of the crossing tracks run before and after the area survey and the density of boulders suitable for use as navigation fixed points. For the first hour, the UUV ran toward the survey area, so there were no overlapping points early in the mission; by then $UUV_{\Delta p}$ had grown to almost 5 meters.

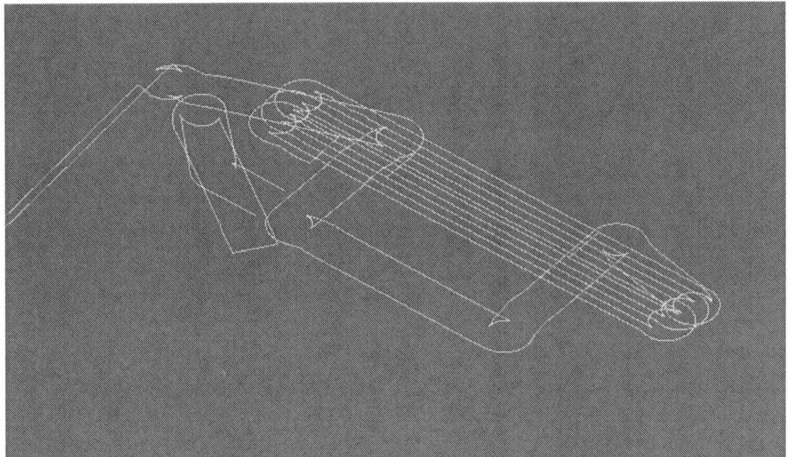

Figure 3: Sonar coverage for the UUV path for mission 15.

4. Results

Table 1 shows each encounter with the ten reference rocks identified in the imagery. The encounters are listed in chronological order to show the monotonic growth of $UUV_{\Delta p}$ with two minor exceptions toward the end of the table. Chronological listing also shows how Δ_{pos} decreases over time, since the IMU has a longer data stream to analyze. Δ_{pos} is the L_2 norm sum of Δ_{head}, Δ_{roll} and Δ_{pitch}, which is approximately 90% determined by Δ_{head} in these missions. One can see that the total position error of the object, $F_{\Delta p}$, is strongly related to the vehicles position error for this UUV, implying that the vehicle is a steady platform for collecting imagery. The final column shows that error at each of these points after each rock has been processed in order from the lowest error rock, number 2, to the highest error rock, number 7. The rate of total error increase has been greatly reduced over the mission period.

Table 1. Table of rocks used. Size, l_o, $UUV_{\Delta p}$, $F_{\Delta p}$, and E_{ob} are in meters. Δ_{pos}, the effective angular error, is in degrees.

Rock	Time	l_o	$UUV_{\Delta p}$	Δ_{pos}	size	$F_{\Delta p}$	E_{ob}
2	16:50:58	64.2	4.790977	0.0495	1.2	4.807966	4.824895
3	16:53:38	17.1	4.974138	0.0496	0.9	4.983199	4.894036
1	16:54:17	35.02	5.028479	0.0496	2.3	5.086678	4.986812
1	16:54:54	16.54	5.081085	0.0497	2.3	5.138619	4.98674
1	17:25:42	8	6.153769	0.0366	2.3	6.201345	4.986722
4	17:26:04	18.34	6.167349	0.0367	1.6	6.190378	4.913853
3	17:26:24	31.72	6.181608	0.0368	0.9	6.188917	4.894056
2	17:28:49	54.59	6.31933	0.0372	1.2	6.332076	4.824706
3	17:30:58	61.22	6.379434	0.0354	0.9	6.386595	4.894159
4	17:30:58	62.61	6.37875	0.0354	1.6	6.401125	4.913991
1	17:31:44	32.98	6.376895	0.0354	2.3	6.422849	4.986761
10	17:39:34	63.52	6.620993	0.0347	0.8	6.626473	5.231762
10	17:45:01	31.17	6.837284	0.0339	0.8	6.842507	5.231653
1	17:52:53	63.7	7.075232	0.0350	2.3	7.116755	4.986872
9	18:07:58	44.2	7.561946	0.0344	1.4	7.576379	5.337535
9	18:10:51	13.39	7.752511	0.0352	1.4	7.766548	5.337475
10	18:12:09	28.13	7.837889	0.0356	0.8	7.842444	5.23165
8	18:27:35	51.93	8.438442	0.0360	1.8	8.459809	5.331037
10	18:33:48	57.42	8.503772	0.0344	0.8	8.508022	5.231734
9	18:35:07	14.11	8.523545	0.0346	1.4	8.536315	5.337476
9	18:38:01	44.29	8.558907	0.0333	1.4	8.571658	5.337531
6	18:43:20	56.35	8.623797	0.0325	1.3	8.634737	5.366855
8	18:45:37	22.03	8.642084	0.0312	1.8	8.662896	5.33095
5	18:51:36	33.69	8.727057	0.0308	0.8	8.731149	5.355192
8	18:54:46	7.46	8.744636	0.0299	1.8	8.765197	5.330938
6	18:57:06	26.32	8.765096	0.0290	1.3	8.775811	5.366777

7	18:59:02	64.52	8.804198	0.0295	1.6	8.8204	5.432225
7	19:08:36	32.97	8.911788	0.0287	1.6	8.927748	5.432149
6	19:10:11	28.3	9.02459	0.0285	1.3	9.034998	5.366779
8	19:12:48	38.03	9.181865	0.0302	1.8	9.20147	5.330974
5	19:16:02	11.3	9.388464	0.0316	0.8	9.392253	5.355165
5	19:18:47	22.38	9.38267	0.0319	0.8	9.386467	5.355176
8	19:22:01	66.49	9.417344	0.0307	1.8	9.436506	5.331056
6	19:24:35	57.95	9.488358	0.0303	1.3	9.498297	5.366848
7	19:26:01	35.64	9.473229	0.0297	1.6	9.488248	5.432156
5	19:43:13	52.58	9.67809	0.0286	0.8	9.681799	5.355226
7	19:53:23	55.71	9.764558	0.0281	1.6	9.77915	5.432193

5. Conclusions

Fixed points may be detected during the mission and used to improve the initial navigation solution. Here, we demonstrated a method for integrating these fixed points into the NavLab software suite, improving the dead reckoning navigation toward that using acoustic transponders. Further work is needed to move from human-assisted fixed point reacquisition to automatic reacquisition.

Acknowledgments

We would like to acknowledge the help and guidance we received for NavLab implementations from Kongsberg and the Norwegian Defence Research Establishment. Furthermore, we would like to thank the Naval Oceanographic Office for allowing us to use their data.

References

[1] S. Razin, "Explicit (noniterative) Loran Solution," *NAVIGATION: The Journal of the Institute of Navigation*, vol. 14, n. 3, Fall 1967.

[2] R. J. Milliken and C J Zoller, "Principle of operation of NAVSTAR and system characteristics," *NAVIGATION: The Journal of the Institute of Navigation*, vol. 25, n. 2, Summer 1978.

[3] A. L. Washburn, "Reconnaissance geology of portions of Victoria Island and adjacent regions, Arctic Canada", vol. 58, n. 12, December 1947.

[4] K. Gade, 'NavLab, a generic simulation and post- processing tool for navigation", *European Journal of Navigation*, vol. 2, no. 4, pp. 51-59, November 2004.

[5] P.E. Hagen and J. Kristensen, "The HUGIN AUV 'plug and play' payload system," *Proc. Oceans 2002*, Biloxi, USA: 2002.

[6] J. Yuh, "Design and Control of Autonomous Underwater Robots: a survey", *Autonomous Robots*, vol 8, n. 1, 2000.

[7] Ø. Midtgaard, R. E. Hansen, T. O. Sæbø, V. Myers, J. R. Dubberley, and I. Quidu, "Change detection using Synthetic Aperture Sonar: Preliminary results from the Larvik trial", *Proc. Oceans 2011*, Kona, US: September 2011.

[8] C. Abbe, "A historical note on the method of least squares." *Amer. J. of Science and Arts 101 (Third series v. 1)*, p411-415, 1871.

[9] M. Gendron, and M. Lohrenz (2007). The Automated Change Detection and Classification Real-time (ACDC-RT) System. *Proceedings of the IEEE Oceans 2007- Europe Conference*. Aberdeen, Scotland. June 18 2007.

[10] D. P. Williams, J. Groen, and W. L. J. Fox, "A fast detection algorithm for autonomous mine countermeasures", *NURC Technical Report NURC-FR-2011-006*, October 2011.

[11] M. Mandt, K. Gade, and B. Jalving, "Integrating DGPS-USBL position measurements with inertial navigation in the HUGIN 3000 AUV", *Proceedings of the 8th Saint Petersburg International Conference on Integrated Navigation Systems,* Saint Petersburg, Russia. 2001.

CHAPTER TWO

DETECTION OF SEABED OBJECTS USING GROUND PENETRATING RADAR AND CONTINUOUS WAVE ELECTROMAGNETIC INDUCTION SENSOR

UROŠ PUC, ANDREJA ABINA, ANTON JEGLIČ, PAVEL CEVC AND ALEKSANDER ZIDANŠEK

Abstract

Utilization of non-destructive and non-invasive methods for real-time remote sensing in underwater environment is one of the challenging tasks in maritime security and safety, including harbour surveillance. The seabed is a complex environment, often covered with sand, dense aquatic vegetation or rocks. Usually, a combination of sonar and video systems is used for detection and classification of underwater targets. In order to improve the detection of hidden objects under the seabed, we tested the operation and efficiency of two electromagnetic (EM) sensors, ground penetrating radar (GPR) and continuous wave electromagnetic induction sensor (CWEMIS). The operation of GPR is based on the observation of EM waves reflections at the interface boundaries where the dielectric permittivity changes. In the CWEMIS method, the primary magnetic field produced by the transmitter coil is changed in such a way that a higher density of magnetic flux lines occur due to the presence of metallic objects. The modified magnetic field is detected by a receiver coil. Additionally, eddy currents occur which originate from the metallic objects and induce the receiver coil field. The CWEMIS has proven to be very effective in detecting both ferromagnetic and nonmagnetic metallic targets lying on the sea bottom or buried in the seabed. The additional benefit of GPR is its ability to detect not only metallic, but also non-metallic objects; however its range in salt water is very short. Digital processing of the acquired data from the CWEMIS generates two-dimensional images, which are easier to analyse and interpret for localization of buried objects and determination of its shape and size. The proposed sensors were integrated into a remotely operated underwater vehicle (ROV) which was equipped with a supplementary optical imaging and navigation system.

Keywords Continuous Wave Electromagnetic Induction Sensor, Ground Penetrating Radar, Remote Sensing, Underwater Sensing.

1. Introduction

Utilization of non-destructive and non-invasive methods for real-time remote sensing in underwater environment is one of the challenging tasks in maritime security and safety, including harbour surveillance. As the seabed is a complex environment often covered with sand, dense aquatic vegetation or rocks, a combination of SONAR (sound navigation and ranging) and video systems [1-3] is usually used for detection and classification of underwater targets.

Currently, we have achieved the last phase of our contribution within the UNCOSS project funded under the 7th Framework Program of the European Union. The main aim of the project is to develop an underwater inspection system composed of video, acoustic, and magnetic sensors, as well as a neutron-based explosive detector. In order to improve the detection of hidden seabed objects, we tested the operation and efficiency of two electromagnetic (EM) sensors: ground penetrating radar (GPR) and continuous wave electromagnetic induction sensor (CWEMIS).

EM sensors have long been recognized as a useful tool for terrestrial geophysical exploration and remote sensing [4-9]. Their applications have been growing rapidly and there was great progress in the development of theory, technique and technology over the past few decades. However, no system currently available on the market is able to accurately survey and map the location of the objects buried under the seafloor sediments or vegetation. Therefore, the aim of this work was to verify and evaluate the advanced EM sensors mounted on a remotely operated vehicle (ROV) and use for object detection in marine environments.

2. A short overview of existing remote sensing methods

Remote sensing technology plays a key role in the investigations of the underwater environment and in the detection of unknown objects.

Nowadays, different techniques are used for non-destructive and non-invasive underwater sensing [3, 10-13]. Some underwater sensing techniques are depicted in Fig. 1, which shows that the technology costs go up with the increased sensors availability and complexity.

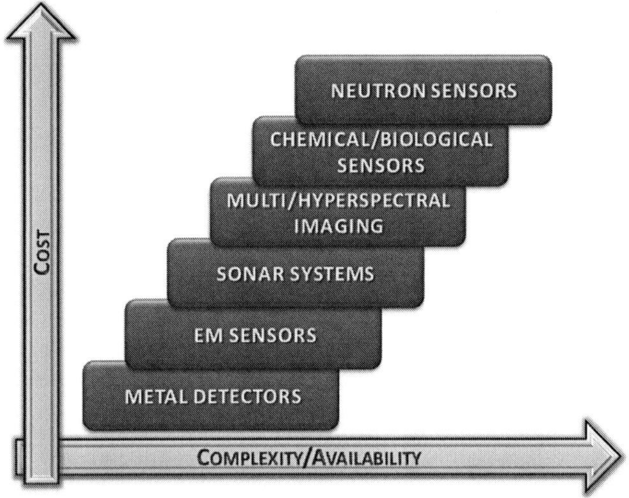

Figure 1: Some underwater sensing techniques.

The most-used techniques in underwater environments are acoustic and optical devices. The priority of acoustic systems originates from the low attenuation of sound in water. On the other hand, two major limits of acoustic technology are the low speed of sound underwater and time-varying multipath propagation in shallow waters which results in the collection of poor quality data [14]. The optical systems, as an alternative option, have another obstacle related to the strong backscattering caused by the suspended matter in the liquid medium [15]. In comparison with acoustic waves, the velocity of the EM waves in water is more than four orders of magnitude faster. Another advantage of EM waves are their lower sensitivity to the reflection and refraction effects in shallow water. In addition, the suspended particles have almost no impact on EM waves, whereas this impact is significant in the case of the optical waves. The comparison between acoustic, EM and optical waves in seawater environments [16] is given in Table 1. Using EM waves at radio frequencies as wireless communication carriers in an underwater environment is still a challenging task for many researchers. A short range transmission could not significantly contribute to the efficient wireless communication among underwater nodes but for remote sensing purposes, even short range detection is suitable.

Table 1: Comparison of acoustic, EM and optical waves in seawater environment [16].

	acoustic waves	optical waves	EM waves
nominal speed (m/s)	~ 1,500	~ 33,333,333	~ 33,333,333
power loss	> 0.1 dB/m/Hz	∞ turbidity	~ 28 dB/1 m/100 MHz
frequency band	~ kHz	~ 10^{14}-10^{15} Hz	~ MHz
antenna size	~ 0.1 m	~ 0.1 m	~ 0.5 m
effective range	~ km	~ 10-100 m	~ 10 m

3. EM propagation in water environments as a basis for underwater EM remote sensors development

The EM propagation in water is extremely different from the propagation through the air due to the high permittivity and electrical conductivity of water. In freshwater, the conductivity is 0.1 – 10 mS/m, whereas in sea water this value increases to around 4 S/m. Another difference occurs due to the very large attenuation loss of the propagating pulses in water, which depends on the selected frequency and the salinity of water. Hence, for freshwater and sea water the attenuation loss at 100 MHz is 0.1dBm^{-1} and 100 dBm^{-1}, respectively, whereas at 1 GHz it increases to 1 dBm^{-1} and 1000 dBm^{-1}, respectively. Since the dielectric constant, ε_r, of saline and freshwater is about 81, the propagation velocity and the corresponding wavelength in water decrease by a factor of about 9 in comparison to the velocity and wavelength in free air [17-19].

The use of EM waves at radio frequencies has several advantages over acoustic waves, mainly due to the faster velocity and high operating frequency. However, there are many limiting factors which inhibit the use of the EM waves in underwater environments. The limiting factors originate from the fact that the EM field propagates very differently in freshwater and seawater. Freshwater is known as a low-loss medium whereas seawater is a high-loss medium. The propagation speed c in freshwater is therefore expressed as [16]:

$$c \approx \frac{1}{\sqrt{\varepsilon\mu}},$$

(1)

where ε is the dielectric permittivity and μ is the magnetic permeability. The absorption coefficient α for EM propagation in freshwater can be approximated as [16]:

$$\alpha \approx \frac{\sigma}{2}\sqrt{\frac{\mu}{\varepsilon}}, \tag{2}$$

where σ is the electric conductivity. Since the absorptive loss in freshwater is frequency independent, the EM waves can easily propagate through the freshwater medium. For instance, GPR has been successfully applied for the lake-bottom sediments exploration from a boat on the lake's surface [20-21]. In seawater, the electrical properties significantly differ from those in freshwater. The major difference is related to the electric conductivity which is about two orders higher than that of freshwater due to the greater salt concentration. In seawater, both the propagation speed and the absorptive loss of EM waves are frequency f dependent and expressed through Equation 3 and Equation 4, respectively [16]:

$$c \approx \sqrt{\frac{4\pi f}{\mu\sigma}}, \tag{3}$$

and

$$\alpha \approx \sqrt{\pi f \mu\sigma}. \tag{4}$$

Hence, this was the primary motivation for using a lower frequency antenna for remote sensing in seawater environment. In the subsequent sections, the operational principle of the EM sensors that we selected for the experimental work is described.

4. Physical principles of GPR

Fundamental to the applications of the ground penetrating radar (GPR) are the propagation characteristics of EM waves through materials, and how these characteristics depend on frequency and material properties. The GPR method images structures in the medium that are related to changes in the dielectric properties. If a very short EM pulse is transmitted by a transmit antenna into the medium, it propagates in the subsurface with a velocity that depends on the electrical properties of the medium. In the case of a layered subsurface or in the presence of any object with contrasting electrical properties, a part of the EM radiation is reflected back to the surface where it is detected by a receive antenna. Synchronization between the transmitter and the receiver systems allows one to determine the time taken for the EM pulse to be reflected back to the GPR system [7, 22].

For remote sensing purposes, we developed a special type of GPR with an operating frequency of 100 MHz. The developed GPR consists of a signal generator, transmitter, receiver and control unit as shown in Fig. 2. The main functions of the control unit are to coordinate the transmitter and the receiver as well as to record and process the received data. This version of the GPR antenna has a detection range of about 5 m in freshwater and of about 0.3 m in sea water.

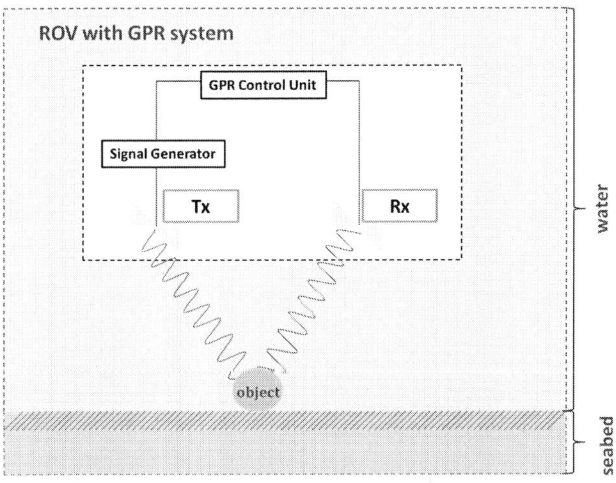

Figure. 2: The GPR underwater operation.

5. Physical principles of CWEMIS

The detection of metallic objects can be performed by using a variety of geophysical sensing techniques. Since the objects lying on the seabed are ferrous as well as non-ferrous, we developed the continuous wave electromagnetic induction sensor (CWEMIS) which is capable of detecting both. In the CWEMIS method, the primary magnetic field is used to illuminate a conducting target. The primary field produced by the transmitter coil induces a higher density of magnetic flux lines on metallic targets which then generate a secondary magnetic field. The secondary magnetic field is detected by a receiver coil. Additionally, eddy currents occur which originate from the metallic objects and have an important effect on the induction of the receiver coil field. The secondary magnetic field is determined by the target's conductivity, magnetic permeability, shape, and size [4, 23-24].

The CWEMIS used in this experimental work consists of a linear array of eight sensing probes as depicted in Fig. 3. The transmitter coil within the array transmits a continuous, digitally controlled EM waveform which is received by the array of receivers. Since the operating principle of the CWEMIS is temperature dependent, the sensor electronics contain a special part for EM waveform adjustment that accounts for the temperature conditions within the surrounding environment. The current version of the sensor is capable of measuring an object's EM induction response at a distance of up to 50 cm. From the received data, one can determine the object's size, shape, orientation, and metallic material composition.

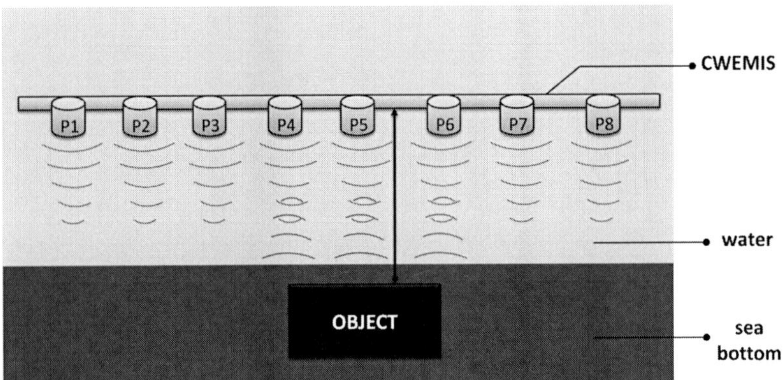

Figure 3: The CWEMIS underwater operation [25].

6. The integration of EM remote sensors into a remotely operated vehicle

Although some underwater remote sensors used for detection in marine environment already exist, there is no multisensory system which offers an all-in-one solution. Therefore, we integrated the developed sensors into an underwater remotely operated vehicle (ROV) which was equipped with a supplementary optical imaging and navigation system.

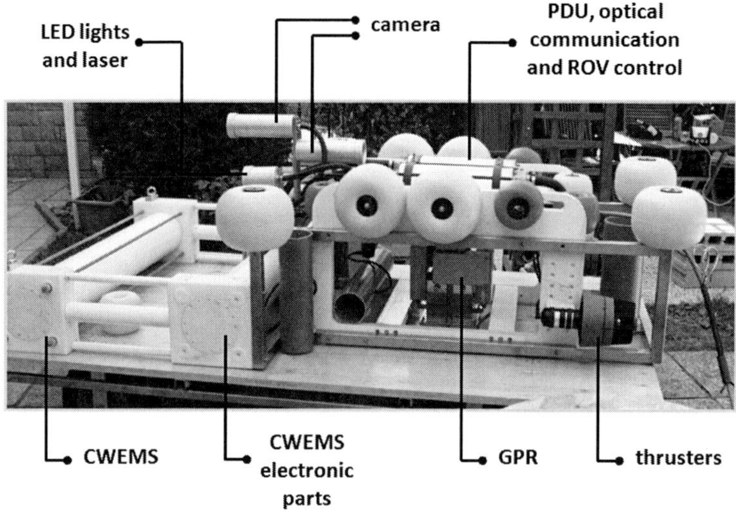

Figure 4: The integration of the EM remote sensors into ROV.

Commercially available ROVs did not meet the requirements for sensor operation due to their high sensitivity to metallic parts. To satisfy these demands, we constructed a compact and portable ROV with low metal content, as shown in Fig. 4. We choose the polyoxymethylene (POM) as a construction material, which is strong enough to sustain the mass of the entire construction and is resistant to salt water environment. Connecting frames and other parts, where plastic construction was not possible, were made from aluminium or sea water resistant iron. The ROV can carry the GPR and other magnetic sensors without causing any interference.

The ROV and EM sensors mounted on the hull of the vehicle are controlled via a tethered laptop from the surface. For easier operation of the ROV, a streaming video is provided from two small cameras. The video signal is transferred to the surface laptop where the image is displayed by the controlling graphical user interface (GUI). In addition, the movement of the vehicle and the communication between the ROV and GUI is controlled by a National Instruments Compact RIO controller (cRIO). The ROV is equipped with seven DC brushless thrusters from Technadyne and is capable of going forward, reverse, up and down. Using software written in LabView, the navigator sends signals to the motor drivers which control the current to the motors. Most objects in water are positively or negatively buoyant. The buoyancy of the current design of the ROV was compensated with additional buoys (red and yellow balloons in Fig. 4). The current version of the ROV is capable of submerging to a maximum depth of 100 m and is suitable for underwater exploration by GPR and other magnetic sensors such as CWEMIS.

7. Results and discussion

We performed integrated GPR and CWEMIS measurements in the northern Adriatic Sea along the Slovenian coast during the spring of 2012. The sensors were mounted on the ROV and submerged at a depth of 5 m (Fig. 5). The primary objective of the experiment was to verify the detection capabilities of the developed underwater remote sensors.

Figure 5: The detection of underwater objects with CWEMIS and GPR mounted on the ROV.

We first tested the CWEMIS above the metal objects submerged in sea water at depth of 5 m. Digital processing of the acquired data from CWEMIS generates two-dimensional images which are easier to analyze in order to determine the objects' shape, orientation, size, and material composition (ferrous, aluminium). In Figs 6(a) and 6(b), one can notice that the CWEMIS is very effective in detecting both ferrous (left small object) and non-ferrous (right, large object) metallic targets lying on the sea bottom. As is observed in Figs 6(a) and 6(b), the CWEMIS is an appropriate tool to discriminate between object sizes.

Figure 6: The results of the detection of seabed objects using the CWEMIS; test objects (a) and CWEMIS images (b).

The results of this research show that GPR is able to detect objects lying on the seabed. We obtained EM signals at three different distances (10 cm, 20 cm, and 30 cm) from the test object. In Fig. 7 one can notice two important effects as a consequence of the object's presence: the shift of the signal peak toward the right; and the reduction of the signal amplitude. We proved that the GPR system operating submerged in water makes use of EM energy to detect the objects in a conductive medium such as seawater, and to provide information about the detected objects. The additional benefit of GPR is its ability to detect not only metallic, but also non-metallic objects; however the detection range of the current version of the GPR antenna is limited to about 30 cm in sea water.

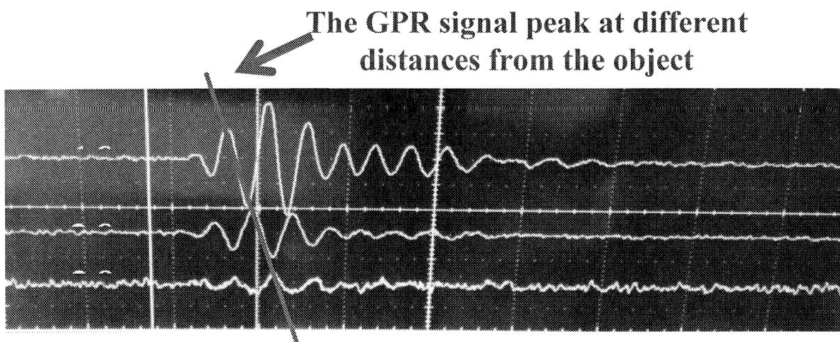

Figure 7: The results of the seabed object detection by the GPR in the form of received signals at different distances from the object.

8. Conclusions

We verified and evaluated two EM sensors mounted on a remotely operated vehicle for the detection of objects in marine environments. In order to improve the detection of hidden seabed objects, we performed integrated GPR and CWEMIS measurements in the northern Adriatic Sea. We found that CWEMIS provides rich data about the detected metallic magnetic or non-magnetic object properties concerning shape, size, orientation, and material composition. The acquired 2D data can be improved with additional digital data processing techniques to form a spatial map indicating object locations and other properties. We also demonstrated that the GPR system operating submerged in the water can detect objects in a conductive medium such as seawater and provide additional information about the detected objects, both metallic and non-metallic objects.

Acknowledgement

The authors would like to thank J. Polanec and V. Eržen for the support at EM sensors development; Slovenian Research Agency grants no P2—0348 and J2—4266 and EC 7th Framework Project UNCOSS for financial support.

References

[1] T. A. Nelson, S. N. Gillanders, J. Harper, and M. Morris, "Nearshore Aquatic Habitat Monitoring: A Seabed Imaging and Mapping Approach," *Journal of Coastal Research,* vol. 27, pp. 348-355, 2011.

[2] A. Lefebvre, C. E. L. Thompson, K. J. Collins, and C. L. Amos, "Use of a high-resolution profiling sonar and a towed video camera to map a Zostera marina bed, Solent, UK," *Estuarine, Coastal and Shelf Science,* vol. 82, pp. 323-334, 2009.

[3] P.-P. J. Beaujean, L. N. Brisson, and S. Negahdaripour, "High-Resolution Imaging Sonar and Video Technologies for Detection and Classification of Underwater Munitions," *Marine Technology Society Journal,* vol. 45, pp. 62-74, 2011.

[4] I. J. Won, D. A. Keiswetter, and T. H. Bell, "Electromagnetic induction spectroscopy for clearing landmines," *Geoscience and Remote Sensing, IEEE Transactions on,* vol. 39, pp. 703-709, 2001.

[5] K. C. Ho, L. M. Collins, L. G. Huettel, and P. D. Gader, "Discrimination mode processing for EMI and GPR sensors for hand-held land mine detection," *Geoscience and Remote Sensing, IEEE Transactions on,* vol. 42, pp. 249-263, 2004.

[6] L. Collins, P. Gao, L. Makowsky, J. Moulton, D. Reidy, and D. Weaver, "Improving detection of low-metallic content landmines using EMI data," in *Proceedings of Geoscience and Remote Sensing Symposium, IGARSS*, 2000, pp. 1631-1633 vol.4.

[7] X. Xu, Q. Zeng, D. Li, J. Wu, X. Wu, and J. Shen, "GPR detection of several common subsurface voids inside dikes and dams," *Engineering Geology*, vol. 111, pp. 31-42, 2010.

[8] W. L. Lai, T. Kind, and H. Wiggenhauser, "Using ground penetrating radar and time-frequency analysis to characterize construction materials," *NDT & E International*, vol. 44, pp. 111-120, 2011.

[9] S. Hubbard, C. Jinsong, K. Williams, Y. Rubin, and J. Peterson, "Environmental and agricultural applications of GPR," in *Proceedings of the 3rd International Workshop on Advanced Ground Penetrating Radar, 2005. IWAGPR 2005*, 2005, pp. 45-49.

[10] C. Eleon, B. Perot, C. Carasco, D. Sudac, J. Obhodas, and V. Valkovic, "Experimental and MCNP simulated gamma-ray spectra for the UNCOSS neutron-based explosive detector," *Nuclear Instruments and Methods in Physics Research Section A: Accelerators, Spectrometers, Detectors and Associated Equipment*, vol. 629, pp. 220-229, 2011.

[11] L. Wu and J. W. Tian, "Automated gravity gradient tensor inversion for underwater object detection," *Journal of Geophysics and Engineering*, vol. 7, pp. 410-416, Dec 2010.

[12] W. Lin, T. Xin, M. Jie, and T. Jinwen, "Underwater Object Detection Based on Gravity Gradient," *Geoscience and Remote Sensing Letters, IEEE*, vol. 7, pp. 362-365, 2010.

[13] W.-M. Tian, "Integrated method for the detection and location of underwater pipelines," *Applied Acoustics*, vol. 69, pp. 387-398, 2008.

[14] M. Stojanovic and J. Preisig, "Underwater acoustic communication channels: Propagation models and statistical characterization," *Communications Magazine, IEEE*, vol. 47, pp. 84-89, 2009.

[15] S. G. Shan Jiang, "Electromagnetic Wave Propagation into Fresh Water," *Journal of Electromagnetic Analysis and Applications*, vol. 3, pp. 261-266, 2011.

[16] S. Z. Lanbo Liu, Jun-Hong Cui, "Prospects and problems of wireless communication for underwater sensor networks," *Wireless communications and mobile computing*, vol. 8, pp. 977–994, 2008.

[17] A. I. Al-Shamma'a, A. Shaw, and S. Saman, "Propagation of electromagnetic waves at MHz frequencies through seawater," *Antennas and Propagation, IEEE Transactions on*, vol. 52, pp. 2843-2849, 2004.

[18] D. Margetis, "Pulse propagation in sea water," *Journal of Applied Physics*, vol. 77, pp. 2884-2888, 1995.

[19] A. Kosinski, "Electromagnetic Waves in a Sea Water Medium," in *The 18th International Conference "Electromagnetic Disturbances EMD'2008"*, Vilnius, Lithuania, 2008.

[20] L. Sambuelli and S. Bava, "Case study: A GPR survey on a morainic lake in northern Italy for bathymetry, water volume and sediment characterization," *Journal of Applied Geophysics*, vol. 81, pp. 48-56, 2012.

[21] M. Pipan, Baradello, L., Forte, E., Gasperini, L., Bonatti, E., and Longo, G., "Ground penetrating radar study of the Cheko Lake area, Siberia," in *Proc. of Eighth International Conference on Ground Penetrating Radar*, p. 329-334, 2000.
[22] R. Knight, "Ground penetrating radar for environmental applications," *Annu. Rev. Earth Planet. Sci.*, vol. 29, pp. 229-255, 2001.
[23] H. Haoping and I. J. Won, "Characterization of UXO-like targets using broadband electromagnetic induction sensors," *Geoscience and Remote Sensing, IEEE Transactions on*, vol. 41, pp. 652-663, 2003.
[24] A. Benavides I, M. Everett, and C. Pierce, "Unexploded ordnance discrimination using time-domain electromagnetic induction and self-organizing maps," *Stochastic Environmental Research and Risk Assessment*, vol. 23, pp. 169-179, 2009.
[25] U. Puc, A. Abina, A. Jeglič, P. Cevc, and A. Zidanšek, "Underwater electromagnetic remote sensing," in *Proceedings of 4th Jožef Stefan International Postgraduate School Students Conference*, Ljubljana, Slovenia, 2012.

SESSION II

TARGET DETECTION

CHAIRED BY YVAN PETILLOT
HERIOT-WATT UNIVERSITY

CHAPTER THREE

AN EXPECTATION-MAXIMIZATION APPROACH APPLIED TO UNDERWATER TARGET DETECTION

TAI FEI, DIETER KRAUS
AND IVAN ALEKSI

Abstract

In this paper, an expectation-maximization (EM) approach assisted by Dempster-Shafer evidence theory (DST) for image segmentation is presented. The likelihood function for the EM approach proposed by Sanjay-Gopal *et al.*, which decouples the spatial correlation between pixels far away from each other, is taken into account. The Gaussian mixture model is extended to a generalized mixture model which adopts the Pearson distribution system, so that our approach can approximate the statistics of sonar imagery with more flexibility. Moreover, an intermediate step (I-step) based on DST is introduced between the E- and M-steps of the EM in order to consider the spatial dependency among neighbouring pixels. Finally, numerical tests are carried out on Synthetic Aperture Sonar (SAS) images. Our approach is quantitatively compared to those methods from the literature with the help of several evaluation metrics for image segmentation.

Keywords: Image Segmentation, Pearson Distribution System, Dempster-Shafer Evidence Theory, Expectation-Maximization Algorithm, Synthetic Aperture Sonar.

1. Introduction

Conventionally, the task of underwater object detection is fulfilled by an experienced human operator due to the high variability of different objects in the sonar imagery. Recently, with the rapid development of autonomous underwater vehicles (AUVs) and the technological maturity of synthetic aperture sonar (SAS) systems mounted on them, a huge volume of high-quality sonar images are required to be processed. Therefore, the automatic target detection (ATD) is not only possible but also indispensable.

ATD systems usually employ image segmentation techniques to group the image pixels into highlight, background and shadow. Then,features will be extracted based on the segmentation results so that a detected target with highlight and shadow can be classified into types such as truncated cone mine, cylinder mine, natural stone, etc. Since the subsequent processing of the sonar data is highly dependent on the results of ATD, a reliable segmentation method with high accuracy is required.

In the last two decades, many segmentation algorithms have been proposed in the literature such as iterated conditional modes (ICM) [1] which provides a solution to the maximum *a posteriori* probability (MAP) estimation [2], as well as the methods associated with expectation-maximization (EM) algorithm, *e.g.* the EM-based segmentation of Zhang *et al.* [3] and the diffused EM (DEM) [4] of Boccignone *et al.* The image pixels are spatially correlated with their neighbours, *i.e.* neighbouring pixels are probably assigned with the same labels. Hence, the MAP estimator incorporates a prior, which describes the spatial correlation through the Gibbs distribution, while Zhang *et al.* substitute the pixel class probability provided by the M-step of the previous iteration with a Markov random field (MRF) based estimate. Furthermore, Boccignone *et al.* introduce an anisotropic diffusion step between each E- and M-step *c.f.* also [5]. According to the *a priori* knowledge that neighboring pixels are likely to be assigned to the same class, the probabilities of neighboring pixels belonging to the different classes should also be similar. Thus, an anisotropic diffusion filter is applied to probabilities in order to exclude the outliers with respect to their neighborhoods, while the real edges of the image are still preserved.

Our approach adopts the macro-structure of DEM and generalizes its diffusion step to an intermediate step (I-step) as presented in Fig. 1. The likelihood function of Sanjay-Gopal *et al.* in [6] is chosen so that the correlation between pixels spatially far away from each other is decoupled. Furthermore, the classical Gaussian mixture model is replaced by a generalized mixture model which includes the Pearson system [7]. There is a set of different types of distributions in the Pearson system. The components of the mixture model are not constrained to a certain distribution type anymore. Therefore, the mixture model is more flexible to approximate the statistics of the given sonar data. In addition, we apply the Dempster-Shafer theory (DST) [8]: The class label of a neighbor is a piece of evidence which provides some support to the event that the pixel belongs to the same class of this neighbour. Information from different pieces of evidence is combined by using Dempster's rule. Finally, numerical tests are carried out using SAS images, and the results of our approach are compared to those from the literature. In order to make the analysis more convincing, a quantitative assessment is made with the assistance of several evaluation measures for image segmentation.

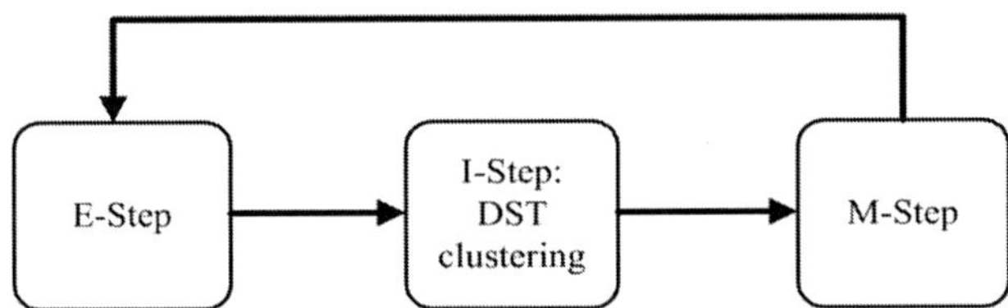

Figure 1: The structure of proposed EM approach.

2. EM-based segmentation approach with generalized mixture model

Let u_i be the observed pixel intensity of pixel i, $1 \leq i \leq N$, and $\{f_j(u_i|\theta_j)\}$ a set of probability density functions (pdf), where θ_j is the parameter vector of function f, with $1 \leq j \leq M$. Furthermore, M denotes the number of classes and in our application $M = 3$. The binary valued vector $r_i = (r_{i,1}, \ldots, r_{i,M})^T$ contains M elements. If $r_{i,j} = 1$, then we have $r_{i,j'} = 0$, $j' \neq j$, $1 \leq j' \leq M$, which means that pixel i belongs to class j. The probability that the i-th pixel belongs to j-th class is given by $p_{i,j} = \text{Prob}(r_{i,j} = 1)$.

The vector $D = (u_1, \ldots, u_i, \ldots, u_N, r_1^T, \ldots, r_i^T, \ldots, r_N^T)^T$ is the complete data, and $\Psi = (p_1^T, \ldots, p_N^T, \theta_1^T, \ldots, \theta_M^T)^T$ is the parameter vector with $p_i = (p_{i,1}, \ldots, p_{i,M})^T$. For the complete data, Sanjay-Gopal et al. proposed the conditional pdf

$$f_D(D|\Psi) = \prod_{i=1}^{N} \prod_{j=1}^{M} [p_{i,j} f_j(u_i|\theta_j)]^{r_{i,j}}, \tag{1}$$

where $f_j \in \Phi$, and we allow a set of 8 types of distributions $\Phi = \{F_1,\ldots,F_8\}$ in this paper. The classification of the type of density function f_j will be detailed in the next subsection.

Pearson System

Delignon *et al.* [9] introduced an approach to determine the type of the density function f_j in Equation (1). Let U be a real random variable whose distribution belongs to Pearson system and let its density function be denoted as $f(u)$. Based on the moments of U given as follows

$$\mu = E[U], \tag{2}$$

$$\zeta_q = E[(U - \mu)^q] \text{ and } q = 2, 3 \text{ and } 4, \tag{3}$$

they calculate the skewness s and the kurtosis ε

$$s = \sqrt{\frac{\zeta_3^2}{\zeta_2^3}}, \tag{4}$$

$$\varepsilon = \frac{\zeta_4}{(\zeta_2)^2}, \tag{5}$$

and also define an additional parameter λ,

$$\lambda = \frac{s(\varepsilon + 3)^2}{4(4\varepsilon - 3s)(2\varepsilon - 3s)(2\varepsilon - 3s - 6)}, \tag{6}$$

so that the type of the density function $f(u)$ can be classified as follows

$$\begin{cases} f \in F_1 \Leftrightarrow \lambda < 0, \\ f \in F_2 \Leftrightarrow s - 0 \text{ and } \varepsilon < 3, \\ f \in F_3 \Leftrightarrow 2\varepsilon - 3s - 6 = 0, \\ f \in F_4 \Leftrightarrow 0 < \lambda < 1, \\ f \in F_5 \Leftrightarrow \lambda = 1, \\ f \in F_6 \Leftrightarrow \lambda > 1, \\ f \in F_7 \Leftrightarrow s = 0 \text{ and } s > 3, \\ f \in F_8 \Leftrightarrow s = 0 \text{ and } \varepsilon = 3, \end{cases} \tag{7}$$

where $F_1,\ldots,F_8$ denote the beta distribution of the first kind, type II distribution, gamma distribution, type IV distribution, inverse gamma distribution, beta distribution of the second kind, Type VII distributions and Gaussian distribution respectively. The expressions of these 8 types of distributions can be found in [7].

As explained in [7], the density functions $f(u)$ of all those 8 different types of distributions satisfy the following differential equation,

$$\frac{1}{f(u)}\frac{df(u)}{du} = -\frac{u+a}{c_0 + c_1 u + c_2 u^2}, \tag{8}$$

where the variation of the parameters a, c_0, c_1,c_2 control the shapes of the solutions, and they can be obtained by

$$a = \frac{(\varepsilon+3)\sqrt{s\zeta_2}}{10\varepsilon - 12s - 18} - \mu, \tag{9}$$

$$c_0 = \frac{\zeta_2(4\varepsilon - 3s) - \mu(\varepsilon+3)\sqrt{s\zeta_2} + \mu^2(2\varepsilon - 3s - 6)}{10\varepsilon - 12s - 18}, \tag{10}$$

$$c_1 = \frac{(\varepsilon+3)\sqrt{s\zeta_2} - 2\mu(2\varepsilon - 3s - 6)}{10\varepsilon - 12s - 18}, \tag{11}$$

$$c_2 = \frac{(2\varepsilon - 3s - 6)}{10\varepsilon - 12s - 18}, \tag{12}$$

where there exists the possibility that for certain types of the distributions some of these 4 parameters are no longer necessary [7]. In those cases, the unnecessary parameters are set to zero when we come to solve (8) for the density function $f(u)$.

EM with Generalized Mixture Model

The classical EM algorithm is composed by an E- and M-step. The E-step provides the estimate of the $r_{i,j}$ in (1)

$$\omega_{i,j}^{(k)} = \frac{p_{i,j}^{(k)} f_j(u_i|\theta_j^{(k)})}{\sum_{m=1}^{M} f_m(u_i|\theta_m^{(k)})}, \tag{13}$$

where $\omega_{i,j}^{(k)}$ is the expectation of $r_{i,j}$ in the k-th iteration, and the parameters of the pdfs of the mixture model are updated in the M-step [9]. When the Pearson system is applied, the type of distribution should be determined according to (7) before estimating $r_{i,j}$ in the E-step. In practice, the moments in (2) and (3) of a certain class are estimated by

$$\mu_j^{(k+1)} = \frac{\sum_{i=1}^{N} u_i p_{i,j}^{(k+1)}}{\sum_{i=1}^{N} p_{i,j}^{(k+1)}}, \tag{14}$$

$$\zeta_{q,j}^{(k+1)} = \frac{\sum_{i=1}^{N}(u_i - \mu_j^{(k+1)})^q p_{i,j}^{(k+1)}}{\sum_{i=1}^{N} p_{i,j}^{(k+1)}}, \tag{15}$$

where $\mu_j^{(k+1)}$ is the mean value of class j and $\zeta_{q,j}^{(k+1)}$ denotes the q-th centralized moment of class j in the $(k+1)$-th iteration. As explained in [6], the $p_{i,j}^{(k+1)}$ can be obtained by

$$p_{i,j}^{(k+1)} = \frac{\omega_{i,j}^{(k)}}{\sum_{m=1}^{M} \omega_{i,m}^{(k)}} = \omega_{i,j}^{(k)}. \tag{16}$$

Equations (14) and (15) are then expressed as

$$\mu_j^{(k+1)} = \frac{\sum_{i=1}^{N} u_i \omega_{i,j}^{(k)}}{\sum_{i=1}^{N} \omega_{i,j}^{(k)}}, \tag{17}$$

$$\zeta_{q,j}^{(k+1)} = \frac{\sum_{i=1}^{N} \left(u_i - \mu_j^{(k+1)}\right)^q \omega_{i,j}^{(k)}}{\sum_{i=1}^{N} \omega_{i,j}^{(k)}}. \tag{18}$$

Dempster-Shafer Theory assisted EM segmentation

The DST has been applied to pixel clustering for a long time. Let the finite set $\mathcal{L} = \{1, 2, 3\}$ be the frame of discernment, which contains all the possible states of the class labels l_i, *i.e.* shadow, background and highlight. Its associated power set is defined as $2^{\mathcal{L}} = \{A | A \subseteq \mathcal{L}\}$. The DST is closely related to the well-known Bayesian probability theory. Their difference is rooted in the assignment of the uncertainty. The Bayesian theory requires the probability should be assigned to every element of the set $\mathcal{L}$ exactly. For instance, in a coin tossing experiment, without any prior assumption, the Bayesian theory assigns 0.5 to both of the outcomes (heads and tails). This operation implicitly incorporates the knowledge that this coin is unbiased. In contrast, the DST will just assign all the belief to the combination of heads and tails and does distinguish which one is more probable than the other. It means that each case is possible and no more information is available under the current condition. Hence, the advantage of the DST is that when the quality of the information source is poor, the 'expert' is no longer required to distinguish those similar cases. This relaxation is called ignorance in DST. The counterpart of the probability mass function in DST is the basic belief assignment (bba) function, *b:* $2^{\mathcal{L}} \rightarrow [0, 1]$. The normal bba of certain evidence fulfills the conditions:

$$b(\emptyset) = 0, \tag{19}$$

$$\sum_{A \subseteq \mathcal{L}} b(A) = 1. \tag{20}$$

If more than one piece of evidence is available, the information coming from different pieces can be combined. The most widely adopted one is called Dempster's rule,

$$b_{1 \oplus 2}(\boldsymbol{a}) = \frac{\sum_{A \cap B = a} b_1(A) b_2(B)}{1 - \sum_{A \cap B = \emptyset} b_1(A) b_2(B)}, \tag{21}$$

where the sets $A, B, \boldsymbol{a} \in 2^{\mathcal{L}}$. Since this combination rule is commutative and associative, evidence can be combined one by one sequentially in any arrangement. The effect of the denominator in (21) is to normalize the resulting combined bba. This operation can induce highly counterintuitive results, as explained in [10], when the 2 pieces of evidence are highly conflicting.

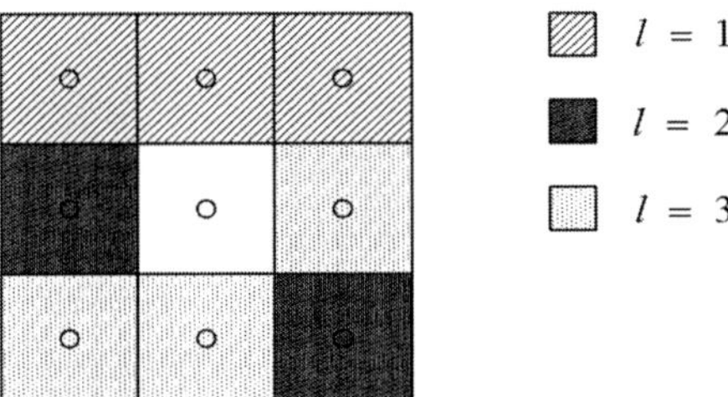

Figure 2: The pool of evidence for the pixel $\boldsymbol{i}$.

The simple bba given as follows is chosen to avoid high conflict,

$$b(\boldsymbol{B}) = \begin{cases} \vartheta_\eta w_\eta, & \boldsymbol{B} \in \mathcal{L}, \\ 1 - \vartheta_\eta w_\eta, & \boldsymbol{B} = \mathcal{L}, \end{cases} \tag{22}$$

where ϑ_η models the quality of the evidence itself and w_η provides the maximum belief that can be obtained from the evidence (pixel η) to support the event that the pixel of interest is assigned with the same label as pixel η. In our application, the evidence pool is composed of the second order neighborhood $\mathcal{N}_i$ of the pixel i, as illustrated in Fig. 2.
The values of ϑ_η and w_η in (22) can be obtained by

$$\vartheta_\eta = \frac{\exp\left(-\gamma_1 \left| u_\eta - med_i \right|\right)}{\max\limits_{\xi \in \mathcal{N}_i} \exp\left(-\gamma_1 \left| u_\xi - med_i \right|\right)}, \tag{23}$$

$$w_\eta = \exp\left(-\gamma_2 \frac{|u_i - \mu_{l_\eta}|}{\sigma_{l_\eta}}\right), \tag{24}$$

where μ_{l_η} and σ_{l_η} are the mean value and standard deviation of the class l_η, med_i is the median of the pixel intensity of $\mathcal{N}_i$, and γ_1, γ_2 are positive constants. The choice of γ_1 and γ_2 will be motivated in Section 3. The idea behind ϑ_η is that the information supplied by an outlier is usually less plausible. Furthermore, since w_η is distance dependent, it is necessary to normalize all the distance measures into the same scale by dividing the measures by σ_{l_η} as in (24).

The decision-making of DST is still open, and there are many proposals in the literature, such as the famous pignistic probability [10]. Because of the fact that the focals of the combined bba's are either elements of $\mathcal{L}$ or $\mathcal{L}$ itself, the results obtained from the pignistic level is identical to those from the bba function. Therefore, the decision-making at location i is given by

$$l_i = \arg\max_{j \in \mathcal{L}} b_{\text{total}}(j), j \in \mathcal{L}, \tag{25}$$

where b_{total} is the bba induced by fusing 8 neighboring pieces of evidence in $\mathcal{N}_i$. During the DST step, we finally turn the label information into $\overline{\omega}_{i,j}$ by

$$\begin{cases} \overline{\omega}_{i,j} - 1, l_i - j, \\ \overline{\omega}_{i,j'} = 0, j' \neq j. \end{cases} \tag{26}$$

The DST assisted EM with generalized mixture model (E-DS-M) can be summarized as follows,

- Initialization
  i.   determine the types of $\{f_j\}$ with the help of (14), (15) and (4)-(7), and determine the distribution density functions with the help of a, c_0, c_1, c_2 using (9)-(12).
  ii.   obtain the estimate of $r_{i,j}$, $\omega_{i,j}^{(k)}$, with the help of (13).
  iii. perform a hard decision on $\{\omega_{i,j}^{(k)}\}$, then get $\{l_i^{(k)}\}$.
  iv. run DST clustering on $\{l_i^{(k)}\}$, and with the help of (26) get $\{\overline{\omega}_{i,j}^{(k)}\}$.
  v.   substitute the $\{\omega_{i,j}^{(k)}\}$ with $\{\overline{\omega}_{i,j}^{(k)}\}$ and update the mean $\mu_j^{(k+1)}$ and $\zeta_{q,j}^{(k+1)}$ by (17) and (18).

- Stop iteration until the mean converges.

3. Numerical study

In order to evaluate the performance of the E-DS-M, we applied our approach to real SAS data. They are small windows of dimension 100×100 pixels cut from a large SAS image. Each one contains an object in it. The pixel intensities range from 0 to 255.

Evaluation metrics

For the sake of quantitative analysis, evaluation metrics are necessary. The Rand index (RI) [12] and variation of information (VI) [13] are adopted to assess the quality of the segmentation results. The RI in statistics is a measure of the similarity between segmentations. Let S be a segmentation of the image, it divides the image $\mathcal{U} = \{u_1, u_2, \ldots, u_N\}$ into subsets $s_1, s_2, \ldots, s_j, \ldots, s_M$ called groups such that

$$s_j \cap s_k = \emptyset \text{ and } \bigcup_{j=1}^{M} s_j = \mathcal{U}, \tag{27}$$

where $j \neq k$ and the pixel number in the group s_j is $N_j = |s_j|$. Let another segmentation be S' and it segments the image into $s'_1, s'_2, \ldots, s'_{j'}, \ldots, s'_{M'}$ with group size of $N'_{j'} = |s_{j'}|$. Then the number of pixels in the intersection of s_j of segmentation S and $s'_{j'}$ of segmentation S' is denoted as $N_{jj'}$,

$$N_{jj'} = \left| s_j \cap s'_{j'} \right|. \tag{28}$$

The RI of the segmentation S' compared to S is defined as

$$i_R(S, S') = \frac{N(N-1) - \left(\sum_{j=1}^{M} N_j^2 + \sum_{j'=1}^{M'} N_{j'}^2 - 2 \sum_{j=1}^{M} \sum_{j'=1}^{M'} N_{jj'}^2 \right)}{N(N-1)}. \tag{29}$$

with $0 \leq i_R \leq 1$. When $i_R = 0$, it means that two segmentations have no similarity. On the other hand, $i_R = 1$ denotes that S and S' are identical. The VI evaluates the difference between 2 segmentations in terms of the information distance between them,

$$I_{\text{VI}}(S, S') = H(S) + H(S') - 2I(S, S'), \tag{30}$$

where the $H(S)$ and $I(S, S')$ are found out in this scene by

$$H(\mathcal{S}) = -\sum_{j=1}^{M} \frac{N_j}{N} \log_2 \frac{N_j}{N}\,, \tag{31}$$

$$I(\mathcal{S}, \mathcal{S}') = \sum_{j=1}^{M}\sum_{j'=1}^{M'} \frac{N_{jj'}}{N} \log_2 \frac{\frac{N_{jj'}}{N}}{\frac{N_j}{N}\frac{N_{j'}}{N}}. \tag{32}$$

The VI measures the dissimilarity of between the two segmentations $\mathcal{S}$ and $\mathcal{S}'$. If they are identical, the sum of the entropy $H(\mathcal{S})$ and $H(\mathcal{S}')$ equals $2I(\mathcal{S}, \mathcal{S}')$ and in this case, $I_{VI} = 0$. In our application, we substitute $\mathcal{S}$ with the ground truth segmentation and $\mathcal{S}'$ denotes the segmentation result we obtain by using different methods. To this end, for an ideal segmentation with respect to the ground truth, we have the evaluation measures $i_R = 1$ and $I_{VI} = 0$.

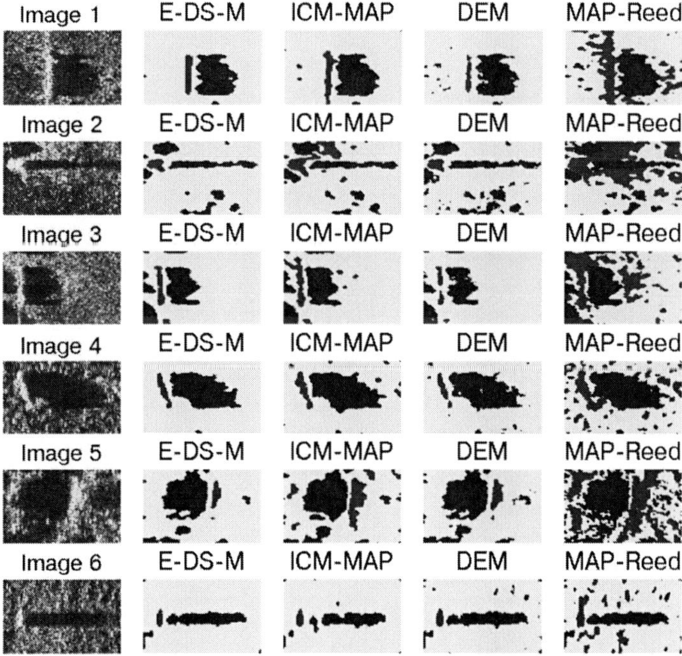

Figure 3: Examples of the segmentation results. From top to bottom they are Image 1 to Image 6.

Experiments on real SAS images

The EM based approaches are very sensitive to the initial inputs. In our study, it is especially dependent on the initial mean value inputs. Fandos *et al.* proposed a robust initialization scheme in [14] which is adopted in this paper. The results of E-DS-M are compared to those of the methods in the literature: MAP estimation solved by ICM algorithm (ICM-MAP) [2], DEM [4] and the segmentation method of Reed *et al.* [15] (MAP-Reed), which is also developed for the sonar application. These segmentation methods are applied to real SAS images provided by ATLAS Elektronik Bremen, and their results are quantitatively evaluated and compared by using the measures RI and VI.

The methods E-DS-M, ICM-MAP, DEM and MAP-Reed are evaluated using six images. The segmentation examples are shown in Fig. 3. The quantitative comparisons are represented in Fig. 4 and Fig. 5. We vary the 2 free parameters γ_1 and γ_2 in E-DS-M to reveal how the E-DS-M reacts to tuning of the parameters. In order to clearly illustrate the comparison of the performance, we define the VI distance (d_{VI}) and RI distance (d_{RI})

$$d_{VI} = I_{VI,E-DS-M} - \max\{I_{VI,ICM-MAP}, I_{VI,DEM}, I_{VI,MAP-Reed}\}, \tag{33}$$

$$d_{RI} = \min\{i_{R,ICM-MAP}, i_{R,DEM}, i_{R,MAP-Reed}\} - i_{R,E-DS-M}, \tag{34}$$

where both distances quantify the performance of E-DS-M against the other three methods. When the distance is positive, it means that the E-DS-M outperforms all the other three methods. Otherwise, there is at least 1 method providing better result than E-DS-M.

The information obtained by RI and VI is consistent: Except for image 4 as shown Fig. 4 and Fig. 5, the E-DS-M outperforms the other three approaches in all of the cases. Even for image 4, its performance degrades only when γ_2 is around 0.1. It can be viewed as an extreme case, so that the choice of γ_2 should always be greater than 0.1. Apparently, the E-DS-M is not very sensitive to parameter variation, as there are only slight alternations in the performance for different parameter values.

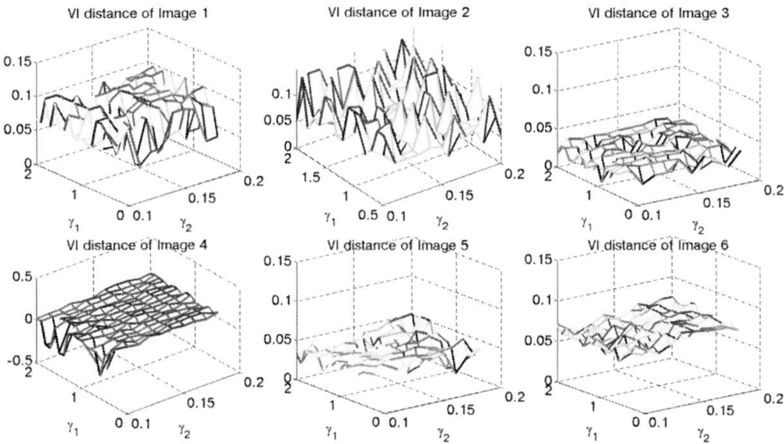

Figure 4: Quantitative comparison of the segmentation results, VI distance.

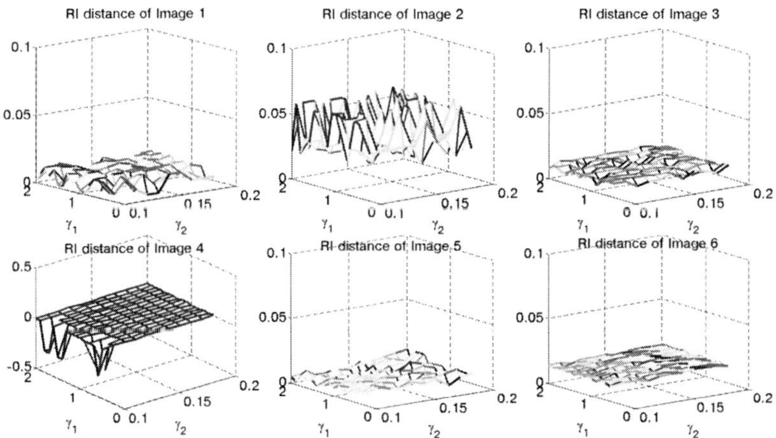

Figure 5: Quantitative comparison of the segmentation results, RI distance.

4. Conclusion

In this paper, we extend the generalized EM approach of Delignon *et al.* by substituting its mixture model with the one proposed by Sanjay-Gopal *et al.* Furthermore, a DST pixel clustering method is incorporated to suppress noisy segmentation. A simple belief structure is proposed to incorporate the belief provided by evidence in the neighborhood of a pixel. It considers not only the amount of the belief that the evidence can provide but also the quality of the evidence itself. The quantitative analysis of the segmentation results shows that the E-DS-M can provide better segmentation and it also demonstrates its insensitivity to the variation of the free parameters, thus alleviating the pressure of parameter optimization. Empirically speaking, the parameters out of the set $\Gamma = \{(\gamma_1,\gamma_2)|0.5 \leq \gamma_1 \leq 2, 0.1 \leq \gamma_2 \leq 0.2\}$ could provide reasonable segmentation results.

References

[1] J. Besag, "On the statistical analysis of dirty pictures," *J. Roy. Stat. Soc.* Series B, vol. 48, No. 3, pp. 259-302, 1986.

[2] O. Demirkaya, M.H. Asyali, and P.K. Sahoo, *Image Processing with Matlab: Applications in Medicine and Biology*, Boca Raton: CRC Press, 2008, ch. 7, pp. 279-310.

[3] J. Zhang, J. W. Modestino, and D. A. Langan, "Maximum-likelihood parameter estimation for unsupervised stochastic model-based image segmentation," *IEEE Trans. Image Process.*, vol. 3, no.4, pp. 404-420, July 1994.

[4] G. Boccignone, M. Ferraro, and P. Napoletano, "Diffused expectation maximization for image segmentation," *Elec. Lett.*, vol. 40, no. 18, pp. 1107-1108, September 2004.

[5] J. Weickert, "Applications of nonlinear diffusion in image processing and computer vision," *Acta Math. Univ. Comenianae*, vol. 70, pp. 33-50, 2001.

[6] S. Sanjay-Gopal and T. J. Hebert, "Bayesian pixel classification using spatial variant finite mixtures and the generalized EM algorithm," *IEEE Trans. Image Process.*, vol. 7, no. 7, pp. 1014-1028, July 1998.

[7] N. L. Johnson and S. Kotz, *Continuous Univariate Distributions*, vol. 1, 2nd ed. New York: John Wiley & Sons. Inc., 1994, ch. 12.

[8] R. Yager and L. Liu, "Classic works of the Dempster-Shafer Theory of Belief Functions: An introduction," in *Classic Works of the Dempster-Shafer Theory of Belief Functions*, Yager and Liu, Ed. Heidelberg: Springer-Verlag, pp. 1-34, 2008.

[9] Y. Delignon, A. Marzouki, and W. Pieczynski, "Estimation of Generalized Mixtures and Its Application in Image Segmentation," *IEEE Trans. Image Process.*, vol. 6, no. 10, pp. 1364-1375, October 1997.

[10] L. A. Zadeh, "Reivew of Books: A Mathematical Theory of Evidence," *A.I. Magazine*, vo. 5, no. 3, 1984.

[11] P. Smets, "Constructiong the pignistic probability function in a context of uncertainty," Proc. 5. *Ann. Conf. Uncertainty in Artifical Intel.*, pp. 29-39, North-Holland, Amsterdam, 1989.

[12] W. M. Rand, "Objective criteria for the evaluation of clustering methods," *Journal of the American Statistical Association*, vol. 66, pp. 846–850, 1971.

[13] M. Meilă, "Comparing clustering by the variation of information," *Proc. 6th Ann.Conf. Compt. Learning Thoery (COLT)*, pp. 173–187, 2003.

[14] R. Fandos, and A. M. Zoubir, "Enhanced initialization scheme for a three-region Markovian segmentation algorithm and its application to SAS images," *Proc. European Conf. Underwater Acous.*, 2010.

[15] S. Reed, Y. Petillot, and J. Bell, "An automatic approach to the detection and extraction of mine features in sidescan sonar," *IEEE Journal of Oceanic Engineering*, vol. 28, no. 1, pp. 90–105, 2003.

IMPROVEMENT OF AUTOMATIC MAN-MADE OBJECT DETECTION IN UNDERWATER VIDEOS USING NAVIGATIONAL INFORMATION

ISABELLE LEONARD, ANDREAS ARNOLD-BOS, AYMAN ALFALOU AND NICOLAS MANDELERT

Abstract

In order to detect man-made objects in underwater video, we propose and validate a novel approach based on background subtraction methods. A second contribution is the introduction of a *priori* elements deduced from positioning sensors. These elements allow one to enhance the visibility of underwater objects thanks to the calculation of the position of the sun in relation to the vehicle's position, the distance from the detected object and post-processing with constraints placed on the vehicle movements. These constraints allow one to reject false detections and to better know the position of the detected object. We tested our algorithm on data acquired at sea and show that we can improve detection results as well as decrease the false alarm rate compared to our former work, with both algorithms having been applied to the same videos. Work remains on increasing the true detection rate while reducing the processing time i.e. the processing time should be close to the video rate.

1. Introduction

Underwater mines represent an important threat; this threat is generally addressed using a system with four steps: a detection step, a classification step, an identification step, and a neutralization step [1]. Nowadays, the trend is to design autonomous systems, such as autonomous underwater vehicles (AUV) to avoid the involvement of clearance divers. Some of these AUVs are equipped with an optical video camera in addition to sonars and positioning sensors. In the case of the identification mission, detection and guidance are done by sonar. When the vehicle is close to the mine, the video camera is activated. However, video images are affected by the underwater medium: Scattering and absorption cause images with weak contrast and objects are difficult to distinguish on the ocean floor. In addition, real-time pre-processing and detection algorithms are necessary to improve identification results and closed-loop vehicle guidance.

In this article, our vehicle is supposed to be able to automatically identify a mine using a video camera. For that, we assume that the vehicle knows approximately the position of the target object using sonar navigational data. Therefore, in a first stage, our system myst detect this object and position the mine exactly.

We present a novel method based on background subtraction and an adaptation of our detection method to make use of navigational information. Videos are analyzed image by image. One of the contributions of this article is the use of navigational information in order to improve the true detection rate. Another key point of our method is to consider the temporal aspect, *i.e.* the link between successive images.

First we will detail our problem and present some performance criteria. Then we will detail our proposed algorithm and our initial experimental results. Finally, we will compare the performances of our algorithm with a state-of-art algorithm.

2. Problem statement

This work takes place in the underwater mine detection domain. The underwater medium affects the light used to illuminate the target scene through absorption and scattering phenomena. The visibility range reaches only a few meters, which limits the use of video cameras in underwater applications. Moreover, underwater images have a weak contrast, require preprocessing steps, and constrain the efficiency of edge detection methods. Accordingly, we are interested in background subtraction methods that are less sensitive to the underwater medium than edge detection methods.

Furthermore, we must take processing time into account, since our system should be embedded on an AUV. This vehicle guides itself depending on the results obtained with the detection and identification steps. Thus, the processing time should be close to the video recording rate.

Our preliminary tests, using experimental data acquired at sea, showed good algorithm performance.

How to measure algorithm performance?

First of all, we have to define some parameters to measure the performance of the detection algorithm. The first parameter is the definition of mine presence zones, while the other parameters are used to calculate the detection probabilities. To compute these probabilities, we create for each experimental image an annotation file, containing among other things, the viewer-object distance and the position of the region of interest located around the target object.

Definition of mine presence zones

We apply our algorithm on underwater video, *a posteriori* rather than during the actual video acquisition. However, in order to guide the underwater vehicle when the algorithm has been embedded on it, we must define the mine presence zone. One solution is to ask a human operator to select zones where there is an object; however this solution is not robust one and is a particularly repetitive method. In fact, the mine presence zone differs in a random way, at the beginning and the end of the zone, depending on the operator and the video. Some people wait for the entire object while others need a few millimeters to detect it. Instead, we are looking for a more objective method. For that, we carefully investigated our videos and chose a distance criterion; we empirically fixed a maximum viewer-object distance to 6 meters. According to visibility and turbidity, this distance is a satisfactory compromise.

Detection probabilities

Our new algorithm is able to detect several objects in an image. For that, we have to distinguish true and false detections. Moreover, we wish to test the detection performance of our algorithm and compare it with another one (our former detection algorithm). To solve this problem (distinguish true and false detections), we defined several probabilities, summarized in Fig. 1.

		Reality	
		Mine	Nothing
Results	Mine	Ptp true positive	Pfp false positive
	Nothing	Pfn false negative	Ptn true negative

Figure 1: Definition of different used probabilities

The probabilities are defined as follows:

- If our algorithm detects an object with the correct location, we have a true positive detection, noted Ptp (*cf.* figure 2)

Figure 2: Example of a true positive detection

- If our algorithm detects an object with wrong location (*cf.* Fig. 3a) or in an empty image (*cf* Fig. 3b), we have a false alarm or a false positive detection, noted Pfp (*cf.* Fig. 3)

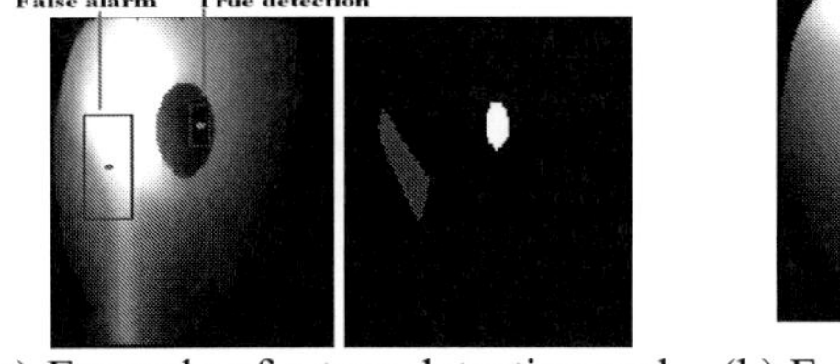

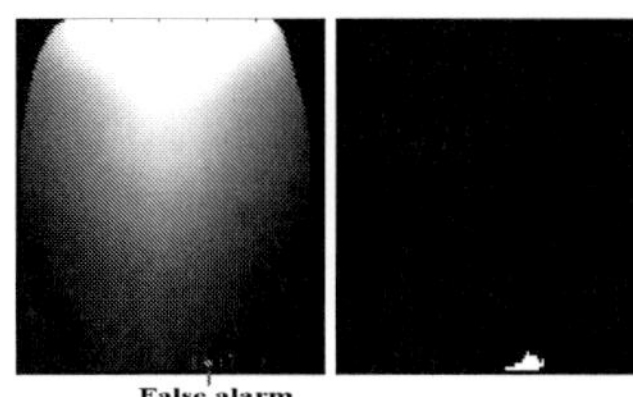

(a) Example of a true detection and a false alarm.

(b) Example of a false alarm

Figure 3: Example of false alarm detection

- If we miss a detection in an image with an object (*cf.* Fig. 4), we have a false negative detection noted Pfn

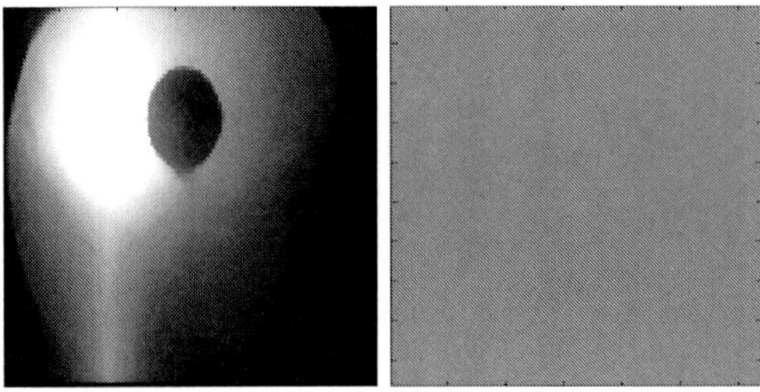

Figure 4: Example of a missed detection

- If no object is detected in an empty image (*cf.* Fig. 5), we have a true negative detection, noted Ptn

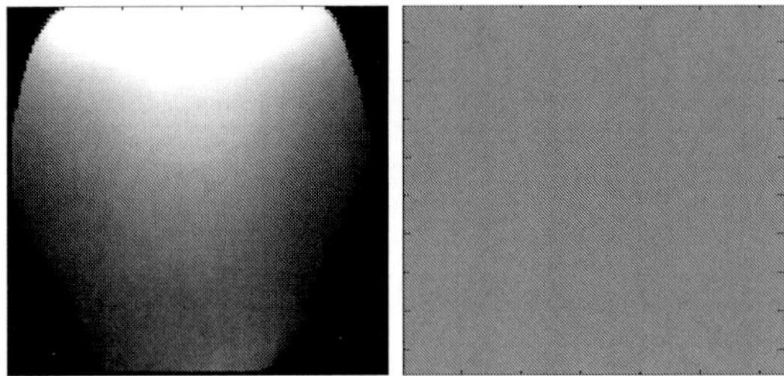

Figure 5: Example of a true negative detection

As we define the mine presence zone parameter according to viewer-object distance, we present our detection results according to the same viewer-object distance. However, we cannot calculate probabilities for each single distance. For that, we group distances by intervals equal to 0.5 meter, *i.e.* we group all our detection results for a given video with a viewer-object distance from 0 meter to 0.5 meter and so on. Thanks to the annotation files, we know the viewer-object distance for each image, thus we know how many images and how many true objects correspond to each distance interval. For each distance interval, each probability is defined as:

$$\frac{\text{number of detection objects in the considered distance interval corresponding to the probability definition}}{\text{number of all objects in the distance interval}} \quad (1)$$

3. Algorithm

Underwater images have a poor contrast caused by light absorption, which increases with water turbidity. To increase the mine detection rate, we need to pre-process the images, which was presented in a previous article [2]. To limit the moiré effect and the processing time, we resize the images. Then, we apply the edge enhancement proposed by Arnold Bos *et al.* [3, 4]. Finally, we use Phong's model [5] to reduce the sun reflection on the seafloor.

According to Phong [5], the received intensity I_r is the combination of the ambient light I_a (a constant), the scattered light I_d and the specular light I_s. In the underwater realm, the absorption balances this combination:

$$I_r = e^{-c.z}(I_a + I_d + I_s), \tag{2}$$

where c represents the absorption coefficient and z the distance between the object and the viewer. The specular intensity depends on the viewer and light source positions, and the scattered light depends on the light source position [5]. Equation 2 can also be written as:

$$I_r = e^{-c.z}(I_a + (-\vec{L}\vec{N})I_e + (\vec{R}\vec{O})I_e), \tag{3}$$

where I_c is the emitted intensity, the vector $\vec{L}$ represents the source-object vector, the vector $\vec{N}$ is the vector perpendicular to the object, the vector $\vec{R}$ represents the reflected light and the vector $\vec{O}$ represents the object-viewer vector. These vectors are explained on Fig. 6.

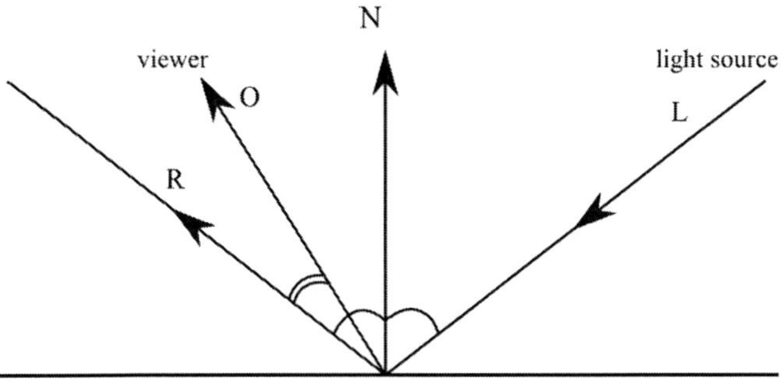

Figure 6: Definition of the angles and vectors used to calculate the received intensity.

The navigational information contains the AUV position and time of the video recording. Thus, we know the viewer position and we can calculate the sun position thanks to the Reda and Andreas algorithm [6]. On Figs. 7(a) and 8(a) we present preprocessed images.

In our previous publication [2], we used the phase of the image spectrum to detect mine edges, and we obtained good results. However, this method has a very low detection rate especially when we have images with weak contrast, as shown on Table 1. The detection probability (Table 1, 4th column) is low (below than 35%) while the false alarm rate (Table 1, 5th column) is very high (above 45%).

Table 1: Results obtained with the method proposed in [2].

Mine	Number of studied images	Number of images with a mine	Ptp	Pfp	Pfn	Ptn
Manta	25205	18275	18.87%	71.64%	42.34%	14.74%
Cylinder	49251	37564	32.42%	46.72%	20.96%	33.21%
Sphere	11376	7919	31.45%	69.94%	25.95%	7.10%
Other objects	13905	10222	17.92%	71.15%	26.90%	14.35%
Empty videos	17389	0		8.97%		74.90%

To improve these rates, we are interested in other kinds of methods. Edge detection methods are not always the most efficient methods when the contrast is limited, however region subtraction and background subtraction methods in particular, can solve this problem. This is not a new method in the underwater domain [7]. Moreover, these methods have demonstrated shown a good detection performance in other domains as well, *e.g.* Edgindton *et al.* [7] proposed and validated a new system based on these methods to detect animals. Thus, we adapted our algorithm based on these methods to correctly detect most of the true objects, increasing the true detection rate. Based on the background subtraction methods, we decided to use several images to correctly create a background image. In fact, we observe that the detection is more robust when we create the background image using mean images instead of using only one image. For that, we select the first hundred images of the video (where there is no object), we pre-processed these images and create the background image by averaging all of the images.

We decided to compare preprocessed images (*cf.* Figs. 7(a) and 8(a)) to pre-processed images with background subtraction (*cf.* Figs. 7(b) and 8(b)). Then, we compared both images and looked for corresponding high intensity and very low intensity zones. Thresholds were fixed empirically. Figs. 7(c) and 8(c) show the results of the different steps.

Figs. 7(a) and 8(a) also show the preprocessed images, along with the images with background subtraction in Figs. 7(b) and 8(b) and the corresponding comparison results in Figs. 7(c) and 8(c). For these examples, mines are clearly visible: On Fig. 7(c), we obtain only the spherical mine. However, on Fig. 8(c), the mine is correctly detected but other zones are also present, corresponding to difference between the seafloor and the images used to create the background at the beginning of a given video, resulting in some false alarms.

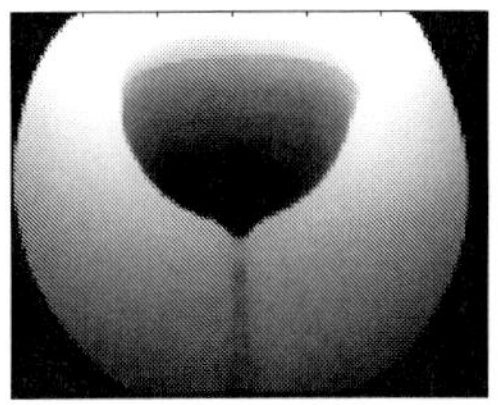

(a) Preprocessed image

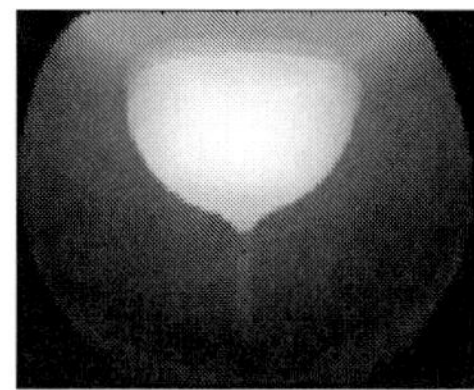

(b) Preprocessed image with background subtraction

(c) Result of the image comparison

Figure 7: Result of our algorithm on an image of a spherical mine.

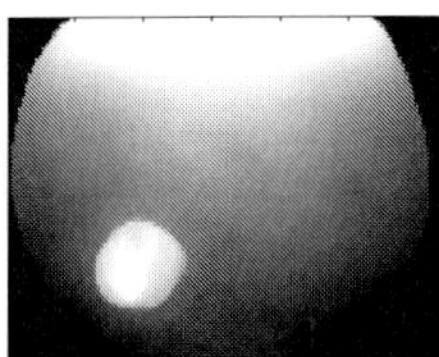

(a) Preprocessed image

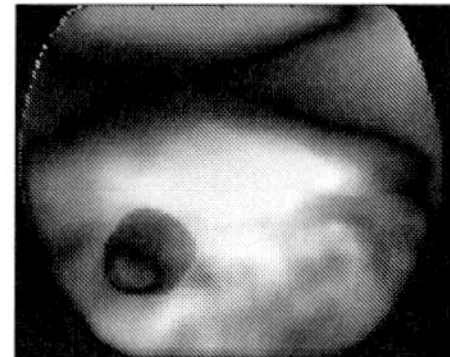

(b) Preprocessed image with background subtraction

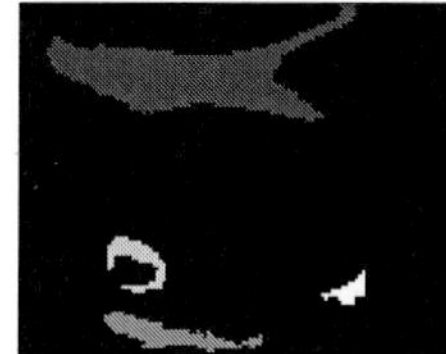

(c) Result of the image comparison

Figure 8: Result of our algorithm on an image of a Manta mine.

The results obtained with this method are presented in Table 2. The detection probability (Table 2, 4th column) is higher than the detection probability previously obtained (cf. Table 1), above 30%, while the false alarm rate (Table 2, 5th column) decreases. The true negative detection rate (Ptn, Table 2, last column) is greater than 90% for both the Manta mine and spherical mine. The different results presented in Table 2 show a good improvement compared to Table 1, but the proposed method is not the best one since all o fthe probabilities are not near the optimal probabilities.

It should be noted that we also improved the processing time. Our algorithm has been run using Matlab, version R2007a, using an 2.66 GHz Intel Core 2 Quad CPU. The processing time is 0.08s per image, which is close to the video rate.

Table 2: Results obtained with our proposed method

Mine	Number of studied images	Number of images with a mine	Ptp	Pfp	Pfn	Ptn
Manta	25205	18275	32.86%	20.83%	26.19%	96.61%
Cylinder	49251	37564	49.41%	62.37%	16.48%	31.61%
Sphere	11376	7919	43.23%	2.10%	56.41%	99.40%
Other objects	13905	10222	46.82%	71.94%	34.72%	13.96%
Empty videos	17389	0		4.13%		95.87%

Further analysis of our results shows that then detection can be changed between two consecutive images when neither the underwater vehicle nor the mine moves. So we thought that we could improve the detection probabilities by applying a special constraint from the navigational information regarding the vehicle movement, specifically position (x, y and z) and orientation (pitch, roll and heading). Under the assumptions that mines are not supposed to move, the vehicle makes no abrupt movements, and that when the mine has been detected in the center of the image under considration that it is not likely to disappear, detection stops can be avoided by an analysis of the navigational information and the detection position.

These results needed a comparison with other results obtained with a state-of-art algorithm. We chose an algorithm developed by Cybernetix and Thales [8]. This algorithm pre-processes the image and segments it to obtain contour images. More details are provided in [8]. The results obtained with state-of-art algorithm are presented in Table 3.

Table 3: Results obtained with a state-of-art method

Mine	Number of studied images	Number of images with a mine	Ptp	Pfp	Pfn	Ptn
Manta	25205	18275	19.78%	3.54%	70.51%	99.02%
Cylinder	49251	37564	42.91%	10.68%	40.42%	84.20%
Sphere	11376	7919	36.05%	3.83%	54.04%	99.64%
Other objects	13905	10222	18.30%	9.63%	73.02%	82.55%
Empty videos	17389	0		8.57%		91.43%

In particular, we worked on videos containing spherical mines. Consequently, our detection probability (Ptp, 4th column in Table 2) and true negative detection probability (Ptn, last column of Table 2) are higher than reference algorithm probabilities (Table 3, columns 4 and 7), and the false alarm and false non-detection rates are lower. Our algorithm also works better on empty videos. For objects on the seafloor, our background image is not well optimized but we reach a false non-detection rate that is lower than the reference algorithm. On the videos used in this work, we detect many false objects, but these false detections can be filtered out during the identification step.

4. Conclusion

In this article, we present a novel method based on background subtraction and comparison as well as on the use of navigational information. Our algorithm works in three steps. First, we pre-processed our images. Besides classical pre-processing using only information present on the image, we use Phong's model and the position of the sun to limit the effects from lighting. Then, we detect objects: To do this we use the background subtraction algorithm. Navigational information is necessary to learn the background when the distance is sufficiently high to be sure of the absence of the object (recall that the object position has been indicated by the sonar detection). Finally, we increase the detection rate and decrease the false alarm rate with post processing. The fusion of navigational information with detection results is a novel method for improving performance. Knowing the vehicle's motion, we can place constraints on the detected object in images.

We tested our algorithm on data acquired at sea and show that we improve the detection results and decrease the false alarm rate compared to our former work. Detection results obtained with the proposed algorithm are better than those obtained with the algorithm based on the phase of the image spectrum and with the reference algorithm. False alarms on empty videos are also reduced. False negative probabilities have also been lowered between the proposed algorithm and the reference algorithm.

There still are some improvements needed to compute the background image, especially when objects are on the seafloor. Future work will consist in identifying the detected objects, which will help to further reduce the false alarm rate.

References

[1] Ocean Studies Board National Research Council, *Oceanography and mine warfare*. National Academy Press, 2000.
[2] I. Leonard, A. Arnold-Bos, and A. Alfalou, "Interest of correlation-based automatic target recognition in underwater optical images: theoretical justification and first results," in *Proc. SPIE*, vol. 7678, 2010.
[3] A. Arnold-Bos, J. Malkasse, and G. Kervern, "Towards a model-free denoising of underwater optical images," in *Proceedings of the IEEE conference on Ocean (Europe)*, 2005.

[4] A. Arnold-Bos, J.-P. Malkasse, and G. Kervern, "A pre-processing framework for automatic underwater images denoising," in *Proceedings of the European Conference on Propagation and Systems*, 2005.
[5] B. Phong, "Illumination for computer generated pictures," *Communications of the ACM*, vol. 18, pp. 311–317, June 1975.
[6] I. Reda and A. Andreas, "Solar position algorithm for solar radiation applications," *Solar Energy*, vol. 76, pp. 577–589, 2004.
[7] D. Edgindton, D. Cline, D. Davis, I. Kerkez, and J. Mariette, "Detection, tracking, and classifying animals in underwater video," in *MTS/IEEE Oceans 2006 Conference Proceedings*, 2006.
[8] N. Mandelert and A. Arnold-Bos, "Joint sonar and video sensing for a fire-and-forget underwater mine disposal munition," in *Proc. 3rd conference on Maritime Systems and Technology*, 2008.

Chapter Five

Acoustic Scattering of a Straight Groove on a Metal Plate Immersed in Water at Low Frequency: Detection and Positioning

Gérard Maze, Fernand Léon,
Dominique Décultot, Farid Chati,
Yaya Sidibé, Fabrice Druaux
and Dimitri Lefebvre

Abstract

As part of ocean development, humans build more and more immersed mechanical systems such as offshore wind turbines and marine current turbines. These mechanical systems can be monitored at any time in situ. Classic methods of nondestructive testing may, of course, be used with sensors continuously at preselected locations on the structure. The present study is an alternative to these classic methods; it is based on acoustic scattering measurements without contact and thus allows a scan of any part of the structure. Perfect knowledge of the structure is however necessary. In this presentation, the study of the acoustic scattering, in a frequency range between 50 kHz and 400 kHz, by a flat plate having a fine groove opening out is performed. The scattering acoustic signals are identified and linked to the Lamb waves A and S0 propagating in the plate. This preliminary study allows the detection and the localization of the groove on the plate.

1. Introduction

A number of studies on the acoustic scattering from simple objects immersed in water such as plates, cylinders, cylindrical shells, spheres or spheroids, have already been published. The relationship between the scattering signals and the propagation of guided waves in these objects has been shown. In the case of plates immersed in water, the symmetric or antisymmetric Lamb waves influenced by the fluid are taken into account to explain the scattering mechanism [1, 2]. In finite length plates immersed in a fluid, quasi Lamb waves are generated at a critical angle, at the extremities or at defects: cracks, arc welding, etc...[3]. Moreover, mode conversions occur at these impedance discontinuities: one propagation mode changes into another mode [4]. The radiations of the guided waves at an extremity of a plate or a tube have also been studied and angular diagrams were obtained [5].

Lamb waves have extensively been used in non destructive evaluation to detect defects in plates and in pipes [6, 7]. Several works by a team from London Imperial College are examples of these applications. In their studies, the team developed a software tool called DISPERSE to calculate the dispersive velocity of these Lamb waves in structures [8].

All these results are used to explain the phenomena observed in the study presented in this work.

The aim of the present study is to set the first stage for the *in situ* monitoring of the operation of a marine current turbine and to detect potential defects, such as cracks or concretions. The propeller of a marine current turbine is made up of a boss with several blades. In this paper, the acoustic scattering from a blade immersed in water is studied and, in order to simplify the problem, the blade is considered as a rectangular plane plate. It is excited by an acoustic impulse at various incidence angles in a horizontal plane, perpendicular to the plate.

In the explored low frequency domain, two types of Lamb waves can be observed when the plate is placed in air: the antisymmetric Lamb wave A_0 and the symmetric Lamb wave S_0 [9]. In this paper, the theoretical propagation of the quasi-Lamb waves in an infinitely long thin plate immersed in water is studied. Special attention is given to the case of the A_0 wave considering the bifurcation of the phase velocity dispersion curve in the vicinity of the speed of sound in water [10]. When the plate is in vacuum, the phase velocity of the A_0 wave rises from zero to the velocity of the Rayleigh wave. When the plate is in water, the velocity dispersion curve of the A_0 wave would rise and cross the value of sound speed in water, which is not possible. A new wave replaces the A_0 wave, the A

wave with a phase velocity which is always smaller than the sound speed in water.

The time signals obtained from a plate with finite dimensions allow us to explain the mechanisms of the acoustic scattering. A 2D problem is considered here, in which the guided waves set up resonances along the width of the plate, whereas no resonance is established along the length of the plate, which is longer than the width. The study also examines conditions for the generation of the A wave. Indeed, since the phase velocity of this wave is smaller than the speed of sound in water, it is not possible to generate it under the Snell-Descartes condition; however, a number of resonances is established from this A wave. Therefore, in order to explain this finding, it is assumed that its generation takes place at the extremities of the plate. In the case of the S_0 wave, two modes of generation in the plate are experimentally observed. The phase velocity of this wave is higher than the speed of sound in water, it can therefore be generated at the critical angle defined by the Snell-Descartes Laws, but it is also generated at the extremities of the plate or at a discontinuity due to a groove.

2. Experimental setup

The plate is vertically hung by two nylon threads in a water-filled cylindrical tank (diameter 3m and depth 2m). A transducer turns around the plate in the horizontal plane, perpendicular to the plate, *i.e.* the axis of the transducer and the vertical axis of the plate cut each other perpendicularly (Fig. 1(a)). The Olympus broadband transducer (V 3507) with a central frequency 200 kHz is excited by a short impulse generator. The scattering time signal is detected by the same transducer and, after amplification, it is digitized and visualized on a Lecroy oscilloscope. The sampling rate is 10 Msamples/s and the number samples in a file for each incidence angle is 10000 pts. This time signal is recorded on a hard disc and is processed on a Personal Computer (PC). The incidence angular signal recording interval is 1° and the angular range is from 0° to 180°. The rectangular plate used in the experiments is made of stainless steel. Its length L_p is equal to 300 mm, its width l_p is equal to 194 mm and its thickness e is equal to 1.5 mm. The position and the dimension of the groove opening out are indicated in Fig. 1(b). The parameter values for the stainless steel used in the computation are the velocity of longitudinal wave $C_L = 5790$ m/s, the velocity of the shear wave $C_T = 3100$ m/s and the density $\rho_{ss} = 7900$ kg/m^3. The parameter values for water in which the plate is immersed are the sound speed $C_w = 1470$ m/s and the density $\rho_w = 1000$ kg/m^3.

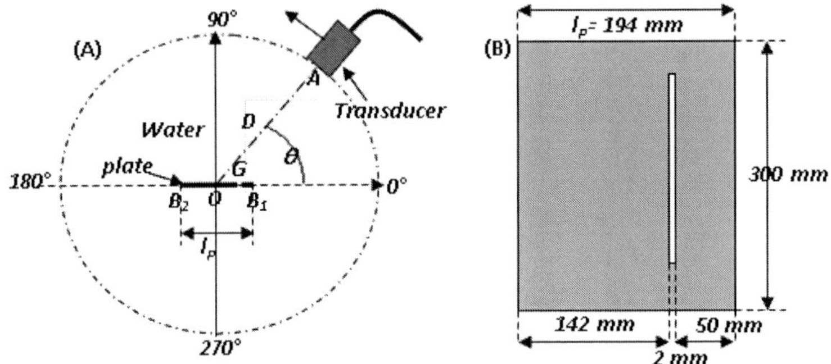

Figure 1: (a) Experimental setup, (b) finite length plate with a groove opening out.

3. Experimental time signals for a plate without a groove

The plate without the groove has the same dimensions that the plate with the groove (length L_p=300 mm, width l_p=194 mm and thickness e=1.5 mm). Figs. 2(a) and 3(a) show the experimental time trajectories as a function of the incidence angle, for incidence angles ranging between 0° and 180° with angular intervals of 1°; all of the time signals are put together to obtain a grey-scale image. On the left side of these figures, echoes related to the extremities B_1 and B_2 of the plate, sparkling lines, are observed. They are indicated by continuous black arrows in the figures and marked (**E₁**) and (**E₂**). A brace bracket designates the elastic echoes related to the propagation of the Lamb waves A and S_0. Figs. 2(b) and 3(b) show the time echo trajectories related to the propagation of the A wave and the S_0 wave, respectively, in the plate as function of the incidence angle. In the case of the A wave, only the generation at the extremities of the plate is possible, the phase velocity of this wave is always smaller than the sound speed in water. In the case of the S_0 wave the two types of generation are possible at the extremities and at the critical angle. These calculated trajectories are obtained with the following equations. The flight times of the two echoes related to the scattering from the extremities of the plate are obtained from Equations (1) and (2) multiplied by 2:

$$T_{AB_1} = [\sqrt{D^2 + \frac{l_p^2}{4} - D\, l_p\, cos(\theta)}\,]/C_w \qquad (1),$$

$$T_{AB_2} = [\sqrt{D^2 + \frac{l_p^2}{4} + D\, l_p\, cos(\theta)}\,]/C_w \qquad (2).$$

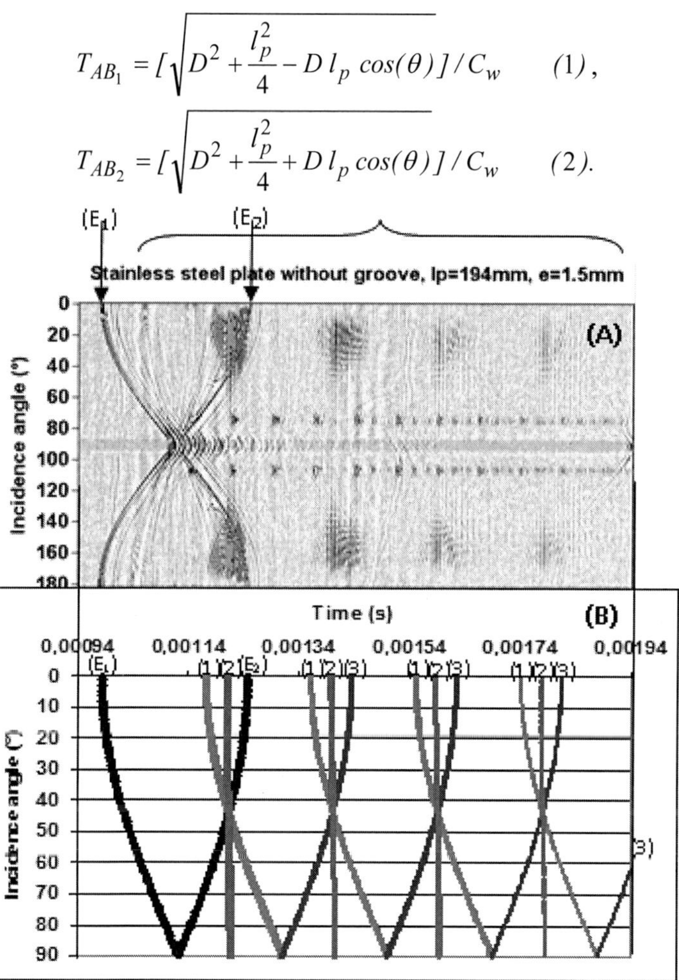

Figure 2: (a) Experimental time echo trajectories in grey level; (b) Trajectories of echoes calculated using group velocity of *A* wave.

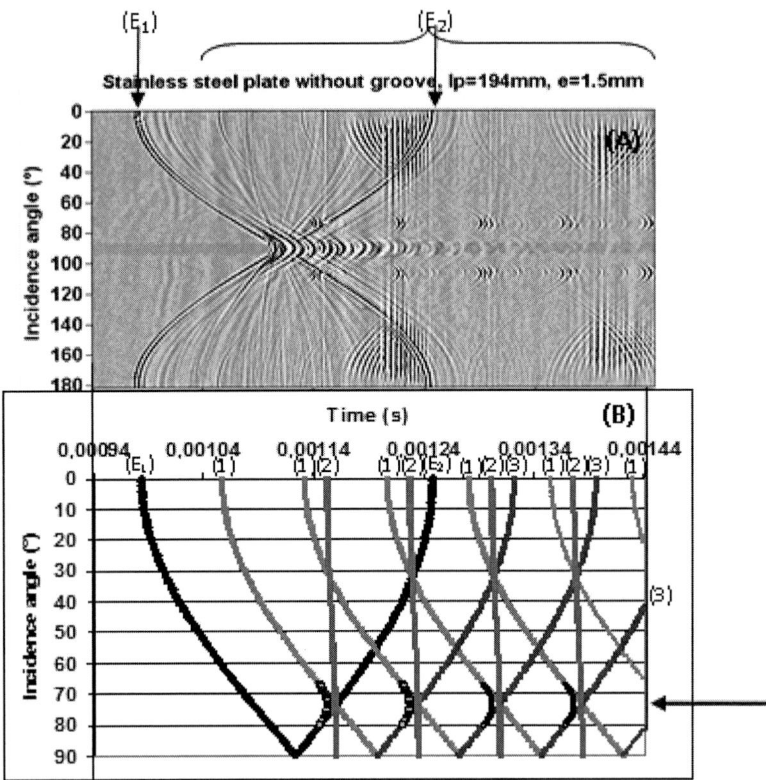

Figure 3: (A) Experimental time echo trajectories in grey level; (B) Trajectories of echoes calculated using group velocity of wave S_0 wave.

where l_p is the plate width, is equal to 194 mm; D is the distance between the transducer and the center of the plate, is equal to 0.82 m; C_w is the speed of sound in water and; θ is the incidence angle (Fig.1). The group velocities used in the computations to determine the flight times is $C_A^{gr} = 2045 \, m/s$ for the A wave and $C_{S_0}^{ph} = 5220 \, m/s$ for the S_0 wave corresponding to a frequency close to 200 kHz [3]. Time echo trajectories indicated by the number (1) in the figure, are obtained from Equation (3).

$$t = 2T_{AB_1} + \frac{2\,i\,l_p}{C_{A,S_0}^{gr}} \quad (3)$$

The Lamb wave A is generated at the extremity B_1 (Fig. 1), it propagates in the plate and undergoes reflection at the extremity B_2, in addition, it radiates some of its energy from extremities B_1 and B_2 into the water. The transducer detects the time signal that radiates at the extremity B_1. The parameter i indicates the path number in the plate $B_1 B_2$. The time echo trajectories indicated by the number **(2)** are obtained from Equation (4). In this case, the Lamb wave A or S_0 is generated at the extremity B_1 (or B_2), it propagates in the plate right up to B_2 (or B_1) where it radiates into water. The parameter j, which takes values 1, 3, 5...., indicates the path number for $B_1 B_2$ (or $B_2 B_1$).

$$t = T_{AB_1} + \frac{j\, l_p}{C^{gr}_{A,S_0}} + T_{AB_2} \quad (4)$$

The time echo trajectories indicated by the numbers **(3)** are obtained from Equation (5). The Lamb wave A or S_0 is generated at the extremity B_2, propagates in the plate and undergoes reflection at the extremity B_1; in addition, it radiates some of its energy from extremities B_1 and B_2 into the water. The transducer detects the time signal radiated at the extremity B_2. The parameter i indicates the path number $B_2 B_1$.

$$t = 2\, T_{AB_2} + \frac{2\, i\, l_p}{C^{gr}_{A,S_0}} \quad (5)$$

The echo trajectories indicated by the black arrow on the right side of Fig. 3(b) and observed at an incidence angle of around 75° are obtained by the generation of the Lamb wave S_0 at the critical angle (73.65°). The angular limitations are determined by the possibility to insonify the plate at the critical angle. In the experimental Figs. 2(a) and 3(a), not all echoes can be identified because they are too numerous.

4. Experimental time signals for a plate with a groove

Influence of the A wave

Fig. 4 (Fig. 5) compares the experimental results of the acoustic scattering by the plate with a groove as described above in a grey level representation. The time signal trajectories are also calculated supposing that the guided wave in plate is the A wave.

The two black trajectories are related to the scattering from extremities of the plate B_1 and B_2. The brown trajectory is related to the scattering from the groove (G).

Three paths are possible with a propagation of the A wave:

- From A to G in water (C_w=1470m/s), from G to B_2 (B_1) and after reflection on the extremity, from B_2 (B_1) to G in the plate ($C_A^{gr} = 2025m/s$) and finally from G to A in water. The path from G to B_2 (B_1) can be done several times, which explains the observed periodicity (Fig. 4, red curves).

- From A to G in water, from G to B_2 (B_1) in the plate and finally from B_2 (B_1) to A in water. The path from G to B_2 (B_1) can be done several times (Fig. 4, green curves).

- From A to B_2 (B_1) in the water, from B_2 (B_1) to G and from G to B_2 (B_1) in the plate and finally from B_2 to A in water. The path from G to B_2 can be done several times, (blue curves).

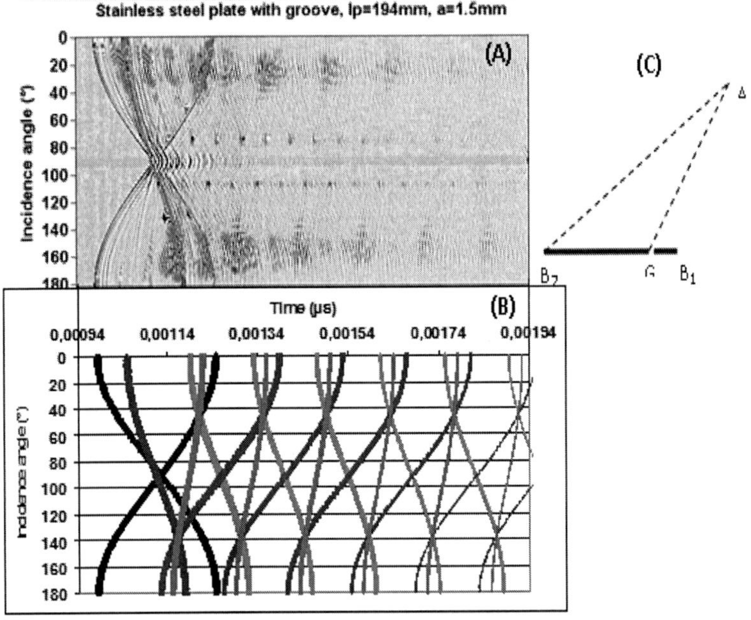

Figure 4: (a) Experimental time echo trajectories in grey level; (b) Trajectories of echoes calculated using group velocity of *A* wave, (c) wave paths.

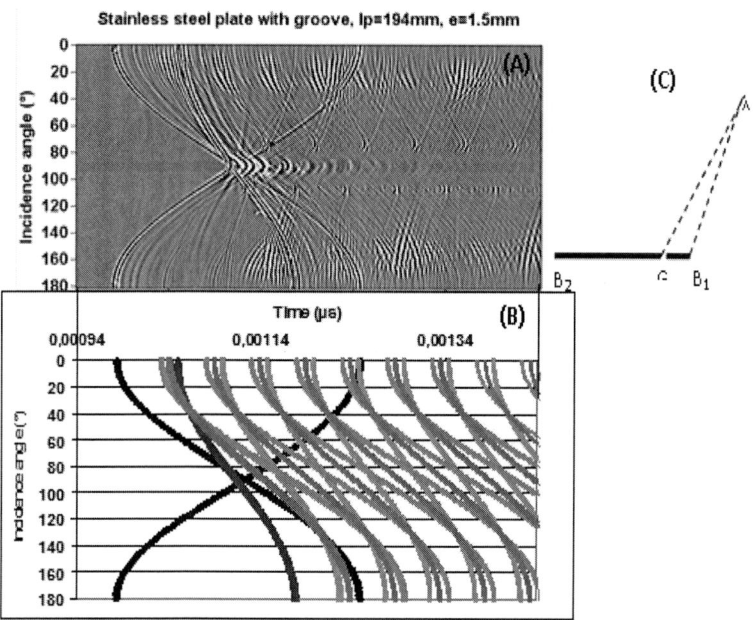

Figure 5: (a) Experimental time echo trajectories in grey level; (b) Trajectories of echoes calculated using group velocity of A wave, (c) wave paths.

A good agreement can be observed between the experimental results and the calculated trajectories.

Influence of the S_0 wave

The same calculus can be realized with a propagation of the S_0 wave in the plate. The results are presented in Figs 6 and 7. A good agreement can be observed. However, given the number of trajectories and their tightening, it is unclear whether they are all experimentally observable.

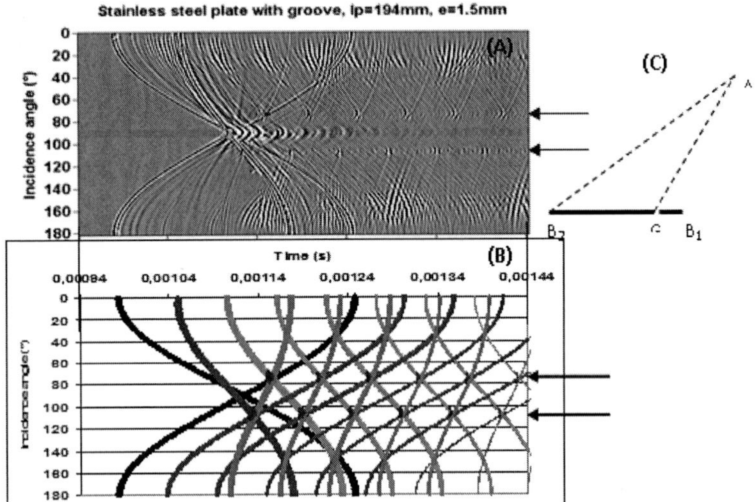

Figure 6: (a) Experimental time echo trajectories in grey level; (b) Trajectories of echoes calculated using group velocity of S_0 wave, (c) wave paths.

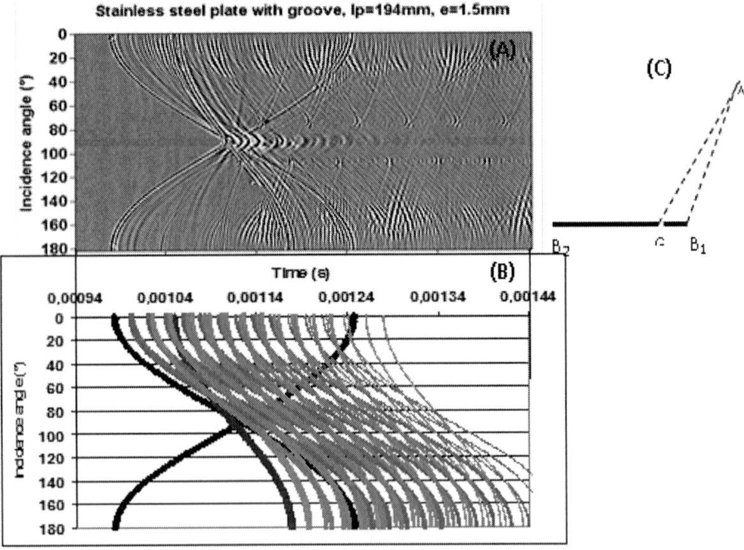

Figure 7: (a) Experimental time echo trajectories in grey level; (b) Trajectories of echoes calculated using group velocity of S_0 wave, (c) wave paths.

In addition, at around 73° and 107°, the presence of bright echoes indicated by black arrows at the critical angle of the wave S_0 is observed in Fig. 6. The critical angle is defined by Snell's Law with Eq. (6):

$$q_c = a\sin(\frac{C_w}{C_{S_0}^{Phase}}) = a\sin(\frac{1470}{5230}) = 16.32° , \quad (6)$$

with the chosen angle origin the critical angles are 73.68° and 106.32°. In the calculation, the angular interval which allows excitation of a point on the plate is taken into account. The experimental results (Fig. 6(a)) show that the echoes corresponding to the excitation angle 73° arrive later than those corresponding to the angle 107°. The time difference between two consecutive echoes is the same for both angles. The echoes for the incidence angle 73° are obtained from the path AGB_2GA. The S_0 wave propagates along the path in the plate GB_2G. The echoes for the incidence angle 107° are obtained from the path AB_2GB_2A. The S_0 wave propagates along the path in the plate B_2GB_2. The delay is due to the propagation in water which is not identical, a dissymmetry is between the two paths; the groove is not at the middle of the plate. The time between two consecutive echoes is Δt = 54.3 µs, It corresponds to the propagation of the S_0 wave along the path GB_2G or B_2GB_2 considering the group velocity of this wave ($C_{S_0}^{ph}$ = 5220 m/s). The time difference between two consecutive echoes is the same for both angles. The length (GB_2) giving the groove position on the plate can be calculated using:

$$l_{GB_2} = 54.3\,10^{-6}\,5220/2 = 0.142m . \tag{7}$$

5. Conclusion

From the acoustic scattering by a finite length plate with a straight groove, it is possible to determine the position of this groove using the characteristics of the A wave or the S_0 wave with good precision.

References

[1] R. Fiorito, W. Madigosky and H. Überall, "Resonance theory of acoustic waves interacting with an elastic plate," *J. Acoust Soc. Am.* 66, 1857-1866, 1979.
[2] L. Shuyu, "Study on the radiation acoustic field of rectangular radiators in flexural vibration," *Journal of Sound and Vibration* 254, 469-479 2002.

[3] N. Cité, F. Chati, D. Décultot, F. Léon, G. Maze, "Acoustic scattering from a finite plate: generation of guided Lamb waves S_0, A_0 and A." *J. Acoust Soc. Am.* In press.

[4] A. Baillard, J. Chiumia, D. Décultot, G. Maze, A. Klauson, J. Metsaveer, "Surface Wave Conversion Analysis on lengthwise Soldered Circular Cylindrical Shell," *J. Acoust. Soc. Am.* 124, 2061-2067, 2008.

[5] F. Luppé, B. Gilles Chatenets and G. Maze, "Diffraction of Lamb waves at the end section of a plate," *J. Acoust. Soc. Am.* 87, 1807-1809, 1990.

[6] M. J. S. Lowe, P. Cawley, J.-Y. Kao and O. Diligent, "The low frequency reflection characteristics of fundamental antisymmetric Lamb wave a0 from a rectangular notch in a plate," *J. Acoust. Soc. Am.* 112, 2612-2622, 2002.

[7] M. J. S. Lowe, D. N. Alleyne, P. Cawley, "Defect detection in pipes using guided waves," *Ultrasonics* 36, 147-154, 1998.

[8] B. Pavlakovic, M. Lowe, D. Alleyne, P. Cawley, "DISPERSE: a general purpose program for creating dispercive waves," *Review of Progress in Quantitative Nondestructive Evaluation* 16, 185-192, Edited by D. O. Thompson and D. E. Chimenti, Plenum Press New York, 1997.

[9] I. A. Viktorov, *Rayleigh and Lamb Waves*, Plenum, New York, chapter I, 67-121, 1967.

[10] J. Dickey, G. Maidanik and H. Überall, "The splitting of dispersion curves for the fluid-loaded plate," *J. Acoust. Soc. Am.* 98, 2365-2367, 1995.

SESSION III

ATR CLASSIFICATION

CHAIRED BY SCOTT REED
SEEBYTE LTD

CHAPTER SIX

MULTI-VIEW CLASSIFICATION WITH THE MIXTURE-OF-EXPERTS MODEL

HERMAN MIDELFART
AND ØIVIND MIDTGAARD

Abstract

The performance of automatic target recognition systems may be improved by classifier fusion if multiple observations of each object are available. The Mixture-of-experts model is a method for fusing classifier outputs which makes it possible to prioritize between the observations. It assigns a weight to each view, and this weight controls the impact the view has on the fused score. This can be used, for example, to subdue low quality observations. In this paper, we examine the performance of the Mixture-of-experts method and compare it to several other fusion methods. We find that most fusion methods improve the classification performance significantly and that the Mixture-of-expert performs slightly better than the other approaches. We find also that an even better performance may be obtained if we introduce a similar type of weighting in Dempster-Shafer fusion.

Keywords: Multi-view Classification, Mixture-of-Experts, Classifier Fusion.

1. Introduction

Classification of underwater objects in sonar images is a challenging task. If the objects have been observed multiple times at different aspect angles or ranges, however, it may be possible to improve the classification performance since more information is available about each object.

Several authors have demonstrated such gains by combining the data from different views of the same object [1-5].

Fusion of views may be performed on different levels. One approach [6] combines the views at the pixel level. In this case, the views are combined into a single image by co-registering the images and computing the average for each pixel. The fused image can then be classified just in the same manner as one would for a single observation. Alternatively, the views can be fused at the feature level by combining the feature values from each view into a single augmented vector. However, this strategy is rarely used since the classifier requires a feature vector of fixed size, while the number of views may vary. More commonly the views are fused on the decision level by merging the classifier outputs. Confidence scores created by the classifier may, for example, be combined by simply choosing the maximum or minimum score for each class [5]. It is also possible to use more complex approaches based on Dempster-Shafer theory of evidence [2], Bayesian methods [7] or voting [4].

Many decision level methods treat each view equally so that they have the same impact on the fused score. However, the quality of the views may vary, and this can greatly impact the classification performance. A poor image may reduce the fused score even if the other views indicated a clear target.

The Mixture-of-expert model [8,9] is a method for fusing classifiers and includes a mechanism for subduing the outputs of a poor classifier. This approach assumes that there is a set of expert classifiers and a gating classifier. The experts predict the probability of each class. The gating classifier assesses the quality of each expert and controls their influence on the fused result. The fused score is computed as a weighted average over the probabilities of the experts where the gating classifier provides the weights. This approach may be applied to the multi-view classification problem if one considers each view as an expert. It may consequently subdue poor views by assigning them a low weight.

In this paper, we examine how the Mixture-of-expert model can improve the classification performance on high-resolution sonar images. We also compare it to several other fusion methods.

This paper is organized as follows: In Section 2, we present the Mixture-of-experts model and the other fusion methods that we used in the comparison. We explain how the evaluation was conducted in Section 3. The results are presented in Section 4 and concluding remarks are made in Section 5.

2. Methods

The mixture-of-expert model

Fig. 1 illustrates the Mixture-of-experts model [8,9] assuming a set of expert classifiers. Each expert classifies an observation by estimating the posterior probabilities of each class. These probabilities are fused by means of a gating classifier, which determines how likely each expert is to produce a correct classification and controls their influence on the fused results.

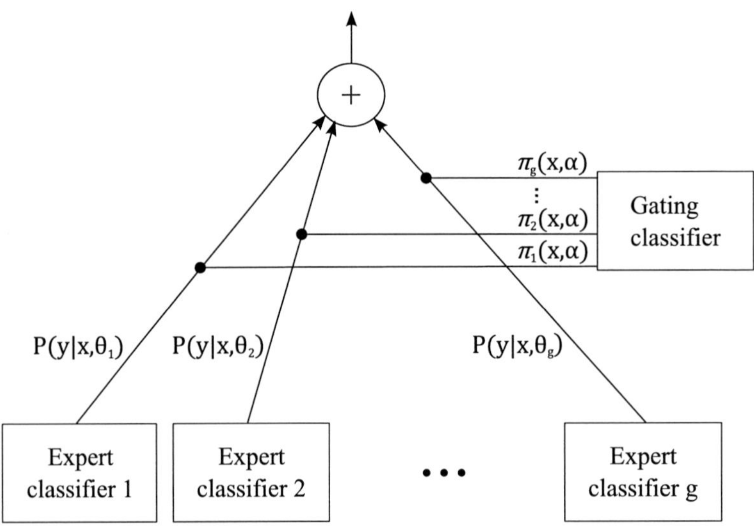

Figure 1: The Mixture-of-experts model.

More formally, we assume that there is a set of observations $\chi = \{(x_j, y_j)|j = 1, ..., n\}$, where x_j is a feature vector with values describing the observation, and y_j is the class label of the observation. Expert classifier $i \in \{1, ..., g\}$ is parameterized by θ_i and produces the (posterior) probability $P(Y_j|x_j, \theta_i)$ when applied to feature vector x_j. The gating classifier takes the parameters $\alpha = \{\alpha_1, ..., \alpha_g\}$ and computes for each expert i the probability $\pi_i(x_j, \alpha)$ that the expert makes a correct decision. The fused probability for class label c is then computed as

$$P(Y_j = c|x_j, \Psi) = \sum_{i=1}^{g} \pi_i(x_j, \alpha) P(Y_j = c|x_j, \theta_i), \qquad (1)$$

where $\boldsymbol{\Psi}$ denotes the complete set of parameters, *i.e.*, $\{\boldsymbol{\theta}_1, ..., \boldsymbol{\theta}_g, \boldsymbol{\alpha}\}$. $P(Y_j|\mathbf{x}_j,\boldsymbol{\Psi})$ is a mixture model where the component distributions $P(Y_j|\mathbf{x}_j,\boldsymbol{\theta}_i)$ are created by the experts, and the mixing weights $\pi_i(\mathbf{x}_j,\boldsymbol{\alpha})$ are created by the gating classifier. The mixing weights must sum to 1 so that the fused probability is a weighted average of the expert probabilities. $P(Y_j|\mathbf{x}_j,\boldsymbol{\theta}_i)$ and $\pi_i(\mathbf{x}_j,\boldsymbol{\alpha})$ may be represented by any classifier, which outputs a set of probabilities. However, they are often represented by the "softmax" function (This is also used in logistic regression). The gating classifier function for expert *i* may for example be represented as

$$\pi_i(\mathbf{x}_j, \boldsymbol{\alpha}) = \frac{e^{\boldsymbol{\alpha}_i^T \mathbf{x}_j}}{\sum_{k=1}^{g} e^{\boldsymbol{\alpha}_k^T \mathbf{x}_j}} \tag{2}$$

The parameters in this model are usually found by maximum likelihood estimation, but there is no analytical solution. Therefore, the solution is estimated with the EM-algorithm [10]. This method introduces as set of indicator variables $\mathbf{Z}_j = \langle Z_{j1}, ..., Z_{jg} \rangle$ with realized values $\mathbf{z}_j = \langle z_{j1}, ..., z_{jg} \rangle$ which specify which experts make the right decision. $\mathbf{Z}_j$ is distributed according to a multinominal distribution with one draw where $\pi_i(\mathbf{x}_j, \boldsymbol{\alpha})$ is the probability of that $z_{ji} = 1$ (*i.e.*, that expert *i* classify example *j* correctly). The probability of $y_j, \mathbf{z}_j$ given $\mathbf{x}_j, \boldsymbol{\Psi}$ is therefore

$$P(y_j, \mathbf{z}_j|\mathbf{x}_j, \boldsymbol{\Psi}) = \prod_{i=1}^{g} [\pi_i(\mathbf{x}_j, \boldsymbol{\alpha})P(y_j|\mathbf{x}_j, \boldsymbol{\theta}_i)]^{z_{ji}} \tag{3}$$

and the log-likelihood (where is $\zeta = \{(\mathbf{x}_j, y_j, \mathbf{z}_j)|j = 1, ..., n\}$) is

$$\log L(\boldsymbol{\Psi}|Z) = \sum_{j=1}^{n} \log P(y_j, \mathbf{z}_j|\mathbf{x}_j, \boldsymbol{\Psi})$$
$$= \sum_{j=1}^{n} \sum_{i=1}^{g} z_{ji}\log \pi_i(\mathbf{x}_j, \boldsymbol{\alpha}) + z_{ji}\log P(y_j|\mathbf{x}_j, \boldsymbol{\theta}_i) \tag{4}$$

The EM-algorithm consists of two steps: the expectation step and the maximization step, which are applied iteratively. The first step takes the conditional expectation of the log-likelihood given the parameter values $\boldsymbol{\Psi}^{(p)}$ from the previous step (p) and the observations χ. This is

$$Q\left(\Psi; \Psi^{(p)}\right) = E\left[\log L(\Psi|\zeta)\,|\chi, \Psi^{(p)}\right]$$

$$= \sum_{j=1}^{n}\sum_{i=1}^{g} \tau_{ji}^{(p)}\log \pi_i\left(\mathbf{x_j}, \boldsymbol{\alpha}\right) + \tau_{ji}^{(p)}\log P\left(y_j|\mathbf{x_j}, \boldsymbol{\theta_i}\right) \tag{5}$$

As the other variables and parameters are fixed, the step requires only the calculation of the conditional expectation of z_{ji}:

$$\tau_{ji}^{(p)} = E\left[Z_{ji}|\chi, \Psi^{(p)}\right] = P\left(Z_{ji} = 1|y_j, \mathbf{x_j}, \Psi^{(p)}\right)$$

$$= \frac{P\left(y_j|\mathbf{x_j}, \boldsymbol{\theta_i}^{(p)}\right)\pi_i\left(\mathbf{x_j}, \boldsymbol{\alpha}^{(p)}\right)}{\sum_{i=1}^{g} P\left(y_j|\mathbf{x_j}, \boldsymbol{\theta_i}^{(p)}\right)\pi_i\left(\mathbf{x_j}, \boldsymbol{\alpha}^{(p)}\right)} \tag{6}$$

The maximization step maximizes $Q\left(\Psi; \Psi^{(p)}\right)$ with respect to the parameters for iteration $p+1$. $\boldsymbol{\alpha}$ and $\boldsymbol{\theta_i}$ may be estimated separately since $Q\left(\Psi; \Psi^{(p)}\right)$ is linear, and $\boldsymbol{\alpha}$ and $\boldsymbol{\theta_i}$ occur in separate terms. Hence, they can be found according to the following equations:

$$\boldsymbol{\alpha_i}^{(p+1)} = \underset{\alpha_i}{\mathbf{argmax}} \sum_{j=1}^{n}\sum_{i=1}^{g} \tau_{ji}^{(p)}\log \pi_i\left(\mathbf{x_j}, \boldsymbol{\alpha}\right) \tag{7}$$

$$\boldsymbol{\theta_i}^{(p+1)} = \underset{\theta_i}{\mathbf{argmax}} \sum_{j=1}^{n} \tau_{ji}^{(p)}\log P\left(y_j|\mathbf{x_j}, \boldsymbol{\theta_i}\right) \tag{8}$$

The solution to these equations cannot be found analytically, but they may be solved with iteratively reweighted least-squares.

When the mixture of expert model is applied to multi-view classification some minor modifications are necessary. Essentially, only one expert classifier is needed as the same classifier can be applied to every view. Hence, the set of parameters is reduced so that there is only one set of parameters $\boldsymbol{\theta}$ for the expert classifier and one set $\boldsymbol{\alpha}$ for the gating classifier. Moreover, the feature vector $\mathbf{x_j}$ is now composed of several feature vectors $\mathbf{x_j} = \left\{\mathbf{x_{j1}}, \dots, \mathbf{x_{jg_j}}\right\}$ where $\mathbf{x_{ji}}$ is the features for view i, and g_j is the number of views. Note that it is also necessary to index the number of views by each object j since the number of times each object has been observed may vary. The gating classifier can thus be represented as

$$\pi_i\left(\mathbf{x_j}, \boldsymbol{\alpha}\right) = \frac{e^{\boldsymbol{\alpha}^T \mathbf{x_{ji}}}}{\sum_{k=1}^{g_j} e^{\boldsymbol{\alpha}^T \mathbf{x_{ji}}}} \tag{9}$$

The expectation and maximization steps become:

$$\tau_{ji}^{(p)} = \frac{P\left(y_j \middle| \mathbf{x}_{ji}, \boldsymbol{\theta}^{(p)}\right) \pi_i\left(\mathbf{x}_j, \boldsymbol{\alpha}^{(p)}\right)}{\sum_{v=1}^{g_j} P\left(y_j \middle| \mathbf{x}_{ji}, \boldsymbol{\theta}^{(p)}\right) \pi_i\left(\mathbf{x}_j, \boldsymbol{\alpha}^{(p)}\right)} \quad \text{and}$$

$$\boldsymbol{\alpha}^{(p+1)} = \operatorname*{argmax}_{\alpha} \sum_{j=1}^{n} \sum_{v=1}^{g_j} \tau_{ji}^{(p)} \log \pi_v\left(\mathbf{x}_j, \boldsymbol{\alpha}\right)$$

$$\boldsymbol{\theta}^{(p+1)} = \operatorname*{argmax}_{\theta} \sum_{j=1}^{n} \sum_{v=1}^{g_j} \tau_{ji}^{(p)} \log P\left(y_j \middle| \mathbf{x}_{ji}, \boldsymbol{\theta}\right)$$

Other fusion methods

We compared the Mixture-of-expert methods to several fusion methods in order to assess its performance. These included standard average fusion (*mean*), maximum fusion (*max*), product fusion (*prod*) and Dempster-Shafer based fusion (*ds*).

The average fusion was very similar to the Mixture-of-expert approach except that no gating classifier was used. It fused the views simply by computing the mean of the views:

$$f_{\mathrm{mean}}(c) = \sum_{i=1}^{g_j} P\left(Y_j = c \middle| \mathbf{x}_{ji}, \boldsymbol{\theta}_i\right) \tag{10}$$

The maximum fusion used the maximum classifier score among the views as the fusion score, *i.e.*

$$f_{\mathrm{max}}(c) = \max_i P\left(Y_j = c \middle| \mathbf{x}_{ji}, \boldsymbol{\theta}_i\right) \tag{11}$$

The product approach used the normalized product of the classifier scores, *i.e.*

$$f_{\mathrm{prod}}(c) = \frac{\prod_{i=1}^{g_j} P\left(Y_j = c \middle| \mathbf{x}_{ji}, \boldsymbol{\theta}_i\right)}{\prod_{i=1}^{g_j} P\left(Y_j = c \middle| \mathbf{x}_{ji}, \boldsymbol{\theta}_i\right) + \prod_{i=1}^{g_j} \left(1 - P\left(Y_j = c \middle| \mathbf{x}_{ji}, \boldsymbol{\theta}_i\right)\right)} \tag{12}$$

This method can be derived from the Bayesian theorem if the prior distribution of the classes is assumed uniform.

The Dempster-Shafer approach was based on Dempster-Shafer theory of evidence and used Dempster's combination rule to fuse the views [11]. For each class, we considered a binary classification problem where the frame of discernment consisted of the class and its complement, *i.e.*, $\Theta = \{c, \bar{c}\}$. The following mass functions were used:

- $m_i(c) = \gamma \cdot P\left(Y_j = c \middle| \mathbf{x}_{ji}, \boldsymbol{\theta}_i\right)$
- $m_i(\bar{c}) = \gamma \cdot \left(1 - P\left(Y_j = c \middle| \mathbf{x}_{ji}, \boldsymbol{\theta}_i\right)\right)$ $\tag{13}$
- $m_i(\Theta) = 1 - \gamma$

The constant γ was chosen to be just below 1, but not exactly 1. This was done in order to avoid issues with contradictory evidence when a class was assigned zero mass in one view and its complement assigned zero mass in another view.

We implemented also a Dempster-Shafer approach (*dsweighted*) where the impact of the view on the fused score was adjusted similar to the Mixture-of-experts. In this case, we used logistic regression to predict a value γ so that more mass was assigned to Θ (*i.e.,* uncertainty) if a view was poor. Poor views were thus assigned lower γ values, making their classification scores contribute less to the fused scores. This model was trained with the same feature as the gating classifier. However, special class labels were used, as we wanted this classifier to predict the performance of the expert classifier. We model this task as a binary classification problem. An observation was assigned class label 1 if the expert classifier correctly classified the observation and class label 0 if an incorrect class was assigned to the observation.

3. Experimental setup

In this study, we deviated slightly from the Mixture-of-expert framework since we used a set of support vector machines (SVMs) as the expert classifier. One SVM was used for each class c, and a sigmoid function was applied to the output from the SVM in order to produce an estimate of the posterior probability, i.e, $P\left(Y_j = c | \mathbf{x}_{ji}, \boldsymbol{\theta}_i\right)$. The SVMs were trained in advance, so that only the gating classifier was fitted with the Mixture-of-expert method. This made comparison with other fusion algorithms easier since the same expert classifier output could be used for every fusion method.

We used several data sets that were acquired with HISAS 1030 on HUGIN 1000 AUVs at several locations on the Norwegian coast. All data sets included some deployed objects. One data set, which was recorded outside of Larvik, Norway was used as a training set for the gating classifier. This included a cylinder and a truncated cone target that were observed multiple times. Another data set was used for testing. This was from a mission outside Bergen, Norway where several cylinder objects and two truncated cone targets were deployed. Both the training set and the testing set were collected in very shallow waters so that the quality of the sonar images was often quite low due to multipath noise.

The SVMs were trained on several data sets acquired with HUGIN outside Horten, Norway as well as one data set from the Colossus II trials. The data from Colossus II were given to us by the NATO Undersea

Research Center (NURC) and were collected with their MUSCLE AUV off the coast of Latvia. All of these missions were performed in relatively deep waters. Thus, the sonar images were usually of much higher quality than the images in training and testing sets of the gating classifier.

The Mixture-of-expert method normally assumes that the same set of features is used by both the expert classifier and the gating classifier. However, these classifiers perform different tasks so that features that work well for the expert classifier may not work well for the gating classifier and vice versa. Hence, we used different features for the expert classifier and the gating classifier. For the expert classifier, we used features that were suitable for describing the target classes. For the gating classifier, we used features that described the quality of the image.

More precisely, the expert classifier used a template matcher. This compared synthetic template images to the sonar images and produced a correlation score for each target class. These correlation scores were given as features to the SVMs. The gating classifier applied a single feature that measured the contrast between the echo and shadow of the object. This feature was used on the assumption that the classifier is more likely to classify an object incorrectly if the echo or the shadow is weak or missing. In order to compute this feature, we segmented each image into echo, shadow and background regions. The feature was then calculated simply as the mean intensity in the echo region divided by the mean in the shadow region.

4. Results

The Mixture-of-expert model computes basically a weighted average. Hence, we compared it initially to a fusion method that computes the standard average to see if its weighted scheme could improve the fusion performance. We also compared it to the original single-view classification made by the expert classifier. These results are shown in Fig. 2. These receiver operating characteristic (ROC) curves show that the Mixture-of-experts outperformed the standard average and the single-view classification. However, the average fusion method also improved the performance considerably, and the difference in performance between the Mixture-of-experts and the average fusion was significantly less than the difference between the Mixture-of-expert and the single-view classifier. Hence, the main performance gain came from fusing views, while the weighting performed by the Mixture-of-experts method produced a modest gain.

Better performance of the Mixture-of-expert model may possibly be achieved by improved correlation between the contrast feature and the performance of the expert classifier. When we used the echo-to-shadow contrast feature in the gating classifier, we assumed the accuracy of the classifier improved with higher contrast. This was also the case for our target objects. However, for non-target objects we witnessed a negative trend between the contrast and the performance of the expert classifier. High contrast images with non-targets were more likely to be incorrectly classified than low contrast images. This is really a weakness of the expert classifier. Hence, it is possible that larger performance gain could be achieved with a better expert classifier. Moreover, the performance gain may also be improved with other features that measure the image quality more accurately.

We also compared the Mixture-of-expert methods to several other fusion methods. These included maximum fusion (*max*), product fusion (*prod*), Dempster-Shafer fusion (*ds*), and weighted Dempster-Shafer (*dsweighted*). The results from this comparison are shown in Fig. 3 and Fig. 4. The first figure shows the ROC curves when all available views were fused. The last figure displays the area under the ROC curve (AUC) when the number of views was restricted. These curves were created by splitting the set of views belonging to an object into several sets of a specified size. In the figures for the cylinder target, the Mixture-of-expert outperformed the product and Dempster-Shafer methods, but had a slightly worse or the similar performance to the maximum and the weighted Dempster-Shafer fusion. For truncated cones, the maximum fusion had the worst performance. Both Dempster-Shafer approaches outperformed the Mixture-of-expert model. The performance of the product fusion varied more, but was sometimes better than the Mixture-of-export model. The best performance for both targets was obtained with the weighted Dempster-Shafer approach.

Note that the AUC curves in Fig. 4., especially the one for truncated clone, showed sometimes a quite large change in the AUC for a small change in the number of views. This effect seemed to affect all fusion methods. It was most likely due to the small number of target objects in the testing set and the splitting of the objects. This splitting could sometime produce some unfortunate sets of views that were difficult to classify correctly. This affected the AUC to a large extent since there were few sets of views so that each misclassification had a large effect.

One reason to the weaker performance of the Mixture-of-experts model is its way of fusing the views by *averaging* the classifier outputs. This means that the fused score, produced by this method, will never be higher than the highest score, or lower than the lowest score. This may lead to an unwanted ranking of the objects when the number of views varies within a data set. For example, if we observe an object three times with a high score of 0.85 each time, the fused score will still be 0.85. An object that is observed once with a score of 0.9, will have fused score 0.9. It is ranked higher than the first object even though we have observed that object three times. This seems counterintuitive since the difference in the score is relatively minor and we have more observations of the first target. It is less likely that all of these observations are incorrect. The Dempster-Shafer approach, on the other hand, will give the first object a higher score than the second and thus produce the desired ranking. This effect could be observed when the fused scores of our test data were inspected. Many of the non-targets that were ranked high by the Mixture-of-experts model were observed only once. These objects were ranked lower by the Dempster-Shafer approach.

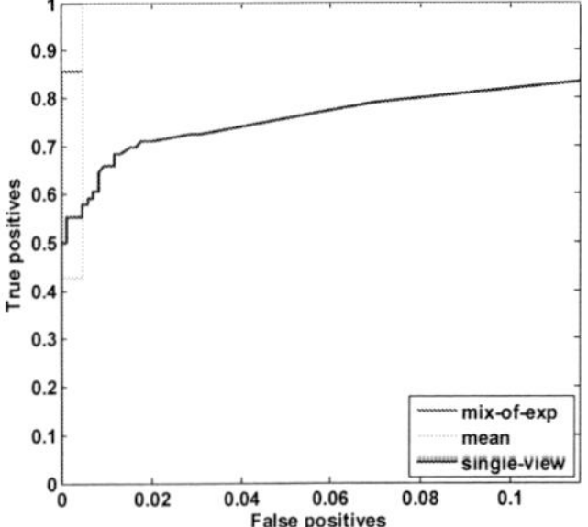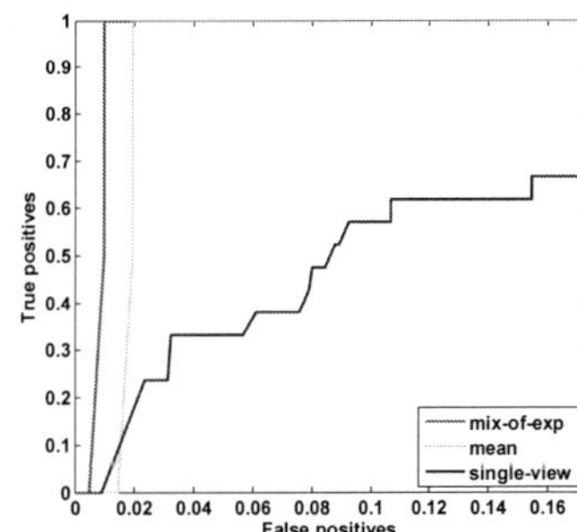

Figure 2: The performance of the Mixture-of-export (mix-of-exp) method for cylinders (left) and truncated cone (right) compared to the standard average method (mean) and the original classification of the expert classifier (single-view). All available views were combined.

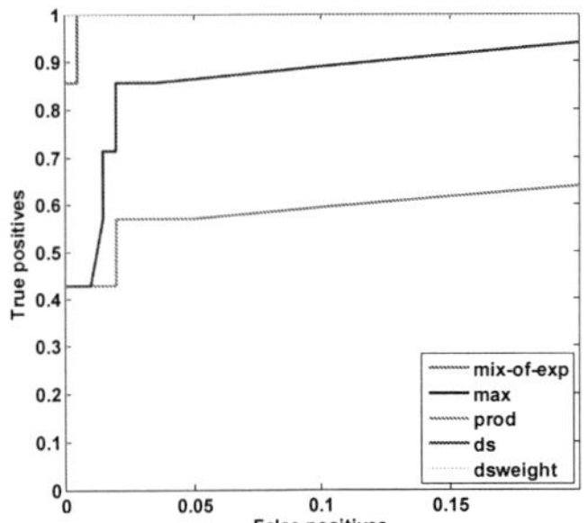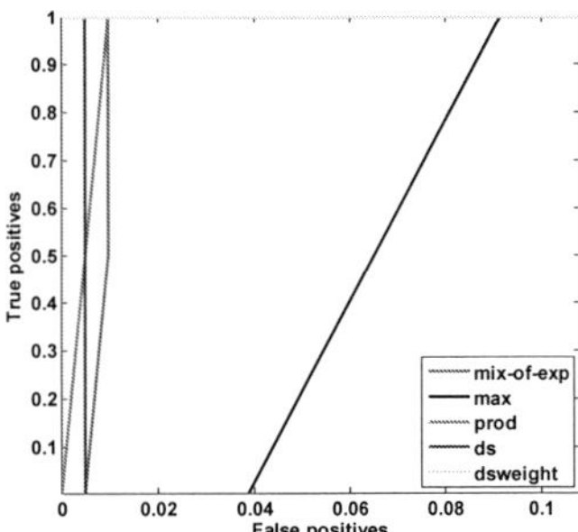

Figure 3: The performance of various fusion methods for cylinders (left) and truncated cones (right). All available views were combined.

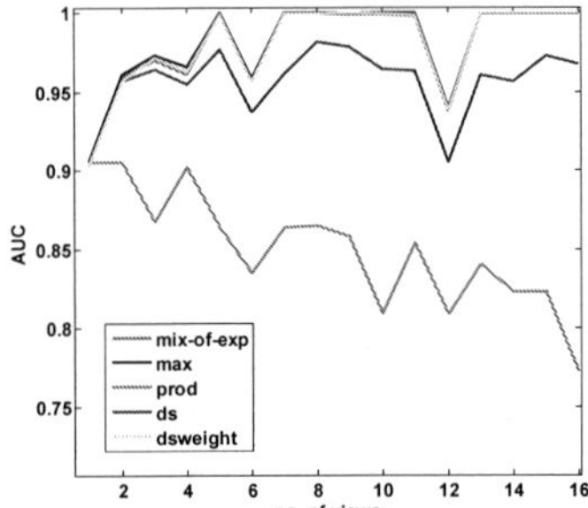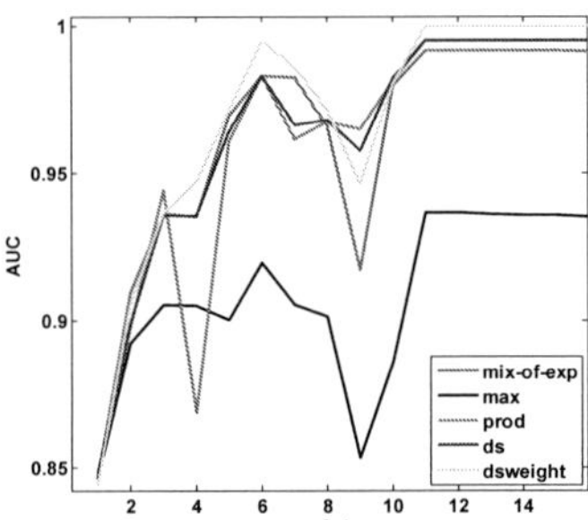

Figure 4: The AUC for several fusion methods when the maximum number of view was restricted. The performance for cylinders and truncated cones are show in left and right image, respectively.

5. Conclusion

In this paper, we have examined the utility of the Mixture-of-experts model for fusing classifier outputs from multiple observations of underwater objects. This method includes a gating classifier that assigns weights to all views. The method may thus allow some views to influence the fused score more than other methods so that low-quality views may be subdued. We found that the method may outperform standard average fusion, but the effect is relatively minor in comparison to the performance gain obtained by most multi-view fusion methods. When we compared the Mixture-of-experts method to other fusion methods, we found that some of these could match its performance in some cases. However, only the weighted Dempster-Shafer approach was consistently better.

The original Mixture-of-experts model assumes that the number of expert classifiers is fixed. It has no mechanism that allows the number of views to be taken into account. When the number of views varies, it may thus produce a ranking where objects that have been observed only once or twice, are ranked too high. This is a drawback since it is nearly impossible to guarantee that all objects are passed exactly the same number of times on realistic surveys.

In this paper, we have only used a single feature in the gating classifier. It is possible that better performance can be achieved with the Mixture-of-expert (and the weighted Dempster-Shafer approach) if one uses other features in the gating-classifier. This method could, for example, improve the performance on a ripple seabed. In this case, the visibility of the ripples and the degree they obfuscate the object depends on the orientation of the sonar with respect to the ripples. One could therefore detect if ripples are present in an image and use the Mixture-of-experts method to assign less weight to it if that is the case.

References

[1] B. Zerr, E. Bovio, and B. Stage, "Automatic mine classification approach based on AUV manoeuverability and COTS side scan sonar," *CAD/CAC 2001*, 2001.

[2] J. Fawcett, V. Myers, D. Hopkin, A. Crawford, M. Couillard, and B. Zerr, "Multiaspect Classification of Sidescan Sonar Images: Four Different Approaches to Fusing Single-Aspect Information," *IEEE Journal of Oceanic Engineering*, vol. 35, no. 4, pp. 863-876, 2010.

[3] S. Reed, Y. Petillot, and J. Bell, "Automated approach to classification of mine-like objects in sidescan sonar using highlight and shadow information," *IEE Proceedings on Radar, Sonar and Navigation*, vol. 151, no. 1, pp. 48-56, 2004.

[4] F. Langner, W. Jans, C. Knauer, and W. Middelmann, "Benefit for screening by automated Acoustic data fusion," *Proceedings of the 4th International conference on Underwater Acoustic Measurement*, pp. 139-150, 2011.

[5] D. P. Williams, "On multi-view mine classification with SAS imagery," NATO Undersea Research Center, NURC-FR-2008-026, 2008.

[6] J. Groen, E. Coiras, and D. P. Williams, "False-alarm reduction in mine classification using multiple looks from a synthetic aperture sonar," *IEEE Oceans 2010 – Sydney*, 2010.

[7] D. P. Williams, "Bayesian Data Fusion of Multiview Synthetic Aperture Sonar Imagery for Seabed Classification," *IEEE Transaction on Image Processing*, vol. 18, no. 6, pp. 1239-1254, 2009.

[8] M. I. Jordan and R. A. Jacobs, "Hierarchical mixtures of experts and the EM algorithm," *Neural Computation*, vol. 6, pp. 181-214, 1994.

[9] G. McLachlan and D. Peel, *Finite Mixture Models*, Wiley, 2000.

[10] A. P. Dempster, N. M. Laird, and D. B. Rubin, "Maximum likelihood from incomplete data via the EM algorithm," *Journal of the Royal Statistical Society B*, vol. 39, pp. 1-38, 1977.

[11] G. Shafer, *A mathematical theory of evidence*. Princeton, NJ, USA, Princeton University Press, 1976.

CHAPTER SEVEN

ANOMALY DETECTION IN SONAR IMAGES USING SCATTERING OPERATORS

NICOLAS VALEYRIE AND YVAN PETILLOT

1. Introduction

Underwater target detection has been performed for the most part with the help of side-looking sonars mounted on both sides of underwater vehicles because such an arrangement quickly provides images of wide areas of the seafloor. Side-looking sonars are active sonars that alternatively transmit an acoustic wave towards the sea bottom and record the wave reverberated by the seafloor. A sonar image is a representation in two dimensions of the energy of the reverberated waves, one dimension being the time between two successive transmissions, and the other being the travel time of the acoustic waves through water. Many environmental and operational parameters contribute to the variation of the level of energy in a sonar image [1].

The primary visual signature of a target in a sonar image is a highlight region next to a shadow region. The highlight region is a region of high energy that comes from the scattering by the target of the transmitted acoustic waves. The shadow region is a region of low energy that comes from the lack of acoustic reverberation from the portion of the seabed which is behind the target with respect to the underwater vehicle. Many target detectors are based on this visual signature. Target detection is performed in [2,3] with Markov Random Fields whose prior probability distributions incorporate information about the geometry of the highlight and the shadow regions. Targets are detected in [4] with the help of the Hilbert transform because this transform helps reveal the highlight regions. Targets are detected in [5] with the help of the first order statistics of sonar images because those statistics also help reveal the highlight regions. The supervised target detector of [6] makes use of a cascade of boosted classifiers and is trained on examples of targets and therefore on examples of highlight and shadow regions. The detector of [6] is also trained on examples of the sea bottom.

In this paper, two algorithms for saliency detection in sonar images are presented. This approach fundamentally differs from the existing target detectors. We do not use any *a priori* information about the targets. We specifically do not use the fact that the primary visual signature of a target is a highlight region next to a shadow region. In order to reveal targets as salient regions in sonar images, we need (1) examples of the types of seabed that are usually found in sonar images; (2) a similarity metric to evaluate the similarity between regions of the sonar images under study and the examples of the types of seabed; and (3) a compact representation of the seabed so that only targets appear as salient regions. We used a similarity metric based on the concept of ensemble of patches [7], and we used a seabed representation based on a scattering operator. We opted for a scattering operator because it leads to a signal representation which is stable with respect to deformations. The signal representation induced by the scattering operator, consequently, is compact. Section 2 introduces the signal representation induced by scattering operators, and Sections 3 and 4 present two algorithms for saliency detection in sonar imagery: the first one based on learning the seabed from examples and the second one looking at the closest response in the image to a given patch of interest.

2. The seabed representation

In this section, we introduc the signal representation induced by scattering operators. We start with presenting the wavelet transform of images because scattering operators are based this transform. The wavelet transform of images represents images in terms of atoms that are obtained by dilations and rotations of a unique function $\Psi(x)$ called a wavelet [8]. The atoms are the functions:

$$\Psi_{k,\gamma}(x) = 2^{-2k}\,\Psi[\,2^{-k}\,r_\gamma^{-1}(x)\,], \qquad (14)$$

where r_γ is the rotation of angle γ. The angle γ takes values in a discrete set of angles $\Gamma \subset [\,0,\pi\,]$ and k is an integer that takes values between 0 and $K \geq 0$. The finest scale and the coarsest scale at which images are analysed correspond to $k = 0$ and $k = K$, respectively. The wavelet $\Psi(x)$ has to be a band pass filter and so, in turn, are the atoms. Low frequencies beyond the coarsest scale are captured by a low pass filter $\Phi_K(x)$. The wavelet transform of an image $f(x)$ is the result of the convolution of the image with every atom and with the low pass filter. The transform corresponds therefore to the set of images:

$$\{ f \star \Phi_K(x) \} \cup \{ f \star \Psi_{k,\gamma}(x) : \ k \leq K \text{ and } \gamma \in \Gamma \}, \qquad (215)$$

where $\star$ denotes a convolution. Scattering operators require complex wavelets; we used the complex Gabor wavelet:

$$\Psi(x) = \Psi(x_1, x_2) = \kappa \exp\left[-\alpha^2 x_1^2 - \alpha^2 x_2^2 + i \, \xi_0 \, x_1 \right], \qquad (3)$$

where κ is a normalisation constant and ξ_0 represents a spatial wave number. The spatial support of the wavelet is controlled by the parameter α. In all numerical experiments, we used $\xi_0 = 3\pi/4$, $\alpha = \pi/4$ and $\kappa = \alpha^2/\pi = \pi/16$. We also used the Gaussian low pass filter:

$$\Phi_K(x) = \Phi_K(x_1, x_2) = \kappa' \exp\left[-\beta_K^{\;2} x_1^2 - \beta_K^{\;2} x_2^2 \right], \qquad (16)$$

where κ' is another normalisation constant. The spatial support of the low-pass filter is controlled by the parameter β_K which depends on the coarsest scale K. In all numerical experiments, we used $\beta_K = (\xi_0 - \alpha)/2^K$ and $\kappa' = \beta_K^{\;2}/\pi$. For example, $\beta_0 = \pi/2$, $\beta_1 = \pi/4$ and $\beta_2 = \pi/8$ when $\xi_0 = 3\pi/4$ and $\alpha = \pi/4$.

We now present the scattering operators and we start with the introduction of a slight change of notation. We denote by $\lambda = (k, \gamma)$ any pair of scale and orientation and we denote by $\Lambda = \{ (k, \gamma) : k \leq K \text{ and } \gamma \in \Gamma \}$ the set of all possible pairs of scales and orientations. A path $p = (\lambda_1, \ldots, \lambda_n) \in \Lambda^n$ of length $n \geq 0$ is defined as an ordered set of pairs of scales and orientations. The path of zero length is denoted by the symbol $\emptyset$ of the empty set. The scattering image calculated along the path p is defined as:

$$S_p f(x) = \underbrace{|\cdots|}_{n \text{ times}} f \, \mathring{a} \Psi_{\lambda_1} \, | \mathring{a} \Psi_{\lambda_2} | \, \cdots \mathring{a} \Psi_{\lambda_n} | \mathring{a} \Phi_K(x), \qquad (5)$$

and is the result of n iterations over the wavelet transform and the complex modulus operator followed by a convolution with the low pass filter. The scattering image calculated over the path of zero length is defined as:

$$S_\emptyset f(x) = f \, \mathring{a} \Phi_K(x), \qquad (617)$$

and is therefore the average of the original image at the coarsest scale of the wavelet transform. The scattering images calculated over paths of unit length contain first order interferences because of the effect of the complex modulus operator is to reveal differences of frequencies [9]. The scattering images calculated over paths of length two contain second order interferences, $i.e.$ co-occurrence information between pairs of scales and orientations [10]. The stochastic variability of the scattering images is controlled by the low pass filter and therefore by the coarsest scale K of the wavelet transform. The higher that scale is, the less variable the scattering images are. The compactness of the signal representation induced by scattering operators comes from such a property.

The scattering transform of the image $f(x)$ corresponds to the set of all scattering images calculated along all possible paths of any length. The scattering transform of the image $f(x)$ corresponds therefore to the set

$$Sf(x) = \{ S_p f(x) : p \in \mathcal{P} \}, \tag{18}$$

where $\mathcal{P} = \cup_{n \geq 0} \Lambda^n = \emptyset \cup \Lambda \cup \Lambda^2 \cup \cdots \cup \Lambda^n \cup \cdots$ is the set of all possible path of any length. The squared norm of the scattering transform is defined as

$$\| Sf(x) \|^2 = \sum_{p \in \mathcal{P}} \| S_p f(x) \|^2 \text{ with } \| S_p f(x) \|^2 = \int_{\mathbf{R}^2} |S_p f(x)|^2 dx. \tag{8}$$

The squared norm of the scattering transform defines a metric which is stable with respect to deformations [9]. We do not enter much more into the details of the stability of scattering operators with respect to deformations and we refer to [9] for all details. We only say that if the image $g(x)$ is a deformed version of the image $f(x)$, the scattering transform of $g(x)$ is not too different than the scattering transform of $f(x)$. In other words, the norm $\| Sf - Sg \|$ of the difference of the two scattering transforms is not too large. The scattering operator was implemented in C with the help of the FFTW library [11].

3. Algorithm 1:
Saliency by learning normality from examples

In this algorithm, a training set of representative seabeds is first selected. From this training set we extract three different seabed types: flat, ripples and complex. The reference signal R is built as the collection of examples of the three types of seabed extracted from our sonar database. In our case, we have used two images containing various seabed types (see Fig. 2). The extracted examples correspond to the white rectangular regions in Fig. 2. Imagine now that one wants to analyse a new signal Q and decide if it is an anomaly compared to the set of examples R. A distance measure between Q and R is required. This metric is introduced in the next section.

The similarity metric

The similarity metric is based on the concept of ensemble of patches as it appears in [7]. We consider a query signal Q which in practice is a rectangular region taken around one pixel of the sonar image under study. The query signal is broken into many overlapping small patches and we denote by N_Q the total number of patches. We do not use the relative spatial arrangement of the patches within the query signal. We consider a reference signal $R = (R_1, R_2, R_3, \dots)$ which is the collection of a given number of examples of the types of seabed that usually appear in sonar images. For example, R_1 can be the example of an area with seaweed and R_2 can be the example of an area with sand ripples, etc.... The reference signal is also broken into many small, overlapping patches. The query signal Q is defined as similar to the reference signal R if most patches of Q are contained in R. This is a simple and yet powerful way of evaluating the similarity between Q and R. The similarity measure between Q and R is formally defined as:

$$D(Q, R) = \frac{1}{N_Q} \Sigma_{q \in Q} \min_{r \in R} \| Sq - Sr \|. \tag{9}$$

For each patch q in Q, we look for the patch r in R which is the most similar to q. The similarity between q and r is evaluated in the signal representation induced by the scattering operator via Sq and Sr. The definition of Sq and Sr was done in Section 2. We expect $D(Q, R)$ to be large when Q is part of a target and $D(Q, R)$ small when Q is part of the seabed. The similarity metric is illustrated on Fig. 1.

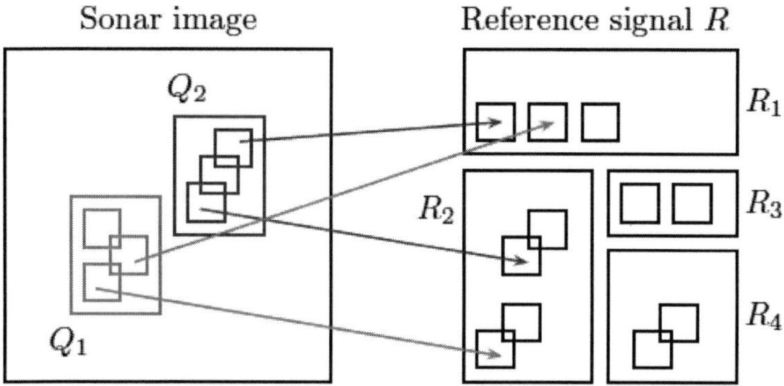

Figure 1: The Sonar image on the left hand side with two query signals Q_1 and Q_2 both broken into small overlapping patches. Reference signal $R = (R_1, R_2, R_3, R_4)$ is on the right hand side, which is a collection of four examples of types of seabed. The examples need not be of the same size. R is also broken into small overlapping patches.

Results

We now present in Fig. 3 two sonar images in which targets are revealed as salient regions. Those sonar images are not the images from which the reference signal R were created and yet only the targets appear as salient regions. The water column also appears as salient because it was not modelled by R.

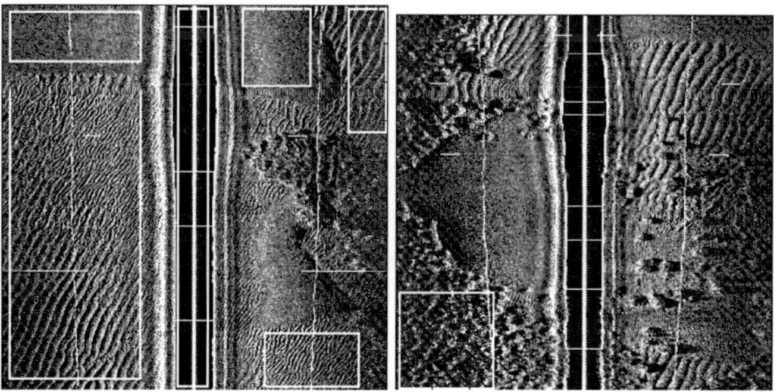

Figure 2: Reference signal R which is a collection of examples of types of seabed extracted from two sonar images. The types of seabed are areas with sand ripples, areas with seabed, flat areas and the water column. The extracted examples correspond to the white rectangular regions.

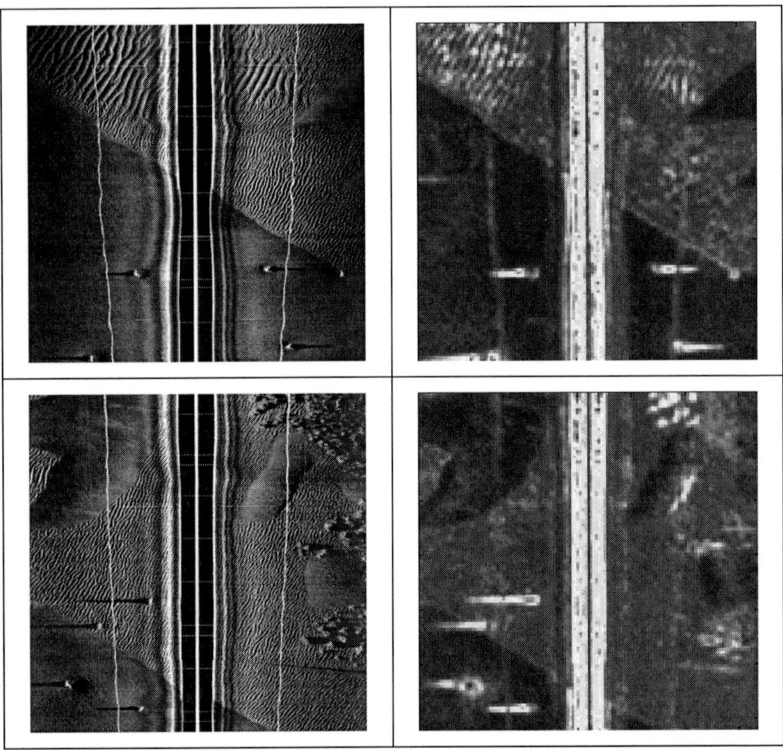

Figure 3: Two sonar images on the left hand side and the corresponding saliency maps on the right hand side. The targets present in the two sonar images appear as salient regions.

4. Algorithm 2: Similarity by composition

In this approach, there is no learning of the seabed *a priori*. A query signal Q is chosen by the operator (or a detection algorithm). The images to which Q belongs is considered as the reference R. Similarly to the previous algorithm, the query and the references are broken down into small patches and scattering operators extracted for each of these sub-patches. Critically, the spatial arrangement of the patches is now taken into account.

Similarity metric

Consider a query signal Q (a rectangular region extracted from the sonar image under study). We consider the rest of the image as a reference R. We look for the signal S^* in the reference which is most similar to the query Q, that is:

$$S^* = \mathrm{argmax}_S P(S|Q), \tag{190}$$

where $P(S|Q)$ quantifies the amount of similarity between any candidate signal S, in the reference R, and the query Q. We use the concept of similarity by composition. The query signal Q is broken into many small overlapping patches, and so are the candidate signals S. Every patch is characterised by a descriptor D (scattering operators) and a position P relative to a pre-defined centre C:

$$Q = (C_Q, D_Q^1, p_Q^1, D_Q^2, p_Q^2, \ldots, D_Q^n, p_Q^n)S = (C_S, D_S^1, p_S^1, D_S^2, p_S^2, \ldots, D_S^n, p_S^n). \tag{11}$$

This is summarized in Fig. 4.

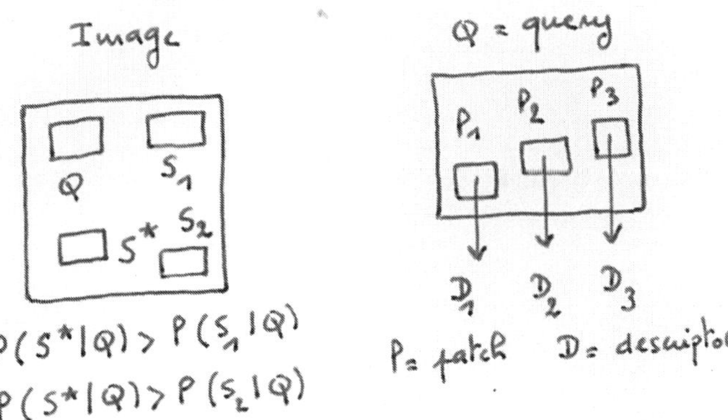

Figure 4: Principle of the algorithm. The Query is composed of P patches. Each Patch p_i has a descriptor D_i associated. A descriptor is a vector of scattering operators extracted from the patch.

The statistical dependencies between the centres, the patches descriptors, and the patches positions are modeled by a Bayesian network described in Fig. 5.

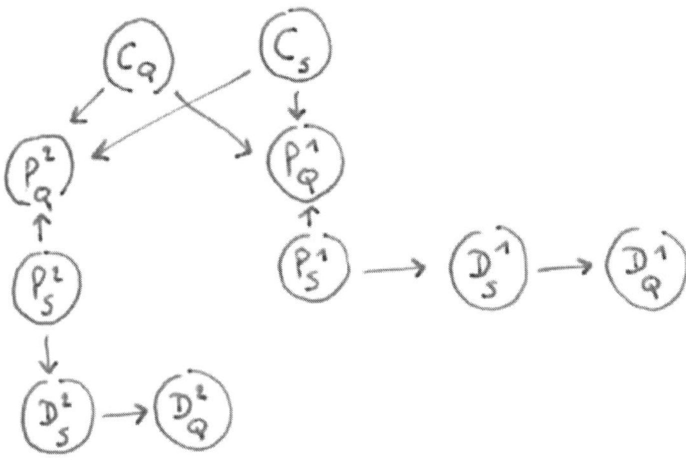

Figure 5: Bayesian Network used for inference of $P(S|Q)$.

A MAP algorithm is used to find S^* such that:

$$S^* = \text{argmax}_S P(S|Q) = \text{argmax}_S P(S,Q)/P(Q) = \text{argmax}_S P(S,Q) \qquad (20)$$

In practice, the maximisation over the set of all possible S is performed using a belief propagation algorithm. Assume that we now have k patches per query and that the patches are independent, we can rewrite $P(S,Q)$ as:

$$P(S,Q) = P(C_S)P(C_Q) \prod_k [P(p_S^k)P(D_Q^k|D_S^k)P(D_S^k|p_S^k)P(p_Q^k|p_S^k,C_S,C_Q)], \qquad (13)$$

where $P(D_Q^k|D_S^k)$ is modelled as a Gaussian distribution, $P(D_S^k|P_S^k)$ is a Dirac and $P(p_Q^k|p_S^k,C_S,C_Q)$ is a uniform distribution.

Results

The algorithm was tested on three different images containing potential targets. the query was set on a flat area of seabed, a rippled area and a target. In each case, the algortihm correctly identified the regions of the seabed closest to the query. This algotithm therefore has the potential to perform anomaly detection in sonar imagery and would be best used after an initial detection phase. The results are presented in Fig. 6.

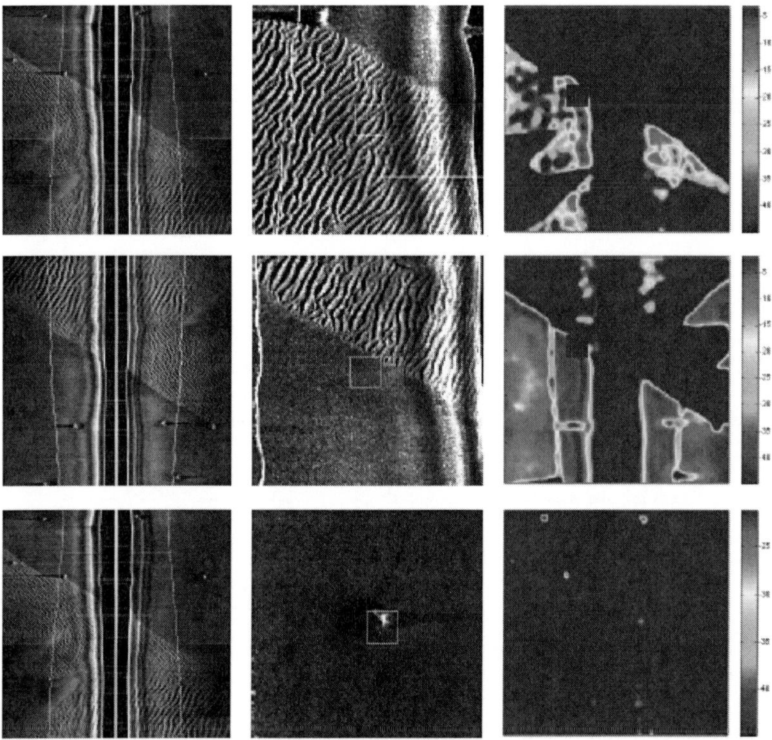

Figure 6: Sonar images are shown on the left; in the middle, the query signal; on the right, $P(S, Q)$ associated with all possible signals S in the image. The score is displayed in a logarithmic scale. Red = high similarity. Blue = low similarity.

5. Conclusion

Most of the current target detectors are based on the fact that the primary signature of a target in sonar images is a highlight region next to a shadow region. We qualitatively showed in this paper that it is possible to make targets appear as salient regions in sonar images, that is to say, as anomalies with respect to the seabed. We first define a robust representation of the image texture using scattering operators. We then proposed two algorithms for saliency detection. We did not use any *a priori* information about the targets unlike most of the present target detectors. Qualitative results on a number of typical sonar images show that targets do appear as salient regions. We believe that this work can be combined with one of the present target detectors so as to improve the overall target detection performance.

Acknowledgments

This work was supported by EPSRC and DSTL under the grant EP/H012354/1.

References

[1] R. J. Urick. *Principles of Underwater Sound*. McGraw-Hill, 3rd edition, 1983.

[2] B. Calder, L. Linnett, and D. Carmichael. "A Bayesian Approach To Object Detection In Sidescan Sonar," In *Proceedings of the International Conference on Image Processing and Its Applications*, vol. 2, pp. 857–861 vol.2, Jul 1997.

[3] S. Reed, Y. Petillot, and J. Bell. "An automatic approach to the detection and extraction of mine features in sidescan sonar," *Oceanic Engineering, IEEE Journal of*, 28(1): pp. 90–105, Jan 2003.

[4] J. Del Rio Vera, E. Coiras, J. Groen, and B. Evans. "Automatic target recognition in synthetic aperture sonar images based on geometrical feature extraction," *EURASIP Journal on Advances in Signal Processing:* pp. 1–9, 2009.

[5] F. Maussang, J. Chanussot, A. Hetet, and M. Amate. "Mean–standard deviation representation of sonar images for echo detection: Application to SAS images," *IEEE Journal of Oceanic Engineering*, 32(4): pp. 956–970, Oct. 2007.

[6] J. Sawas, Y. Petillot, and Y. Pailhas. "Target detection and classification using cascades of boosted classifiers," In *European Conference on Underwater Acoustics*, 2010.

[7] D. Simakov, Y. Caspi, E. Shechtman, and M. Irani. "Summurizing Visual Data Using Bidirectional Similarity." In *CVPR '08*, 2008.

[8] B. Torréssani. *Analyse Continue par Ondelettes*. EDP Sciences, 1995.

[9] S. Mallat. Group Invariant Scattering. *ArXiv e-prints*: pp. 1–76, January 2011.

[10] J. Bruna and S. Mallat. Classification with Scattering Operators. *ArXiv e-prints*: pp. 1–18, November 2010.

[11] M. Frigo and S. G. Johnson. "The design and implementation of FFTW3," *Proceedings of the IEEE*, 93(2): pp. 216–231, 2005. Special issue on "Program Generation, Optimization, and Platform Adaptation".

Chapter Eight

Cascade of Boosted Classifiers for Automatic Target Recognition in Synthetic Aperture Sonar Imagery

Jamil Sawas and Yvan Petillot

1. Introduction

Sonar devices are the sensors of choice for underwater sensing in commercial and military applications. A common and critical application of sonar systems is underwater object detection, which is a major challenge to a variety of underwater applications (off-shore, archeology, marine science, mine detection). This task is traditionally carried out by a skilled human operator. However, automated approaches are required in order to tackle the large amount of data produced, help the operators in decision-making and increase on-board autonomy. With the advances in autonomous underwater vehicle (AUV) technology, automated approaches have become more important to process the incoming data on-board and in real time to enable on the fly adaptation of the missions and near real-time update of the operator.

Automatic object detection in sonar imagery turns out to be a difficult task due to the large variability of the appearance of the same scene in images as well as the high level of noise usually present in the images. Object detection and classification in sonar imagery is a well-researched area [1-8]. Most techniques use the characteristics of the acoustic shadows projected by the objects on the seabed [1, 2]. Other approaches make use of the echoes for detection [3] where objects are filtered or isolated by segmentation. Machine learning techniques have also been tried for underwater object detection, such as neural networks [4] and eigen-analysis [5]. In [6], the Hilbert Transform is used to segment the object and shadow regions after which a curve fitting algorithm is used to extract features for classification by decision trees. In most of the algorithms mentioned above, *a priori* fixed features and models are used for object detection. In addition, these approaches are not computationally efficient and can result in high false alarm rates. In [7] we proposed a new method for object detection in sonar imagery based on the Viola and Jones cascade of boosted classifiers [8]. Unlike most previously proposed approaches based on a model of the target, this method is based on in-situ learning of the target responses and of the local clutter. Learning the clutter is vitally important in complex terrains to obtain low false alarm rates while achieving high detection accuracy. Our method learns features and models directly and automatically from the data and minimizes computation time. Computationally efficient detection approach is required in order to operate on real-time without a need for any special hardware. With the large amount of data that we get from novel sonar systems such as SAS (Synthetic Aperture Sonar), DIDSON and BlueView, computationally efficient detection approaches become more critical than ever before.

In this paper we extend the work we have presented in [7] and apply it to a real dataset of SAS imagery. SAS offers the promise of high-resolution imagery out to large ranges. Initial commercial SAS systems are now available where the increased resolution offers the opportunity of more conventional image processing techniques. In Section 2, our approach is investigated from the prospective of sonar imagery. A new mechanism to measure the prediction confidence is proposed in Section 3. In Section 4, we introduce an improved structure of the cascade capable of achieving higher detection rates. Results obtained on a real set of SAS data on a variety of challenging terrains are presented in Section 5 to show the discriminative power of such an approach.

2. Cascade of Boosted classifiers

The framework of the cascade of boosted classifiers was first introduced by Viola and Jones [8] in 2001 and extended later in several publications such as [9, 10]. Since then it has attracted much attention because of the tremendous speed and high detection rate it offers. Recently, this framework has been reinvestigated and applied to sonar imagery in [7] and proved to perform very well on synthetic data. This framework combines three main interesting concepts. The first concept is a new image representation called the integral image, which allows computing simple rectangle features very quickly. The second concept is an efficient variant of AdaBoost, which also acts as a feature selection mechanism. Finally and most importantly [8] introduces interestingly a simple combining classifier model referred to as the *cascade*, which speeds up the detection by rejecting most background images in the very early stages of the cascade and working hard only on object like patches. This framework is revised concisely in the following subsections within the context of sonar imagery.

Feature space

Using features rather than pixels for classification can be motivated by the fact that features may provide better encoding of the domain knowledge, especially with finite training data that is inevitable in underwater applications. In addition, a classifier built using features could run faster if only few simple features need to be calculated. Can simple features indicate the existence of an object in a sonar image (Fig. 1)?

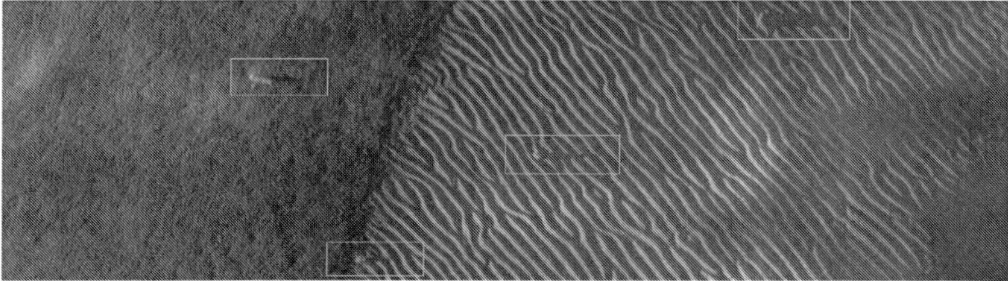

Figure 1: SAS image including four different underwater man-made objects in bounding rectangles, from left to right cylinder, truncated cone, wedge, and cylinder.

Most objects lying on the seafloor share some similar properties. The object region is associated with a shadow region. The object region is brighter than the shadow and the seafloor. The shadow region is darker than the seafloor. This is useful domain knowledge that we need to encode. Features of related sizes, locations (object/shadow), and values (darker/brighter) are required to encode such domain knowledge. Very simple rectangle features reminiscent of Haar basis functions used in [11] could be sufficient to encode those properties. A collection of such features (Fig.2(a)) were first effectively presented in [8]. These feature prototypes are scaled independently in vertical and horizontal direction in order to generate a large set of features. Having a very large number of features, an efficient mechanism has been found to compute them rapidly, called the *integral image* [12]. Once the integral image is computed, any one of the simple rectangle features can be computed in a constant time with very few references to the integral image.

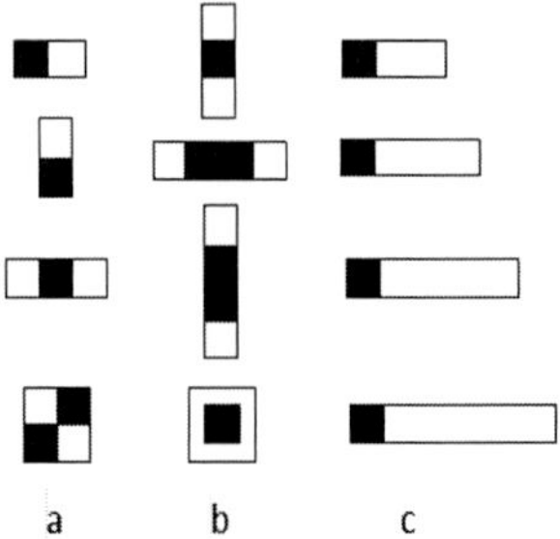

Figure 2: Rectangle Features (a) used in [8] (b) used in [9] (c) used in [7].

Given a detection resolution of 125x55 pixels (the smallest sub-window used in our experiments), a very large set of rectangle features (22,797,621) is generated by shifting and scaling only the four prototypes in Fig. 2(a). This is really an enormous number of features that needs to be evaluated for all positive and negative samples and passed to the feature selection algorithm (AdaBoost) at each stage of the cascade. This is an issue just in the training phase as only a very low number of those features will be selected in this phase and used later in the normal run of the detector. This issue results in a training phase that may take from hours to days or even weeks based on the size of the training set, the training goals, and the processing machine used. Are all those features useful? How different are they from each other? Very small features capture fine details in the image which are below the resolution of the sonar imaging process and therefore more likely to capture variations introduced by noise. Perhaps. In addition, shifting and scaling by only one pixel generates some very similar features in shape and value. Hence, we have put a restriction on the minimum area to be evaluated and increased the shift step and the scale step. Experimental results prove that applying those restrictions does not only expedite the training process by a factor of 10, but also improves the performance of the resulting detector.

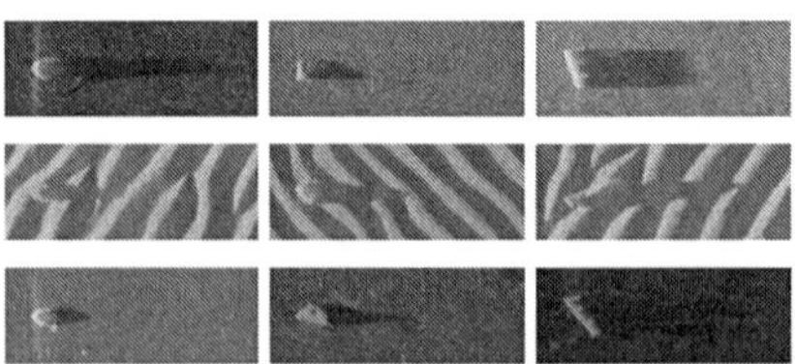

Figure 3: SAS snapshots of objects on the seafloor.

Haar-like features are quite primitive in comparison with other features, but their computational efficiency compensates for their limited flexibility. Several extended sets of Haar-like features have been introduced in literature such as the set introduced in [9] (Fig.2(b)). Our collection comprises some of the previously introduced features (Fig. 2(a, b)) in addition to some new features we have previously presented in [7] (Fig. 2(c)). This collection has enhanced the expressional power of the classification system and consequently improved the performance. Introducing those features has been inspired by the consistent association between the highlight and the shadow in all target samples generated by SAS (Fig. 3).

Feature selection

Given a large feature set associated with each image sub-window, a number far greater than the number of pixels, computing the complete set for each sub-window is still prohibitively expensive; even so, the computation can be carried out very efficiently. Intuitively, a small number of features needs to be found. Several feature selection approaches have been proposed [13]. However, an aggressive mechanism is needed to discard the majority of features leaving only a small subset. Papageorgiou et al. [11] has proposed a solution for a similar problem based on feature variance, but a reasonably large number of features still need to be evaluated for each sub-window. In [8], Viola and Jones used a variant of AdaBoost (Adaptive Boosting) both to select the best features and to train the classifier. The training error of AdaBoost was proved to exponentially approach zero in the number of iterations [14]. In addition, several results proved that AdaBoost achieves large margins and consequently good generalization performance.

The AdaBoost procedure can be easily interpreted as a greedy feature selection process. However, AdaBoost, in its original form, boosts the classification performance by combining a set of weak classifiers. Weak classifiers are constructed each using a single feature. At every round, training examples are re-weighted to emphasize those which were incorrectly misclassified by the previous weak classifier. The final strong classifier is the weighted combination of the weak classifiers where each weak classifier weight is inversely proportional to its training error.

Several variants of AdaBoost have been proposed in the literature looking for better performance. Lienhart et al. [10] experimentally evaluated different boosting algorithms (namely Discrete, Real and Gentle AdaBoost) and different weak classifiers. They argued that Gentle

AdaBoost [15] with small CART trees as base classifiers had the best performance. Therefore, in all our experiments in this paper we use gentle AdaBoost with single node decision trees, known as decision stumps in the machine learning literature.

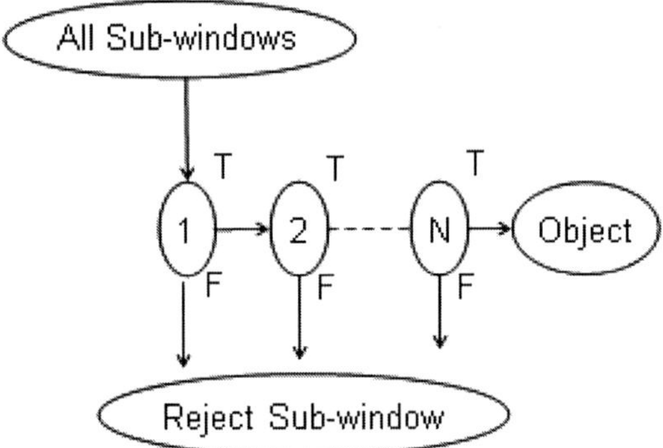

Figure 4: Schematic depiction of the detection cascade.

The cascade

In general, most of the data is not relevant and mechanisms to focus attention (complex features) and processing power (classically limited) to the promising areas of the image is very useful. Within any single image an overwhelming majority of sub-windows are negative (non-target). The cascade achieves this objective by rejecting as many negatives as possible at the earliest stage possible [8]. The overall form of the cascade is that of a degenerate decision tree [16], where at each stage a classifier is trained to detect all objects of interest while rejecting a given fraction of the non-object patterns. Fig. 4 shows a schematic depiction of the detection cascade. An input patch is classified as a target only if it passes the tests in all stages. Much like decision trees, subsequent classifiers are trained using those examples which pass through all the previous stages. Thus, more difficult tasks are faced by classifiers appearing at later stages. Stages of the cascade investigated in this paper are constructed by training classifiers using AdaBoost. The key insight is that smaller and therefore more efficient AdaBoost classifiers can be constructed to detect almost all positive examples (99%) while rejecting a large proportion of the negatives (50%). Cascade detectors have demonstrated impressive detection speed and high detection rates.

3. Cascade score

During the multi-scale scanning mechanism in the detection phase of the cascade, multiple detections normally appear around target-like patches in the image. The cascade structure does not associate these detections with confidence levels. An input sub-window is classified as a target only if it passes the tests in all stages of the cascade. Hence, co-located detections are normally grouped to produce one bounding box around the object. The minimum number of co-located detections in a group is usually set as a criterion to declare a final detection in an area. Increasing this threshold may help suppress some false detections by requiring that the target object be detected multiple times during the scanning phase. This may also reduce the probability of detection for some targets. This is usually the criterion used to evaluate the performance of the cascade by generating the ROC (Receiver Operating Characteristic) curve. Setting this threshold is difficult as it depends on other parameters such as the shift step and the scale factor. This also makes the ability to convert this number to a normalized confidence level even harder. Intuitively, this criterion is ill-founded as it does not take into account the confidence for the classification of the target at each level of the cascade in the final decision process.

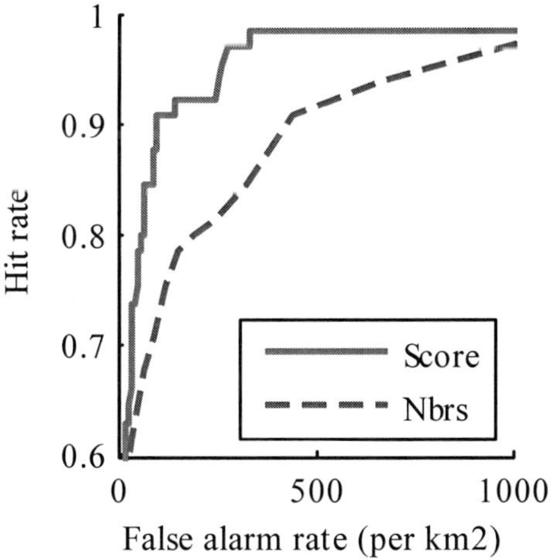

Figure 5: Score and Neighbours ROC curves for a truncated cone detector.

This motivated the definition of a new measure of confidence. At each step of the cascade, an AdaBoost classifier is used to determine if a sample will proceed to the next step. As discussed in section 0, AdaBoost is a weighted combination of weak classifiers. Gentle AdaBoost, used here, outputs a confidence-rated predictions rather than the {-1,1} output of the traditional Discrete AdaBoost. In Gentle AdaBoost each weak classifier returns a value lying in the range [-1,1]. The sign of this value gives the classification and its absolute gives a measure of the confidence in the prediction. At each stage of the cascade the combination of weak classifiers is compared against a threshold learnt and set for this stage during the training phase. Let's call this combination the AdaBoost score. Intuitively the combination of all AdaBoost scores that a sample achieves at all stages of the cascade provides a good measure of the confidence in the prediction.

However, as discussed in section 0, classifiers appearing at later stages of the cascade use more complex features and have more discriminating power. Hence, the score associated to a sample in the later stage of the cascade is probably more important than a score given at an earlier stage and should be given more weight in the final score calculation. Therefore, a weighted combination of AdaBoost scores, where the weight is the stage number is used here. We call this weighted combination the cascade score.

Fig.5 shows two ROC curves generated for the same detector, one using the neighbor detections criterion and another using the cascade score criterion. As expected the score provides a much better confidence measure than the neighbors. Empirical evidence has also shown that the weighted score calculation is more effective than allocating the same weight for each stage of the cascade.

The score does not only provide a good confidence level to every detection, but also reduces the false alarm rate significantly. It is also worth mentioning that the cascade score can also be exploited in the training phase to better select training samples. Intuitively, the score can be computed for all positive and negative samples at the beginning of each training stage. These scores can then be associated with the samples as initial weights for AdaBoost training.

4. Cascade

As discussed in the previous sections, the majority of false alarms are rejected in the first few stages of the cascade and very few of them reach the last stages. Experiments show also that almost all positives pass the first stages of the cascade. The missed detections normally occur in the last few stages of the cascade and affects targets either affected by poor image coherence (SAS case) or strong background interactions. The later and stricter cascade stages will reject them.

In critical applications such as underwater mine detection, the cost of a missed detection is much higher than a few extra false alarms. In this application, sidescan sonar and synthetic aperture sonar are normally used and typically provide only one view of the scene. Therefore a target is typically scanned by the sensor only once. This makes the cost of missing a detection even higher. To guarantee that all targets are detected, a cascade detector with relaxed training goals (fewer stages) should be employed. However such a detector will also result in a very high number of false alarms, which makes the process of mine countermeasures prohibitive to automate.

To confront this issue we propose to split the cascade into two parts. Suppose that the cascade is composed of M stages. It is split into the first N stages (N<M) and the last K stages (N+K=M). The first N stages are used classically, passing and rejecting samples, while the final K stage do not reject samples (Fig. 6). In the second part of the cascade, samples that do not pass AdaBoost test are passed directly to the end of the cascade. However, the score that the sample achieves at each stage is still added to its final score as usual. This structure guarantees that all samples that pass the first part of the cascade are kept and only their scores are affected in the second part of the cascade.

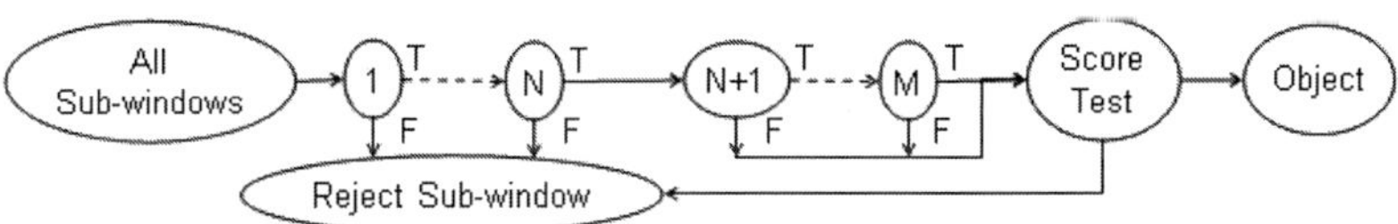

Figure 6: Schematic depiction of the score.

To test this structure, a cascade of two parts has been built. The training goal of the first part is set to 10^{-5} false alarm rate (per sub-window), while the training goal of the second part is set to 10^{-8} false alarm rate. All stages are trained to reject at least 50% of the false alarms and pass at least 99.5% of the targets. In our examples, the first part needed 8 stages to achieve its training goals. An additional 8 stages were needed on top of the first part to build the second part of the cascade. Fig. 7 shows three ROC curves: one for the first part, one for the second part, and finally one for the two parts combined using the new proposed structure, which we call the score cascade. It is clear how the score cascade outperforms the first part of the cascade that normally has high false alarm rates at high detection rates. The score cascade also outperforms the second part of the cascade that normally rejects few targets and is unable to achieve high detection rates.

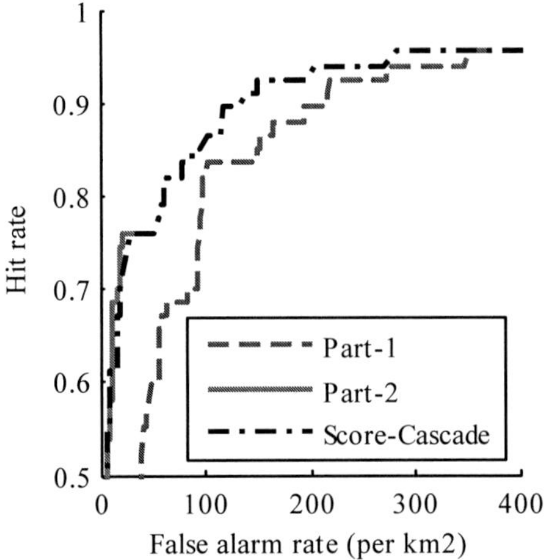

Figure 7: Three ROC curves: one for the first part, one for the second part, and finally one for the score cascade (for a wedge detector).

5. Experimental results

To evaluate the performance of our approach, a real set of SAS data was provided by DSTL (Defence Science and Technology Laboratory). The dataset was collected by NURC (NATO Undersea Research Centre). The system used was the MUSCLE system, an AUV (Autonomous Underwater Vehicle) equipped with synthetic aperture sonar. A number of mine-like targets were deployed and surveyed from different aspects. The targets consisted of a truncated cone shape with a 1.0 m diameter base and 0.5m height, a wedge shape of length of roughly 1.0 m by 0.6m by 0.3 m, and a cylinder of length 2.0 m by 0.5 m diameter, with some protrusions such as fins. A large number of rocks, boulders and other clutter objects were also surveyed. Fig. 1 shows an example of a SAS image, including views of four different targets lying on the seabed.

Images were generated from SAS data matrices that represent an acoustic scan of the seabed from both port and starboard sides of the AUV. The dataset covers around 1 km^2 comprising 201 images of approximately 7000x2000 pixels and 1.5x2.5 cm pixel resolution. The dataset covers 3 separate regions, with similar targets and target distribution patterns but with different seabed characteristics as follows:

- Area B: uncluttered background (flat) (69 images, containing 159 target views).

- Area C: cluttered background (ripples, rocks and weed) (61 images, containing 141 target views).

- Area D: cluttered background (rocks and tracks) (71 images, containing 141 target views).

Each area contains 9 targets (3 from each target type) arranged in a similar pattern. Although the target types are classified as one of three distinct shapes, they actually differ as they may be filled with different materials leading to different acoustic responses. Fig. 3 shows several snapshots of the three different types of targets taken from the three separate regions.

Dataset have been split equally into two subsets, one for training and another for testing. A cascade detector of two parts has been trained for each type of the targets mentioned above (truncated cone, wedge, and cylinder) in addition to a generic detector to detect all types together. The positive samples (targets) have been extracted from the training set using the ground truth. The negative samples (non-target) used to train each classifier in the cascade are selected randomly from a copy of the training set with the targets excluded.

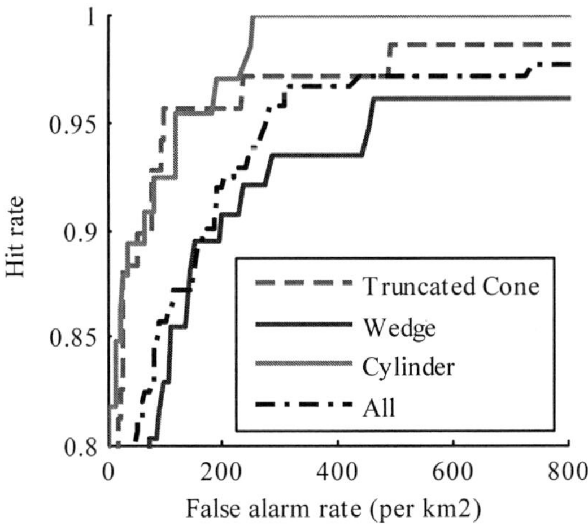

Figure 8: Three ROC curves for truncated cone, wedge, cylinder, and all (generic) detectors.

Our experiments follow the general form, though differ in details, from those presented in [8, 7]. In each round of boosting, a Haar-like feature is selected until the stage training target of minimum hit rate and maximum false alarm rate is achieved. Stages are added to the cascade until either the overall training target (detection rate and false alarm rate) is achieved, or a maximum number of stages has been reached. Wegde, Cylinder and the generic detectors have all been trained under identical training goals, 0.995 min stage hit rate, 0.5 max stage false alarm rate, a maximum of 14 stages for the first part of the cascade and a maximum of 20 stages for the second part. The Truncated cone is the only target that is symmetric in shape from the sidescan point of view, and consequently has a lower variance between its responses. This is why a harder training goal was assigned to the truncated cone detector (0.998 min stage hit rate, 0.25 max stage false alarm rate, a maximum of 7 stages for the first part of the cascade, and a maximum of 14 stages for the second part) to improve the performance. Fig. 8 shows the ROC curves for the resulting detectors on the test datasets. Table 1 lists some details about the results achieved by each detector at around 95% detection rate. The processing time required to run any of these detectors on an image of approximately 7000x2000 pixels using a 3 GHz Intel Xeon with 4 GB of memory is approximately 200 milliseconds.

To show the complexity level of the problem we are dealing with, Fig. 9 displays examples from the test dataset. An example of a target (Wedge) that can be very hard to recognise even by a human expert operator but detected by our approach is shown in Fig. 9(a). Another example of a target (Wedge) that is hard to detect, but this time missed by our detector is presented in Fig. 9(b). Fig. 9(c) shows a false alarm very similar in shape to target samples and consequently picked by all the detectors.

Figure 9: Examples from the results: (a) true detection by wedge detector, (b) target missed by wedge detector and the generic detector, (c) false alarm by all detectors.

It is important to mention that the ability to achieve 100% detection rate was an essential design requirement in all our experiments. This condition has been specified because of the higher cost of missing a target than having fewer extra false alarms. Therefore, all train and test parameters were chosen carefully. Relaxing this requirement can result in detectors that generate ROC curves with lower false alarm rates at the expense of the detection rate.

Table 1: Results achieved by all detectors at around 95% detection rate.

Detector	Truncated Cone	Wedge	Cylinder	All
Number of detected targets	66 (of 69)	72 (of 76)	63 (of 66)	200 (of 211)
Number of false alarms	52	242	66	145
False alarm rate per sub-window	1.5E-07	7.2E-07	2.0E-07	4.5E-07
False alarm rate per km^2	98	454	124	272

6. Conclusions

In this paper, a novel method for object detection in SAS imagery was presented. This method is based on the classifier cascade framework used previously in computer vision domain for face detection. It has also been revisited recently in [7] and applied to the problem of target detection in sidescan sonar data. Unlike most previously proposed approaches for object detection in sonar imagery based on a model of the object, our method is based on in-situ learning of the target responses and of the local clutter.

Several contributions that improve the classification performance have been introduced and discussed. Results obtained on a real dataset of Synthetic Aperture Sonar images on a variety of challenging terrains were presented to show the discriminative power of such an approach. When compared against the state-of-the-art methods, results indicate reasonably competitive performance. Although, we have only tested the extended framework on sonar imagery, the extensions we have presented can also be useful in other applications.

Future works in this domain concern first object identification. This can be performed either by using a generic detector for all objects followed by a specific detector for each object, or using other pattern recognition techniques applied to the detected candidate region. We will also explore using complex features at the last few stages of the cascade. This is justified by the fact that only a very low number of sub-windows pass all these stages, so evaluating computationally expensive features will not affect computational efficiency.

Acknowledgments

We wish to gratefully acknowledge DSTL for providing the data.

References

[1] M. Mignotte, C. Collet, P. Perez and P. Boutherny, "Unsupervised Markovian Segmentation of Sonar Images," in *22nd IEEE International Conference on Acoustics, Speech, and Signal Processing*, Munich, 1997.

[2] S. Reed, Y. Petillot and J. Bell, "An automatic approach to the detection and extraction of mine features in side scan sonar," *IEEE Journal of Oceanic Engineering,* vol. 28, no. 1, 2003.

[3] F. Maussang, J. Chanussot and A. Hetet, "Automated Segmentation of SAS images using the Mean-Standard Deviation Plane for the Detection of Underwater Mines," in *OCEANS*, California, 2003.

[4] S. W. Perry and L. Guan, "Pulse-Length-Tolerant Features and Detectors for Sector-Scan Sonar Imagery," *IEEE Journal of Oceanic Engineering,* vol. 29, no. 1, pp. 138-156, 2004.

[5] P. Saisan and S. Kadambe, "Shape Normalized Subspace Analysis for Underwater Mine Detection," *IEEE ICIP,* vol. 1, pp. 1892-1895, 2008.

[6] J. Del Rio Vera, E. Coiras, J. Groen and B. Evans, "Automatic target recognition in synthetic aperture sonar images based on geometrical feature extraction," *EURASIP Journal on Advances in Signal Processing,* pp. 1-9, 2009.

[7] J. Sawas, Y. Petillot and Y. Pailhas, "Cascade of boosted classifiers for rapid detection of underwater objects," in *European Conference on Underwater Acoustics*, 2010.

[8] P. Viola and M. J. Jones, "Rapid Object Detection using a Boosted Cascade of Simple Features," in *IEEE CVPR*, 2001.

[9] R. Lienhart and J. Maydt, "An Extended Set of Haar-like Features for Rapid Object Detection," in *IEEE ICIP*, 2002.

[10] R. Lienhart, A. Kuranov and V. Pisarevsky, "Empirical Analysis of Detection Cascades of Boosted Classifiers for Rapid Object Detection," in *Proceedings of the 25th DAGM Symposium on Pattern Recognition*, Magdeburg, Germany, 2003.

[11] C. Papageorgiou, M. Oren and T. Poggio, "A general framework for Object Detection," in *International Conference on Computer Vision*, 1998.

[12] P. Viola and M. Jones, "Robust real-time object detection," in *Workshop on Statistical and Computational Theories of Vision*, 2001.

[13] A. Webb, Recognition, Statistical Pattern, New York: Oxford University Press, 1999.

[14] R. E. Schapire, Y. Freund, P. Bartlett and W. S. Lee, "Boosting the margin: A new explanation for the effectiveness of voting methods," in *Proceedings of the Fourteenth International Conference on Machine Learning*, 1997.

[15] Y. Freund and R. E. Schapire, "Experiments with a new boosting algorithm," in *Machine Learning: Proceedings of the Thirteenth International Conference*, 1996.

[16] J. Quinlan, "Induction of decision trees," *Machine Learning*, no. 1, p. 81–106, 1986.

CHAPTER NINE

SAS AND BATHYMETRIC DATA FUSION FOR IMPROVED TARGET CLASSIFICATION

DAVID P. WILLIAMS

Abstract

An algorithm is proposed for the fusion of multiple views of an object from each of two information sources – a synthetic aperture sonar (SAS) image and a bathymetric map. A parameter tied to the success of interferometric processing, and hence the reliability of the bathymetric estimates, automatically weights the relative contribution of each information source. The variation in fused images, measured by the Laplacian, is used to determine the image translation needed to align multiple views. The algorithm is completely model-free and requires no *a priori* knowledge about the types of objects that will be considered. As a result, the method has potential to be particularly useful for reducing false alarms generated by clutter objects, and in turn, for improving classification performance. The proposed fusion algorithm is demonstrated on three objects using real, measured data collected at sea.

Keywords: Data Fusion, Multi-View, Synthetic Aperture Sonar (SAS), Bathymetry, Classification.

1. Introduction

Mine countermeasures (MCM) operations depend on the ability to reliably classify objects on the seafloor as targets (*i.e.,* mines) or benign clutter. The use of high-resolution synthetic aperture sonar (SAS) imagery [1] to accomplish this task has allowed a leap in performance over that which was previously possible with lower resolution sidescan sonar imagery.

However, it is well-known that an object's appearance in a SAS image can depend heavily on the relative aspect at which the object is interrogated. The classic example of this aspect-dependence is that of a cylinder on a seafloor; a cylinder viewed at broadside will look markedly different than the same cylinder viewed at endfire. In fact, even with high-resolution imagery, it may not be possible to correctly classify an object with only a single ("unlucky") view. This fact highlights the value of collecting multiple views of an object at different aspects. With view diversity, a more comprehensive understanding of the object can be obtained, and in turn, a more informed and confident classification decision can be made [2,3].

In this work, we aim to aid classification performance by combining individual SAS views of an object into a single multi-view SAS image. Since this fusion is in fact the overlaying of multiple images of the same object, it can more properly be called image registration, which has a long history in many different fields and with many different sensor modalities (see [4] for a survey). However, the nature of SAS imagery – and the manner in which the sonar data is collected – presents several unique challenges that are not commonly encountered in other domains.

Sonar data for MCM operations is typically collected by an autonomous underwater vehicle (AUV). Because GPS cannot be used while underwater, the navigation accuracy of the AUV is limited [5]. (This should be contrasted with the GPS-aided accuracy achievable in synthetic aperture radar (SAR) applications.) Consequently, registering objects based on navigation information is not feasible because the errors can be large relative to the size of the target.

As an example, Fig. 1 shows the SAS image-fusion result of two views of a torus-like object using only navigation information. The two views were collected by an AUV executing a survey composed of a series of parallel tracks; the views were obtained from different tracks (*i.e.,* passes). It can be seen that the error between the two views of the object is about 2.5m, an unacceptable amount in this context.

One popular class of registration approaches, referred to as *feature-based* techniques [4], rely on the use of landmarks (*i.e.,* prominent features) to align images. This approach is frequently employed to mosaic multiple large-scale sonar images [5,7], but it cannot achieve the fine precision needed for aligning object images. An example of fusing the two views of the torus-like object based on the location of a landmark (in this case, the location of the object itself, obtained from the output of an automatic detection algorithm [8]) is shown in Fig. 1(b). Although the object alignment is better than in the navigation-based approach, it can readily be seen that the two views still do not coincide sufficiently. Computer vision applications, such as object recognition in scenes [9], employ feature-matching methods with great success, but the non-repeatability of features owing to aspect dependence in SAS images (unlike the distinct, repeatable details that can be captured in photographs) disqualifies such approaches for our task.

The other major class of registration techniques are referred to as *area-based* methods [4]. This group is composed of correlation-based and template-matching approaches. Unfortunately, the nature of SAS images – namely, that the fundamental appearance of an object changes with aspect – makes image fusion via direct correlation-based methods infeasible. For example, the parts of an object that are characterized by shadows or highlights in a SAS image will be determined by the viewing aspect. As a result, the same object can look completely different in SAS images from different aspects, which contradicts the basic premise for employing a correlation-based approach.

This obstacle is partially circumvented in [10] by comparing a given SAS image to *models* of several known targets at numerous aspects. (The use of a model reference image for template matching is also common in many medical imaging applications such as brain scan registration [11].) However, such an approach is feasible only if the unknown object belongs to the set of targets for which a model is possessed. In practice, the unknown object may be something unexpected that has never previously been encountered. Hence, the approach is ill-suited for fusing multiple views of objects in the clutter class, to which the vast majority of detected objects typically belong [12]. Moreover, the computation required for this approach grows exponentially with the number of target-models considered.

The failure of common registration approaches and the inapplicability of others motivate the need for a new SAS-specific image-fusion algorithm. We contend that the ill-posed nature of the SAS image-fusion task – owing to the fact that the fundamental appearance of an object changes with aspect – suggests that in order to successfully fuse multiple views, it is necessary to have access to an auxiliary source of information. In this work, this second information source is bathymetric maps, which provide height estimates of the object, obtained from interferometric processing of the sonar data.

Bathymetric maps are a particularly valuable source of information in this fusion task because they measure intrinsic features of the object – the heights at specific locations – that should be invariant to viewing aspect [13]. (In contrast, we know *a priori* that the SAS image of an object will –

and should – indeed vary with aspect; this means that features found in the SAS images will not be robust.) However, because the availability of the bathymetric maps is predicated on the ability to successfully perform interferometric processing, one cannot rely solely on the bathymetry to perform the image registration. (Successful interferometric processing cannot always be guaranteed for data collected at sea [14].) Therefore, in this work, we develop a (model-free) algorithm to determine the correct image registration – specifically, the correct translation – to align multiple SAS images of an object by exploiting both the SAS images themselves and, when they are reliable, bathymetric maps from those same views.

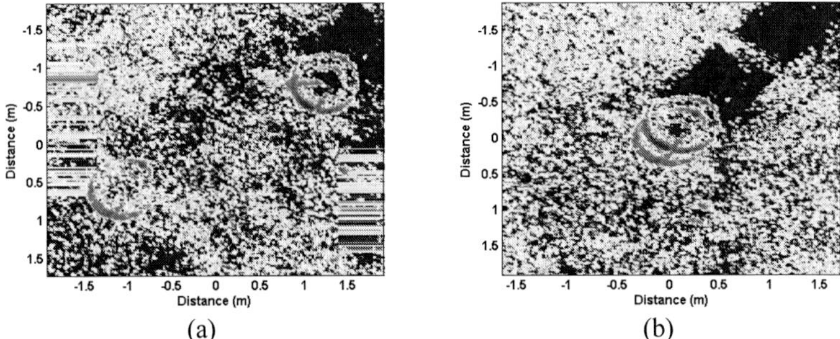

Figure 1: Motivating example: Unsatisfactory SAS image-fusion result of two views (at the same aspect) of the torus-like Object A when the fusion is performed using (a) navigation information, or (b) landmark (*i.e.,* contact-location) information.

The remainder of this paper is organized as follows. In Section 2, the proposed multi-view fusion algorithm is described. Section 3 presents experimental results of this method on real, measured SAS data. Concluding remarks and directions for future work are given in Section 4.

2. Multi-View Fusion

Consider the case in which an object of unknown identity has been interrogated by each of two – not necessarily statistically independent – sensor "modalities" (or, more generically, information sources) multiple times. Assume spatial data (*e.g.,* imagery) related to the object can be produced from a single view with either information source independently (*i.e.,* without having any knowledge of the other source). In this work, the two sources of information representing the object are assumed to be (i) a SAS image and (ii) a bathymetric map obtained from interferometric processing. Our objective is to use the multiple views from these two data sources to create a single fused SAS image. The intent is that this fused image incorporating multiple views simultaneously will be more informative than the set of individual views, in terms of classifying the object.

Let I_i^s be the SAS image of the object obtained from the ith of $N > 1$ views. Let I_i^b be the estimated bathymetric map of the area centered around the object obtained from the ith view. We perform the desired multi-source, multi-view fusion in the following manner.

First, each image is rotated in order to transform the data from the N views into a common reference system. The rotation applied is determined from the heading recorded on the AUV during the data collection. Examples of this rotation step are shown in Fig. 2. After this rotation, the only remaining element in the fusion that is still unknown is the relative translation (*i.e.,* shift) that should be applied to the images in order to align them.

To determine the appropriate translation, we exploit both the SAS images and the bathymetric maps. Specifically, we seek to minimize an objective function that expresses the collective variation that results after fusing translated images. The rationale for this approach is that low variation should correspond to a proper image alignment. The objective function is constructed to depend on the *variation*, rather than the original raw image, partially to circumvent the fact that SAS images of a given object will naturally look different when interrogated at different aspects.

The Laplacian operator, which is the second unmixed partial spatial derivative, has proven useful for detecting rapid intensity changes in an image [15], and therefore, we employ it in this work to measure the variation in the fused image. The Laplacian of an image with pixel values $I(x, y)$ is given by

$$\mathcal{L}(I) = \frac{\partial^2 I}{\partial x^2} + \frac{\partial^2 I}{\partial y^2},\tag{1}$$

with this calculation performed on a discrete image using a finite difference method. (For the sake of brevity and clarity, the (x, y) argument of images are suppressed hereafter.)

For a given row and column translation, $\tau \equiv \{r, c\}$, let $I_{i,j}^{s(\tau)}$ be the fused SAS image that results from combining the SAS images from the ith view and jth (translated) view. The fusion is effected in this work by taking the *maximum* pixel value of the two views at each pixel location (after translation has been applied to the second image). This form of fusion using the maximum operator is chosen with consideration for the nature of SAS imagery, and in particular, the shadows that are created due to the object-sonar geometry. For example, averaging the pixel values would unfairly penalize portions of the object characterized by shadow in a view. Our choice also suggests that in the limit of an infinite number of views spanning all aspects, the resulting fused image would be similar to a circular SAS image [13].

Let $V_{i,j}^{s(\tau)}$ denote the image-variation from fusing the SAS images from the ith and jth views (with translation τ), defined by

$$V_{i,j}^{s(\tau)} = \sum_x \sum_y |\mathcal{L}(I_{i,j}^{s(\tau)})|, \tag{2}$$

with the summations over all pixels in the image.

The bathymetric maps are fused in a slightly different manner. For a given translation, τ, let $I_{i,j}^{b(\tau)}$ be the fused bathymetric map that results from combining the bathymetric maps from the ith view and jth (translated) view. The fusion is effected in this work by taking the *mean* pixel value of the two views at each pixel location (after translation has been applied to the second image). This form of fusion is chosen with consideration for the nature of the bathymetric maps, which represent relative heights (with respect to an arbitrary reference point that is different for each view's map) rather than absolute heights. It is for this reason that alternative choices, such as selecting at each pixel location the larger height or the height associated with the larger coherence, is not sensible.

Let $V_{i,j}^{b(\tau)}$ denote the image-variation from fusing the bathymetric maps from the ith and jth views (with translation τ), defined by

$$V_{i,j}^{b(\tau)} = \sum_x \sum_y |\mathcal{L}(I_{i,j}^{b(\tau)})|. \tag{3}$$

It should be noted that there will be one scalar $V_{i,j}^{s(\tau)}$ and one scalar $V_{i,j}^{b(\tau)}$ for each possible translation, τ. The minimum fused bathymetric map variation achieved by any translation will be denoted $\tilde{V}_{i,j}^{b}$. The minimum fused SAS image variation achieved by any translation will be denoted $\tilde{V}_{i,j}^{s}$.

The elegantly simple objective function we seek to minimize is then given by

$$Q(\tau) = w \frac{V_{i,j}^{b(\tau)}}{\tilde{V}_{i,j}^{b}} + (1 - w) \frac{V_{i,j}^{s(\tau)}}{\tilde{V}_{i,j}^{s}}, \tag{4}$$

where $w \in [0,1]$ is a weight that controls the relative contribution of the SAS images and the bathymetric maps. This key weight is calculated as

$$w = \min(f_i, f_j), \tag{5}$$

where f_i is the fraction of pixels in the ith view for which the coherence (from interferometric processing) is above a threshold, ρ. (In this work, $\rho = 2/3$.) As such, f_i represents a rough measure of confidence about the bathymetric height estimates because a high coherence (above ρ) suggests the interferometric processing was successful. In (5), the *minimum* is selected because it makes sense to fuse two bathymetric maps only if both views are of good quality. That is, there is little (or no) benefit in attempting to fuse one accurate bathymetric map with one that is inaccurate (or unreliable).

In (4), the variations of the fused bathymetric map and fused SAS image are each normalized by the minimum variation achieved (by any translation) to ensure that the contribution of each term to the objective function is comparable in magnitude. We normalize by the *minimum* variation achieved instead of the *maximum* variation achieved because the latter approach would still have the potential to wildly skew the relative magnitudes.

The translation, τ, that minimizes the objective function in (4) is selected as the correct translation needed to properly align the multiple views of the object and produce an accurate fused image. Upon determining this best translation, the two SAS image views are fused (keeping the maximum pixel value at each location, as above), the bathymetric maps are fused (averaging the height estimates at each location, as above), and the coherence maps are fused (taking the minimum value at each location, for reasons outlined above).

If an additional view is possessed (*i.e.,* $N > 2$), all of the above procedure can be repeated treating the new fusion result as an input "view." We choose to perform the fusion sequentially to ensure that the computational load scales only linearly with N; if the fusion were to be performed in parallel, the computation would instead scale exponentially with N.

3. Experimental Results

The Centre for Maritime Research and Experimentation (formerly NATO Undersea Research Centre) has an AUV called MUSCLE that is equipped with an interferometric SAS (InSAS), which permits both synthetic aperture sonar processing and interferometric processing. As a result, multiple sources of information are available with which to aid classification for a given object detected on the seafloor. Using data collected by this AUV at sea, we demonstrate the proposed fusion algorithm outlined in Section 2 on three different clutter objects of unknown identity. Admittedly, in the absence of ground truth, it is difficult to rigorously evaluate the efficacy of the algorithm. The results here act merely as an initial proof-of-concept.

The first object, denoted Object A, has been viewed three times, twice at the same aspect and a third time at a different aspect. The aspects of the three views are $\theta_1 = 126°$, $\theta_2 = 126°$, and $\theta_3 = 37°$. We first perform fusion using views 1 and 2. For this case, the interferometric processing was very successful, yielding high coherence values. Since the bathymetric maps are reliable in this case, they should play a strong role in the fusion process. This is precisely what occurs, as the weight controlling the relative contribution of each information source (SAS image and bathymetric map) in the fusion process was calculated to be $w = 0.84$. The result of the fusion procedure, as well as the data used to undertake it, is shown in Fig. 2. This fusion result should be compared to the (unsatisfactory) fusion results in Fig. 1 that would be achieved using navigation data or contact-location data.

After fusing these two views, the third view, which was at a different aspect, was also fused. This view was characterized by low coherence, and as a result, more importance was automatically placed on the SAS image during the fusion process via the weight, calculated to be $w = 0.37$. The result of this tri-view fusion is shown in Fig. 2(n).

Next, we demonstrate the fusion on an irregularly shaped object, denoted Object B. The aspects of the two views are $\theta_1 = 214°$ and $\theta_2 = 306°$. The fusion result of this object and the data used to achieve it are shown in Fig. 3. In this case, the coherence was again strong, so more importance was placed on the bathymetric fusion via the weight, calculated to be $w = 0.88$. This case is interesting because the SAS images from the two views are significantly different. The fusion result is also shown in a three-dimensional plot in Fig. 3(j) by draping the fused SAS image on top of the fused bathymetry map.

Lastly, we demonstrate the fusion on a third object, denoted Object C, Fig. 4. The aspects of the two views are $\theta_1 = 124°$ and $\theta_2 = 254°$. In this case, the coherence was very weak, so more importance was placed on the SAS image fusion via the weight, calculated to be $w = 0.15$. Although plausible, the fusion result is difficult to quantify objectively without ground truth.

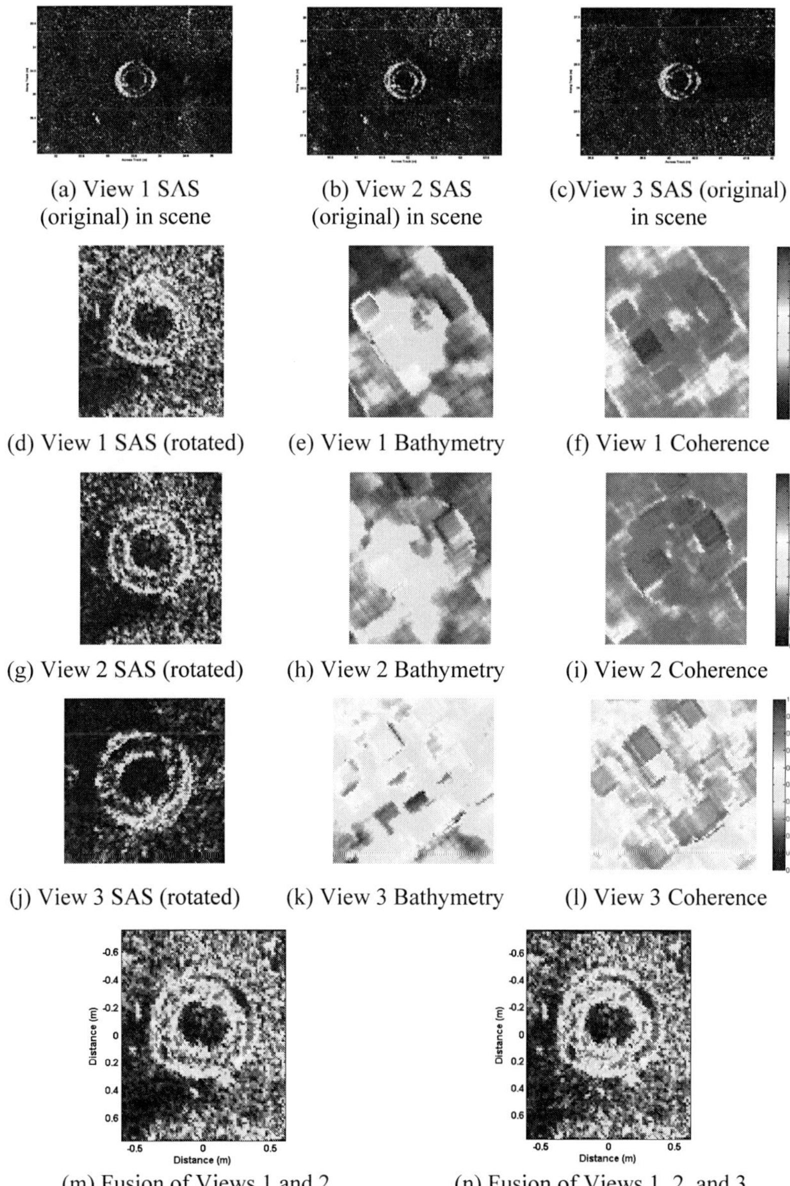

(a) View 1 SAS (original) in scene

(b) View 2 SAS (original) in scene

(c) View 3 SAS (original) in scene

(d) View 1 SAS (rotated)

(e) View 1 Bathymetry

(f) View 1 Coherence

(g) View 2 SAS (rotated)

(h) View 2 Bathymetry

(i) View 2 Coherence

(j) View 3 SAS (rotated)

(k) View 3 Bathymetry

(l) View 3 Coherence

(m) Fusion of Views 1 and 2

(n) Fusion of Views 1, 2, and 3

Figure 2: Object A data and fusion results. The aspects of the three views are $\theta_1 = 126°, \theta_2 = 126°$, and $\theta_3 = 37°$.

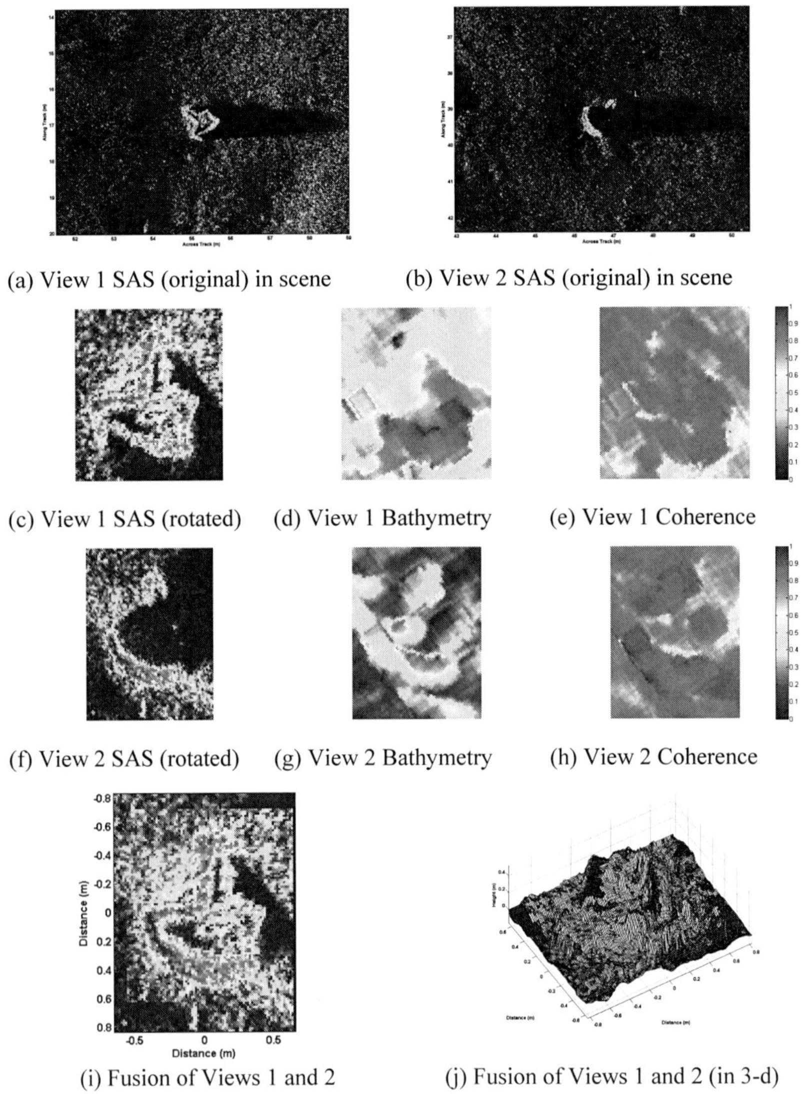

(a) View 1 SAS (original) in scene   (b) View 2 SAS (original) in scene

(c) View 1 SAS (rotated)   (d) View 1 Bathymetry   (e) View 1 Coherence

(f) View 2 SAS (rotated)   (g) View 2 Bathymetry   (h) View 2 Coherence

(i) Fusion of Views 1 and 2   (j) Fusion of Views 1 and 2 (in 3-d)

Figure 3: Object B data and fusion results. The aspects of the two views are $\theta_1 = 214°$ and $\theta_2 = 306°$.

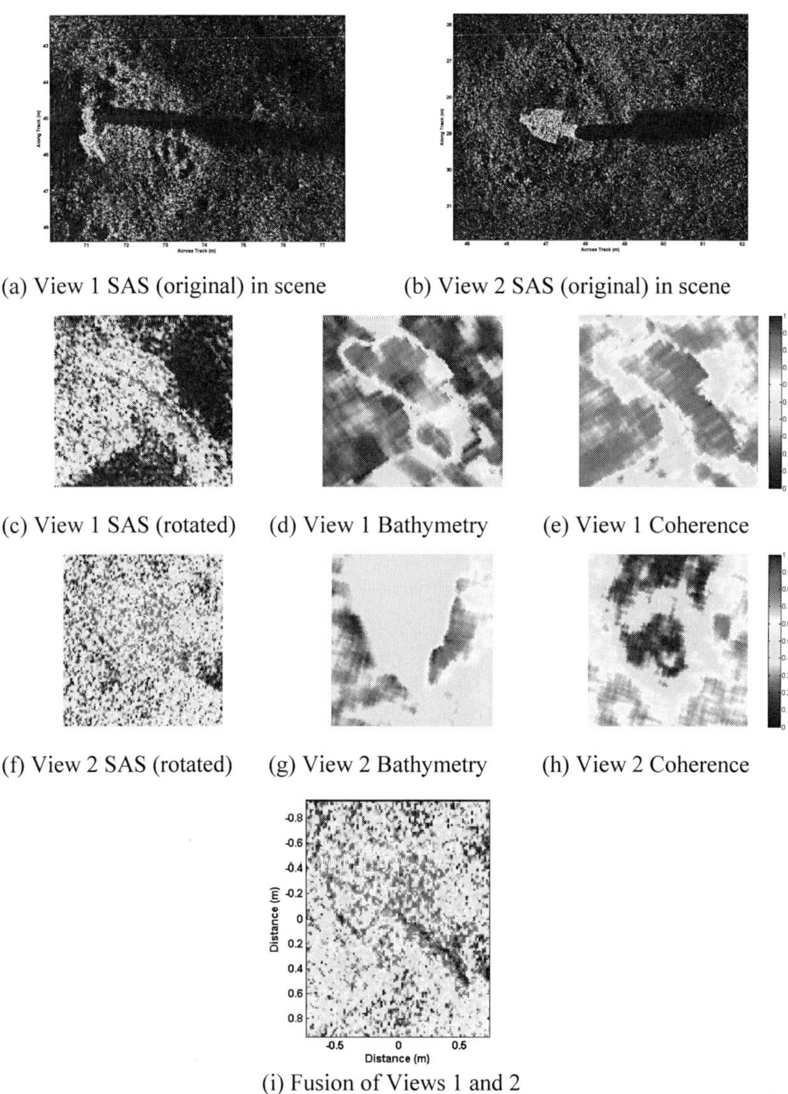

(a) View 1 SAS (original) in scene   (b) View 2 SAS (original) in scene

(c) View 1 SAS (rotated)   (d) View 1 Bathymetry   (e) View 1 Coherence

(f) View 2 SAS (rotated)   (g) View 2 Bathymetry   (h) View 2 Coherence

(i) Fusion of Views 1 and 2

Figure 4: Object C data and fusion results. The aspects of the two views are $\theta_1 = 124°$ and $\theta_2 = 254°$.

One appealing aspect of the proposed algorithm is that the data quality is automatically taken into account in the fusion procedure. If the interferometric processing is successful, the additional information provided by the bathymetric maps is exploited. If the interferometric processing is not successful, the algorithm knows to ignore that information source and instead base the fusion on the SAS images alone. However, it should be noted that relying solely on the SAS images may not produce a satisfactory fusion result in general. Indeed, it was for this very reason that the proposed algorithm was formulated to exploit the bathymetric maps.

4. Conclusion

An algorithm for the fusion of multiple views of an object from each of two information sources – a SAS image and a bathymetric map – was proposed. The technique is completely model-free and requires no *a priori* knowledge about the types of objects that will be encountered. Preliminary results demonstrated the promise of the technique, but the multi-view fusion problem is still far from solved.

Future work will seek to improve the robustness of the algorithm and see its application to larger data sets with known targets so fusion performance can be measured quantitatively. Additional research will aim to determine the best way to fuse data when $N > 2$ views are possessed. For example, it may make sense to fuse images from similar aspects first, or to first fuse images for which the interferometric processing was most successful.

References

[1] M. Hayes and P. Gough, "Broad-band synthetic aperture sonar," *IEEE Journal of Oceanic Engineering*, vol. 17, no. 1, pp. 80–94, 1992.

[2] P. Runkle, L. Nguyen, J. McClellan, and L. Carin, "Multi-aspect target detection for SAR imagery using hidden Markov models," *IEEE Transactions on Geoscience and Remote Sensing*, vol. 39, no. 1, pp. 46–55, 2001.

[3] S. Ji, X. Liao, and L. Carin, "Adaptive multiaspect target classification and detection with hidden Markov models," *IEEE Sensors Journal*, vol. 5, no. 5, pp. 1035–1042, 2005.

[4] B. Zitova and J. Flusser, "Image registration methods: a survey," *Image and Vision Computing*, vol. 21, pp. 977–1000, 2003.

[5] R. Hansen, H. Callow, T. Sæbø, and S. Synnes, "Challenges in seafloor imaging and mapping with synthetic aperture sonar," in *Proceedings of the European Conference on SAR*, 2010.

[6] E. Coiras, I. Tena-Ruiz, Y. Petillot, and D. Lane, "Fusion of multiple side-scan sonar views," in *Proceedings of IEEE OCEANS*, 2004.

[7] E. Coiras, D. Williams, and J. Groen, "Mosaicking synthetic aperture sonar images using dynamic constraints," in *Proceedings of IEEE OCEANS*, 2011.

[8] D. Williams, "On adaptive underwater object detection," in *Proceedings of IEEE/RSJ International Conference on Intelligent Robots and Systems*, pp. 4741–4748, 2011.

[9] H. Bay, T. Tuytelaars, and L. V. Gool, "SURF: Speeded up robust features," in *Proceedings of European Conference on Computer Vision*, 2006.

[10] J. Groen, D. Williams, and W. Fox, "A model-based multi-view image registration method for SAS images," in *Proceedings of Underwater Acoustic Measurements*, 2011.

[11] J. Ashburner, J. Andersson, and K. Friston, "High-dimensional image registration using symmetric priors," *NeuroImage*, vol. 9, pp. 619–628, 1999.

[12] D. Williams, V. Myers, and M. Silvious, "Mine classification with imbalanced data," *IEEE Geoscience and Remote Sensing Letters*, vol. 6, no. 3, pp. 528–532, 2009.

[13] H. Callow, R. Hansen, S. Synnes, and T. Sæbø, "Circular synthetic aperture sonar without a beacon," in *Proceedings of Underwater Acoustic Measurements*, 2009.

[14] S. Synnes, R. Hansen, and T. Sæbø, "Assessment of shallow water performance using interferometric sonar coherence," in *Proceedings of Underwater Acoustic Measurements*, 2009.

[15] D. Marr and E. Hildreth, "Theory of edge detection," *Proceedings of the Royal Society of London. Series B, Biological Sciences*, vol. 207, no. 1167, pp. 187–217, 1980.

Chapter Ten

Unsupervised Seafloor Classification for Automatic Target Recognition

Oliver Daniell, Yvan Petillot and Scott Reed

Abstract

The performance of Automatic Target Recognition (ATR) algorithms in Sidescan Sonar (SSS) is largely dependent on the texture of the sea-floor. In regions of heavy clutter or sand ripples at target like scales, the majority of current ATR algorithms produce a large number of false alarms. This paper presents a novel approach to the characterisation of seafloor textures in SSS. Unlike existing seafloor classification algorithms, the authors derive a continuous measure of the complexity and anisotropy of seafloor texture. These properties are directly related to the difficulty of evaluating a region with an ATR algorithm. False alarms from an ATR can influence the performance of autonomous surveys where the vehicle adapts its mission plan to survey each detection. The algorithm presented in this paper can be applied in real time to eliminate these areas from the survey.

Keywords: Sidescan Sonar, Seafloor Classification, Target Recognition.

1. Introduction

This paper presents a method for the determination of the complexity and anisotropy of seafloor regions in sidescan sonar (SSS). The technique is used to evaluate Automatic Target Recognition (ATR) performance and to define regions in which the ATR performance is likely to be poor. ATR performance is known to suffer due to textures such as ripples and in regions with a high density of non-target clutter [1]. To predict ATR performance in these regions, a measure of the 'difficulty' of classifying an object with respect to the local seafloor texture is required. The complexity of the seafloor is defined as the average of a filter response in a region and the anisotropy as the variance of the filter response with respect to direction. This provides a continuous measure of both the clutter density and the ripplicity of a region. The wavelet scale can be chosen such that the image is evaluated at target like scales and it is shown that this correlates to the difficulty of evaluating a region with an ATR algorithm.

Regions which may result in a high false alarm rate are a serious problem both for autonomous missions and for operators. In an autonomous survey, the vehicle is programmed to perform a closer inspection of objects detected by the ATR. In regions of high clutter density this will result in unacceptable mission durations. This technique allows the vehicle to flag danger areas from an initial survey and it can then decide whether to return to those regions. For an operator a high false alarm rate can reduce confidence in the performance of an ATR. It is more desirable for the ATR to flag a 'no-go' area, than to return hundreds of contacts that the operator will have to search manually.

It is well established that wavelet features are a good descriptor of seafloor textures [2,3], both for supervised and unsupervised classification. These techniques can be used to evaluate the performance of ATR algorithms with respect to seafloor type. However, the results are dependent on the training set, or in the case of unsupervised clustering on the testing set. Therefore they are best applied to post-processing. The algorithm presented in this paper provides a continuous metric which is independent of the sonar type and data set, and can therefore be used to evaluate unseen seafloor textures during the mission.

The technique is similar to that of Williams [4] where the 'ripplicity' of a region is defined as the maximum difference between a directional filter and the 90 degree rotated version of the filter. While the filter set used by Williams is better suited to detecting ripples, it is not as well suited for general clutter detection. The Haar filters described in this paper are more prone to achieve false ripple detections due to objects, however these detections can be eliminated in the post-processing stage. Additionally, the authors measure of ripplicity requires a lower number of directional filters. The use of a few fast features provides a significant increase in performance and allows the algorithm to be run in real time on an embedded processor.

In the following sections, the theory is presented independently from the filter basis before specific implementation using Gabor and Haar filters are explored. It is demonstrated how the algorithm can be applied at multiple scales as a fast unsupervised seafloor classification algorithm and at a single scale to evaluate the performance of an ATR. Finally the authors discuss how the algorithm can be used to select the best ATR algorithm for a specific seafloor type and explore the use of the algorithm for vehicle autonomy.

2. Theory

Complexity and Anisotropy

Defining an angular resolution $\Delta\theta$ and an index k such that the angle $\theta = k \times \Delta\theta$. A set of filters $\psi_{s,k}$ are formed from the convolution of a 1D periodic function oriented along direction k with period $2s$ convolved with a 2D windowing function. The complexity C_s at scale s is defined by the energy of the filter response averaged over the set of directions k.

$$C_s(x,y) = \frac{\sum_{k=1}^{n} |\psi_{s,k}|^2}{n} \tag{1}$$

The anisotropy at scale s is defined by the variance of the filter responses over the set of directions k, divided by the complexity

$$A_s = \frac{\sum_{k=1}^{n} (|\psi_{s,k}|^2 - C_s)^2}{C_s(n-1)} \tag{2}$$

A mean filter is applied to the complexity and anisotropy maps. The filter is of a similar size to the the minimum seafloor regions which should be retained. We have implemented the technique using two different filters.

Complex Gabor Filters

The 2D Gabor filter is formed from a Gaussian window function modulated by a sinusoidal plane wave. A filter bank can be generated at scale s and direction k as

$$\psi_{s,k}(x,y) = \exp\left(-\frac{x'^2 + \gamma^2 y'^2}{2\sigma^2}\right) \exp\left(i\left(2\pi\frac{x'}{s/2}\right)\right) \tag{3}$$

where $x' = x\cos\theta + y\sin\theta$, $y' = -x\sin\theta + y\cos\theta$ and γ defines the ellipticity of the support of the Gabor function.

Positive results were achieved with an angular resolution of 30 degrees forming 6 directional filters per scale (Fig. 1). The naive approach to calculating the Gabor filter response at a pixel is found by convolving the filter with the image. This is computationally very expensive, however the

Gabor filters can be approximated as Haar filters. Haar filters are simple 2-level filters which can be calculated efficiently from integral images. This reduces the filter calculation to 6 lookups of the integral image.

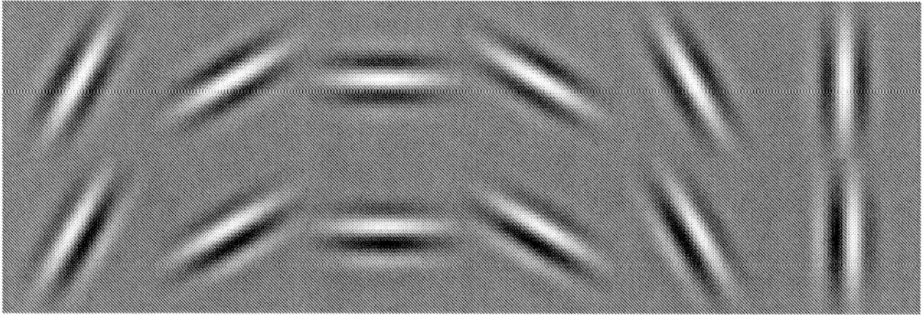

Figure 1: The complex Gabor filter bank.

Haar Filters

The 2D Haar filter is a rectangular window function modulated by a 1D step function.

$$\psi_{s,k}(x,y) = \begin{cases} 1 & 0 \leq x' < s \text{ and} -\gamma s \leq y' < \gamma s \\ -1 & -s \leq x' < 0 \text{ and} -\gamma s \leq y' < \gamma s \\ 0 & \text{otherwise.} \end{cases} \quad (4)$$

where $x' = x\cos\theta + y\sin\theta$, $y' = -x\sin\theta + y\cos\theta$ and σ defines the elongation of the support of the function.

The filters have the property that they can be calculated as the difference of the sum of two rectangular regions. As such they can be calculated directly from an integral image. An integral image is required for each rotation of the filter. To minimise the computational requirements a 0 degree and a 45 degree rotated integral image are created. This enables the calculation of 4 filters at 0,45,90 and 135 degree orientations (Fig. 2). This could be extended to other angles using the technique in [5].

Figure 2: The Haar Filter Bank.

Image Normalisation

The wavelet energy will be proportional to the amplitude of the original signal. Therefore, for consistent results to be achieved across all images the raw sonar signal should undergo the same pre-processing. In practice each sonar system applies a different preprocessing algorithm. This can be compensated for by normalising the mean background intensity across the test set. For seafloor classification it is desirable to remove sonar artefacts such as beam pattern while for ATR evaluation these artefacts should be treated as complex regions which are likely to degrade ATR performance. For seafloor classification a normalisation algorithm based on that of Capus et. al. [6] is used. While this mostly provides good results, small inaccuracies in the estimation of the altitude of the vehicle can sometimes result in the beam pattern being classified as ripples. For ATR evaluation, it is sufficient to estimate the TVG curve using polynomial approximation [7] or more simply a median filter in the across track direction.

A common problem for seafloor classification algorithms is that targets will influence the classification of the local seafloor. Approximating the anisotropy and complexity maps as a series of contours, target sized regions can be removed from the image by placing a threshold on the minimum contour area.

ATR Evaluation

It is common for ATR algorithms to generate a large number of false alarms in rippled regions or regions of high clutter density. While this is an inconvenience for an operator it can cause serious problems for autonomous surveys. The vehicle needs a method for ignoring regions which are likely to cause a large number of false alarms. A supervised ATR was trained on a data set with a largely flat seafloor and then applied to a different sonar type with large rippled and cluttered regions. This simulates a very poor ATR system. Without any post-processing the ATR achieves a false alarm density of 500 km^{-2}. A false alarm density of greater than 100 km^{-2} will result in an unacceptable mission duration due to the vehicle being required to perform a closer inspection of every target. Regions in which the false alarm density is unacceptable can be identified by plotting the seafloor complexity and anisotropy against the false alarm density. These regions can be removed from the survey or flagged for attention from an operator.

3. Results and Analysis

The complexity and anisotropy maps for the Gabor and Haar filters applied to the same image are shown in Fig. 3. The filter outputs were scaled linearly between 0 and 1 and mapped to intensity values. The complexity maps for both sets of filters are very similar with a clear differentiation between the complex and non-complex regions. The anisotropy map produced using the Gabor filters identifies most of the rippled regions but is not robust in regions where the ripples change direction, or do not have a constant period. The Gabor filters are also sensitive to anisotropic regions of the seafloor which would not be identified as ripples. This can easily be eliminated by only considering anisotropic regions which are also complex as ripples. Unlike the Gabor filter the Haar filter is only sensitive to a single period of the ripples. Therefore it is not as effected by changes in the direction or the period of the ripples. Conversely it is much more likely to produce false alarms due to objects on the seafloor, however these can easily be removed in the post-processing stage.

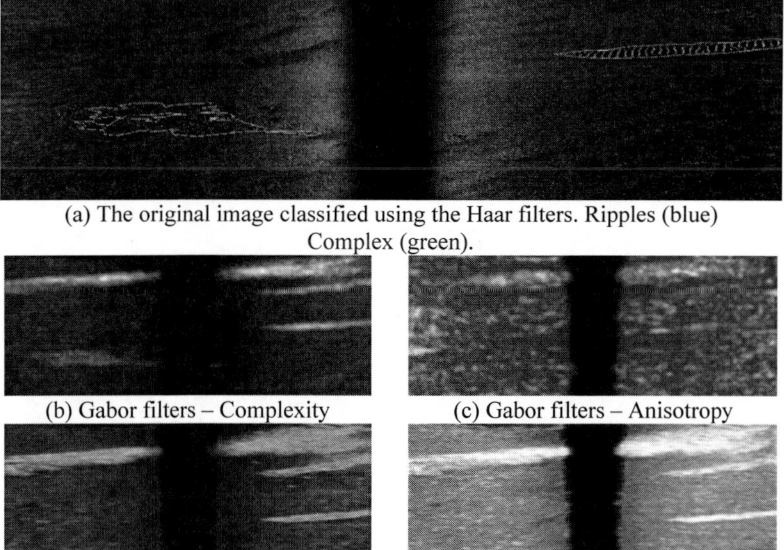

(a) The original image classified using the Haar filters. Ripples (blue) Complex (green).

(b) Gabor filters – Complexity

(c) Gabor filters – Anisotropy

(d) Haar filters – Complexity

(e) Haar filters – Anisotropy

Figure 3: Multi-scale filtering of seafloor with rippled and cluttered regions. The filters were run with scale s = 0.2m to 1m in increments of 0.2m.

Seafloor Classification

The complexity and anisotropy measure can be used to generate a robust seafloor segmentation and classification algorithm. A threshold can be applied to the filter output to identify the contours surrounding the complex regions as shown in Fig. 3(a). The threshold is dependent on the filter type and was set by finding the values that produced the best fit to a test data set of 10 images. This could be optimised by using an error minimisation technique but in practice a visual assessment is sufficient. The same threshold was applied to classify a test set consisting of 50 Edgetech, Klein and Marine Sonic images. A representative sample is shown in Fig. 4. Some of the ripples in the Edgetech image have been misclassified, this can be attributed to the fact that the scale of the ripples is similar to that of the resolution of the image.

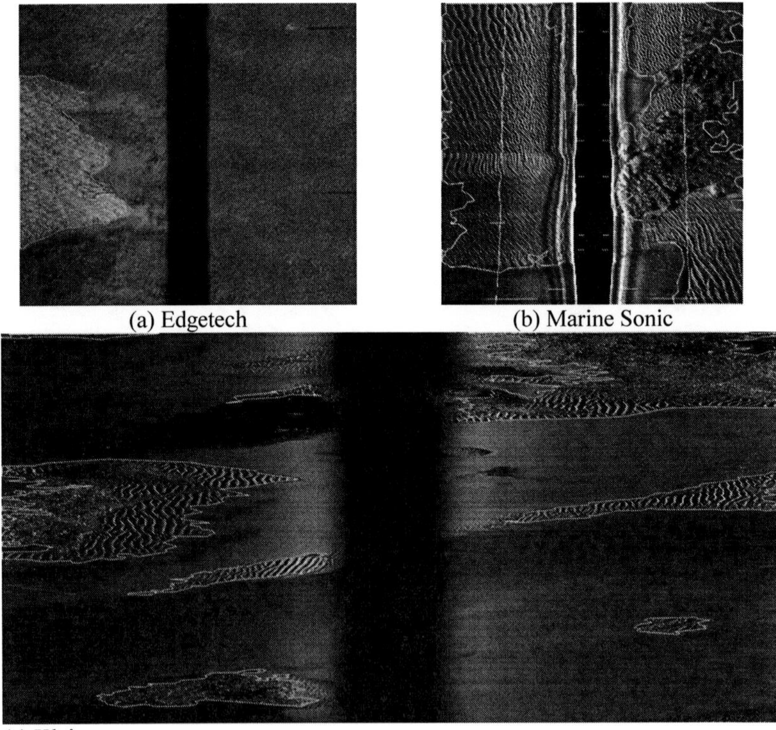

(a) Edgetech   (b) Marine Sonic

(c) Klein

Figure 4: Seafloor classification by applying a threshold to the complexity and anisotropy maps. The same threshold is robust across all sonar types. Ripples (blue) Complex (green).

Evaluation of ATR Results

An ATR algorithm was trained such that it has a high probability of generating false alarms, thereby producing sufficient statistics over a test set of 10 Klein images. The number of false alarms per km^2 with respect to the complexity and anisotropy of the seafloor is shown in Fig. 5. The authors measure of complexity and anisotropy are invariant between sonar type and dataset, therefore seafloor textures which are likely to produce an unacceptably high number of false alarms can be simply eliminated from the data set. In the authors data set this is best achieved by applying a threshold on the anisotropy score. In practice a joint optimisation on the complexity and anisotropy thresholds would be performed to maximise the coverage while obtaining a target false alarm rate. In this evaluation we have only considered false alarm density, however we intend to extend the evaluation to consider both false alarm density and the probability of detecting an object on a given seafloor.

We have assumed that running the algorithm at target-like scales will produce the results that best correlate with the false alarm density. Currently, we have not yet investigated the effect of running the algorithm at multiple scales for ATR evaluation. The complexity and anisotropy provide a very good measure of the difficulty of evaluating a region of the seafloor with our ATR. However, as both the ATR and the seafloor classification use similar Haar-like features we should apply some caution in extrapolating the results to other ATR systems.

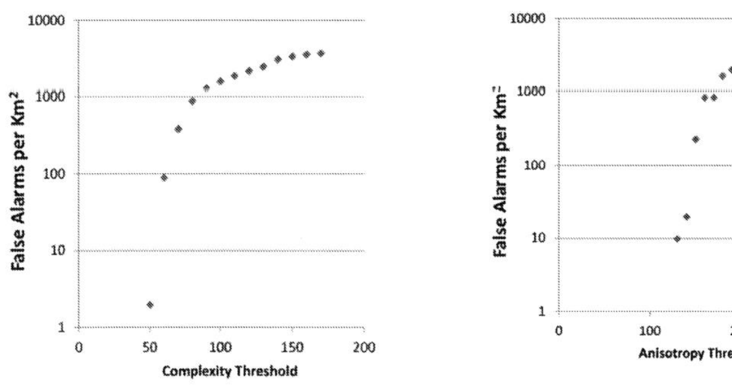

(a) Complexity   (b) Anisotropy

Figure 5: False alarm density for an ATR where the ATR is run only on regions which have complexity or anisotropy less than the threshold.

4. Conclusion

It has been demonstrated how two intrinsic properties of the seafloor can be used to evaluate the performance of an ATR algorithm on a specific region of seafloor. The majority of existing ATR algorithms suffer from a high false alarm density in rippled or cluttered areas of the seafloor. While this can be an inconvenience for an operator it is a serious problem for autonomous surveys where every detection must be investigated. By performing a joint optimisation on the complexity and anisotropy of a region with respect to the false alarm density the area than can be surveyed by the vehicle can be maximised, while achieving an acceptable number of false alarms.

The anisotropy and the complexity of regions of the seafloor can be characterised by the algorithm, at multiple scales. This allows simple seafloor classification by applying a threshold to the two measures. The threshold has been shown to be robust across data sets and sonar types. By combining the two measures with the intensity of the seafloor it is believed that a very fast and robust seafloor classification algorithm can be produced. This will be the subject of future work.

References

[1] J. Nelson and N. Kingsbury, "Fractal dimension based sand ripple suppression for mine hunting with sidescan sonar," in *Proc. SPIE*, pp. 1–6, 2010.

[2] D. P. Williams, "Unsupervised seabed segmentation of synthetic aperture sonar imagery via wavelet features and spectral clustering," *2009 16th IEEE International Conference on Image Processing (ICIP)*, pp. 557–560, Nov. 2009.

[3] I. Karoui, R. Fablet, J.-M. Boucher, and J.-M. Augustin, "Seabed Segmentation Using Optimized Statistics of Sonar Textures," in *MTS/IEEE Proc. Oceans Conf.*, vol. 47, pp. 1621–1631, June 2009.

[4] D. Williams and E. Coiras, "On sand ripple detection in synthetic aperture sonar imagery," *Acoustics Speech and Signal Processing (ICASSP), IEEE International Conference on*, pp. 1074 – 1077, 2010.

[5] C. Messom, "Fast and efficient rotated haar-like features using rotated integral images," *Australasian Conference on Robotics*, 2006.

[6] C. Capus, I. Ruiz, and Y. Petillot, "Compensation for changing beam pattern and residual tvg effects with sonar altitude variation for sidescan mosaicing and classification," in *Proc. European Conference on Underwater Acoustics*, 2004.

[7] P. Cervenka and C. de Moustier, "Sidescan sonar image processing techniques," in *MTS/IEEE Proc. Oceans Conf.*, vol. 18, pp. 108–122, Apr. 1993.

Session IV

Survey and MCM Operations

Chaired by Michel Couillard
Centre for Maritime Research and Experimentation

CHAPTER ELEVEN

ATR:
AN ENABLER FOR MULTI-VEHICLE AUTONOMOUS MCM OPERATIONS

SCOTT REED, PEDRO PATRON,
JOSÉ VASQUEZ AND OLIVER DANIELL

Abstract

Unmanned Underwater Vehicles (UUVs) are routinely used in Mine Countermeasures (MCM) operations as data collecting assets. Current on-board autonomy and decision-making capabilities are limited. This is predominantly due to current limitations in Automatic Target Recognition (ATR) algorithms which produce unacceptable levels of false alarms within complex or new environments.

The first part of the paper will present SeeByte's ATR system for sidescan sonar systems. Results are presented on real data from a variety of sidescan sonar models including Edgetech and Marine Sonic. The issue of ATR training and how ATR performance is often strongly correlated to the similarity between the training and test data is also discussed.

The second section of the paper considers the importance of ATR as a key autonomy enabler. Results are presented from SeeByte's recent MCM multi-vehicle operations. In these operations, the ATR is used to dynamically add mission objectives to the plan, requesting that a capable and available vehicle re-inspects each target to confirm identity. SeeByte's NEPTUNE product allows multiple vehicles to collaboratively execute different components of a MCM mission in parallel. The ATR provides key input into the mission plan. This highlights the need for on-board ATR systems to produce reliable results with an acceptable false alarm rate.

Keywords: ATR, Autonomy Enabler, Multi-Vehicle Operations.

1. Introduction

Unmanned Underwater Vehicles (UUVs) are used routinely in Mine Countermeasures (MCM) operations. Commercial off-the-shelf (COTS) UUVs are available which are man portable and can carry multiple payloads. These include Sidescan Sonar (SSS), Forward Looking Sonar (FLS), video and Synthetic Aperture Sonar (SAS). The UUVs can conduct their operations close to the seafloor, are easily deployable and provide high resolution, long range sensor data. This sensor data is of sufficient resolution to allow an operator or autonomy module to identify mine-like threats. Navigation sensors allow mine threats to be localized and re-acquired.

Autonomy relies on the vehicle being able to localize itself within its environment which may be cluttered, changing and unknown. The vehicle's raw sensor data must be converted into meaningful information upon which autonomous decisions can be made. This process is often called Automatic Target Recognition (ATR).

Historically, research into ATR has focused on developing monolithic classifiers which are slow to train and require huge amounts of example data. These models are generally static, performing well in simple scenarios but unable to adapt to changing environments or object appearance. The first section of this paper will detail SeeByte's current ATR capabilities for Autonomous Underwater Vehicle (AUV) mountable sensors.

MCM operations currently include a human operator in the loop. The mission is programmed as a series of waypoints. The UUV SSS data is analysed post-mission by a human operator. Any response requires that the UUV is re-deployed. Extensive research has been conducted in developing on-board ATR [1-4] which can process the sensor data in real-time and identify possible mine threats. Integrating further autonomy into MCM operations, with multiple vehicles, requires that the UUVs are able to make decisions, re-plan and allocate mission tasks dynamically [5]. The ATR provides critical input to the autonomy system for MCM operations since much of the dynamic mission re-planning will be based on possible mine threats. The success of the on-board autonomy is dependent on the input from the ATR being reliable and not containing multiple false alarms.

Moving mission planning from operator-driven waypoint planning to goal based mission planning [6] allows the operator to provide the high-level aim of the UUV mission. Specific tasks relevant within the Search Classify Map (SCM), Reacquire Inspect (RI), Neutralise (N) phases of an operation, are allocated for each vehicle based on capability and mission constraints [7].

The second component of the paper looks at SeeByte's NEPTUNE product. This is a goal based mission planning module allowing multiple, heterogeneous vehicles to be run in parallel to complete a MCM mission. The role of the ATR module within this system is discussed with results from recent UUV trials presented.

2. ATR

The majority of ATR algorithms operate using separate detection and classification phases. The detection phase highlights possible objects. The classification phase considers each detection and makes a decision on whether a mine is present. Commonly used detection methods include statistical algorithms [8], geometric algorithms [9] and saliency [10].

Classification algorithms can broadly be split into supervised and unsupervised approaches. Unsupervised methods typically require a model of the target. Since the algorithm is not trained, the decision making algorithms are usually simple and versatile to changes in sonar [2,11]. Supervised algorithms require a representative sample of target images. These classifiers can learn the background feature distribution as well as the object features, improving performance on seafloor types which are similar to those contained in the training data. There is no guarantee that these results will generalize and transfer to other seafloor types. The performance of the supervised classification algorithm is heavily dependent on the features used. Typical features involve statistical, geometric [11], filter responses [12] and spectral responses.

SeeByte use a model-based ATR approach to a supervised model using filter responses. Previous work into the use of Haar features [12] has shown that these features demonstrate strong performance on simple symmetric objects. However they are not invariant to grazing or aspect angle. A reduced performance is seen for objects which change appearance considerably under rotation or changes to range. Cylindrical shapes typically see a reduction in performance due to the extreme variability in appearance under rotation (see Fig.1).

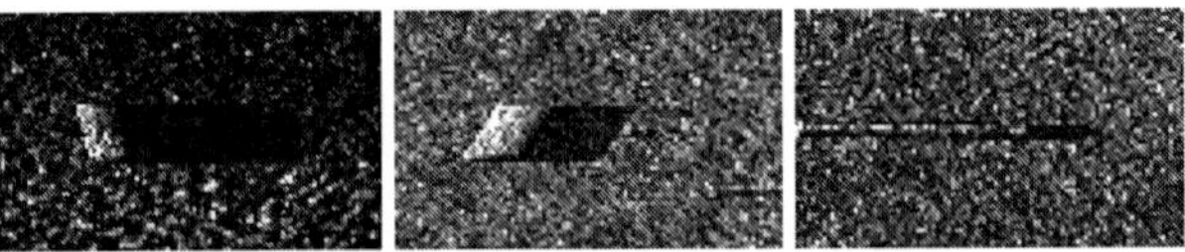

Figure 1: Simulated cylinders at different angles of rotation. The appearance of the cylinder changes significantly under rotation.

The reduction in performance observed for objects which are not symmetric with regard to rotation is dealt with by using a second stage of classification. A rule-based classification system uses geometrical and statistical features extracted from the highlight and shadow regions of each target to dismiss false alarms.

The SeeByte ATR has been trained on data from multiple sidescan sonar systems. Examples from Edgetech and Marinesonics imagery may be seen below in Fig. 2. The Marinesonics image shows a cylindrical target that has not been detected due to it being rotated perpendicular to the direction of the vehicle.

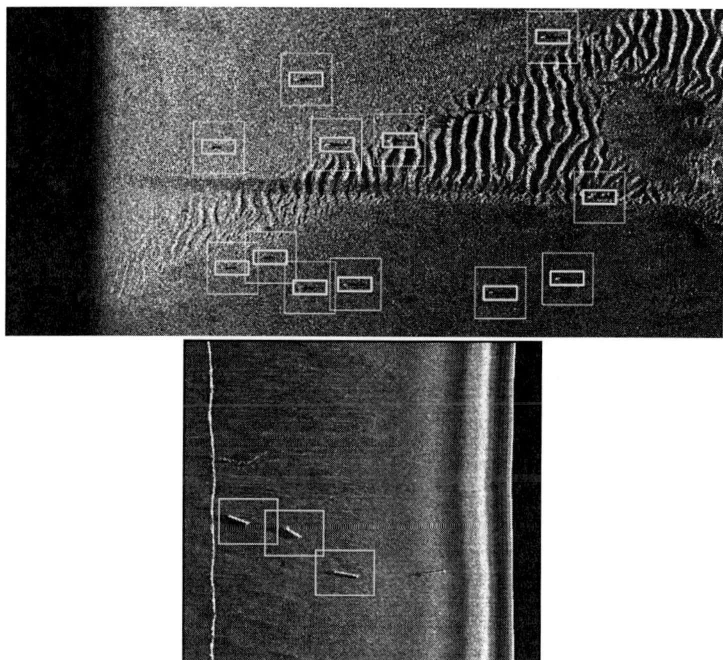

Figure 2: Examples of the ATR on Marine Sonic and Edgetech imagery.

3. ATR training and evaluation

Supervised classification is heavily dependent on using representative data to train the system. Obtaining large quantities of real mine targets is time-consuming and expensive.

SeeByte are evaluating the feasibility of training the ATR using a mixture of real and simulated data. PATT is an augmented reality based approach for the evaluation of MCM capabilities [13]. It may be used to assess the performance of either an operator or an ATR system. It may also be used for training; either as an operator aid or as a provider of ground truth data for supervised ATR models. The system has three principle modes of operation. In the first, targets are randomly placed across the battlespace, with multiple targets inserted into the sidescan imagery from a mission. This mode is principally used for providing robust, quantitative statistical information on either the operator or ATR capabilities, producing a PD/PFA output for the environment being considered. In the second mode, more realistic conditions are employed with fewer mines inserted into the data. This mode operates more as a realistic "war game" but can also be used to test data association and fusion work; the mission navigation information of the mission is respected during the mine insertion process so that targets appear in all relevant imagery at the appropriate range and orientation. In the third mode, the sonar simulator component of PATT is not used and no targets are added. The operator may input ground truth files from a real MCM operation which may be used to assess an operator or ATR. In this mode, PATT's analysis modules are used to provide statistical information that would be otherwise very difficult and laborious to obtain.

The augmented reality approach of PATT relies on accurately adding simulated man-made objects into real sidescan data while respecting the seafloor topology. Producing realistic simulated data that is representative of the huge diversity of clutter and seafloor observed in sidescan image is very hard and PATT gets around this by using real sidescan data. PATT therefore takes advantage of the "best of both worlds" – targets may be readily simulated for meaningful results while real sonar data alleviates the need to fully simulate a complex and unknown environment. Examples of the sonar rendering process may be seen below in Fig.3.

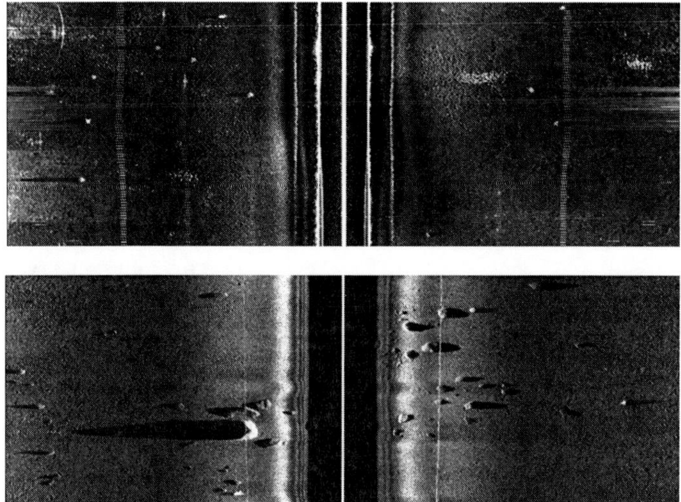

Figure 3: Examples of the mine rendering processing in PATT.

4. ATR and collaborative vehicle operations

SeeByte's SeeTrack NEPTUNE (Navy EOD Planning Tool for UMS Network) is an adaptive planning tool for optimizing the execution of multi-vehicle UUV operations. NEPTUNE supports high-level goal-based mission descriptions and matching of mission requirements against vehicle(s) capabilities. It also includes behaviours capable of adapting the mission based on changes in the environment, assets and c) mission objectives. The system is built around open interfaces to generic embedded services, and vehicles.

Within the MCM domain, typical UUV operations revolve around an initial Search-Classify-Map (SCM) phase of operations where the collected sensor data is processed by an operator or an ATR module to highlight possible mine threats. These identified targets are then re-inspected using a Re-acquire / Identify (RI) search pattern. The process is time consuming and sequential. On-board ATR offers the opportunity to run the SCM and RI components of the MCM mission in parallel with different vehicles taking on mission tasks based on their availability and capabilities. The entire process is based on the ATR providing a low false alarm rate. If a high false alarm rate is observed, the vehicle(s) will be requested to conduct RI search patterns on non-mine threats, increasing mission time and reducing the benefits provided by the multi-vehicle autonomy framework. The dependency on ATR is discussed after a summary of NEPTUNE.

NEPTUNE capabilities

The NEPTUNE framework provides an open architecture system that allows the integration of third party autonomy behaviours, functions and vehicles. The adaptive, goal based mission planning tool receives a high level mission goal and allocates task based on the individual vehicle capabilities. New tasks may be added in-mission (for example by the ATR), and the execution of a task may be dynamically re-planned based on external factors such as the environment. Key capabilities are listed below:

- Reduction of the cognitive load on the operator by enabling high-level description of mission objectives using a goal-based mission planning approach.
- Automated discovery of asset capabilities that detaches operator from the specifics of the individual assets; allowing him/her to concentrate on 'what' he/she wants from the mission rather than 'how' to execute the mission.
- Coordination of asset capabilities for dynamic in-stride asset management while in water in order to identify the best solution for accomplishing the mission objectives.
- The operator is able to simply define convex irregular polygonal shapes for performing searches over complex areas that do not fit into the classical rectangular-shape lawnmower patterns.
- Minimise of the opportunity for stranding the vehicle on the beach by providing shallow water turn around.
- Maximisation of sensor data quality for survey patterns by dynamically adapting lawnmower patterns to sensed water current direction.
- Maximisation of the survivability of the vehicles by defining exclusion zones that the assets cannot enter during the execution of the mission.
- Minimisation of the opportunity of collision between assets sharing common water space by performing transits between objectives at different depths and broadcasting dynamic exclusion zones over on-going mission objectives.

- Increase of operational tempo by enabling simultaneous Search and Re-acquisition phases by providing embedded ATR capabilities and coordination of multiple assets on a single mission.
- Maximising information exchange and operator awareness by enabling acoustic communications relays between assets located beyond the acoustic communication maximum range.
- Maximising the number of contact views for target identification by providing spiral-shaped variable range multi-aspect RI pattern.
- Reduction of time needed for post-mission analysis by generating a single common report from all the logs of the assets involved in the mission using a common operator interface.

NEPTUNE results

This section shows collaborative behaviour between multiple UUV's using the NEPTUNE system. Results are presented using two simulator scenarios which allow some of the different NEPTUNE functionality to be described. Within Figs 4 and 5, common representations are used. Firstly, the heading of each vehicles is described by a green line. The trajectory of each vehicle is shown by a dark blue line. Deployment points for the two vehicles are shown as a green open circle. The final recovery point for each vehicle is shown as a red open circle. Static exclusion zones which neither vehicle may enter at any time are described as purple polygons. These have been entered by the operator *a priori*, as unsafe areas for the vehicles. Targets, either known in advance or detected dynamically by an ATR, are represented by filled red circles.

Within Fig. 4, vehicle A is conducting a lawnmower inspection behaviour within an irregularly shaped survey region and has only completed the bottom section of the mission. The remaining portion of the survey region becomes a dynamic exclusion zone for the second vehicle. This is represented in the figure as a cyan polygon within the RI vehicles image. Each vehicle checks for the presence of dynamic exclusion zones prior to carrying out a task to ensure there is no chance of a collision. Within Fig. 4, vehicle B is conducting a RI behaviour of an object. The area around the object becomes a dynamic exclusion zone for the other vehicle and is represented by a cyan polygon in vehicle A image. Similarly, the *a priori* known target within vehicle A's SCM survey region may not be re-acquired and identified by Vehicle B until vehicle A has completed its inspection.

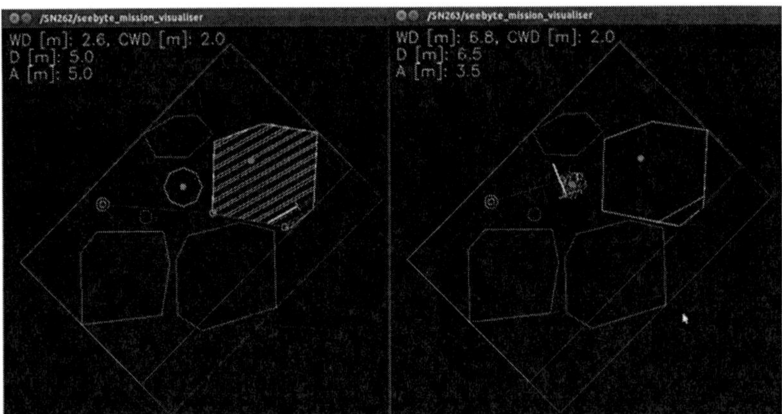

Figure 4: Two vehicles conducting a MCM mission. The image on the left is the visualization for the SCM vehicle (A). The image on the right describes the RI vehicle (B).

Fig. 5 shows 2 vehicles conducting autonomy behaviours around static exclusion zones. Vehicle A within Fig. 5 is conducting the SCM survey. As before, static exclusion zones are described by purple polygons. Vehicle A can be seen transiting around the exclusion zones to approach the area that needs to be surveyed. Vehicle B can be seen inspecting an *a priori* known target that sits within Vehicle A's survey region. Vehicle B is allowed into this area because Vehicle A's survey has been completed and the initial dynamic exclusion zone that would have existed for vehicle B has been removed.

Other vehicle autonomy behaviours are running concurrently. One example is the avoid-short mechanism that persistently monitors the vehicle depth. If either of the vehicle assets approach critical water depth, the avoid short behaviour takes pre-cautionary action and issues behaviour waypoints that lead the asset back into deeper water. If no suitable waypoints can be found, the behaviour will be terminated. Examples of other behaviours that will be input into NEPTUNE include aligning the assets with sea current and /or sand ripples.

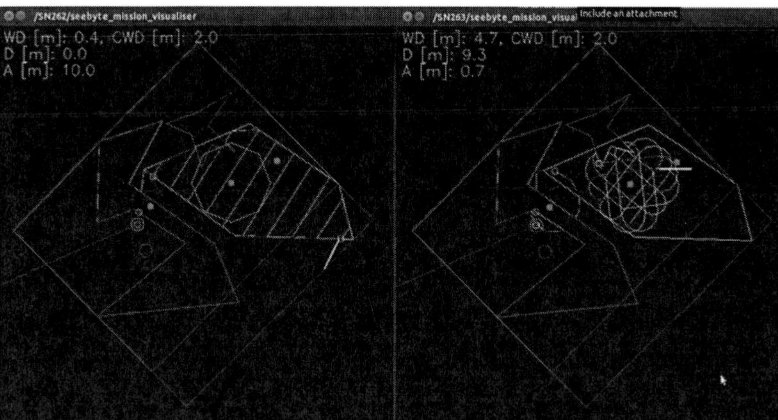

Figure 5: Two vehicles conducting behaviours around static exclusion zones. Vehicle A (left image) is the survey vehicle. Vehicle B (right image) is the RI vehicle.

ATR for Autonomy Operations

Successful autonomy operations where the on-board ATR is able to add new mission objectives is dependent on the ATR not flagging multiple false alarms. A high density of false alarms will result in many automated RI tasks being requested, increasing mission time and reducing operator trust into the system. One area of research within SeeByte is the automated measurement of clutter density [14]. ATR systems are now able to provide robust PD/PFA results on flat, simple seafloors. As the seafloor becomes more complex and the scale of the clutter approaches that of the mine targets being searched for, the number of false alarms increases dramatically. Autonomous operations using ATR modules will require that the clutter density is automatically determined and used to modify the ATR output. One possible initial scenario is that the ATR is automatically disabled for high clutter areas and alerts the operator during PMA of the areas not processed in-mission. SeeByte are actively researching this area and looking to insert this into NEPTUNE as a behaviour. An example of clutter density estimation may be seen below in Fig. 6. This will be discussed in more detail in [14].

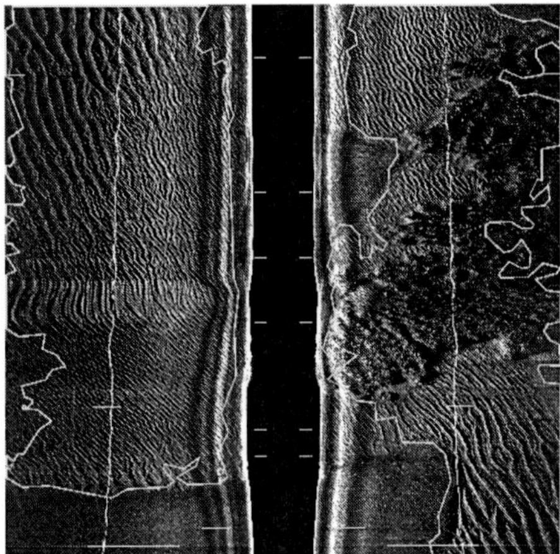

Figure 6: Clutter density estimates are required to modify ATR output during autonomous operations.

5. Conclusions

This paper first presented the SeeByte ATR for sidescan sonar systems with results shown on Edgetech and MarineSonics Sidescan data. The section was concluded with looking at the issues around training and evaluating supervised sidescan sonar systems. The second part looked at multi-vehicle autonomous operations and the importance of on-board ATRs providing robust detection rates while maintaining a low false alarm rate. The need for a robust clutter density measurement was highlighted so that the ATR's behaviour can be adapted in-mission based on the environment.

References

[1] M. Mignotte, C. Collet, P. Perez, and P. Bouthemy, "Hybrid genetic optimization and statistical model-based approach for the classification of shadow shapes in sonar imagery," *IEEE Trans. Pattern Anal. Machine Intell.*, vol. 22, no. 2, pp. 129–141, Feb. 2000.
[2] S. Reed, Y. Petillot, and J. Bell, "A model based approach to the detection and classification of mines in sidescan sonar," *Applied Optics*, 2003.
[3] I. Quidu, P. Malkasse, G. Burel, and P. Vilbe, "Mine classification using a hybrid set of descriptors," *OCEANS MTS/IEEE Conf. and Exhibition,* vol. 1, pp. 291–297, 2000.
[4] J. A. Fawcett, "Image-based classification of side-scan sonar detections," presented at *CAD/CAC Conf.*, Halifax, Nova Scotia, Canada, Nov. 2001.

[5] S. Reed, J. Wood, P-Y. Mignotte, "SeeByte Autonomy delivers Smart ROV for Successful Ship Hull Inspection", *AUVSI North America*, Denver, USA, August 2010.

[6] P. Patrón, D. M. Lane, and Y. R. Petillot, "Continuous mission plan adaptation for autonomous vehicles: balancing effort and reward" in *4th Workshop on Planning and Plan Execution for Real-World Systems, 19th International Conference on Automated Planning and Scheduling*, Greece, September 2009, pp. 50–57.

[7] C. Sotzing, D. M. Lane, "Improving the Co-ordination Efficiency of Limited Communcation Multi-Autonomous Underwater Vehicle Operatons using a Multi-agent Architecture", *Journal of Field Robotics,* 27(4), pp. 412-429, 2010.

[8] J. Bell, Y. Petillot, S. Reed, E. Coiras, P.Y. Mignotte, and H. Rohou. Target Recognition in Synthetic Aperture and High Resolution Sidescan Sonar", *in IET Proc. High Resolution Imaging and Target Classification*, pp. 99-106, 2006.

[9] C. Rao, K. Mukherjee, S. Gupta, A. Ray, and S. Phoha, "Underwater Mine Detection using Symbolic Pattern Analysis of Sidescan Sonar Images," *in Proceedings of the American Control Conference*, 2009.

[10] L. M. Linnett, S. J. Clarke, C. St. J. Reid, and A. D. Tress, "Monitoring of the seabed using sidescan sonar and fractal processing," *Proceedings of the Underwater Acoustics Group*, pages 49-64, 1993.

[11] E. Dura, J. Bell, and D.M. Lane, "Superellipse Fitting for the Recovery and Classification of Mine-Like Shapes in Sidescan Sonar Images", *IEEE Journal of Oceanic Engineering*, 33[4]:434-444, 2008.

[12] J. Sawas, Y. Petillot, and Y. Pailhas, "Cascade of Boosted Classifiers for Rapid Detection of Underwater Objects", *In Proc. European Conference on Underwater Acoustics*, 2010.

[13] P.Y. Mignotte, J. Vazquez, S. Reed, "PATT: A Performance Analysis and Training Tool for the Assessment and Adaptive Planning of Mine Counter Measure (MCM) operations, *IEEE OCEANS,* 2009.

[14] O. Daniell, Y. Petillot, S. Reed, "Unsupervised seafloor classification for automatic target recognition", *iCoURS 2012 International Conference on Underwater Remote Sensing*, 2012.

CHAPTER TWELVE

PERFORMANCE ASSESSMENT OF AN ADAPTIVE AUV SURVEY

MICHEL COUILLARD AND DAVID P. WILLIAMS

Abstract

Traditional underwater surveys employing side-looking sonars are designed by assuming quality data will be collected out to a fixed range. However, environmental factors at sea introduce variability into the coverage actually achieved. To address this issue, the NATO Undersea Research Centre (NURC) has developed an adaptive survey algorithm for an autonomous underwater vehicle (AUV) equipped with a synthetic aperture sonar (SAS). This algorithm allows the AUV to react to *in situ* data and adjust its route accordingly to ensure complete coverage of the area of interest is achieved. This adaptive strategy, which assumes no *a priori* knowledge, is compared to pre-planned approaches in an extensive performance assessment. The study demonstrates the power of the adaptive strategy, which in certain scenarios can match the optimal pre-planned survey that assumes perfect knowledge of sonar performance. Results show that the adaptive survey algorithm outperforms traditional surveys designed with a fixed sonar range, by guaranteeing complete coverage while limiting the travel distance (or time) required to do so. The assessment is supported by real data collected at sea.

Keywords: Autonomous Underwater Vehicle (AUV), Performance Assessment, Autonomy, Adaptive Surveying, Sonar Data.

1. Introduction

Autonomous underwater vehicles (AUVs) equipped with synthetic aperture sonar (SAS) systems are quickly becoming fundamental tools for seabed mapping applications, as they provide high resolution imagery independent of range from the sensor, with high area coverage rates. These side-looking sonar systems can be used for a wide range of applications, including habitat mapping [1], seabed classification [2], mine detection [3] and pipeline monitoring [4]. The standard approach to seabed mapping is to conduct a pre-planned survey consisting of parallel tracks based on the assumption that satisfactory sonar coverage is achieved for a fixed range on either side of the AUV's tracks. In reality, environmental and operational conditions such as multipath [5] and adverse vehicle motion [6] introduce variability in the range to which quality sonar data can be collected. If this range is underestimated in a pre-planned survey, the same area of seabed is imaged multiple times, decreasing the coverage rate and causing more time and resources to be expended during the mission. If this range is overestimated, there will be a lack of sonar data for portions of the mission area, thereby making tasks like object detection and classification [7, 8] impossible in these regions. An example of a SAS image with degraded quality at long range is shown in Fig. 1.

To account for the variability of sonar performance during a mission and to address the limitations of pre-planned surveys, the NATO Undersea Research Centre (NURC) has developed an adaptive route planning algorithm that exploits through-the-sensor data collected during a mission and guarantees full coverage of a search area [9]. This algorithm takes advantage of the ping-to-ping cross-correlations generated by the SAS displaced phase center antenna (DPCA) motion estimation algorithm [6]. These correlation coefficients can be used as real-time estimates of the quality of the sonar images being collected. By using this *in situ* sonar performance information, the algorithm adaptively selects which AUV tracks to execute with the goal of ensuring sufficient quality of the resulting sonar data.

This paper quantifies the performance of the NURC adaptive survey algorithm when compared to traditional pre-planned surveys. First, a baseline performance assessment is conducted by deriving analytically optimal pre-planned surveys when perfect knowledge of the true sonar ranges is assumed. Then, real data collected at sea are used to assess the operational performance of the adaptive algorithm for real operations. The unique dataset used for this analysis was collected during three sea trials conducted under different environmental and operational conditions.

The remainder of this paper is organized as follows. Section 2 describes traditional pre-planned surveys, while Section 3 summarizes the adaptive survey algorithm. Section 4 introduces the empirical dataset collected at sea and used in this study. Section 5 presents a performance assessment of the new adaptive survey algorithm when compared to traditional surveys. Concluding remarks are made in Section 6.

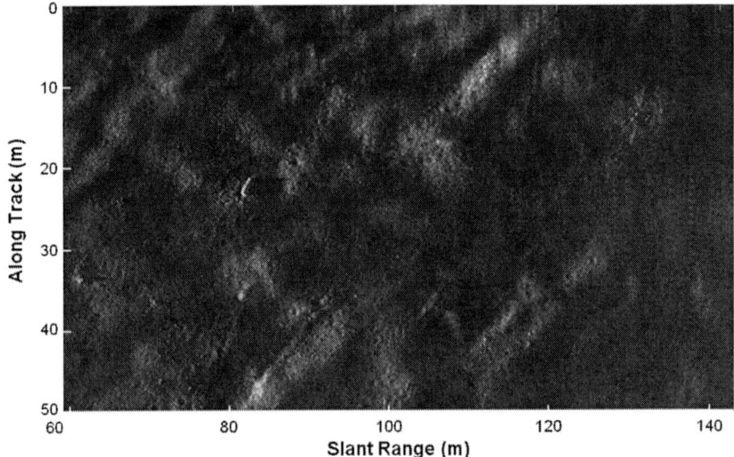

Figure 1: An example of a SAS image. A cylindrical object can be seen at short range with its characteristic highlight and shadow. Deterioration of the image quality can be seen at long range.

2. Traditional survey planning

The traditional survey planning approach when using an AUV equipped with a side-looking sonar is to create a series of parallel tracks referred to as a "lawn-mowing" pattern [10, 11]. Each vehicle track enables imaging of the regions to the port and starboard side of the vehicle, and these regions are referred to as "swaths." On each side, there exists a pair of minimum and maximum plan ranges, $r_{\min}$ and $r_{\max}$, bounding the region where quality data can be collected. As $r_{\min} > 0\ m$, each track executed by the AUV leaves a gap in coverage, so an additional track is needed to fill this gap. This is illustrated in Fig. 2. When $r_{\min}$ and $r_{\max}$ are fixed, one can analytically derive the number and positions of the tracks needed to completely cover a given rectangular search area.

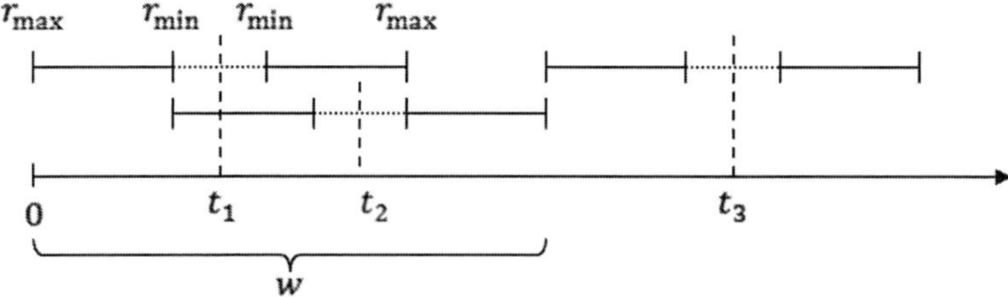

Figure 2: Traditional survey planning conducted with side-looking sonars. The search area begins at $t_0 = 0$ and the position of each track is given by t_i, $i = 1, \dots, N$. Around each track, r_{min} and r_{max} define the regions where quality data can be collected and this creates coverage gaps around $t_i \pm r_{min}$. These gaps can be covered by a minimum number of tracks n ($n = 2$ in this example), covering a width w.

Let N be the total number of tracks needed to cover the total search area width W. This width W is perpendicular to the direction in which the AUV tracks are oriented. Also, denote by $\lceil x \rceil$ and $\lfloor x \rfloor$ the ceiling and floor functions, respectively. Fig. 2 shows that a minimum number of survey tracks will need to be grouped in order to fill in the gaps left between $\pm r_{min}$ around each track. This minimum number of grouped tracks, n, is given by:

$$n = \left\lceil \frac{2r_{min}}{r_{max} - r_{min}} \right\rceil + 1 \, . \tag{1}$$

Each group of n tracks completely covers a width w given by:

$$w = (n - 1)(r_{max} - r_{min}) + 2r_{max} \, . \tag{2}$$

To design a survey covering the entire search area, one simply needs to add groups of tracks covering a width w until the total search area width W is reached. Using (1) and (2), the total number of tracks needed to cover the total width W is given by:

$$N = n \left\lfloor \frac{W}{w} \right\rfloor + \min\left(\left\lceil \frac{R}{r_{max} - r_{min}} \right\rceil , n \right) , \tag{3}$$

where R is the remainder of the total width W not covered by a whole number of widths w and is given by:

$$R = W - w \left\lfloor \frac{W}{w} \right\rfloor \, . \tag{4}$$

If the total width W can be covered by a whole number of widths w, then (4) yields $R = 0$. Finally, if the survey is assumed to begin at the left edge of the survey area, identified by $t_0 = 0$, the position of track i, $i = 1, \ldots, N$ is given by t_i:

$$t_i = \left\lceil \frac{i}{n} \right\rceil (r_{\max} + r_{\min}) + i(r_{\max} - r_{\min}) - r_{\max}. \tag{5}$$

Being able to derive pre-planned surveys analytically allows one to investigate the area coverage achieved by a survey designed with an assumed maximum sonar range that may differ from the true maximum sonar range. Results for a standard survey area of 2 km by 2 km and a fixed minimum sonar range of 40m are shown in Fig. 3. First, let r_a be the assumed maximum sonar range to which quality data are collected and let r_t be the true maximum sonar range. If $r_a = r_t$, represented by the diagonal of the matrix shown in Fig. 3, the pre-planned survey will yield the minimum number of tracks needed to achieve complete coverage and the area will be covered completely. This is the optimal case as no alternative survey strategy can achieve complete coverage while using fewer tracks. If $r_a < r_t$, the sonar coverage is underestimated. Although complete coverage will still be achieved in this scenario, as shown by the area above the diagonal in Fig. 3, the survey will include extra tracks beyond the minimum number required to achieve complete coverage. Finally, if $r_a > r_t$, the sonar coverage is overestimated, causing the survey to result in incomplete coverage. This is shown in Fig. 3 by the area below the diagonal where the fraction of the survey area covered is smaller than 1. Coverage gaps are not operationally acceptable as they require secondary surveys to fill-in the gaps and result in significantly increased mission time.

These results for a survey conducted with $r_a \neq r_t$ motivate the use of an adaptive survey algorithm able to take into account *in situ* information about the true maximum sonar range. Such an adaptive algorithm was designed by NURC and is briefly described in the next section.

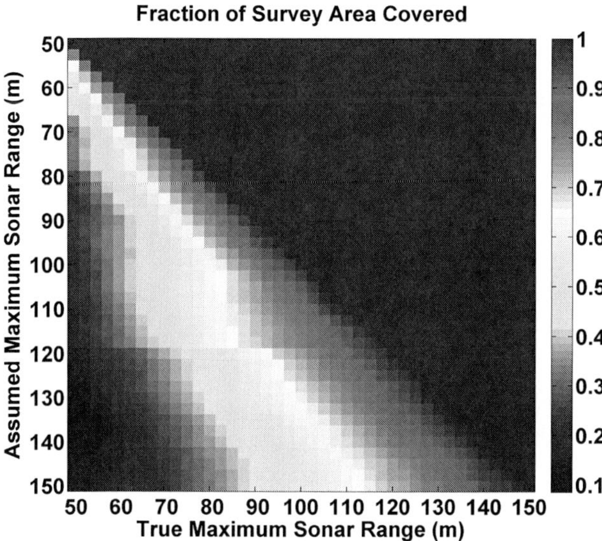

Figure 3: Area coverage for a pre-planned survey as a function of the assumed and true maximum sonar ranges. The minimum sonar range is fixed at **40 m**.

3. Adaptive survey algorithm

To account for the limitations of traditional pre-planned surveys, NURC developed an adaptive algorithm determining the track locations of a survey based on *in situ* data collected as the mission progresses [9]. Ping-to-ping correlation values, as a function of range, are used to adaptively determine the true maximum sonar range to which quality data is achieved, and the locations of subsequent tracks are based on that information. First, the mission area is discretized into a finite set of parallel regions, or swaths, and the line segments demarcating these swaths form the set of admissible tracks. User defined increments of 10m are typically used to discretize the search area. The set of tracks is the universe of possible tracks from which the AUV is allowed to adaptively choose during the survey. Since there is no human supervision during the onboard decision-making process, this discretization provides a layer of safety that prevents unexpected commands from being made.

To begin the survey, an initial track near one edge of the mission area is selected. As the vehicle is executing a track, the AUV's onboard processor computes the correlation value between consecutive pings at a given range, on each side of the sonar. The range and sonar side associated with a correlation value, when coupled with the track information, uniquely determine the swath to which each correlation value corresponds. As the mission progresses, the algorithm keeps track of the mean correlation coefficient value for each swath. If this mean value is above a set image quality threshold, the corresponding swath is considered to have been imaged successfully.

Once the current mission coverage has been updated, a new track must be selected. In order to do so, the utility of running each track in the track universe is calculated. This utility is defined as the difference between a benefit term and a cost term. The benefit expresses the improved coverage expected to be achieved by the next track and is based on the historical imaging success rate [9]. This success rate is the ratio of the number of tracks that resulted in quality data for a given range and sonar side over the total number of tracks executed up to that point. That is, the benefit of each track is adapted *in situ* based on the data quality collected during the mission thus far. The cost of running each particular track is a function of the transit distance required to reach the new track from the vehicle's current location. This distance cost is weighted by a scaling factor designed to reduce the transit penalty as the mission progresses, and more and more of the seabed swaths are covered.

Finally, the track for which the utility is maximized is selected as the next track to be executed. This entire process is repeated until quality sonar data has been collected for the entire mission area. It is worth noting that the track selection process in the version of the NURC adaptive algorithm used in this study differs from [9] by considering only potential tracks that would have a non-zero probability of covering the "first" uncovered swath. This uncovered swath will be the left-most uncovered swath if it is assumed that the AUV begins the mission on the left side of the survey area. With this constraint, the mission progresses in such a way that a gap in coverage is immediately filled in by the subsequent track. Therefore, it effectively eliminates the need to transit back across the survey area to fill in gaps, since the gaps are immediately filled on the initial pass.

4. Data collected at sea

Since 2008, NURC has collected a large set of high-resolution SAS data in various underwater environments using the MUSCLE AUV (shown in Fig. 4) equipped with a 300 kHz interferometric SAS with a 60 kHz bandwidth. These data include DPCA ping-to-ping correlation coefficients [6] for various sonar parameters, bottom types and water depths. Three SAS sea trials are of special interest for assessing the performance of the adaptive survey algorithm. The representative subsets of ping-to-ping correlation coefficients as a function of range selected from each sea trial are summarized in Fig. 5. The variability of the correlation coefficients is summarized by using the median (solid line), the 25th and 75th percentiles (dashed lines) and the 9th and 91st percentiles (dotted lines) of each dataset. If the observed distributions were Gaussian, these five curves would be uniformly spaced. This variability is due in part to the motion of the AUV, the variation of the surface condition and the variation of the local seabed composition.

Figure 4: The MUSCLE AUV being deployed.

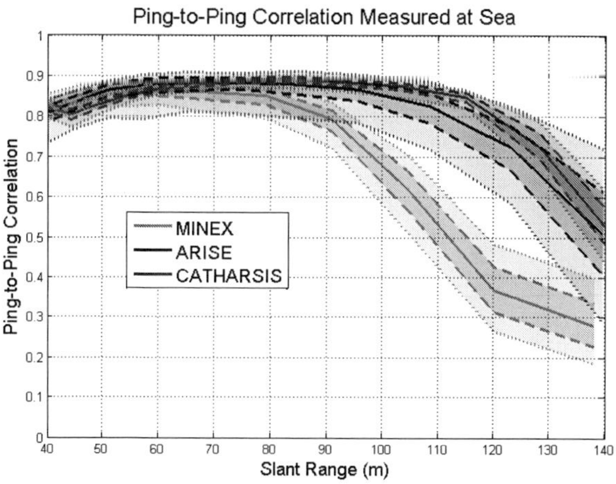

Figure 5: Correlation coefficients measured at sea during three sea trials.

The first sea trial, CATHARSIS, was held in March 2009 in a water depth of 34 m. In contrast, the second sea trial, ARISE, was held in May 2011 in a shallow water area having a maximum water depth of 17 m. CATHARSIS and ARISE were chosen as they illustrate the impact of the water depth on the multipath contribution, which reduces the quality of the sonar images [6]. Multipath returns are the result of reflections from seabed objects traveling to the sea surface and then to the sonar receiver, as opposed to directly back to the sonar [8]. They overlap in time with arriving bottom returns and reduce the value of the ping-to-ping correlations. This multipath phenomenon can be very significant when operating in a shallow water environment. This can be seen in Fig. 5 as the values of the correlation coefficients at long range tend to be smaller for ARISE compared with CATHARSIS. The CATHARSIS dataset contains 4837 correlation coefficient curves, while the ARISE dataset contains 4108 curves.

In addition to multipath, significant vehicle motion can also have a negative impact on the quality of the data collected and reduce the value of the correlation coefficients. In particular, large variations in sway and yaw can severely degrade the quality of the sonar coverage [6]. To illustrate this phenomenon, the third sea trial chosen for this study was the Italian Navy Mine Hunting Exercise held in November 2011 (MINEX). This sea trial was held in the same area as the ARISE sea trial, but increased currents induced adverse vehicle motion and decreased the maximum imaging range achievable. This phenomenon can be clearly observed in Fig. 5. The MINEX dataset includes 4032 correlation coefficient curves.

5. Performance Assessment

In this section, the performance of the NURC adaptive survey algorithm is compared with the performance achieved by traditional pre-planned surveys. First, a baseline performance assessment is conducted by assuming constant imaging ranges. Then, simulations based on the real data introduced in Section 4 are used to assess the operational performance of the adaptive survey algorithm. For this performance assessment, the minimum imaging range is assumed to be fixed at 40 m on both the port and starboard sides of the sonar. This is done in order to isolate the performance dependence on $r_{\max}$, as much larger variations of data quality are observed at long range than at short range.

Performance Assessment with Constant Range

The first step in assessing the performance of the adaptive survey algorithm described in Section 3 is to compare this algorithm to pre-planned surveys based on perfect knowledge of the maximum imaging range. Furthermore, this maximum range is assumed to be constant for all tracks and for both the port and starboard sides of the sonar. Using ping-to-ping correlation coefficients, this is expressed mathematically by setting the values of the correlation coefficients at range r from each side of the sonar to 1 within the interval $r_{\min} \leq r \leq r_{\max}$, and to 0 elsewhere. A representative survey area of 2 km by 2 km is chosen for this performance assessment. The total distance travelled is based on the real design of seabed mapping surveys and includes the length of each track, a 30 m lead-in and lead-out for each track and optimal turning manoeuvres between tracks given by Dubins curves [13]. A turning radius of 40 m was used for the AUV.

Fig. 6 shows the total distance to be travelled to achieve 100% coverage for the adaptive and pre-planned surveys as a function of the true maximum imaging range. The results for the pre-planned surveys are based on perfect knowledge of the sonar performance, and as such provide a bound on the performance that can be achieved. No other strategy can reach complete coverage in a shorter distance. It can be observed that the adaptive approach, assuming no *a priori* knowledge, can sometimes match this theoretical optimum.

As perfect knowledge is never truly available, these results indicate that the NURC adaptive survey algorithm can yield a better performance than a pre-planned approach constructed with $r_{\max}$ different from the true sonar range, r_t. This is illustrated in Fig. 6 by the dash-dot blue line representing the distance to be travelled for a pre-planned strategy based on $r_{\max} = 100$ m. This line begins at the optimal case $r_t = 100$ m on the perfect knowledge curve (in red), and extends to the right. It remains horizontal as the distance to be travelled for this pre-planned strategy does not change as r_t increase, for $r_t \geq 100$ m. Also, as this strategy does not achieve complete coverage for $r_t < 100$ m, the line is not extended to the left of its starting point. It can be observed that for a true maximum sonar range between 100 and 102.5 m, the pre-planned strategy outperforms the adaptive survey. However, for the interval between 102.5 and 105 m, the performances of both strategies are identical and for a true sonar range greater than 105 m, the adaptive survey outperforms the pre-planned strategy by yielding shorter distances to be travelled to achieve 100% coverage. Furthermore, for true sonar ranges shorter than 100 m, the adaptive survey also outperforms the pre-planned strategy as the latter fails to achieve 100% coverage by overestimating the true sonar range.

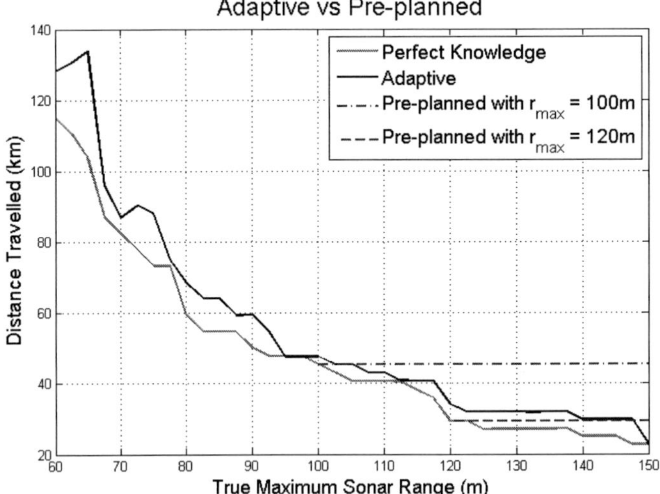

Figure 6: Total distance needed to be travelled as a function of the true imaging range to achieve 100% coverage for adaptive and pre-planned surveys. The pre-planned strategies with $r_{\mathbf{max}} = \mathbf{100}$ $\mathbf{m}$ and $r_{\mathbf{max}} = \mathbf{120}$ $\mathbf{m}$ do not achieve 100% coverage for true sonar ranges shorter than $r_{\mathbf{max}}$.

Finally, Fig. 6 also shows that in some instances, one has to recognise that the adaptive approach will not always produce significant gains over a pre-planned strategy. This is illustrated by the dashed blue line representing the distance to be travelled for a pre-planned strategy based on $r_{\mathrm{max}} = 120$ m. It can be seen that the adaptive survey outperforms the pre-planned strategy for true sonar ranges shorter than 120 m and greater than 148 m. However, the pre-planned strategy outperforms the adaptive algorithm for a large range interval from 120 to 148 m.

Simulations

The performance assessment of the adaptive survey algorithm needs to be extended to real operations at sea where the maximum range varies between tracks and between the port and starboard acoustic arrays. A standard way of achieving this operational performance assessment would be to conduct a series of adaptive and pre-planned surveys during the same sea trial and compare their performance in terms of coverage achieved and distance travelled. However, multiple surveys would have to be completed to build a large statistical sample, and this would take a significant amount of time. The alternative to at-sea testing is to use simulations based on the real data introduced in Section 4 to recreate the environmental and operational conditions experienced during the trials and generate a large number of surveys synthetically.

As described in Section 3, the adaptive survey algorithm is designed to achieve 100% coverage of a search area. As such, in order to compare the performance of an adaptive survey with the performance of the pre-planned surveys, the fundamental constraint that satisfactory pre-planned surveys have to achieve 100% coverage is imposed. A survey not achieving 100% coverage is not operationally desirable as it would require a secondary survey to fill in the coverage gaps. This additional survey would require a significant amount of additional time and resources as the AUV would need to be recovered, the raw data from the first survey would have to be downloaded and analysed to locate the coverage gaps, the second survey would have to be designed and the AUV would have to be redeployed. The optimal survey is therefore the one that achieves 100% coverage with the shortest total distance travelled. As SAS-based surveys are usually conducted at a constant speed, this shortest distance objective is equivalent to a shortest time objective. In the case of the MUSCLE AUV, this constant mission speed is usually set to 1.5m/s.

For each sea trial dataset shown in Fig. 5, the performance of the adaptive approach is compared with the performance of a finite set of pre-planned surveys, designed with a fixed r_{max} going from 60 m to 150 m, in increments of 10 m. This finite set of pre-planned surveys is chosen as a realistic set of potential options an operations planner would consider. This is also in line with the decision of discretizing the search area in increments of 10 m for the adaptive planning algorithm. Therefore, for each dataset, eleven survey designs are compared: one adaptive and ten pre-planned. For each of these eleven survey designs, 5000 simulations are used to conduct the performance assessment. During a given simulation, each track selected within a survey is associated with two curves of correlation coefficient values as a function of range. These two curves are used as the mean correlation coefficient curves from the port and starboard sides of the sonar. Each correlation curve is randomly drawn with repetition from the sea trial dataset. In the case of the adaptive approach, a given track can be revisited and when this happens, different correlation coefficient curves are drawn. As in [12], the image quality threshold is set to a minimum correlation coefficient value of 2/3 and the regions within the search area associated with correlation coefficient values exceeding this threshold are considered to have been imaged successfully. Once again, a search area of 2 km by 2 km is used.

Fig. 7 compares one of the pre-planned surveys, one based on $r_{max} = 150$ m, to a survey obtained with the adaptive algorithm for the ARISE case. It can be seen that the legs of the pre-planned survey are grouped in pairs and ordered in an increasing manner from west to east. In contrast, the legs of the adaptive survey are not uniformly spaced and the ordering of the tracks is not monotonically increasing from west to east. For the adaptive survey, the algorithm processes the simulation inputs and builds survey solutions achieving a fixed 100% coverage. Each solution can have a different total distance to be travelled. This situation is reversed for the pre-planned approach. The surveys have a constant distance to be travelled as the selected tracks do not change from one simulation to another. However, the final area coverage achieved will differ between simulations as the pre-planned surveys are designed independently of the correlation curve inputs. This is illustrated in Fig. 8 for the ARISE case. The grouping of distances around increments of about 2.5 km in the adaptive survey case illustrates the fundamentally discrete nature of the distances to be travelled based on the number of tracks to be visited.

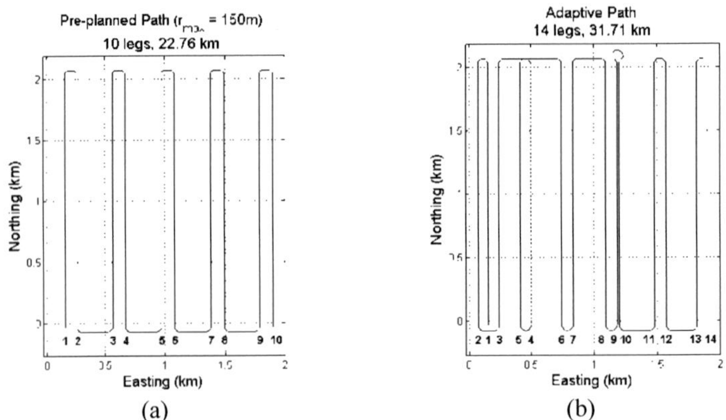

Figure 7: Examples of survey paths for different strategies (the order of the tracks is shown by the numbers at the bottom of each track): (a) pre-planned survey; (b) adaptive survey.

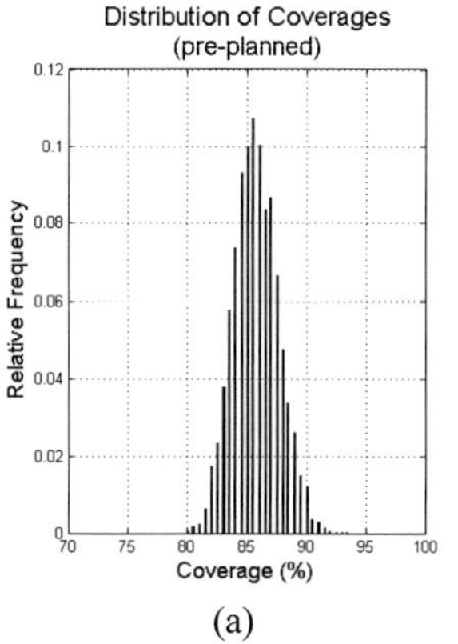

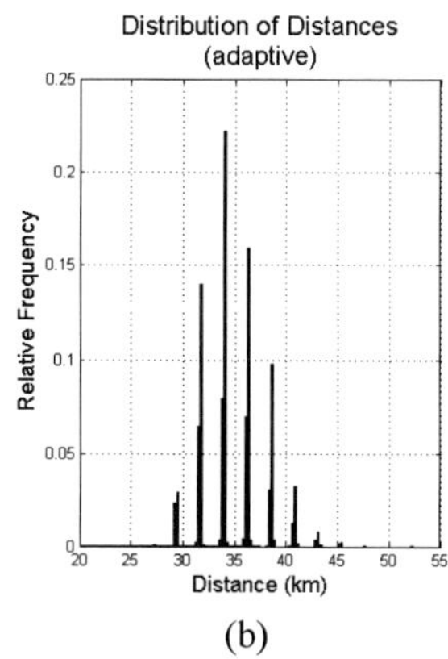

Figure 8: Examples of simulation results. (a) The pre-planned surveys have a fixed distance to be travelled (22.76 km), but a variable area coverage; (b) the adaptive survey provides a fixed 100% coverage, but a variable distance to be travelled.

Performance Assessment with Variable Range

The performance assessment of the simulation results from the previous section are summarized in Figs. 9 to 12. The results for the CATHARSIS scenario are summarized in Figs 9 and 10. The CATHARSIS scenario is of particular interest as it is a standard example of a deep water environment allowing for a greater imaging range than shallower environments. Also, the variability of the correlation coefficient curves is smaller than for the ARISE and MINEX cases. First, the performance of the selected set of pre-planned strategies is considered. Fig. 9 shows the probability of achieving 100% coverage for each of the pre-planned strategies (for each sea trial considered). This probability of achieving complete coverage corresponds to the number of simulations where 100% coverage was achieved by a given strategy over all 5000 simulations. The 100% coverage constraint for pre-planned surveys means that for a given pre-planned strategy to be considered satisfactory, it has to be associated with a probability of 1 of achieving 100% coverage. For instance, the CATHARSIS results in Fig. 9 show that the pre-planned strategy based on $r_{max} = 130$ m had a 0.94 probability of achieving 100% coverage. While this probability is high, the pre-planned strategy with $r_{max} = 130$ m cannot always guarantee complete coverage, as would the adaptive strategy, and therefore has to be rejected.

For the CATHARSIS scenario, the distribution of the coverage achieved as a function of the total distance travelled for each pre-planned strategy considered is shown in blue in Fig. 9. Each strategy is represented by a vertical error bar delimited by the minimum and maximum coverages achieved for each fixed distance to be travelled. The solid blue line connects the median coverages achieved by each strategy. It can be seen that if the chosen r_{max} is greater than 120 m, the 100% coverage constraint is violated and these pre-planned strategies must be discarded. For r_{max} less than or equal to 120 m, 100% coverage was always achieved. Therefore, the pre-planned strategy with $r_{max} = 120$ m is the best strategy within the finite set of pre-planned strategies as it minimizes the distance to be travelled. This pre-planned strategy must then be compared to the performance of the adaptive survey algorithm. In Fig. 10(a), the perfomance of the adaptive survey is represented by a red horizontal error bar delimited by the minium and maximum distances to be travelled to reach 100% coverage. The black circled star represents the median distance achieved over all 5000 simulations.

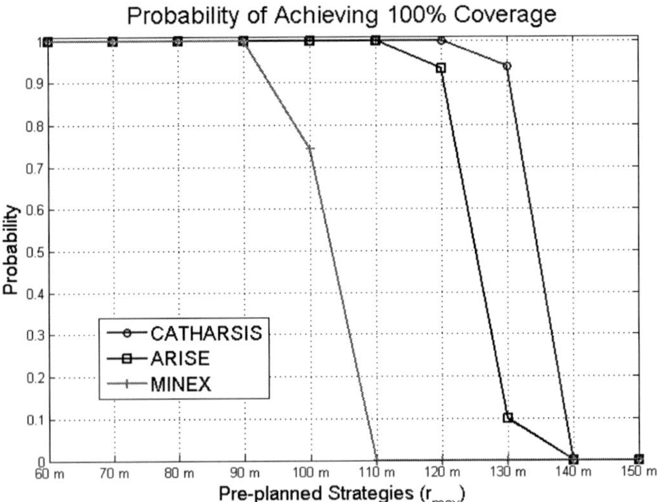

Figure 9: Probability of achieving 100% coverage for various pre-planned strategies.

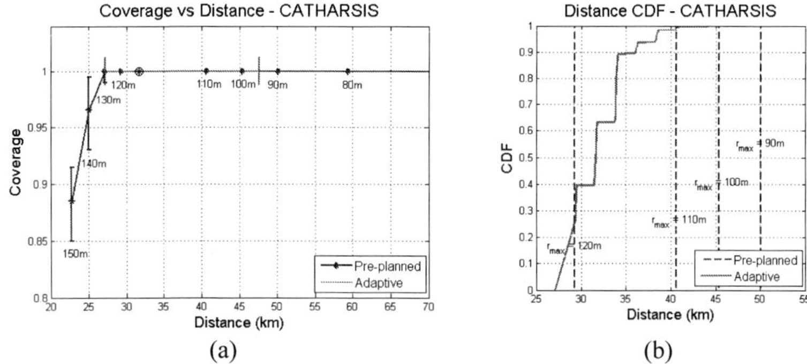

Figure 10: Results for CATHARSIS. (a) Coverage and distance variability; (b) distance CDF for the adaptive survey, compared with the distances of pre-planned surveys achieving 100% coverage.

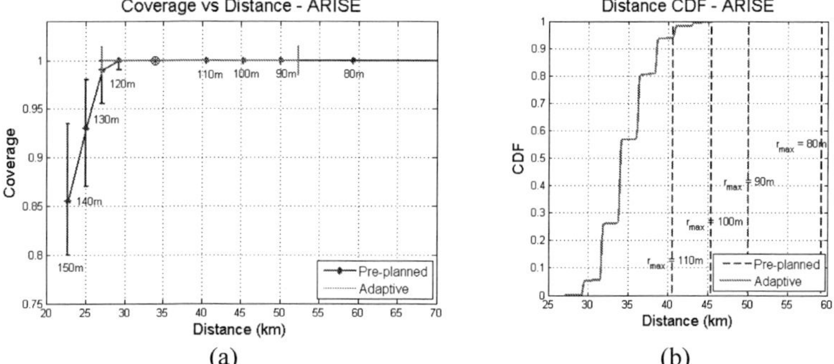

Figure 11: Results for ARISE. (a) Coverage and distance variability; (b) distance CDF for the adaptive survey, compared with the distances of pre-planned surveys achieving 100% coverage.

To facilitate the comparison between the adaptive and pre-planned surveys, Fig. 10(b) shows in red the cumulative distribution function (CDF) of the distances obtained with the adaptive algorithm. This CDF is compared with the distances to be travelled for the pre-planned surveys achieving 100% coverage with probability 1 (represented by vertical dashed blue lines). It can be seen that the median distance achieved by the adaptive survey is 31.68 km, 8.3% longer than the 29.25 km to be travelled with the best pre-planned strategy based on $r_{max} = 120$ m. Furthermore, there is a 0.26 probability that the adaptive algorithm will yield a solution with a shorter distance than the pre-planned strategy with $r_{max} = 120$ m and a 0.99 probability that the distance to be travelled will not exceed the distance of the second best pre-planned strategy with $r_{max} = 110$ m (40.60 km). Given that in a real life scenario the best r_{max} for a pre-planned strategy is unknown, these results demonstrate the added-value of the adaptive survey algorithm as a form of insurance policy guaranteeing that 100% coverage will be achieved. Under conditions similar to the CATHARSIS sea trial, the adaptive survey would reach 100% coverage at the cost of a total distance travelled comparable to the distance that could be achieved if the best maximum imaging range was known *a priori*.

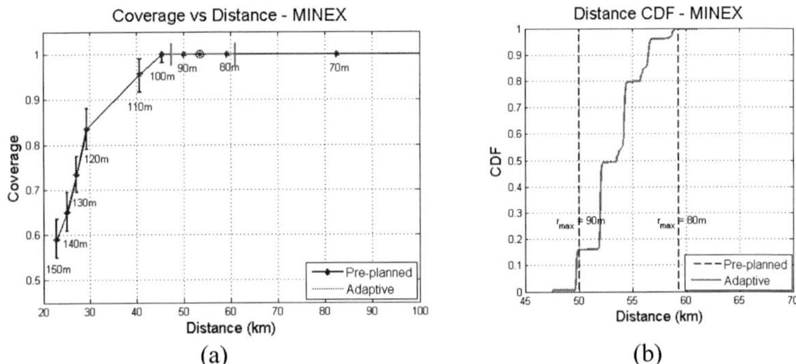

Figure 12: Results for MINEX. (a) Coverage and distance variability; (b) distance CDF for the adaptive survey, compared with the distances of pre-planned surveys achieving 100% coverage.

The performance results for the ARISE sea trial are summarized in a similar way as for the CATHARSIS scenario in Figs. 9 and 11. The ARISE trial is of significant interest as it is a representative example of a littoral environment with shallow water where multipaths degrade the imaging performance of SAS systems and reduce the maximum imaging range achievable. The results shown in Fig. 5 also indicate that the variability of the correlation coefficient curves is much higher than in the CATHARSIS case. While the best pre-planned strategy for the CATHARSIS case was based on $r_{max} = 120$ m, Figs. 9 and 11(a) show that the best pre-planned strategy for ARISE was based on a shorter range $r_{max} = 110$ m, which is consistent with the presence of multipath effects. This is particularly interesting when compared to the adaptive survey results shown in Fig. 11(b). It can be seen that the median distance to be travelled for the adaptive survey is 33.99 km, 16.3% shorter than the distance to be travelled for the best pre-planned strategy (40.60 km). Furthermore, there is a 0.94 probability that the adaptive approach will yield a solution having a shorter distance to be travelled than the $r_{max} = 110$ m solution. Under a real life scenario like the ARISE sea trial, and when using a finite set of pre-planned stagies and a discretization in increments of 10 m, it therefore appears that the adaptive survey algorithm can outperform the traditional pre-planned survey approach based on a fixed sonar range.

The results for our last scenario, MINEX, are shown in Figs. 9 and 12. As was mentioned before, the MINEX exercise was conducted in the same shallow water area as the ARISE sea trial, but currents caused adverse vehicle motion and the imaging range was significantly reduced. This scenario is a clear illustration of the benefit of using an adaptive survey algorithm, as can be seen when comparing Figs. 11(a) and 12(a). If one was to use the results from ARISE and base the pre-planned survey on $r_{max} = 110$ m, the coverage achieved would never satisfy the 100% coverage constraint. Fig. 12(b) shows that the median distance achieved by the adaptive survey is 53.54 km, 7.0% longer than the 50.05 km achieved by the best pre-planned strategy based on $r_{max} = 90$ m. Also, there is a 0.16 probability that the adaptive algorithm will yield a solution with a shorter distance than the best pre-planned strategy and a probability of 1 that the distance to be travelled will not exceed the distance of the second best pre-planned strategy with $r_{max} = 80$ m (59.31 km). These results once again show that the adaptive survey algorithm guarantees 100% coverage, even under adverse operating conditions, at the cost of a total distance travelled not much higher than could be achieved if the best pre-planned survey was known.

6. Conclusions

This paper quantified the performance of the new NURC adaptive survey algorithm when compared to traditional pre-planned surveys. First, after deriving traditional pre-planned surveys analytically, a baseline performance assessment was conducted using constant maximum sonar ranges. It was found that the adaptive strategy assuming no *a priori* knowledge could sometimes match the optimal case in which perfect knowledge of the sonar performance was assumed. Then, real data collected at sea with the MUSCLE AUV were used to obtain an operational performance assessment. It was found that when the maximum sonar imaging range is variable, the adaptive survey algorithm can outperform traditional surveys based on a fixed maximum sonar range. Using an adaptive survey guarantees 100% coverage for a total distance to be travelled comparable to the minimum distance that could be achieved if the best fixed range pre-planned survey was known. Given that in a real life scenario this best fixed range strategy is unknown, the results demonstrate the added-value of the adaptive survey algorithm as a form of insurance policy guaranteeing that complete coverage will be achieved.

The NURC adaptive survey algorithm has already been implemented on the MUSCLE AUV and preliminary experiments were held in 2011. More rigorous testing of the algorithm at sea will be performed during the ARISE 2012 sea trial planned for October 2012.

References

[1] S. Williams, O. Pizarro, M. How, D. Mercer, G. Powell, J. Marshall, and R. Hanlon. Surveying nocturnal cuttlefish camouflage behaviour using an AUV. In *Proc. IEEE Int. Conf. Robotics and Automation*, pages 214–219, 2009.

[2] Z. Reut, N. Pace, and M. Heaton. Computer classification of seabeds by sonar. *Nature*, 314:426–428, 1985.

[3] G. Dobeck, J. Hyland, and L. Smedley. Automated detection/classification of seamines in sonar imagery. In *Proc. SPIE Int Soc Opt*, volume 3079, pages 90–110, 1997.

[4] Y. Petillot, S. Reed, and J. Bell. Real time AUV pipeline detection and tracking using side scan sonar and multi-beam echo-sounder. In *Proc. IEEE OCEANS*, pages 217–222, 2002.

[5] M. A. Pinto, A. Bellettini, L. S. Wang, P. Munk, V. Myers, and L. Pautet. A new synthetic aperture sonar design with multipath mitigation. In *Proc. AIP Conference*, volume 728, pages 489–496, 2004.

[6] A. Bellettini and M. A. Pinto. Theoretical accuracy of synthetic aperture sonar micronavigation using a displaced phase-center antenna. *IEEE J. Oceanic Eng.*, 27(4):780–789, 2002.

[7] D. Williams. Label-alteration to improve underwater mine classification. *IEEE Geoscience and Remote Sensing Letters*, 8(3):487–491, 2011.

[8] J. Fawcett, M. Couillard, D. Hopkin, A. Crawford, V. L. Myers, and B. Zerr. Computer-aided detection and classification of sidescan sonar images from the Citadel trial. In *Proc. Institute of Acoustics*, volume 29, pages 3–10, 2007.

[9] D. Williams. AUV-enabled adaptive underwater surveying for optimal data collection. *Intelligent Service Robotics*, 5(1):33–54, 2012.

[10] United States Naval Academy. *Naval Operations Analysis*, pages 129–132. Naval Institute Press, Annapolis, Maryland, second edition, 1977.

[11] M. Couillard, J. Fawcett, and M. Davison. Optimizing constrained search patterns for remote mine-hunting vehicles. *IEEE J. Oceanic Eng.*, 37(1):75–84, 2012.

[12] J. Groen, M. Couillard, and W. L. Fox. Synthetic aperture sonar array gain measured at sea. In *Proc. Euro. Conf. SAR*, 2012.

[13] L. E. Dubins. On curves of minimal length with a constraint on average curvature, and with prescribed initial and terminal positions and tangents. *American Journal of Mathematics*, 79:497–516, 1957.

SESSION V

CHANGE DETECTION

CHAIRED BY ØIVIND MIDTGAARD
NORWEGIAN DEFENCE RESEARCH ESTABLISHMENT (FFI)

CHAPTER THIRTEEN

DETECTION OF MINE-LIKE OBJECTS AND CHANGE DETECTION USING SONAR IMAGERY FROM AUTONOMOUS UNDERWATER VEHICLES

PHILIP CHAPPLE, ANDREW GONG, WEIZHEN ZHOU AND STUART ANSTEE

Abstract

Automated processing of high-resolution sonar imagery from autonomous underwater vehicles (AUVs) can enhance the vehicles' autonomy and allow them to respond to the presence of significant objects on the seabed. The Australian Defence Science & Technology Organisation (DSTO) has used automated processing onboard an AUV and also in post-processing software to detect mine-like objects. Depending on the nature of the seabed, detection probabilities greater than 80% can be achieved with acceptably low false alarm rates. The software conducts image-by-image detections and allows the user to analyse why an object detected in one image is not detected in another pass over the same patch of seabed. The detection performance depends strongly on the nature of the seabed and the orientation of the mine-like objects with respect to the sonar. Knowledge of this dependence motivates improvements in detection algorithms and strategies for effectively surveying the seabed.

Recently DSTO conducted an AUV experiment to demonstrate change detection, using seabed images collected at different times in the same geographic locations. The software compares the "before" and "after" images in the vicinity of automatic detections, and highlights the locations of objects that were present at one time but not the other, providing potentially important information about changes in the seabed.

Keywords: Automatic Target Recognition, CAD/CAC, Sonar image Processing.

1. Introduction

High-resolution imaging sonars produce imagery that is suitable for the detection of mine-like objects (MLOs) on the seabed. In sidescan sonar imagery, an object that sits proud of the seabed is characterised by a highlight with an adjacent acoustic shadow. Automated data processing provides an attractive means of detecting such objects, reducing the burden and delays connected with manual processing of the data. When an autonomous underwater vehicle (AUV) is used to collect the data, it is possible to process the data in real time to increase the autonomy of the vehicle, enabling it to respond to detected objects by sending a message to another vehicle or platform, or by returning to the object to conduct a closer inspection using different orientations or different sensors.

Researchers have used a variety of approaches for automatic target detection and classification, as reviewed in [1, 2]. These techniques can be broadly divided into supervised and unsupervised image processing techniques. Supervised processing [3-7] relies on training datasets with images containing MLOs in known locations to train the detection algorithms. Unsupervised techniques [8] do not rely explicitly on training data, although they are designed and tested using sonar image data containing MLOs.

The present paper describes research into unsupervised processing of sonar imagery using software written by the Defence Science & Technology organisation (DSTO). The software uses image statistics in local areas within each sonar image, and identifies mine-like objects using highlights and adjacent acoustic shadows which are different from their local backgrounds. The software is described in more detail in Section 3. While the software has been tested with numerous datasets, this paper concentrates on the results of three survey activities that took place in 2011 and 2012. They are an onboard target detection experiment (Section 4), an angular dependence study (Section 5) and a demonstration of change detection (Section 6).

2. Sonar image acquisition

A REMUS 100 AUV, fitted with Marine Sonic Technology sidescan sonars operating at 900 kHz and 1800 kHz, collected the sonar imagery described in this paper. The maximum sonar range was 30 m on each side. Two data sets were gathered in Jervis Bay, NSW, Australia (Fig. 1). The survey for the change detection study (Section 6) took place in coves within Sydney Harbour, where the seabed was cluttered by debris from shore-side construction activities over many years.

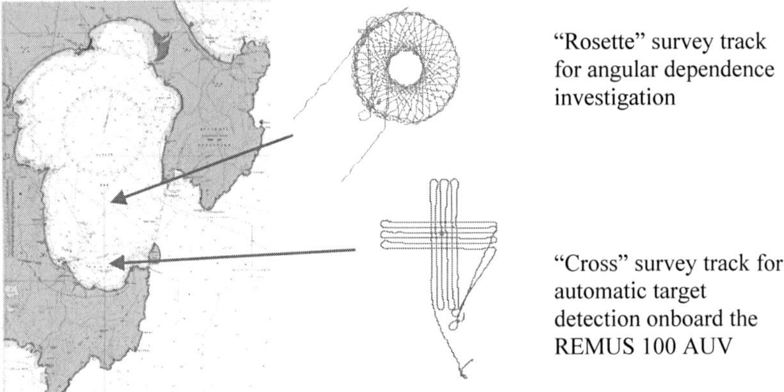

Figure 1: Survey locations in Jervis Bay, and corresponding survey tracks

3. Image analysis for target detection

The unsupervised target detection technique for the work of this paper has been described in [2], although there have been some further developments. The most important steps in this process are:

Data file preparation

For each sonar survey mission, the AUV's sonar data files in Marine Sonic Technology Ltd's MST format are converted to bitmap images. Navigational data for each ping (latitude, longitude, heading, vehicle altitude and vehicle depth) are written to an ASCII file, and another ASCII file contains several operational parameters of the vehicle. The software creates an Excel database to store the metadata and to record detection results. Altitude values are used to mask the water-column region from each sonar image. The software also masks areas where the heading is varying rapidly, indicating that the vehicle is turning, as the sonar imaging is ineffective in these areas (Fig. 2).

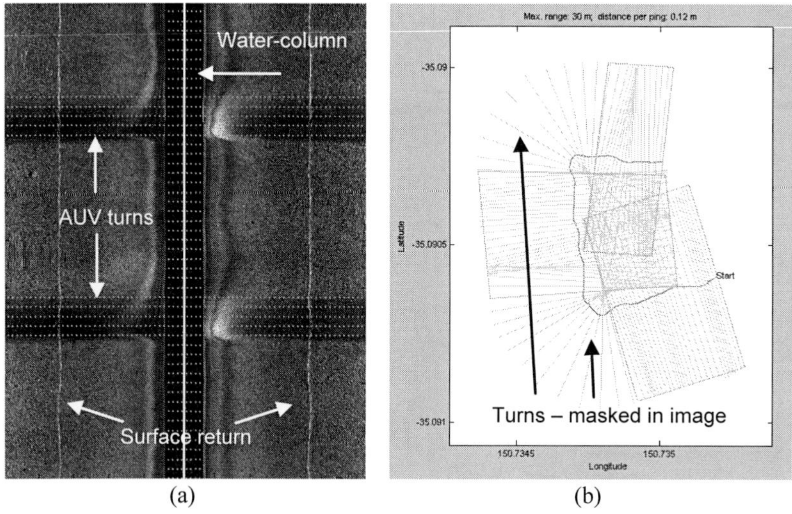

(a)   (b)

Figure 2: (a) Sidescan sonar image showing masked areas (dotted) – the water-column and vehicle turns. (b) Corresponding navigational view of the vehicle track and sonar swath.

Surface return mitigation

In order to reduce the number of false alarms, it is often necessary to mitigate against the effects of surface returns, which are apparent in data obtained when the sonar was closer to the seabed than to the surface and when the distance to the surface was less than the maximum range of the sonar. These conditions prevail for most of the data discussed here, and the surface return is manifest as a bright, irregular fragmented line on both sides of the water-column region (Fig.3).

The software fits a line from the start ping to the end ping of each sonar image, favouring high intensity pixels close to the locations where the surface return is anticipated from vehicle depth data. A cost function is minimised to favour paths through bright pixels from one end of the image to the other, minimising (in a sum-of-squares sense) the size of jumps between these bright pixels. After calculating the port and starboard surface return lines in this way, a local threshold is determined for each row of the image, based on pixel brightness values close to each surface return line. Pixels in the neighbourhood of the surface return with brightness values exceeding these thresholds are replaced by lower-valued pixels from the same neighbourhood. Fig. 4 shows a sonar image before and after mitigation of the surface return.

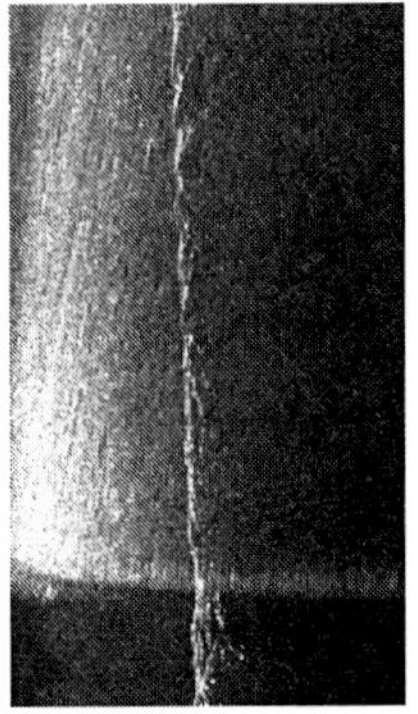

Figure 3: Surface return

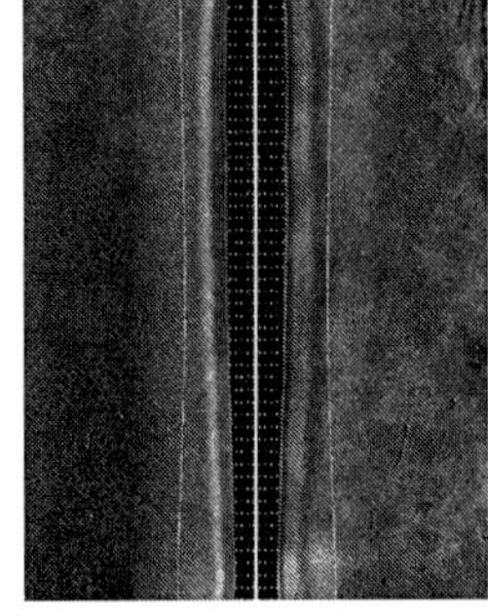

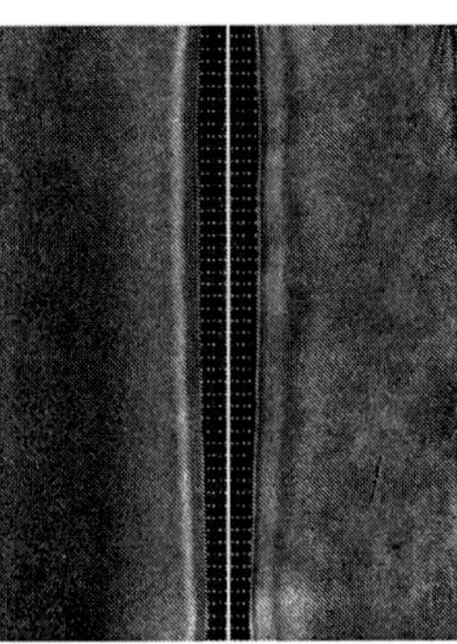

Figure 4: Sonar image before and after removal of the surface return

Replacement of surface return pixel values in this way reduces the false alarm rate of the software without adversely affecting the detection performance. When the surface return crosses the shadow of an MLO, surface return mitigation partially restores the shadow and increases the likelihood of detecting the object. When the highlight of an MLO coincides with the surface return, however, the software sometimes fails to detect the object, either with or without surface return removal.

Positions of the surface return pixels and the replacement values are stored in an ASCII file, so that they do not have to be recalculated each time the image file is loaded.

Spatial filtering of images

The images are treated within the software as having two layers: the original image and a filtered version of the image used for the detection of shadows. For shadow detection, clusters of low brightness pixels are formed, as described in Section 3.4. Low-pass filtering speeds up the processing and reduces the number of false alarms, because there are fewer shadow clusters to process when high spatial frequency variations in the image are reduced. Highlights tend to be smaller and more fragmented than their corresponding shadows. For this reason, the image is not low-pass filtered for highlight detection.

Detection of highlights with associated shadows

The software divides each image into an array of local areas, and the brightness values of each local area are sorted, both for the original image and for the filtered image. Pixels in the top few percentiles of brightness in the original image are marked as potential highlights and pixels in the lowest range of percentiles of brightness in the filtered image are marked as potential shadows. This process is then repeated with a differently positioned array of local areas, with area boundaries between the boundaries of the former local areas, in order to detect highlight and shadow regions that would otherwise be split across boundaries. The software aggregates the highlight pixels and forms clusters of connected highlight pixels. Similarly, clusters of connected shadow pixels are formed from the filtered layer of the image.

For each shadow cluster, the software tests whether there is an adjacent highlight cluster indicating the presence of an object protruding above the seabed. The shadow must appear further from the sonar than the highlight. Highlights and associated shadows must also have similar locations in the along-track direction.

The following parameters have default values and can be set by the user:

- the numbers of local area subdivisions in the across-track and along-track directions;
- the percentile cut-off for regarding bright pixels as potential highlights;
- the percentile cut-off for regarding low brightness pixels as potential shadows;
- the maximum number of pixels separating highlights and adjacent shadows;
- the minimum and maximum lengths of highlights;
- minimum and maximum lengths of shadows in the along-track dimension;
- the minimum and maximum heights of detected objects above the seabed, as deduced from the lengths of their shadows;
- a threshold for scores indicating how well a quadrilateral can be fitted to each shadow; and
- parameters describing the filtering of images.

Some of these parameters and the detection algorithm are described in more detail in [2].

The software carries out this detection process on each image file, as part of a batch process. Detection results are stored in the variables operating within the software, and, during a batch run, the detection results are recorded in the database.

Detection analysis

Once the detection batch process has been carried out for each data file in the sonar survey mission, the detection analysis section of the software groups detections by geographic location. The user is then able to designate each detected feature as an MLO, a non-mine-like object (atypical of the background but not mine-like) or a false alarm. For each site where there is a detection, the software reports all other data files covering the same geographic location. This is particularly useful for analysing results for sonar missions involving multiple looks at the same site. In this case, the software lists all the files where the feature was detected and those in which it was not detected, and provides links for the user to view the relevant sonar images. The software is also able to include features in particular image files that have been previously marked using Sea Scan PC Review software (from Marine Sonic Technology Ltd.), so that the ability to detect these features can be tested. The software takes into account the fact that features are not readily detected in certain parts of a sidescan sonar image:

- in the masked areas corresponding to vehicle turns;
- in the nadir region (sonar incidence angles less than about 60°) in which the shadows are short and the spatial resolution is poor; and
- close to the maximum range part of the image, where shadows may be clipped by the edge of the image.

Detections and false alarms in these parts of the images are not included in the detection statistical analysis.

Once all the detected features and previously marked features have been designated, the software reports on the automatic target detection performance and the false alarm statistics for the mission.

4. Onboard target detection experiment

In June 2012, DSTO conducted a survey using the REMUS 100 AUV with the previously mentioned automatic target detection software running on an embedded computer. The vehicle followed the "cross" track depicted in the lower inset in Fig.1, involving 12 passes of a cylindrical MLO. The software detected the mine in 8 images and created the snapshots shown in Fig. 5(a). Human analysts examining the data afterwards also detected the MLO in the two images in Fig. 5(b), but here the object appeared on the edge of the images and the shadow was clipped. The software rejected these objects as not having suitable shadows to indicate an MLO protruding 0.1 m or more above the seabed. In post-processing, the software reported a 100% success rate in finding all 8 MLOs in the included parts the imagery. Analysis of the shadows associated with the detections indicates that the object was protruding 0.36 ± 0.02 m above the seabed.

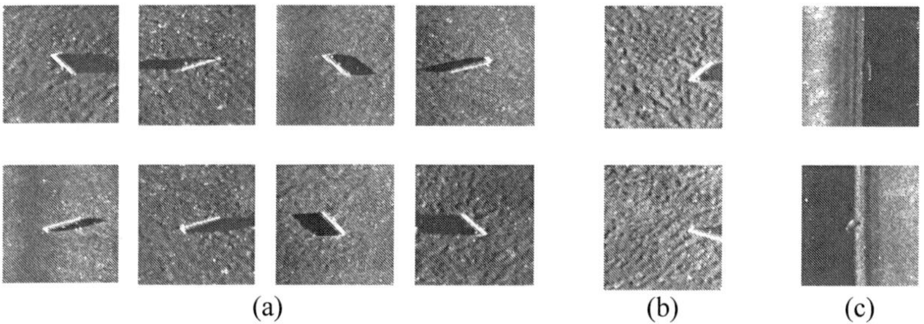

(a)   (b)   (c)

Figure 5: Onboard target detection results. (a) Thumbnail images of 8 detected MLOs. (b) 2 MLOs undetected because of proximity to the edge of the image. (c) 2 MLOs undetected in the water-column region.

The post-processing software reported two further passes over the geographic location of the mine, but in these images the vehicle passed directly over the mine, which appeared only in the masked-out water-column region (Fig. 5(c)). The MLO was observable there in a retrospective examination, but the human analysts did not recognise the object in these files prior to this analysis.

During the trial, there were 6 false alarms from 33 files (0.2 false alarms per image), but some of these were in the nadir region that is excluded in normal processing of results. Subsequent refinement of the detection parameters and algorithms demonstrated that the software could be configured so as to generate no false alarms in running through the dataset.

5. Angular dependence of target detection

DSTO conducted an earlier survey in May 2011 to determine the variability in detection performance for a cylindrical MLO viewed from different look angles. The REMUS vehicle was programmed to follow a "rosette" survey path as shown in Fig. 1.

The object in the rosette survey did not stand out as clearly in the imagery as the object in the cross survey, for two reasons:

(i) The highlights of the MLO in the rosette imagery were not much brighter than the background, in contrast with images from the cross survey described in Section 4, suggesting a different seabed type.

(ii) The shadows were significantly shorter. Analysis of the shadows indicates that the object was protruding only 0.13 ± 0.02 m above the seabed in the rosette survey.

Anderson, Brooke, Radke, McArthur and Hughes [9] reported on seabed habitat types in southern Jervis Bay, as illustrated in Fig. 6. This figure and Fig. 1 indicate that the seabed in the location of the rosette survey is likely to be sandy, with subtle sand waves or ripples. Sand ripples have some facets facing towards the sonar, increasing the bottom reverberation and reducing the contrast of the MLO's acoustic return above the background. Because of the mobility of the sandy bottom, it is also likely that the MLO was partly buried, reducing the shadow length. For the cross survey, the seabed was flatter and harder, and acoustic reflection from the seabed was presumably more specular, allowing the MLO highlight to contrast well with the seabed.

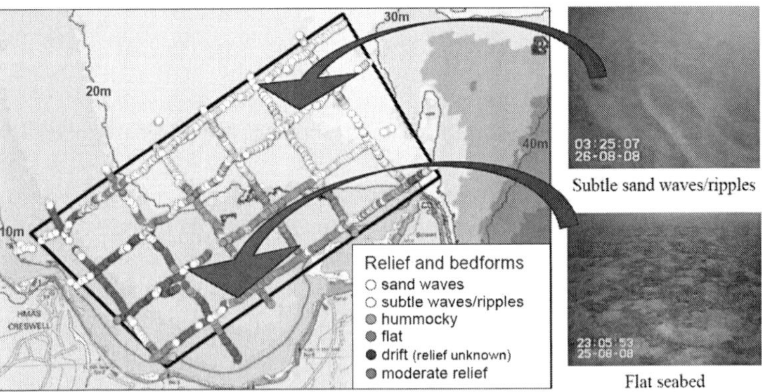

Figure 6: Seabed characterisation of southern Jervis Bay from a towed video survey [9]. Images used by kind permission of Brendan Brooke, Geoscience Australia, 2012.

Two views of the object are shown in 7(a). Clearly, the MLO stands out above its background much better when side-insonified than when end-insonified. This is borne out in the target detection statistics. Fig. 7(b) shows a plot of detections and misses of the MLO, for one particular set of values of the detection parameters. The radial dimension is the range from the sonar to the object (maximum 30 m) and the angle is the direction from the sonar to the target (with north at the top). The MLO was orientated in an approximately east-west direction. This plot shows that target detection operates significantly more effectively for side-insonification than for end-insonification of the MLO.

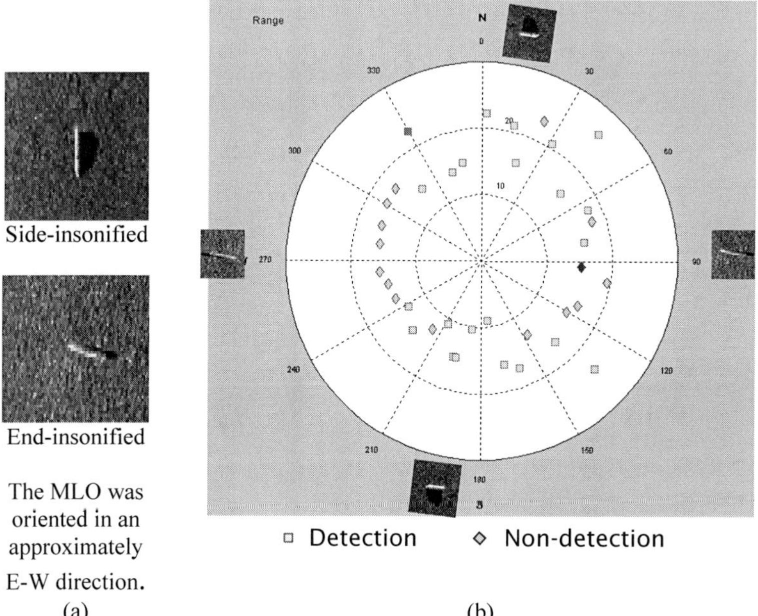

Figure 7: Angular dependence of detection. (a) MLO images. (b) Range vs. bearing from the sonar to the MLO.

DSTO has further developed the target detection software algorithms to improve the detection of MLOs in this situation. The filtering of the images described in Section 3.3 was extended by using simple step-function filters (like a Haar wavelet), one for the left-hand side of the images (the port side) and its mirror image for the right-hand side (the starboard side), to favour a bright object with an adjacent shadow. With this approach, 23 out of 31 MLOs are detected   a probability of detection of 0.74. Two non-mine-like objects are also detected in the imagery, and the false alarm rate is 0.09 per image.

It may be of interest that when the detection parameter values used for the cross dataset are applied to the rosette dataset, the detection rate drops to 0.61, with one non-mine like object detected and a false alarm rate of 0. This detection rate is too low for reliable detection, so these parameter values are unsuitable for this detection problem. However, when the parameter values used for the rosette dataset are applied to the cross dataset, the false alarm rate increases from 0 to 4.9 per image, with many false alarms apparently arising from fish, shells or rocks. (The calculated detection probability remains at 1.) This false alarm rate is intolerably high. It appears that the ideal parameter mix depends on the seabed habitat and the reverberation levels, suggesting the need for adaptivity in tuning the detector to the seabed background for which it is employed. Further research is needed to establish how to make the parameters adaptive.

6. Change detection

Automatic target detection provides a means of comparison of seabed images collected at different times covering the same locations. In January 2012, DSTO used the REMUS AUV to obtain seabed images before and after laying objects on the seabed (Fig. 8), employing identical mission plans. The automatic detection software was run on the imagery, with the detection parameters chosen to detect numerous features per image in cluttered images. Initially, the software identified areas of overlap between the *before* and *after* images. Then, for each detected feature in the *after* image, the software analysed the same geographic location in the *before* comparison image to determine whether the same feature was present. (The two images can have the same underlying features, regardless of whether the automatic target detection routine finds the same features in both images.)

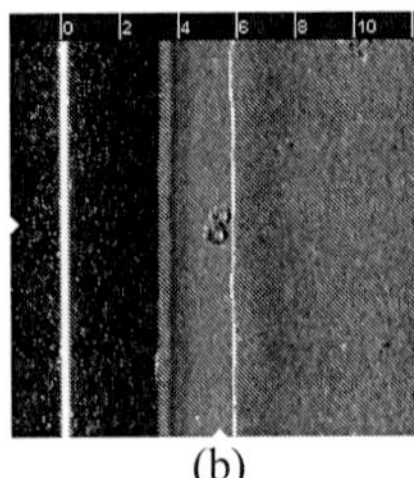
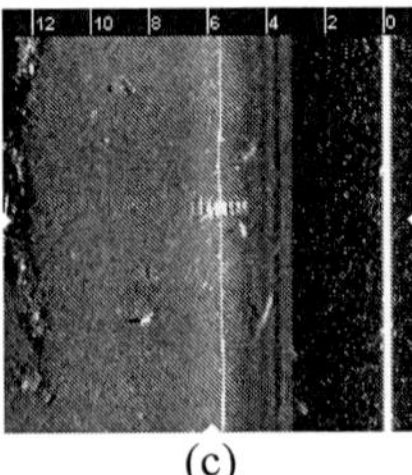

(a)   (b)   (c)

Figure 8: Objects deposited on the seabed: (a) Pair of tyres and a step-ladder; (b) 900 kHz image of the tyres; (c) 900 kHz image of the ladder

A tool frequently used for comparison between an image $f(x, y)$ and an often smaller image or template $t(x, y)$ of the same scaling and orientation, is the normalised cross-correlation [10, 11]:

$$\gamma(u,v) = \frac{\sum_{x,y}\left[f(x,y)-\bar{f}_{u,v}\right]\left[t(x-u,y-v)-\bar{t}\right]}{\left\{\sum_{x,y}\left[f(x,y)-\bar{f}_{u,v}\right]^2\sum_{x,y}\left[t(x-u,y-v)-\bar{t}\right]^2\right\}^{0.5}} \tag{1}$$

where $\bar{t}$ is the mean of $t(x, y)$ and $\bar{f}_{u,v}$ is the mean of $f(x, y)$ under the template. For identical images, $\gamma(u, v) = 1$; in general $\gamma(u, v)$ ranges between $+1$ and -1 and is independent of the mean values or multiplicative factors applying to the image or template.

The software operated using the following procedure:

(1) Identify areas of overlap in the geographic coverage of the two images.
(2) Remove the surface returns from both images.
(3) Detect features in the *before* and *after* images and create corresponding binary images that are nonzero only at highlights of detected features.
(4) For each binary highlight in the *after* image, use Equation (1) to calculate its normalised cross-correlation with the binary *before* image. Here $f(x, y)$ is equal to the binary *before* image and $t(x, y)$ is a binary sub-image in the neighbourhood of each highlight in the *after* image. If $\gamma(u,v)$ exceeds a certain threshold for any value of (u,v), the corresponding highlights from the two images are regarded as matching, with the location of the peak indicating any positional offset between the two images.
(5) If the highlights are not matching in the binary images, compare the original images. Equation (1) is applied with $f(x, y)$ equal to the *before* image and $t(x, y)$ equal to a sub-image in the neighbourhood of each highlight in the *after* image. Again, if $\gamma(u, v)$ exceeds a certain threshold for any value of (u, v), the two images are regarded as matching. If not, the software has identified a feature in the *after* image that is not present in the *before* image.

Fig. 9 shows two 900 kHz sonar images that have been compared in this way. For the images shown, there was almost complete overlap between the geographic areas covered. Although the automatic target detection detected different features in the two images, the software used step (5) above to establish that the ladder was the only feature detected in the object image that was not common to both images.

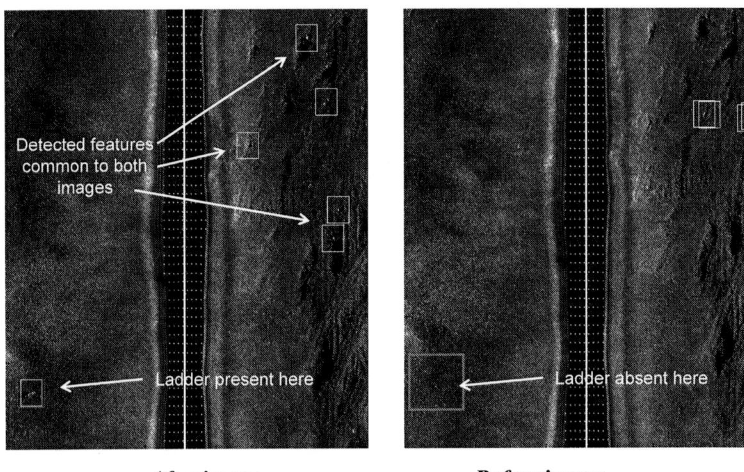

After image   **_Before_ image**

Figure 9: Results of change detection with 900 kHz sonar images. Red rectangles mark the detected differences between the features in the images.

Fig. 10 shows a similar result for 1800 kHz sonar images with and without the ladder on the seabed. The shaded area in the object image is the part of it that overlaps with the comparison image. Here, because of the shorter range and higher spatial resolution attainable with this sonar, several rungs of the ladder have been detected as separate features. Again, the software found that these features are present only in the object image. On processing other images collected before and after laying the pair of tyres on the seabed, the software also detected these differences between the images.

In this initial work, the software only deals with images that are oriented parallel or anti-parallel. Further work will investigate change detection analysis with differently orientated sidescan sonar images.

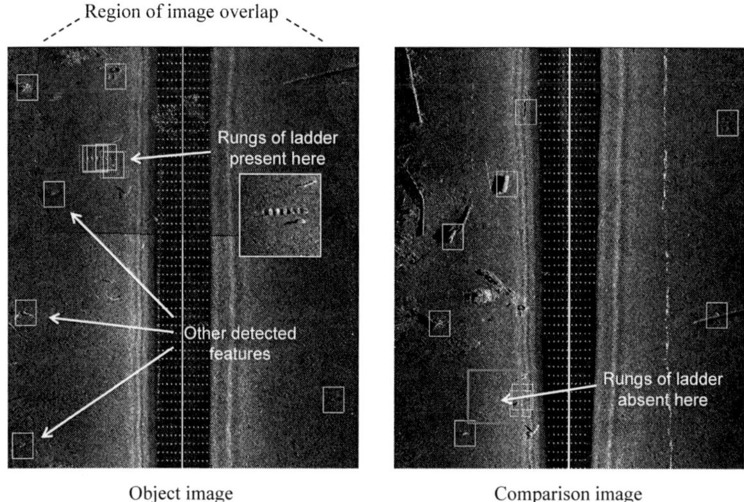

Object image

Comparison image

Figure 10: Results of change detection with 1800 kHz sonar images

7. Conclusion

Using unsupervised target detection software, this work has demonstrated that automatic target detection is effective in the situations tested and is capable of providing increased autonomy to AUVs. For some situations, as in the onboard target detection experiment, the software is able to detect all the MLOs with few or no false alarms. With more challenging seabed conditions, the probability of detection declines. In these situations, the software detects cylindrical objects considerably better when they are viewed side-on than end-on. Further investigation is needed to determine the best operating parameters over a broad range of conditions and how these parameters should be adjusted to take account of the image backgrounds and the nature of the seabed.

This work has also demonstrated that automatic detection of features can detect changes between objects appearing in images from similar surveys conducted at different times and covering the same geographic locations. This capability can provide potentially important information about changes in the seabed.

Acknowledgements

The authors thank Mr. Michael Bell, Mr. Nicholas Rypkema and Mr. Peter Formby for their considerable assistance in trial logistics and the operation of the AUV. They also thank Mr. Les Hamilton for informative discussions about the nature of the seabed in Jervis Bay.

References

[1] P. Chapple, "Automated detection and classification in high-resolution sonar imagery for autonomous underwater vehicle operations," DSTO GD-0537, 2008 http://dspace.dsto.defence.gov.au/dspace/bitstream/1947/9897/1/DSTO-GD-0537%20PR.pdf

[2] P. B. Chapple, "Unsupervised detection of mine-like objects in seabed imagery from autonomous underwater vehicles", *Proc. OCEANS '09 MTS/IEEE,* Biloxi, 2009.

[3] G. J. Dobeck, J. C. Hyland, and L. Smedley, "Automated detection/ classification of sea mines in sonar imagery," *Proc. SPIE*, vol. 3079, pp. 90–110, 1997.

[4] J. A. Fawcett, "Image-based classification of sidescan sonar detections," *Proc. CAD/CAC 2001*, Halifax, Canada, November 2001.

[5] M. R. Azimi-Sadjadi, D. Yao, A. A. Jamshidi, and G. J. Dobeck, "Underwater target classification in changing environments using an adaptive feature mapping," *IEEE Trans. Neural Networks*, vol. 13, pp. 1099–1111, 2002.

[6] E. Coiras, P.-Y. Mignotte, Y. Petillot, J. Bell and K. Lebart, "Supervised target detection and classification by training on augmented reality data," *IET Radar, Sonar & Navigation*, vol. 1, pp. 83–90, 2007.

[7] J. Fawcett, M. Couillard, D. Hopkin, A. Crawford, V. Myers and B. Zerr, "Computer-aided detection and classification of sidescan sonar images from the CITADEL trial", DRDC Atlantic TM 2006-115, 2006.

[8] S. Reed, Y. Petillot and J. Bell, "Automated approach to classification of mine-like features in sidescan sonar using highlight and shadow information," *IEE Proc. Radar, Sonar & Navigation*, vol. 151, pp. 48–56, 2004.

[9] T. Anderson, B. Brooke, L. Radke, M. McArthur and M. Hughes, "Mapping and characterising soft-sediment habitats, and evaluating physical variables as surrogates of biodiversity in Jervis Bay, NSW", Jervis Bay Post-Survey Report, Geoscience Australia Record 2009/10, 2009.

[10] J. P. Lewis, "Fast Normalized cross-correlation", *Industrial Light & Magic*; http://scribblethink.org/Work/nvisionInterface/nip.pdf

[11] R. M. Haralick and L. G. Shapiro, *Computer and Robot Vision*, Volume II, Addison-Wesley, pp. 316–317, 1992.

Chapter Fourteen

Change Detection for MCM Survey Mission

Julien Ferrand
and Nicolas Mandelert

Abstract

In this paper, we present an overview of a high-level change detection approach for Mine Countermeasures survey missions in known areas. This approach has been designed to make best use of the high quality data generated by synthetic aperture sonar (SAS). This high-level algorithm extracts sonar observations and manages a database of mine warfare contacts. At any time, changes can be easily detected by searching new or non-updated contacts from the contact database.

First, we introduce a real time Automatic Target Recognition (ATR) algorithm for high-resolution sidescan sonar data. This algorithm detects any relevant observations from the waterfall images and then extracts robust features needed by the second step. We then explain the second step of the algorithm which aims at aggregating observations into contacts. In the case of a survey mission, a contact database is available and this step allows one to automatically update the database by adding new observations to known contacts. We explain how this step uses pattern matching and simultaneous localization and mapping (SLAM) techniques to perform a robust association.

Finally, we present two applications of this algorithm on real data. The first one is an embedded "contact management system" in the Autonomous Underwater Vehicle (AUV) in order to increase the decisional autonomy level and to produce better contact classification and localization results. The second application is to use this algorithm in mine warfare data analysis software as a decision aid component in the highly time consuming process of mine warfare contact database update.

Keywords: Change Detection, Pattern Matching, Decisional Autonomy, Mine Warfare Contact Manager, Simultaneous Localization and Mapping.

1. Introduction

Mine warfare survey missions are currently used by several nations in home port protection and clearance operations. This efficient operational concept is based on sonar data recording and comparison with a large database of mine warfare information. Only man-made change detection is performed by operational forces. In low to medium bottom complexity areas, change detection can be performed in real-time at low coverage rates with a high-level approach a using minehunter equipped with a hull-mounted sonar. In these cases, the operator extracts the sonar contact from the sonar image and then searches for it in a contact database. The search criteria are mainly absolute position and contact classification. In more complex seabeds (that generally represent smaller areas compared to low and medium complexity areas) the use of synthetic aperture sonar (SAS) is preferred, in order to produce and record high-resolution data. These data are then post-processed and analyzed at a shore-based centre by specialized operators who search for changes directly at the image level. A good probability of detecting a new contact can be achieved, but this task is very time consuming.

The next generation of mine warfare systems will likely make use of unmanned underwater vehicles (UUVs) equipped with a SAS payload in order to reduce the risk to personnel and address new underwater threats. In this context, we are currently developing a high-level automatic change detection algorithm. Low-level change detection algorithms could appear better by the fact that they should be able to detect very small changes [1]; however, associated constraints may drastically reduce the operational employment of this type of approach. Incoherent image-based methods need very accurate track repetition to be able to perform image registration. Difficulties appear as soon as the seafloor is not flat, like in Fig. 1, which shows holes roughly 10 m in diameter by 1 to 2 m depth. In this quite frequent case, any position, altitude or azimuth difference between two acquisition tracks can produce unexpected image differences. Then, the required navigation precision (better than a few meters) appears not currently available for any AUV without special external positioning systems. Coherent image-based methods additionally need very little changes in the seafloor in order to be able to use phase information. This reduces the available time between two acquisitions at a few days. Thus, while these kind of methods have a reduced operational use, they nevertheless seem to be appropriate for automatic attrition operations. Indeed, during these kind of MCM operationss, the risk of minefield re-seeding is high and previously cleared areas need to be frequently re-checked, up to several time a week, in order to be sure that no new mines have been deployed.

Our high-level change detection algorithm is based on Automatic Target Recognition (ATR) processing. It is designed to improve the autonomy level and minehunting performance of AUVs deployed in low to medium complexity areas. It is based on using real-time embedded automatic ATR and pattern matching algorithms.

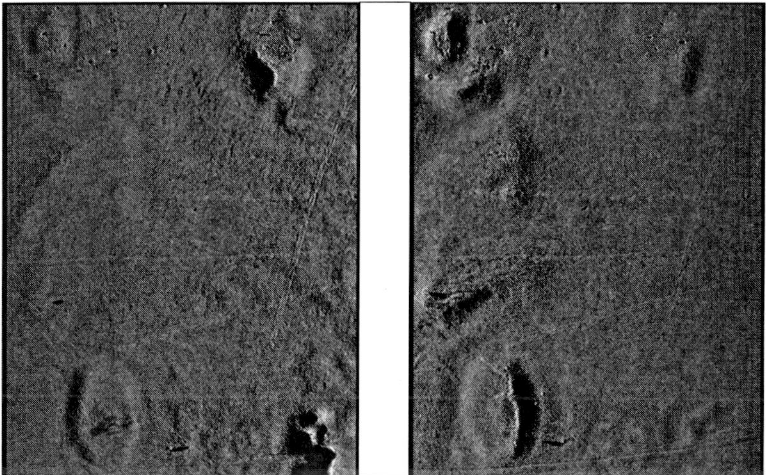

Figure 1: Exactly same medium complexity areas (about 150 x 75 m) acquired with opposite tracks. This extreme case shows how image information depends on the sonar trajectory.

2. Automatic Target Recognition

The automatic target recognition algorithm is designed to be used in real-time on high-resolution sidesscan sonar data. It is currently deployed on several operational systems such as autonomous underwater vehicle AUV or command and control (C2) mine warfare systems.

The ATR architecture is a classical two-step structure as explained in [4]. A first stage processes raw sidescan sonar waterfall images in order to generate detections. These detections are buffered and then classified with a template matching technique. The template matching compares observation shadows to those from a simulated mask database produced by a projection of 3D representations of known contacts.

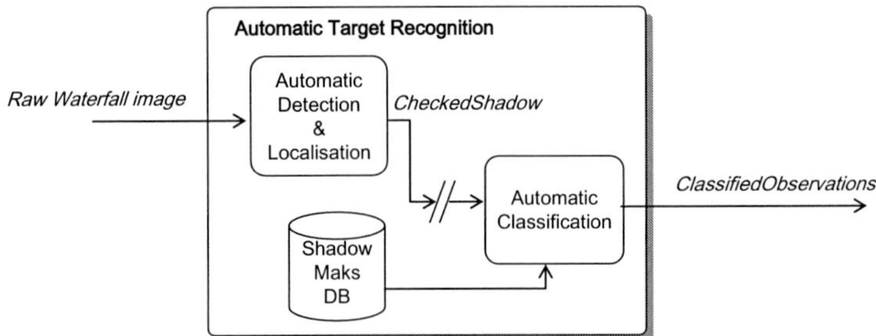

Figure 2: The ATR architecture.

The detection stage in based on shadow detection. In the first step, we use an innovative function of grazing normalization that allows efficient real-time implementation. The grazing normalization aims at morphing the waterfall image in order to obtain a constant shadow dimension in the range axis.

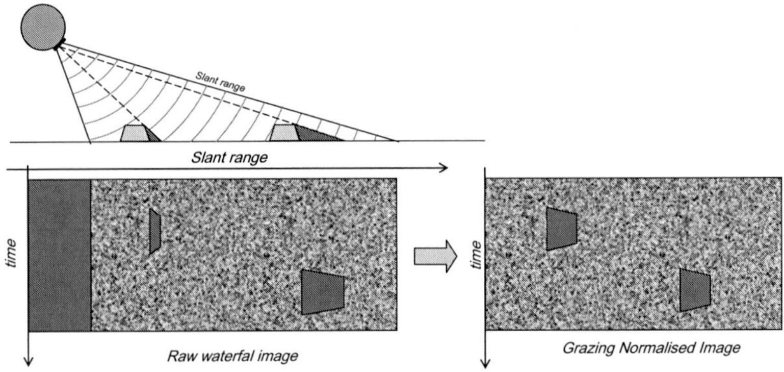

Figure 3: Grazing angle normalization.

The normalized image is then smoothed by using two filters in order to reduce the effect of bottom type on the image intensity. The first filter is a low-pass filter that estimates the mean image intensity along the range axis. This mean intensity is updated with a recursive temporal filter and is used to normalize the whole image intensity to a predefined value.

The next stage is a segmentation function that converts gray level image in two binary images that represent shadows and echoes areas. It consists in applying a median filter with a window size depending on the size of the smallest contact of interest. Then, the medianized image is segmented into 0/1 with threshold levels function for the expected reverberation to shadow contrast H_{RS} and echo to reverberation H_{ER} contrast. Considering the optimal detection threshold definition and the fact that the relevant shadow contact in the grazing-normalized image is composed of at least 200 independent points, we obtain shadow and echo thresholds (T_s and T_e) with expression (2):

$$\sigma_r = \frac{\bar{I}}{\sqrt{\pi/2}} \qquad \sigma_o = \frac{\sigma_r}{10^{\frac{H_{RS}}{20}}} \qquad \sigma_e = \sigma_r . 10^{\frac{H_{ER}}{20}} \tag{1}$$

$$T_s = \bar{I} . \frac{2}{\left(\frac{\sigma_r}{\sigma_o}+1\right)} \qquad T_e = \sigma_e . \sqrt{-2\ln(Pd_e)} \tag{2}$$

where Pd_e is the echo probability detection and $\bar{I}$ is the mean of image intensity.

The shadow extraction stage uses morphological operations to mark relevant shadows. The previous grazing normalization step allows one to use the same morphological kernels on the full waterfall sonar image. Shadows are marked using an erosion operation (with an 8-connected neighbourhood). Shadow markers are used to isolate close contacts as standalone contacts (Fi).

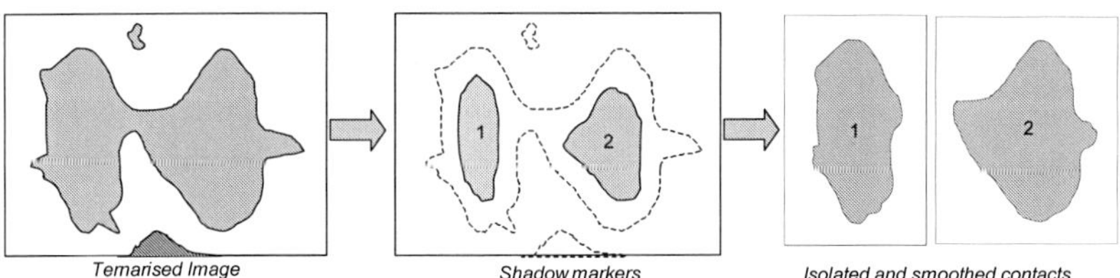

Temarised Image   Shadow markers   Isolated and smoothed contacts

Figure 4: The contact isolation process.

The last detection stage consists in computing a refined shadow segmentation using statistical snakes and then to check the quality of the extracted shadows based mainly on contrast, dimensionality and compactness criteria.

Then, template matching is used to classify contacts. In this process, the classification of the contact is a function of the distance between the shadow of the contact and the best template found in database. The database is populated with simulated masks of known threats. Those masks are generated from many viewpoints with small variations in azimuth and grazing angle. The matching rate between a mask and a contact is a function of the distance map. This distance map is computed with a non-linear distance transform of the differences between a contact and the best alignment of the mask onto it (Fig. 5).

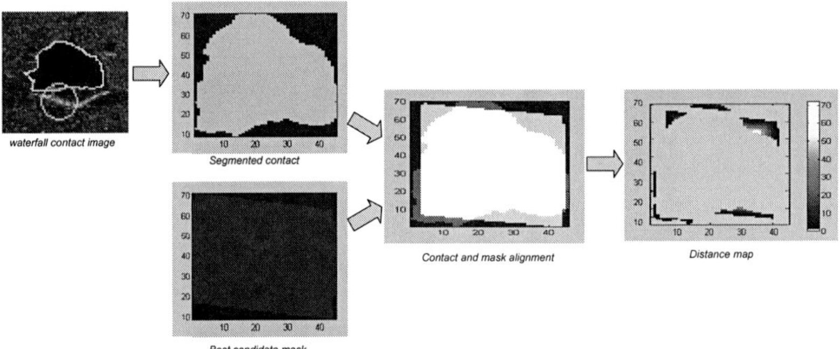

Figure 5: The template matching process.

3. Pattern Matching

The pattern matching stage is an iterative method that uses a contact pairing function with at very low false pairing rate, followed by a contact relocation function. After contact relocation, contact pairing attempts to find new pairing, and so on (Fig. 6).

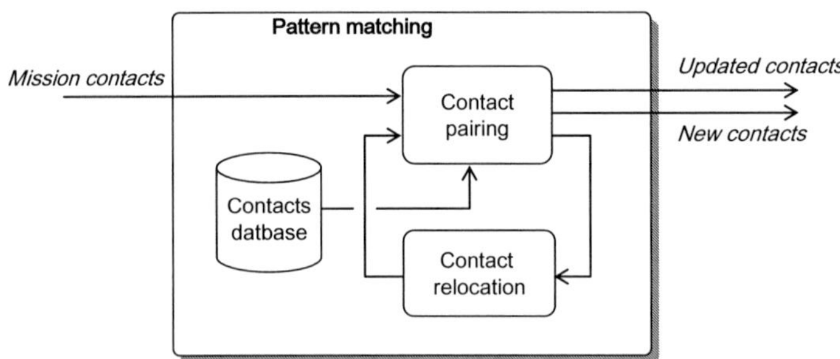

Figure 6: The pattern matching architecture.

Contact pairing

The contact pairing algorithm is composed of four sequential functions.

The first consists to rationalize reference and current mission contact signatures. A contact signature χ_C is a constellation defined by as many branches as contacts within a neighbourhood *Wr*. A branch χ_C^n is defined using the distance between positions, the height difference between contacts, and their relative azimuth (Fig. 7). Signatures are computed for every mission *(M)* and known contact *(C)*.

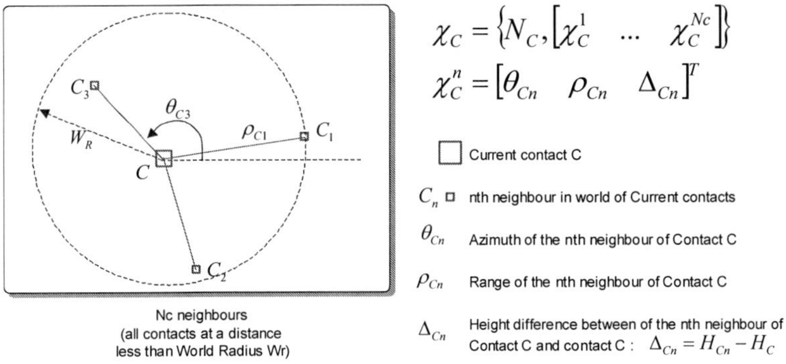

$$\chi_C = \left\{ N_C, \left[\chi_C^1 \quad \cdots \quad \chi_C^{Nc} \right] \right\}$$

$$\chi_C^n = \left[\theta_{Cn} \quad \rho_{Cn} \quad \Delta_{Cn} \right]^T$$

Figure 7: Contact signature definition.

Secondly, a search function selects every known contact at a distance of less than the operational parameter from the analysed mission contact. For a mission contact we get *n* candidate known contacts in a new space:

$$K = \left\{ R_1, ..., R_n \right\}$$

Third, for each pair of known mission contacts, we estimate a matching distance with a modified Haussdorff distance, often used in pattern recognition techniques. A Haussdorff distance is used to make the contact pairing method have a low sensitivity to non-detected mission contacts. On the other hand, it requires a high quality and exhaustive contacts database.

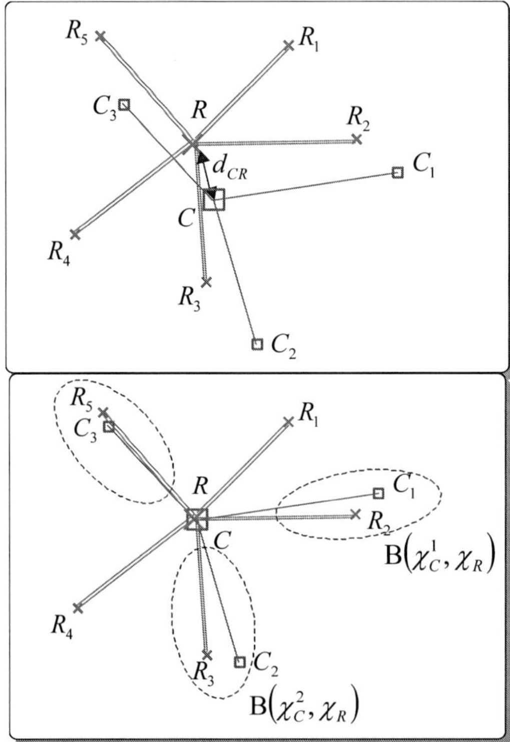

Figure 8: Signature distance example.

The matching distance uses the Mahalanobis distance for the relative position, height, azimuth and measured positional error between the two contacts.

The last stage of the pairing decision step consists in determining the known contact b that is the best math (*i.e.* with the smallest matching distance) and then to check if the matching distance is lower than some fixed threshold.

Contacts relocation

The contact relocation algorithm is derived from a simultaneous localization and mapping (SLAM) function designed for AUVs [2]. This method consists in modeling the relative contact position uncertainty as a spring net and contact pairing as constraints in this spring net.

To get a mathematical representation of the spring net, we define:

- A position vector P of all the known *(Nk)* and mission *(Nm)* contacts

$$\vec{P} = \left[\underbrace{C_K(i)}_{i=1...Nk} \quad ... \quad \underbrace{C_N(i)}_{i=1...Nm} \quad ... \quad \underbrace{0}_{Nk} \quad ... \right]^T . \tag{3}$$

- A mesh matrix M that represents absolute contact position uncertainty. The function $\Gamma(C_K(c))$ stands for spring stiffness of the cth known contact. It is used to defined every contact anchoring by (9) and (10).

$$M = 10^{-5} . \left. \begin{bmatrix} 1 & ... & 0 \\ ... & ... & ... \\ 0 & ... & 1 \end{bmatrix} \right\} 2.Nk + Nm . \tag{4}$$

$$M(c,c) = M(c,c) + \Gamma(C_K(c)) \text{ for } c=1...Nk. \tag{5}$$

$$M(c + Nk, c + Nk) = M(c + Nk, c + Nk) + \Gamma(C_M(c)) \text{ for } c=1...Nm \tag{6}$$

- The relative contact positioning uncertainty ε is used in to define the stiffness spring connection $\Gamma(\varepsilon)$ between contacts (11).

$$\begin{cases} M(c + Nk, c + Nk) = M(c + Nk, c + Nk) + \Gamma(\varepsilon) \\ M(c + Nk, c + Nk + 1) = M(c + Nk, c + Nk + 1) - \Gamma(\varepsilon) \\ M(c + Nk + 1, c + Nk + 1) = M(c + Nk + 1, c + Nk + 1) + \Gamma(\varepsilon) \\ M(c + Nk + 1, c + Nk) = M(c + Nk + 1, c + Nk) - \Gamma(\varepsilon) \end{cases} . \tag{7}$$

- A matrix of constraints C that represents the contact pairing (12). We use (13) and (14) to establish a null initial length connection between known and mission contacts. The initial spring length is null to represent the fact that those two contacts should have the same (or very close) absolute position.

$$C = \left. \begin{bmatrix} 1 & ... & 0 \\ ... & ... & ... \\ 0 & ... & 1 \end{bmatrix} \right\} 2.Nk + Nm . \tag{8}$$

$$\begin{cases} C(k,k) = C(k,k) + \dfrac{1}{\delta_k^2} \\[2mm] C(k,k+Nk+Nm) = C(k,k+Nk+Nm) - \dfrac{1}{\delta_k^2} \\[2mm] C(k+Nk+Nm,k+Nk+Nm) = C(k+Nk+Nn,k+Nk+Nn) + \dfrac{1}{\delta_k^2} \\[2mm] C(k+Nk+Nm,k) = C(k+Nk+Nm,k) - \dfrac{1}{\delta_k^2} \end{cases} \quad . \tag{9}$$

$$\begin{cases} C(Nk+m,Nk+m) = C(Nk+m,Nk+m) + \dfrac{1}{\delta_m^2} \\[2mm] C(Nk+m,k+Nk+Nn) = C(Nk+m,k+Nk+Nn) - \dfrac{1}{\delta_m^2} \\[2mm] C(k+Nk+Nn,k+Nk+Nn) = C(k+Nk+Nn,k+Nk+Nn) + \dfrac{1}{\delta_m^2} \\[2mm] C(k+Nk+Nn,Nk+m) = C(k+Nk+Nn,Nk+m) - \dfrac{1}{\delta_m^2} \end{cases} \quad . \tag{10}$$

where δ_k stands for the detection position uncertainty of a known contact k. δ_m stands for the detection position uncertainty of a mission contact m.

The mesh matrix takes into account the very high relative position accuracy for close contacts in SAS sonar images. The constraints matrix represents the fact that, if a mission contact is found in the known contacts database it should be shifted to get closer to this known contact. Moreover, others nearby mission contacts that are present in the same waterfall should be shifted by "somewhat" the same value.
The potential global energy of the net could be expressed in the quadratic form shown in (15). The Q vector represents contacts shifts.

$$E_{pot} = \frac{1}{2}.Q^T.M.Q + \frac{1}{2}.(P+Q)^T.C.(P+Q). \tag{11}$$

In these conditions, the optimal position of all contacts is obtained at the lower energy state of the spring net by (16).

$$P^* = P + \arg\left(\min_Q\left(E_{pot}\right)\right) = P - \left[M+C\right]^{-1}.C.P. \tag{12}$$

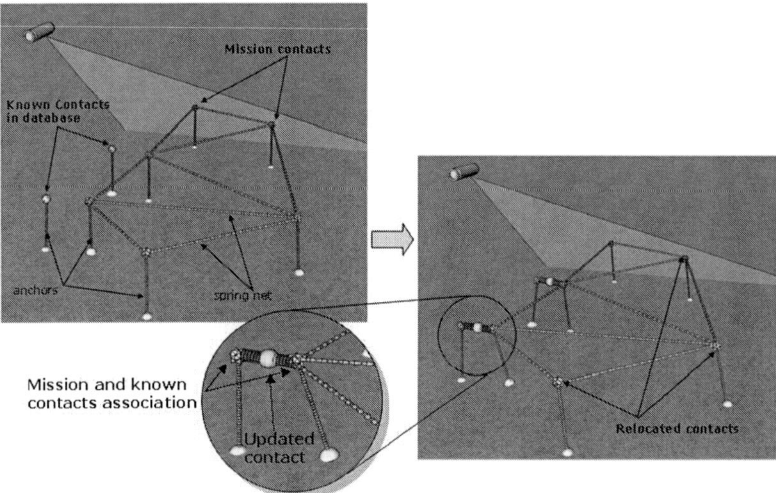

Figure 9: schematic view of contact relocation spring net.

This two-stage iterative algorithm leads to a highly reliable contact pairing method as shown in Fi10. Monte-Carlo simulations and tests on real data have shown a very low false pairing rate with a good probability of correct pairing. The use of the contact relocation algorithm results in a very low sensitivity to the global positioning bias which has to be taken into account for AUV-based missions.

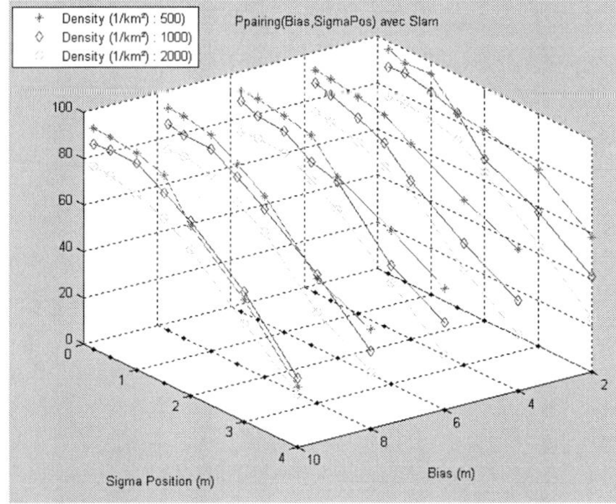

Figure 10: The contact paring probability is a function of relative contact position uncertainty and global positioning bias.

4. Applications and results

This change detection algorithm has been designed to be embedded into the next generation MCM AUVs, like ASEMAR [3] in order to improve its decisional autonomy. This generation of AUVs is fitted with real time SAS and ATR embedded processing. In MCM survey mission, the AUV should be setup with a known contact database; as shown in Fig. 11 a known database could be initialised using ATR output, but this result should be reviewed by a sonar operator in order to obtain precise contact position information. In addition, as explained previously, no contact should be missing in this database.

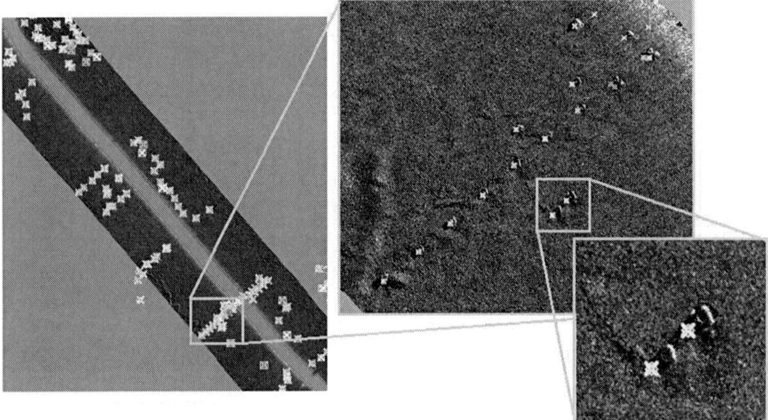

Figure 11: ATR results considered as known contact database.

A typical AUV survey mission is composed of two phases. The first consists in exploring the area with a typical parallel-track pattern. At the end of each track, the change detection algorithm is executed in order to update known contacts with observations (or mission contacts) detected during the track. In the second phase, at the end of the initially-planned tracks, the AUV could decide autonomously to re-acquire the new contacts, depending on available energy and mission time constraints. The advantage of this high autonomy level is that the AUV can produce more sonar views of the suspicious contacts and could even undertake a camera inspection fully autonomously, thus decreasing the need of additional missions to fulfill the identification task. The objective is to provide relevant data with regards to suspicious contacts to the operator for action.

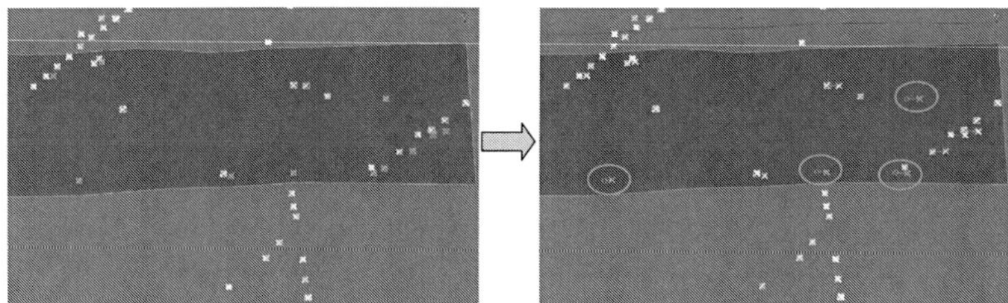

Figure 12: White crosses indicate known contacts, coloured ones indicate mission contacts. On the left, known and mission contacts before change detection has occurred. On right, new contacts are circled after change detection; relocated known contacts are updated, *i.e.* new observations are added to known contacts.

For exploratory MCM missions, a known contact database is not available but the same algorithm could still be used. In this case, the known database is initially empty, but at the end of each track it is filled with ATR detections. The next tracks performed partially on the same area (due to the overlap between two sonar passes) will produce new observations of previously detected contacts. The algorithm performs contact association and is used in the SLAM processing to correct the AUV's internal position. This automatic contact association allows one to perform embedded, multi-view classification to obtain better overall mine detection and classification results.

The same change detection algorithm could be used in a mine warfare C2 system or analysis software. It can be used as a standard pattern matching function to help the operator update the known contact database.

We can also use the intermediate results of the ATR and contact pairing to produce automatically co-registered high-quality sonar data mosaicks (Fig. 13). The principle is to project the sonar data as a function of the sonar's trajectory, and then to apply morphing techniques to the mosaic such that the contacts in the mosaic fit exactly with those in the known contacts database.

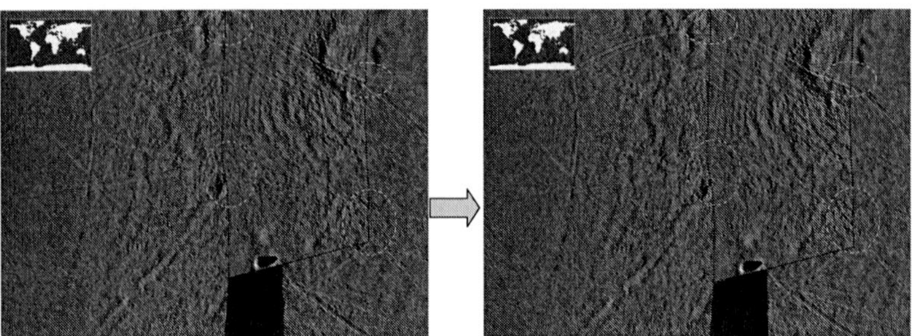

Figure 13: On the left is the initial data mosaic. On the right, an automatically registered mosaic using ATR pattern matching results.

References

[1] Ø. Midtgaard, R. Hansen, T.Sæbø 1, V. Myers, J. Dubberley, I. Quidu, "Change Detection Using Synthetic Aperture Sonar: Preliminary Results from the Larvik Trial", *OCEANS 2011 MTS/IEEE conference*, Konaj, United States, 2011.
[2] J. Ferrand, "Simultaneous localisation and mapping system by non linear elastic filtering", Brevet (Patent) WO 2011048224 (A1)
[3] J. Ferrand, "Système de recalage sur amers dans le projet ASEMAR", *SeaTech Week 2010, MOQSEM,* Brest, 2010
[4] F. Fohanno, N. Mandelert, F. Florin, "Automatic Processing for AUV", *Oceans 2006 IEEE conference*, Singapore, 2006.

CHAPTER FIFTEEN

SUBPIXEL IMAGE REGISTRATION FOR COHERENT CHANGE DETECTION BETWEEN TWO HIGH RESOLUTION SONAR PASSES

ISABELLE QUIDU, VINCENT MYERS, ØIVIND MIDTGAARD AND ROY E. HANSEN

Abstract

The use of phase coherence between two pings is used in many underwater imaging applications, in particular the micronavigation algorithms used in correcting receiver positions when focussing a synthetic aperture sonar (SAS) array. Recently, interest has turned to using the phase coherence between two sonar images that consist of two repeated passes over the same area in order to co-register the images and perform coherent change detection, meaning the detection of differences in two areas that causes a decorrelation between the two images. Such techniques are used in synthetic aperture radar (SAR) applications, and can detect subtle changes that are not immediately detectable by visual inspection or other traditional methods. Before computing the coherence the two images have to be accurately co-registered. Indeed remaining misregistrations after a 2D rigid translation lead to a loss of phase coherence. This can be due to navigational disturbances or data processing defects. The problem of non-rigid and subpixel sonar image registration is achieved here in two main steps. The first step aims to estimate the displacement field from which a warping function is derived; then, the repeat-pass image is resampled using the warping function to co-register it to primary image.

Keywords: Elastic Registration, Change Detection, Coherence, SAS Images.

1. Introduction

Change detection between two repeated sonar passes over the same area is a well-known tactic for detecting targets on the seafloor, and is the most reliable method for detecting objects of an improvised nature meaning that little or no prior knowledge of size and shape is available or that it has been altered or disguised in some way. Two modes of change detection can be considered: incoherent and coherent change detection [1]. Incoherent change detection methods aim to identify changes in the mean backscatter power that can be estimated by the pixel intensity. This method has been widely used in SAR imagery [2,3] and recently applied to high-frequency sonar imagery [4,5]. Coherent change detection, on the other hand, identifies changes in both the amplitude and phase of the image data. By using the information that is provided by the phase, it is possible to detect very subtle changes, even those not visually detectable. However, preserving coherence is made difficult by the natural temporal decorrelation and by the stringent navigational accuracy requirements for minimizing differences in the imaging geometry between the primary and repeat pass [1,6]. In this paper, these issues are examined using a data set collected in April 2010 by the Norwegian Defence Research Establishment (FFI) in an area outside of Larvik, Norway with the HUGIN 1000-HUS AUV equipped with a HISAS 1030 interferometric SAS, deployed from the research vessel HU Sverdrup II [4,7]. Coherent change detection also requires that the primary and repeat pass images are registered to sub-resolution accuracy, typically a tenth of a resolution cell [1]. This requirement, together with the problem of local misregistration, is addressed in three steps: A large scale translation is first applied to the data, which is presented in Section 2, along with a method for estimating the subpixel displacement field; then, two warping procedures are proposed in Section 3 for performing an elastic co-registration. Section 4 shows experimental results on the HiSAS data set, which contains different objects on different types of seabeds.

2. Displacement field estimation

Registration is the process of aligning two images: the primary image Ip and the repeat pass image Irp. Finding the spatial transformation to apply to Irp is generally the key to any registration problem. Sometimes a rigid transformation is not sufficient and local misregistrations remain. In SAS images, it is usually due to a change in the sensor position or viewpoint. In that case, an elastic registration following a rigid one must be performed. The displacement field which gives a feature-to-feature correspondence between the primary image and the repeat pass image, is estimated by finding matching features extracted in both images. Many matching techniques are available and recent techniques have focussed on extracting local invariant features such as the Scale Invariant Feature Transform (SIFT) method and Speeded Up Robust Features (SURF) [8,9]. However these techniques do not use the phase of the image, which is a key component when using coherence to detect changes. Moreover the sonar image formation process leads to a different sampling of a given scene at different times. This is the source of the motivation for evaluating subpixel correlation-based matching methods. Two methods are presented here. For both, in order to speed up the cross-correlation computation over the area to register, the repeat pass M × N image is divided into a number of non-overlapping chips $C_{rp} = I_{rp}(x, y, m, n)$ of size $m \times n$ centred at the image indices where $m \ll M$ and $n \ll N$.

Coarse shift and re-navigation

The first step in the displacement field estimation is a compensation for global translation, as described in [4,7], and shown in Fig. 1.

Corresponding SAS images are produced from the primary and repeat pass sonar data, using the vehicle navigation solutions. As preprocessing for feature point extraction, these images are down sampled by a factor of two in both dimensions using the mean operator, and the resulting magnitude values are transformed onto a logarithmic scale. Anisotropic diffusion is applied to reduce the image speckle, thus creating more uniform magnitude regions while preserving region edges. Feature points are then extracted from both images by the SURF algorithm and matched using a similarity score. The SURF feature points typically correspond to image high-light and shadow "blobs" of various sizes. An outlier filtering stage has been included, as false matches sometimes occur. The filter only accepts matches that are part of the main match cluster in the parameter space. The parameters for a rigid spatial transformation (translation, rotation and dilation) of the images can then be found from the set of resulting point pairs.

The estimated translation between the two images are then applied to the navigation solution of the repeat pass data to regenerate that image (Note that even though the method also estimates rotation and dilation, only the translation was used in this study). The method managed to bring the global relative position error down from around five meters to a few centimeters.

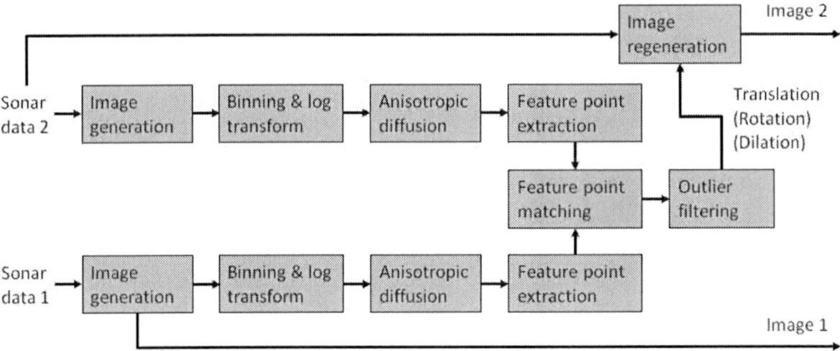

Figure 1: Data flow for the coarse shifting method. After the features are extracted and matched, the SAS imaging process is repeated with the corrected navigation solution.

Subpixel complex correlation

As proposed in [10], the cross-correlation of the two small chips $C_p = I_p(x,y,m,n)$ and $C_{rp} = I_{rp}(x,y,m,n)$ of the same size is achieved into two steps. It starts with an initial estimate of the location of the cross-correlation peak obtained to within a fraction ½ of a pixel by the usual fast Fourier transform (FFT) approach. This approach consists in: (i) computing the fast Fourier transforms of each chips $FC_p = FFT(C_p)$ and $FC_{rp} = FFT(C_{rp})$; (ii) embedding the element-wise product $FC_p \times FC_{rp}^*$ in a larger array of zeros of dimension $(2m{\times}2n)$; (iii) computing an inverse FFT to obtain an upsampled (by a factor of 2) cross correlation; and (iv) locating its peak. This peak is a starting point, the initial estimate, around which a new upsampled cross-correlation (by a factor k) is computed in a $1.5{\times}1.5$ pixel neighbourhood. This is due to the following property:

$$IFFT\left(FC_p \times FC_{rp}^*\right) = FFT^*\left(FC_p^* \times FC_{rp}\right) = FFT^*(h) = H^*,$$

where H can be computed using a Matrix Fourier Transform such that [11]:

$$H(U,V) = e^{-2\pi j UX^T} . h(X,Y) . e^{-2\pi j YV^T}$$

$$\text{where} \quad \begin{cases} U = V = \dfrac{\left[0...\text{ceil}(1.5k)-1\right]^T}{k} & \text{around the initial peak} \\[2em] X = \dfrac{\left[0...m-1\right]^T}{m} - \dfrac{1}{2}, \quad Y = \dfrac{\left[0...m-1\right]^T}{m} - \dfrac{1}{2} \end{cases}$$

The output H is a $1.5k \times 1.5k$ array in units of upsampled pixels. The searched subpixel displacement $(\Delta x, \Delta y)$ is given by the location of the output peak in the complex modulus $|H|$, then in the phase angle $\arg(H^*)$, if necessary.

Possible outliers or erroneous displacement estimates can simply be suppressed by thresholding the value of the output peak. From the remaining estimates two sets of ncp corresponding feature points $\mathbf{x_p} = [x_k], \mathbf{y_p} = [y_k]$ on the primary image and $\mathbf{x_s} = [u_k^{'}], \mathbf{y_s} = [z_k^{'}]$ on the repeat pass image with $k = [1, \ldots, n_{cp}]$ can be derived where: $u_k^{'} = x_k + \Delta x_k$ and $z_k^{'} = y_k + \Delta y_k$.

Amplitude correlation with parabolic interpolation

Unlike the previous one, this method takes as inputs the amplitude of the sonar images. The correlation procedure works as follows: a normalized cross-correlation is performed in a chip, centred at the same image indices x, y with an area in the primary image:

$$\gamma(x, y) = \frac{1}{(mn) - 1} \sum \frac{\overline{C}_p \, \overline{C}_{np}}{\sigma_p \sigma_{rp}} \, ,$$

where $\overline{C}_p = C_p - \mu_p$ is the mean subtracted primary chip and σ_p is the standard deviation of $\overline{C}_p$. The index $\gamma(x, y)$ of the maximum correlation over the central part (that is, where the cross-correlation is valid) of the primary chip is found. Then, a parabolic interpolation is used to estimate the sub-pixel position of the peak indenpendently in the u and z dimensions [1, 12]:

$$u' = u + 0.5 \frac{(u-v)^2 \left|\gamma(u,z) - \gamma(w,z)\right| - (u-w)^2 \left|\gamma(u,z) - \gamma(v,z)\right|}{(u-v)\left|\gamma(u,z) - \gamma(w,z)\right| - (u-w)\left|\gamma(u,z) - \gamma(v,z)\right|}$$

where $v = u - 1$ and $w = u + 1$. An analogous method is used to find z'. The maxima $\gamma(u,z)$ can also be filtered using a threshold τ. What remains are two sets of n_{cp} corresponding feature points $\mathbf{x_p} = [x_k], \mathbf{y_p} = [y_k]$ on the primary image and $\mathbf{x_s} = \left[u'_k\right], \mathbf{y_s} = \left[z'_k\right]$ on the repeat pass image, with $k = \left[1,\ldots,n_{cp}\right]$.

3. Warping procedure

From the displacement field a warping procedure has to be derived. The warping function specifies the pixel-to-pixel correspondence, namely the spatial mapping, between the primary image and the repeat pass image. Registration is performed by resampling the repeat pass image onto the primary image by applying the spatial mapping along with an interpolation technique. The spatial mapping is frequently expressed parametrically as two approximation functions f_x and f_y so as to compute the transformed image I_{rpw} [13]:

$$I_{rpw}(x,y) = I_{rp}\left(f_x(x,y), f_y(x,y)\right)$$

The two approximation functions f_x and f_y must be computed from the estimated displacement field. On the one hand, the displacement field is a set of n feature points $(x_i, y_i)_{i=1\ldots n}$ in the repeat pass image to be displaced by some value $(dx_i, dy_i)_{i=1\ldots n}$. On the other hand, the warp function relates the (x,y) points in the original image to their counterparts $(x',y') = \left(f_x(x,y), f_y(x,y)\right)$ in the warped image. The warping procedure tries to estimate two smooth surfaces from two sets of scattered data: X that passes through $(x_i, y_i, dx_i)_{i=1\ldots n}$ and Y that passes through $(x_i, y_i, dy_i)_{i=1\ldots n}$. The two approximation functions provide a displacement to every pixel of the repeat pass image:

$$f_x(x,y) = (x,y) + X(x,y),$$

and

$$f_y(x,y) = (x,y) + Y(x,y).$$

After the feature matching procedure from Section, 2, the set $(dx_k, dy_k)_{k=1\ldots n_{cp}} = \left(x_k - u'_k, y_k - z'_k\right)_{k=1\ldots n_{cp}}$ can be used to estimate f_x and f_y .

Multilevel B-spline approximation

Cubic B-splines have many properties, such as local control, smoothness and computational efficiency that make them widely used in surface modeling [14]. Moreover, in order to deal irregularly spaced feature points, multilevel B-splines, proposed by Lee *et al* for generating a smooth surface by interpolating the scattered data points [15], was implemented. This approach was chosen over thin-plate splines, introduced by Bookstein [16], as they have two major drawbacks in the present application: firstly, the estimation requires the inversion of a matrix made of data point coordinates and can be computationally expensive; secondly it is based on radial basis functions that cannot adapt themselves to the data point density.

The basic idea is to estimate the approximation function f as a uniform bicubic B-spline function by minimizing (in the least-squared sense) the error between this function and the feature points. The function f is defined in terms of sixteen control points ϕ_{ij} weighted by a product of uniform cubic B-spline basis functions $B_k, k = 0...3$:

$$f(x,y) = \sum_{k=0}^{3}\sum_{l=0}^{3} B_k(s)B_l(t)\phi_{i+k,j+l}, i = \lfloor x \rfloor - 1, j = \lfloor y \rfloor - 1, s = x - \lfloor x \rfloor, t = y - \lfloor y \rfloor,$$

with

$$B_0(t) = \frac{(1-t)^3}{6}, B_1(t) = \frac{(3t^3 - 6t^2 + 4)}{6}, B_2(t) = \frac{(-3t^3 + 3t^2 + 3t + 1)}{6}, B_3(t) = \frac{t^3}{6}$$

$$, 0 \le t < 1.$$

Let Φ be the control lattice that spans the integer grid in a rectangular domain Ω of the xy-plane and the set of scattered points $P = \{(x_c, y_c, z_c)\}$, where (x_c, y_c) is a point of Ω as shown in Fig. 2. The objective is to determine the control points of Φ that provide the value of the approximation function f at every (x_c, y_c) that is closest to z_c. This is found by solving the minimization problem:

$$\min_{\phi_{ij}} \sum_c \left(z_c - f(x_c, y_c)\right)^2 + \sum_{ij} \phi_{ij}^2,$$

where

$$z_c = \sum_{k=0}^{3}\sum_{l=0}^{3} B_k(s)B_l(t)\phi_{i+k,j+l}^c, i = \lfloor x \rfloor - 1, j = \lfloor y \rfloor - 1, s = x - \lfloor x \rfloor, t = y - \lfloor y \rfloor$$

and $\sum_c$ is the sum of the feature points (x_c, y_c, z_c) that influence the value of ϕ_{ij}.

The solution is given by:

$$\phi_{i+k,j+l} = \frac{\sum_c \left(w_{k,l}^c\right)^2 \phi_{k,l}^c}{\sum_c \left(w_{k,l}^c\right)^2}$$

where $\phi_{k,l}^c$ is the contribution to the control point $\phi_{i+k,j+l}$ to the feature points (x_c, y_c, z_c) that are within a 4×4 neighborhood. $\phi_{k,l}^c$ is found by using pseudoinverse method:

$$\phi_{kl}^c = \frac{w_{kl} z_c}{\sum_{a=0}^{3}\sum_{b=0}^{3} w_{ab}^2}$$

with $w_{kl} = B_k(s)B_l(t), k,l = 0...3$, and $k = i+1-\lfloor x_c \rfloor$, $l = j+1-\lfloor y_c \rfloor$, $s = x_c - \lfloor x_c \rfloor, t = y_c - \lfloor y_c \rfloor$

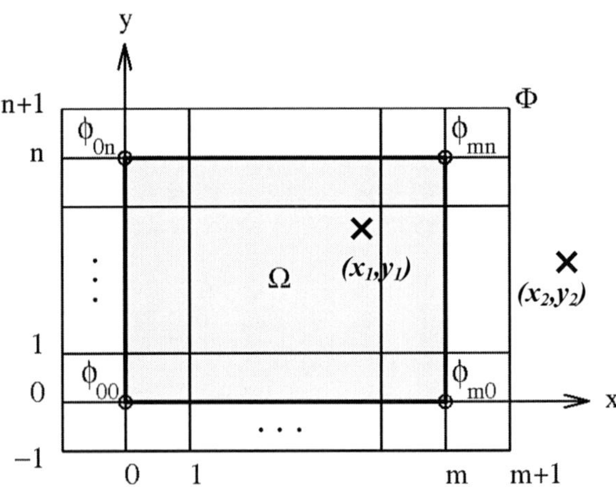

Figure 2: Control lattice Φ overlaid on domain Ω [4] and two features points (x_c, y_c)

Algorithm 1: Multi-level B-spline pseudo-code.

$h \leftarrow$ the number of levels

$P \leftarrow \left\{ \left(x_c, y_c, z_c \right) \right\} \Rightarrow$ The set of scattered points

$f_0 \leftarrow$ result of applying B-spline approximation to P with coarsest control lattice Φ_0.

for each feature point

$$\Delta^1 z_c \leftarrow z_c - f_0 \left(x_c, y_c \right)$$

endfor

$\Psi' \leftarrow 0 \Rightarrow$ Initialize the control lattice

for $k = 1$ to h

Compute Φ_k using $P_k = \left\{ \left(x_c, y_c, \Delta^k z_c \right) \right\} \Rightarrow \Phi_k$ is twice as fine as Φ_{k-1}

    for each feature point

$$\Delta^{k+1} z_c \leftarrow \Delta^k z_c - f_k \left(x_c, y_c \right)$$

    end for

$\Psi = \Psi' + \Phi_k \Rightarrow$ Update the control lattice

$\Psi' \leftarrow \Psi$, where the control point spacing is half as large as Ψ

endfor

This B-spline approximation is parameterized by the size of the control lattice. A coarse lattice leads to a smooth but inaccurate approximation. Conversely with a fine lattice, local peaks near feature points appear. In order to circumvent this tradeoff between smoothness and accuracy a multi-level B-spline approximation has been proposed by Lee et al. [4]. The method is summarized in Algorithm 1, below. The refinement consists in deriving from Ψ a larger control lattice Ψ' so that they both generate the same B-spline functions. It is less computationally expensive than keeping the approximation function of all levels to add them at the end.

Polynomial warp

Another method for computing the warping function is to fit a polynomial of the points $\left(\mathbf{x_p}, \mathbf{y_p} \right)$ and $\left(\mathbf{x_s}, \mathbf{y_s} \right)$. For a 2D polynomial fit of order p, the Vandermonde matrix V must be constructed, where:

$$V = \begin{bmatrix} 1 & u'_1 & z'_1 & u'_1 z'_1 & u'^2_1 & \cdots & z'^p_1 \\ 1 & u'_2 & z'_2 & u'_2 z'_2 & u'^2_2 & \cdots & z'^p_2 \\ 1 & \vdots & \vdots & \vdots & \vdots & \ddots & \vdots \\ 1 & u'_{n_{cp}} & z'_{n_{cp}} & u'_{n_{cp}} z'_{n_{cp}} & u'^2_{n_{cp}} & \cdots & z'^p_{n_{cp}} \end{bmatrix}$$

which is an $n_{cp} \times (p+1)(p+2)/2$ matrix. The coefficients of the least-square fitted polynomial can then be computed as

$$a = V^+ \mathbf{x_p},$$

and

$$b = V^+ \mathbf{y_p},$$

where V^+ is the Moore-Penrose pseudo-inverse of V. The polynomial defined by the coefficients in a and b can be used to compute the required warping to interpolate and co-register the repeat-pass image with the primary image.

Interpolation

The previous warping function gives a shift for every pixel of the image to be co-registered. This warped grid must be interpolated between points of the mesh grid that overlay the expected registered image. Here, a 2D cubic data interpolation is performed, which avoids phase jumps that can happen by a nearest neighbor interpolation.

4. Results

Data set

The data set used in this experiment was gathered in April 2011 in an area near Larvik, Norway using the by the HUGIN 1000-HUS Autonomous Underwater Vehicle, equipped with the HISAS 1030 Synthetic Aperture Sonar, which operates in the 60-120 kHz frequency range with up to 50 kHz in bandwidth. The resolution of the beamformed image is better than 5 × 5 cm and the pixel size is 2 × 2 cm. An area of high clutter was chosen specifically for these experiments: the area was first surveyed without any objects on April 8th, after which four targets were deployed and the area resurveyed on April 10th. The objects were: 2 concrete cubes of 40 × 40 × 40 cm (one rough, one smooth), a underwater glider, and a large water-filled "bag". Fig. 3 and Fig. 4 show the primary and the repeat pass areas respectively. The vehicle track is along the y-axis, and sonar range is along the x-axis. On the repeat pass area, four boxes surrounding the four deployed objects give the specific regions on which the proposed algorithms are assessed.

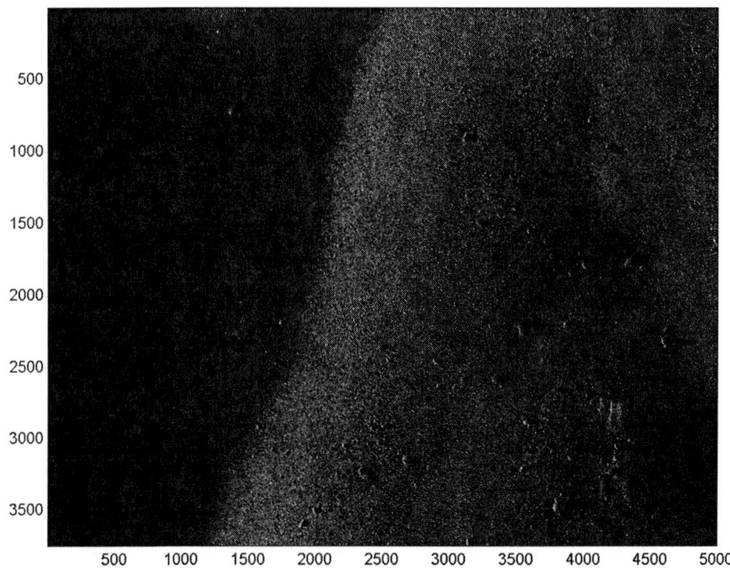

Figure 3: Primary SAS image of Area 2. The image size is 100m (range) by 75m (azimuth). The four studied regions are bounded by a rectangular box with the named object to be detected.

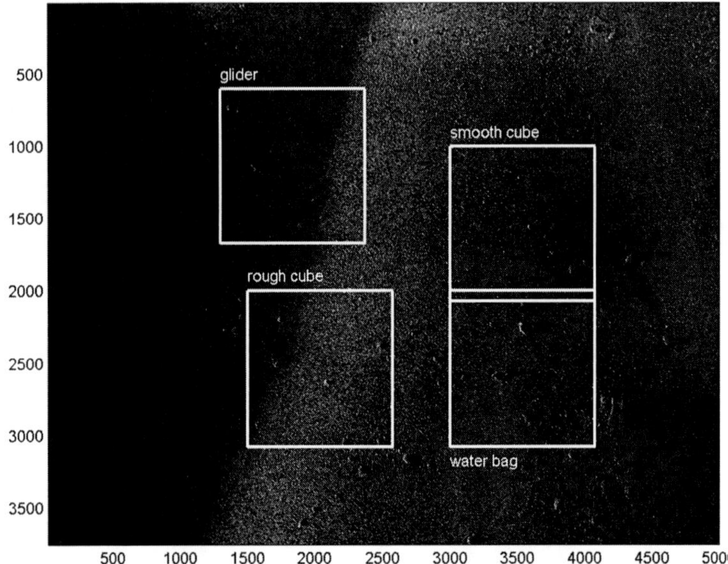

Figure 4: Repeat-pass SAS image of Area 2. The image size is 100m (range) by 75m (azimuth). The four studied regions are bounded by a rectangular box with the named object to be detected.

Displacement field estimation

Cross-correlation is performed using a squared chip of $m=51$ by $n=51$ pixels. The primary and repeat pass images are $M=1024$ by $N=1024$ pixels in size. Local displacements estimated by both methods were fused so as to provide a better estimate of the field. The cross-correlation of complex-valued chips ensures that the phase component also contribute to the alignment process, however where coherence is too weak, displacement can be estimated by correlating the amplitude. For complex subpixel correlation, the upsampling factor k is set to 10 and only displacements for which the peak is over the maximum less 0.2 are kept. For amplitude correlation, the threshold is fixed to 0.5.

Fig. 5 shows the result of the displacement field estimation for the region surrounding the water bag. Extracted feature points have been plotted on the primary (left) and the repeat pass (right) images. At the bottom of the figure, the estimated displacements can be seen. The amount of displacement has been exaggerated in order to be visible. Blue arrows are displacements estimated by both methods but for which the amplitude found by the complex cross-correlation has been kept. Magenta arrows are displacements estimated by the complex cross-correlation only. And the red arrows show displacements estimated by the amplitude cross-correlation only. As expected, these last are found even if the coherence is very weak.

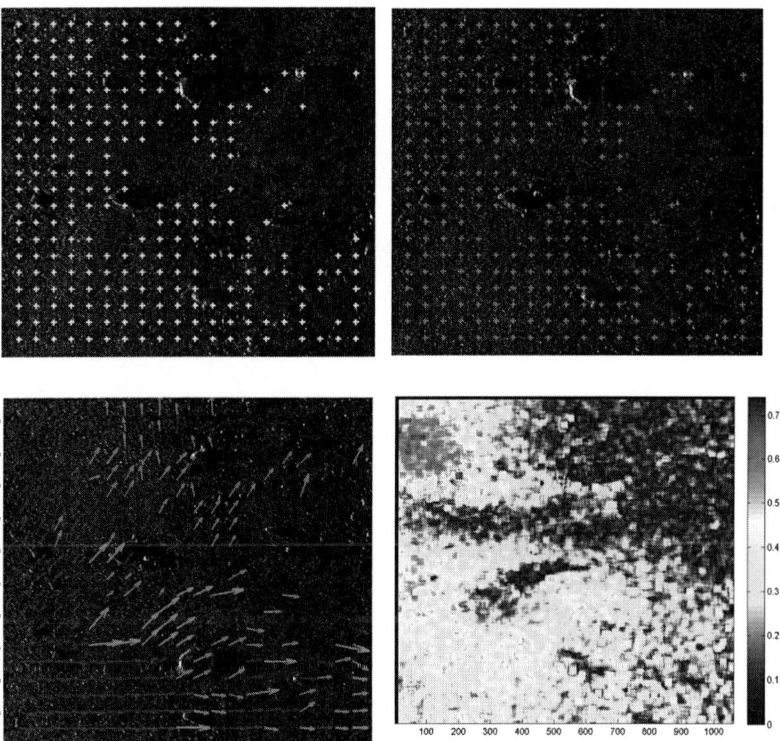

Figure 5: Results for the "water bag" region. In the first row, feature points on the primary (left) and the repeat pass (right) images are plotted. In the second row, on the left the estimated displacements are shown in arrows (length exaggerated to be visible); the coherence between the two images is shown on right.

Warping and interpolation

Here, the coherence used to detect changes between the two sonar passes is defined. First, the cross-correlation between two time series $s_1(t)$ and $s_2(t)$ is defined as:

$$\rho\left(s_1,s_2,\tau\right)=\int_{-\infty}^{+\infty}s_1^{*}\left(t\right)s_2\left(t+\tau\right)dt,$$

where $s^{*}(t)$ represents the complex conjugate of $s(t)$. The complex coherence function between $s_1(t)$ and $s_2(t)$ is defined as:

$$\Gamma(s_1,s_2,\tau)=\frac{\rho(s_1,s_2,\tau)}{\sqrt{\int_{-\infty}^{+\infty}|s_1(t)|^2\,dt}\sqrt{\int_{-\infty}^{+\infty}|s_2(t)|^2\,dt}}.$$

The absolute value of $\Gamma(s_1,s_2,\tau)$ is the maximum likelihood estimator for coherence. It is here computed using a sliding window of 21×21 pixels. In order to avoid aliasing problem while interpolating, the image phase was modified such that the fast fluctuation of the phase in the range direction was corrected by subtracting the fluctuation due to the carrier frequency. This gives a slower fluctuation due to the along-track sonar resolution.

In the multilevel B-spline approximation algorithm, the size of the finest control lattice is determined by the size of the image to register. In other words, the last level h is reached when the control lattice size cannot be refined without oversizing the input image.

Fig. 6 shows the two surfaces (one for estimated displacements along the x-axis, one for estimated displacements along the y-axis) that are estimated by the two warping methods given the feature points extracted in the "water bag" region that were shown in Fig. 5.

In Figs.7, 8, 9 and 10 the two warping methods are compared in terms of phase registration, amplitude registration and coherence. For the phase registration, the phase difference (pixel by pixel) is shown. For the amplitude registration the log-ratio of averaged images (by an average filter of size 20 by 20 pixels) before and after elastic registration [5] are compared. The change-detected object(s) should be visible in the log-ratio image. The first column gives results after only the rigid (coarse) registration. The second column shows results after elastic registration based on polynomial warp. The third column shows results with elastic registration based on the multilevel B-spline approximation.

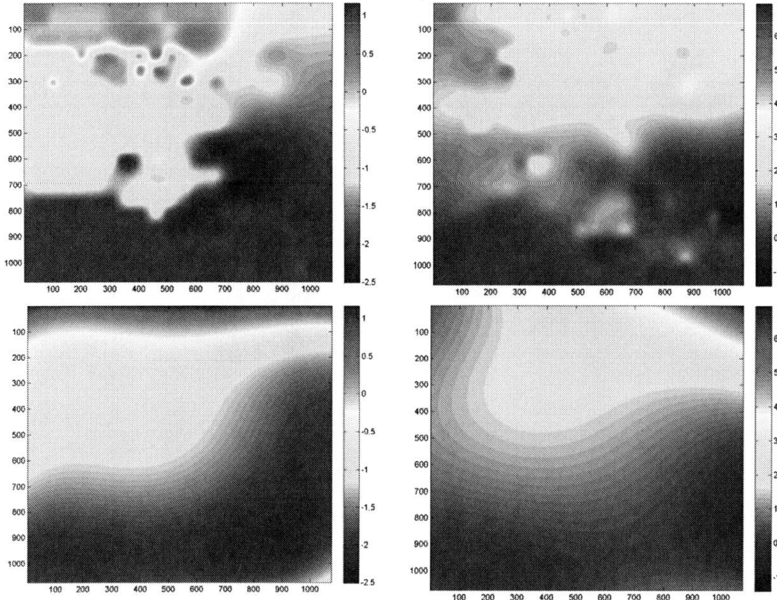

Figure 6: Estimated displacements along the x- and y-axes for the "water bag" region. Above is the field given by the multilevel B-spline warping and below is that computed by polynomial warping.

This case shows the potential of using change detection to detect objects without *a priori* knowledge of size and shape. The water bag target is quite stealthy by nature and had been deployed very near to a rock, which is a very difficult scenario in real-world applications. In spite of these difficulties, it can be detect here by taking the log-ratio of the two images. In this case, the elastic registration step did not provide a noticeably better log-ratio image.

Fig. 8 shows the case of the area surrounding the smooth cube. In this case, the elastic registration provides a significant boost in coherence that is required to detect it by a coherent change detection. The log-ratio image is also improved by the elastic registration step; however the target is easily detectable in all three cases.

In Fig. 9, more dramatic improvements in coherence can be observed in the region surrounding the "rough cube". As was the case for the smooth cube, the rough cube that was invisible in the coherence image after the rigid registration appear clearly with a very weak coherence surrounded by high coherence after the elastic registration. Moreover the remaining false alarms after the rigid registration disappear after the elastic registration. Looking at the phase difference image, the phase rotation is well retrieved, or denoised, over the whole region. Note that the vertical stripes in the coherence and phase difference are probably due to an incorrect wavenumber shift in the image formation and can be corrected.

Finally, Fig. 10 shows a significant amount of coherence gain the "glider" region, however the target, along with a smaller object just below it (which was an anchor used for keeping the glider in place) are in an area where coherence was not maintained, resulting in not a great deal of benefit for coherent change detection. Moreover, we can notice here a border defect of the polynomial warp that appears in the left part of the image leading to a loss of coherence conjugated with a noisy phase difference. The objects are visible in the log-ratio image.

5. Conclusions and future work

This paper examined a number of methods for feature matching, estimating the displacement field and warping to coregister two synthetic aperture sonar images over the same area. The methods were tested on image gathered by the HISAS-equipped HUGIN AUV during experiments at sea in an area near Larvik, Norway, in 2011. In all the cases, the elastic registration provided an increase in coherence between the two images, an in a few cases were need to coherently detect the deployed objects. However, it was also possible to detect the objects using purely amplitude-based methods. This is to be expected, since the true strength of coherent change detection is to be able to identify very small changes those not immediately perceptible by visual inspection, and in the case of the targets deployed in the Larvik trial, a combination of object size and good sensor resolution results in the lack of coherence not being strictly necessary to detect the targets. However, more importantly, it was found to be in fact possible to maintain some amount phase coherence over the seafloor after two days. This suggests that a study on the coherence would be of significant value. In fact, the data collected during the Larvik trial could be used for this purpose as sediment samples were taken and analyzed, and areas were surveyed in such a way as to provide time intervals of one day to over five days between surveys. The temporal coherence of the seabed determines the practical limitations of using coherent change detection (or any other kind of multi-pass coherent processing) and thus needs to be better understood. Also, the phase coherence allows one to envision the use of multiple passes over an area to create very high precision bathymetric maps using interferometry from two passes. Both are suggested as avenues for future research.

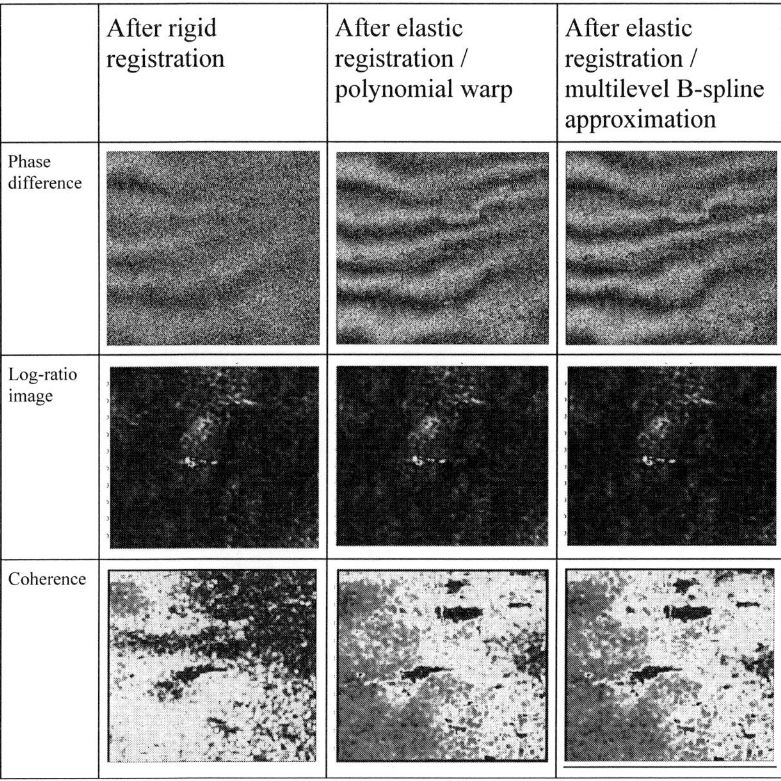

	After rigid registration	After elastic registration / polynomial warp	After elastic registration / multilevel B-spline approximation
Phase difference			
Log-ratio image			
Coherence			

Figure 7: Registration results for the "water bag" region, for coarse registration, polynomial warping and B-spline approximation. The resulting phase difference, log-ratio and coherence for the three methods are shown.

	After rigid registration	After elastic registration / polynomial warp	After elastic registration / multilevel B-spline approximation
Phase difference			

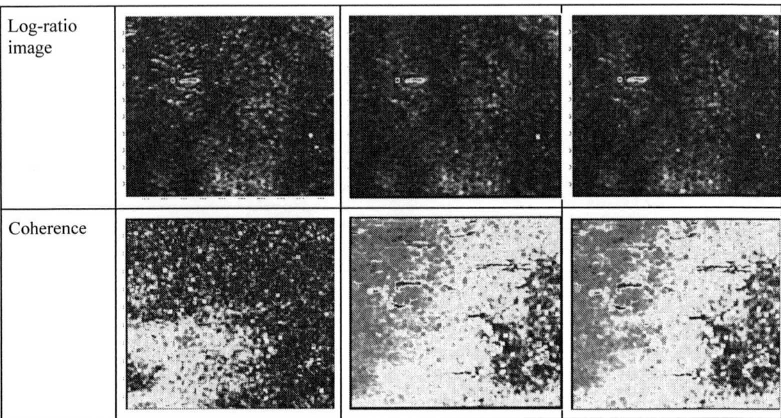

Figure 8: Registration results for the "smooth cube" area.

	After rigid registration	After elastic registration / polynomial warp	After elastic registration / multilevel B-spline approximation
Phase difference			
Log-ratio image		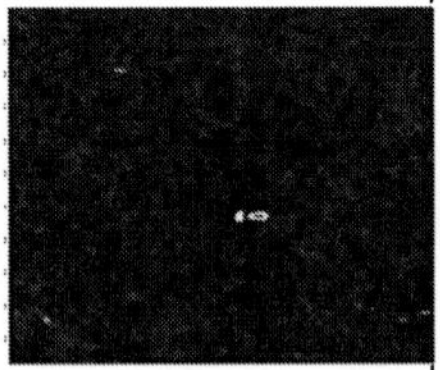	
Coherence	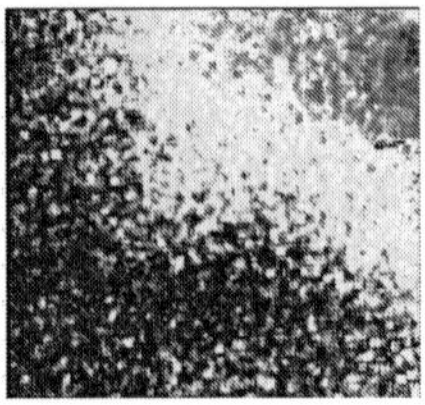	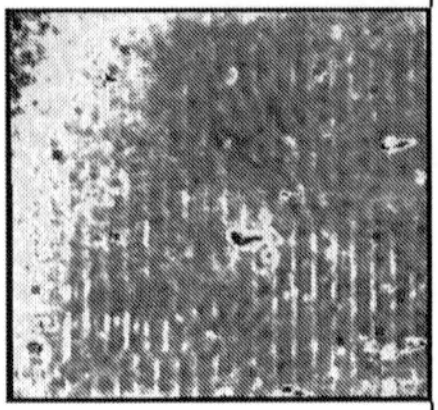	

Figure 9: "Rough cube" region, registration results.

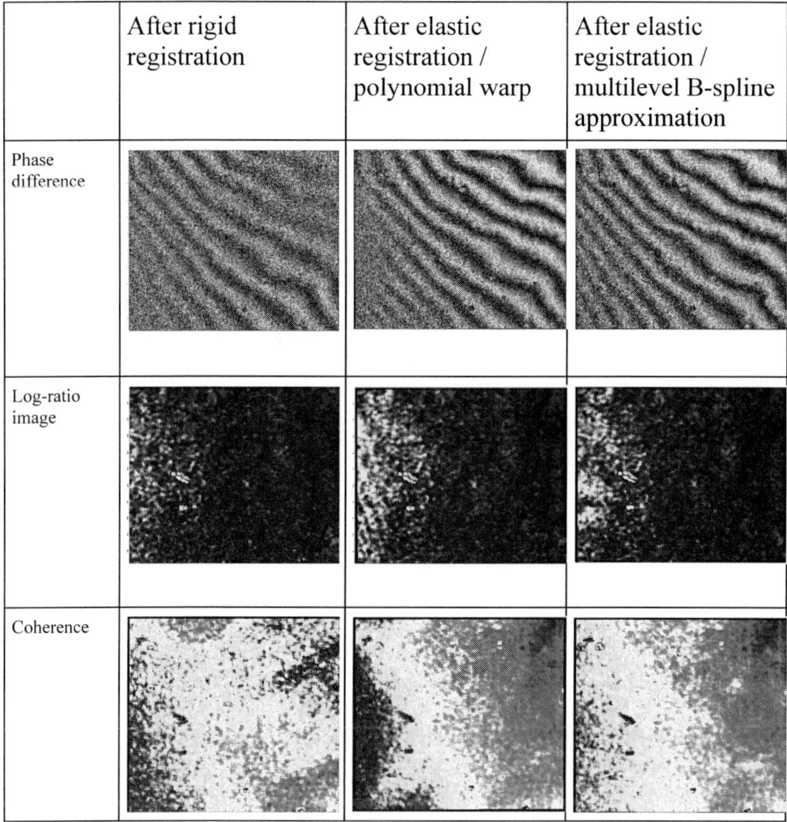

Figure 10 –Registration results for the glider area.

References

[1] M. Preiss and N. Stacy, *Coherent Change Detection: Theoretical Description and Experimental Results*, technical report DSTO–TR–1851, August, 2006.
[2] A. Singh, "Digital change detection techniques using remotely sensed data," *Int. J. Remote Sensing*, vol. 10, pp. 989-1003, 1989.
[3] E. Rignot and J. Van Zyl, "Change Detection Techniques for ERS-1 SAR Data", *IEEE Transactions on Geoscience and Remote Sensing*, Vol. 31, No. 4, July 1993.
[4] Ø. Midtgaard, T. O. Sæbø, R. Hansen, V. Myers, J. R. Dubberley and I. Quidu, "Change Detection Using Synthetic Aperture Sonar: Preliminary Results from the Larvik Trial", OCEANS'2011 MTS/IEEE, Kona, Hawaï, Sept 19-22, 2011.

[5] I. Quidu, "Incoherent change detection using amplitude sidescan sonar images", *11th European Conference on Underwater Acoustics (ECUA)*, 2nd and 6th July, 2012.

[6] T. Lyons and D. Brown, "Temporal variability of seafloor roughness and its impact on coherent change detection," *Proceedings of the International Conference on SAS and SAR*, Lerici, Italy, 2010.

[7] T. O. Sæbø, R. E. Hansen, H. J. Callow, S. A. V. Synnes, "Coregistration of synthetic aperture sonar coregistration of synthetic aperture sonar Images from repeated passes", proceedings of the *4th International Conference on "Underwater Acoustic Measurements: Technologies & Results"*, 2011.

[8] D.G. Lowe "Distinctive image features from scale-invariant keypoints". *International Journal of Computer Vision*, 60(2), pp. 91-110, 2004.

[9] H. Bay, T. Tuytelaars, L.V. Gool, "Surf: Speeded Up Robust Features", *In: 9th European Conference on Computer Vision (ECCV'06)*, May 2006.

[10] M. Guizar-Sicairos, S. T. Thurman, and J. R. Fienup, "Efficient subpixel image registration algorithms," Optics Letters, Vol. 33, pp. 156-158 (2008).

[11] J. O. Smith, *Mathematics of the Discrete Fourier Transform (DFT)* (W3K Publishing, http://www.w3k.org/books/), 2007

[12] W.H. Press, B.P. Flannery, W.A. Teukolsky, W.T Vetterling, *Numerical Recipes in C,* Cambridge University Press, 1988, pp. 299.

[13] L. G. Brown, "A survey of image registration techniques", *ACM computing Surveys*, vol. 24, No 4, pp. 325-376, 1992.

[14] Z. Xie and G. Farin, "Image registration using hierarchical B-splines", *IEEE Transaction on Visualization and Computer Graphics*, 10(1), pp. 85–94, 2004.

[15] S. Lee, G. Wolberg and S. Y. Shin, "Scattered data interpolation with multilevel B-splines", IEEE transactions on visualization and computer graphics, Vol. 3, No; 3, July-September 1997.

[16] F.L. Bookstein, "Principal warps: thin-plate splines and the decomposition of deformations", *IEEE Trans Pattern Anal Mach Intell*, vol. 11, no 6, pp. 567–585, 1989.

POSTER SESSION

CHAIRED BY VINCENT MYERS
DEFENCE R&D CANADA

CHAPTER SIXTEEN

MULTI-FREQUENCY SONAR DATA ANALYSIS:
APPLICATION TO THE DEEP-SEA WRECKAGE
SEARCH OF THE AIRBUS AF447 AIRPLANE
(MID-ATLANTIC RIDGE REGION)

STÉPHANIE DUPRÉ, BENOIT LOUBRIEU,
DELPHINE PIERRE, PIERRE LÉON,
RAYMOND GUILLOU, MICHAEL PURCELL,
GREGORY PACKARD, ANDREW SHERRELL
AND OLIVIER FERRANTE

Abstract

The crash of the Airbus AF447 the 1st of June 2009 in the Equatorial Atlantic Ocean led to a series of geophysical surveys, in particular with the use of multibeam and sidescan sonars to image the seabed. The region investigated during the French Bureau d'Enquête et d'Analyses (BEA) expeditions is associated with a rough seabed morphology characteristic of mid-oceanic ridge areas. Multi-scale or multi-frequency analysis greatly helps in the classification of the echoes by discriminating between some of them, in particular echoes produced by geo-related structures such as volcanic rock outcrops (*e.g.* rooted, buried structures, and rocks partially covered with sediments) and man-made objects.

Keywords: Backscatter, Sidescan Sonar, AUV, AF447, BEA.

1. Background

The A330 Airbus (flight AF447) airplane crashed on the 1st of June 2009 in the Equatorial Atlantic Ocean. The plane took off in Rio de Janeiro heading to Paris with 228 persons onboard. The last known position (LKP) of the airplane was also called ACARS point (Aircraft Communications Addressing and Reporting System). Only the latitude and longitude were known without any constraint on the altitude. The region of the crash is located close to the Mid-Atlantic Ridge. At the time of the accident, no bathymetry data were available except for a very low resolution dataset derived from satellite. The investigation focused on a 40 nm circle around the LKP point corresponding to 17 000 km^2 (Fig. 1).

The search of the wreckage was difficult for several reasons:

- Very little information on either the crash or the time/location of the impact of the plane at the sea surface were available.
- The area of investigation was relatively wide and in water depths of up to 4000 m (Fig. 2).
- The rough seafloor morphology (steep slopes associated with the ridges) was, in many areas, an obstacle for a full coverage, implying several insonifications through different survey dives.
- The rock outcrops characterized by high backscatter amplitude made the interpretation of the backscatter data regarding the plane debris challenging.

BEA reports and information relative to the crash and the subsequent investigation are available at: http://www.bea.aero/en/index.php

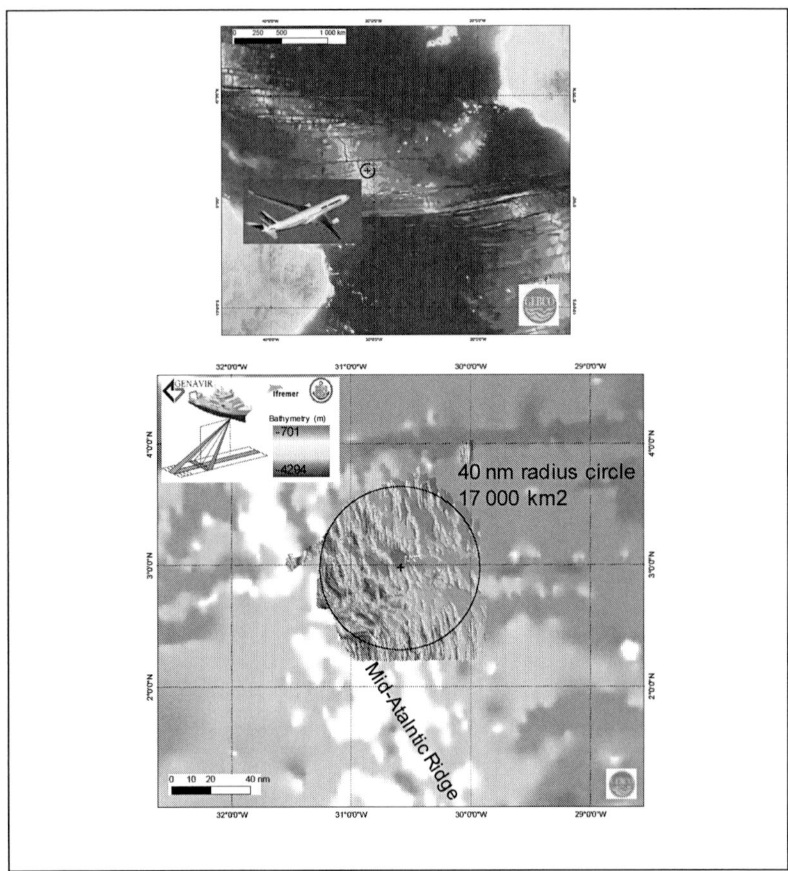

Figure 1: a) Atlantic Ocean map with position of the LKP (upper panel); b) Focus on the crash area with low resolution bathymetry (background) and ship-borne multibeam bathymetry acquired during the first BEA expeditions (lower panel).

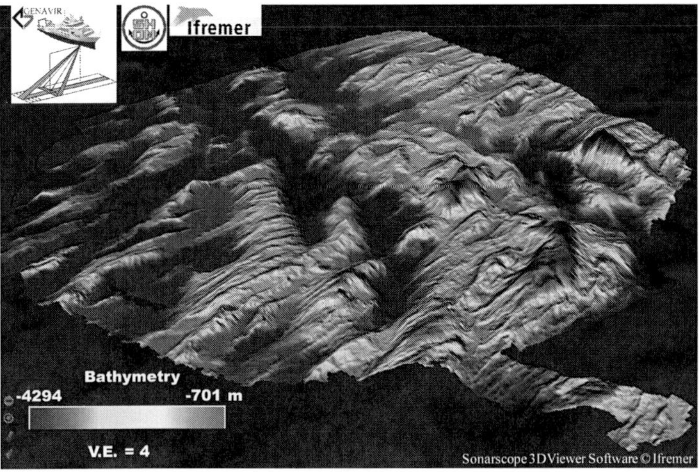

Figure 2: 3D bathymetry data of the investigated area revealing a rough seabed morphology characteristic of mid-oceanic ridge areas. Multibeam data acquired during the phases 1 and 2 (SHOM, IFREMER).

2. Data acquisition and processing

Marine expeditions and geophysical tools

The crash of the Airbus AF447 in the Equatorial Atlantic Ocean led to a series of geophysical surveys with in particular multibeam and sidescan sonars to image the seabed (Fig. 3). Ship-borne multibeam data were first acquired in the region, followed by a series of high-resolution seabed surveys. We report here only the investigation regarding the acoustic seabed imagery.

Several marine expeditions took place:

- Phase 1: 2 June to 15 July 2009 with seabed acoustic mapping using a ship-borne multibeam echosounder Reson 8150 onboard the R/V *Pourquoi pas ?* and *Nautile* submersible and *VICTOR 6000* ROV (Remotely Operated Vehicle) dives
- Phase 2: 23 July to 21 August 2009 with near-bottom acoustic surveys with the SAR deep-towed sidescan sonar from IFREMER and *VICTOR 6000* ROV surveys
- Phase 3: Leg1 23 March to 28 April 2010 and Leg2 30 April to 27 May 2010, using REMUS 6000 AUVs (Autonomous Underwater

Vehicle) (2 from WHOI and 1 from IFM-Geomar) and the TRITON ROV from Seabed onboard the *Seabed Worker* (Norway) and the ORION deep-towed sidescan sonar (Leg1 only) onboard the *Anne Candies* (USA)

- Phase 4: 25 Mars 2011 to 12 April 2011 using REMUS 6000 AUVs with sidecan sonars and electronic still camera with operations from the R/V *Alucia* (former R/V *Nadir*)

Figure 3: Deployed sonar equipment 1.SAR and 2.ORION deep-towed sidescan sonars and deep-water vehicles: 3.REMUS 6000 AUV, 4.VICTOR 6000 ROV, 5.NAUTILE submersible, 6.TRITON ROV.

Acquisition and processing

Multibeam data provide two types of seabed information, the relief/morphology (with the bathymetry) and the texture/nature (with the backscatter). Multibeam surveys were performed with a Reson system mounted on the hull of the R/V *Pourquoi pas ?* operating at a frequency of 12 (and 24) kHz. Bathymetric maps were produced at 50 m and 20 m pixel grid resolution, respectively, for the two frequencies (Fig. 4). Seafloor backscatter mosaics were processed at 20 m and 5 m, respectively. Although the resolution of the 12 kHz multibeam bathymetry/backscatter data is not the most suitable for the detection of airplane debris, the availability of this dataset is essential to 1) gather information on the relief and morphology, and on the nature of the seabed (*e.g.* volcanic rocks versus sediments, rocks partially covered with sediments); and 2) to plan near-bottom surveys with deep-towed, cabled, autonomous vehicles and submersibles as they were carried out during the different phases of the investigation.

High-resolution seafloor mapping was conducted to detect the debris of the airplane using sidescan sonars, either towed (SAR/180kHz, ORION/58kHz) or mounted on REMUS 6000 AUVs (EdgeTech/113 kHz). Up slope, the SAR deep-towed sidescan and the REMUS 6000 AUVs have the capability to climb along a maximum slope of 30° and 20°, respectively. When the AUV is getting close to the seabed and the altitude goes below 10 m, photo imagery of the seabed is automatically obtained. High-resolution, metre-scale seabed pictures are very convenient for i) calibration of the backscatter signature and ii) visual inspection – although narrow – for plane debris. AUV surveys were planned to optimize the seabed insonification in areas of acoustic shadows.

Several software packages were used to process the multibeam and sidescan sonar data:

- CARIS by the SHOM
- CARAIBES (CARtography Adapted to Imagery and BathymEtry of Sonars and multibeam echosounders software, ©Ifremer) by IFREMER
- 20/20 and 30/30 suites by WHOI
- Sonar Wiz 5 software by Phoenix

Processed backscatter mosaics provide very detailed images of the seabed with a resolution range of 1-5 m: 1.25 m for the 180 kHz SAR data, 1 m for the 113 KHz EdgeTech sonar and 3 to 5 m pixel grids for ORION data (Fig. 4).

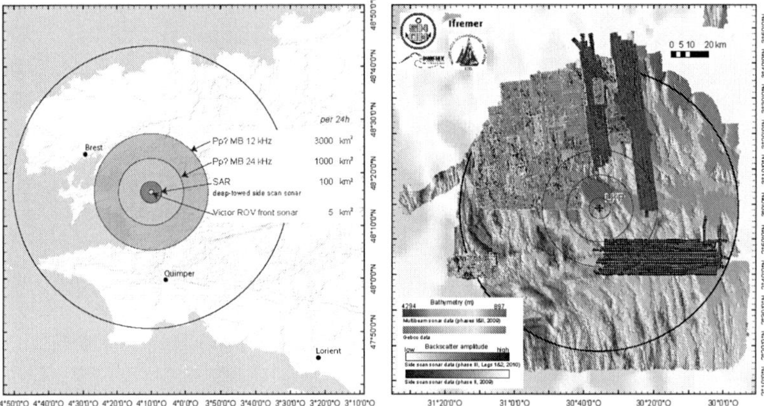

Figure 4: a) The left panel shows seabed coverage investigated per 24h for each different equipment. Note the surface of the investigated area compared to the size of (French) Brittany. b) The right panel shows the seafloor mapping conducted during the BEA expeditions. Shown are the ship-borne multibeam map and the high-resolution sidescan sonar mosaics. The Reson 7150 mounted on the hull of the R/V *Pourquoi pas ?* insonified ~9000 km^2, the SAR system ~1230 km^2, the ORION sonar ~2800km^2, and the REMUS 6000 AUVs ~4700 km^2. The black circle in both images stands for the 40 nm circle around the LKP point.

3. Data methodology and analysis

The region investigated during the BEA expeditions is associated with a rough seabed morphology characteristic of mid-oceanic ridge areas. There are volcanic rocks outcrop in many places, sometimes partially or totally covered with sediments. Seafloor acoustic detection is difficult in areas where 1) high backscatter rocks appear to outcrop over wide areas and 2) steep and large/elevated reliefs (*e.g.* ridges, volcanoes) that produce acoustic shadows (Fig. 5).

Raw and processed sidescan sonar records were analyzed to define and identify acoustic echoes potentially produced by plane debris lying on the seabed.

Conventional analysis for wreckage search was performed, with special attention to:

a) The geometry, dimensions, contour and height of the echo or the identified object as well as the acoustic shadow.
b) The spatial distribution of the echoes.

From the conclusions drawn by the aviation experts, the airplane was supposed to have impacted the sea surface more or less horizontally, leading subsequently to a relatively wide debris field at the seabed (in the order of a few km) with a relatively strong dispersion.

The investigated zone is located very close to the Mid-Atlantic Ridge, and therefore exhibits very steep reliefs and numerous areas with outcroppings of volcanic rocks. It was considered that the debris could have been on hard substrate. In this case, the acoustic discrimination between the rocks and the debris is difficult, if not impossible. Therefore, acoustic anomalies in association with strong reliefs (e.g fault plane), even when they were isolated at the foot of the slopes, have required our attention.

c) The backscatter amplitude of the echoes.

The data analysis focused on high amplitude backscatter patches, especially in areas that were relatively flat and located within a sedimentary environment that backscatter much less energy. This view is not as valid in areas where both rock outcrops (or even partially sedimented) and relief strongly modify the signal amplitude.

Besides these above mentioned parameters, we applied data analysis usually conducted in deep-sea 'academic' research [see *e.g.* 1, 2], thus focusing on:

d) The seabed morphology in the surroundings of the detected echoes (using the 12 and 24 kHz bathymetric data).
e) The multi-frequency acoustic signatures of the echoes (Figs. 6 to 8).

Combining all available backscatter data is very useful. High-resolution acoustic signatures (backscatter amplitude, geometry, contour...) from the SAR/180 kHz, the EdgeTech/113kHz and the ORION/58 kHz, were compared to the ones obtained with 12 and 24 kHz sonars. A multi-frequency dataset provides distinct images of the same object due to the variation in penetration depth of the signal with the emitted frequency. Low-frequency signals from ship-borne data penetrate slightly deeper than the higher frequency signals from the sidescan sonars. In this view, multi-scale or multi-frequency analysis greatly helps in the classification of the echoes by discriminating some of them, in particular echoes produced by geo-related structures, volcanic rock outcrops (*e.g.* rooted, buried structures, and rocks partially covered with sediments) and man-made objects.

The different deep-sea vehicles and sonars have demonstrated a very good complementariness for multi-scale and multi-frequency data analysis during the investigation.

The sequence of sonar data analysis was the following:

- Review and analysis of the raw data.
- Identification of potential and/or intriguing echoes/targets.
- Visualization of acoustic shadows that provide constraints for optimization of the ongoing surveys (with insonification of the same area with different angles and ranges).
- Analysis of the processed backscatter mosaics (1 to 5 m pixel grid size).
- Multi-scale and multi-frequency analysis with integration of all available geo-referenced data with an ArcGis project.
- Review of ground truth data when available (REMUS high-resolution photos and ROV videos) to gain experience in backscatter interpretation.

The data analysis led to i) the identification of targets and ii) a classification of these echoes. Some are interpreted to be related to rock outcrops while others are «undefined» in origin. «Undefined» means that they cannot be interpreted as geological related features (no evidence from the available dataset) and that they may instead correspond to man-made objects (Figs. 9 and 10). Some echoes are interpreted, with a high degree of confidence, to be produced by man-made objects lying on the seafloor (*e.g.* garbage, trash thrown overboard) (Figs. 11 and 12).

Examples of rough terrain areas

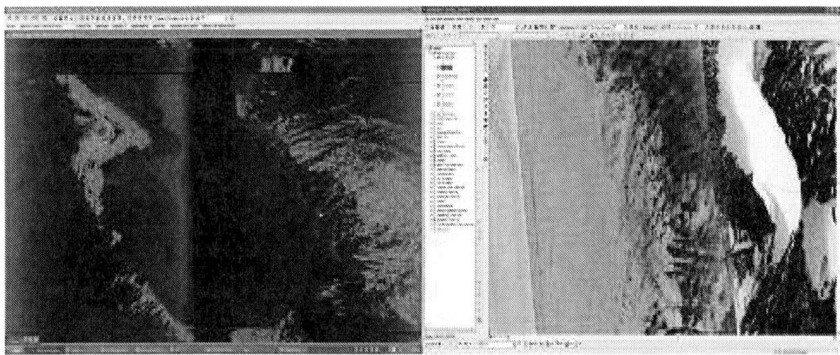

Figure 5: Rough terrain as imaged by a 113 kHz sidescan sonar (raw and processed data in the left and right panel, respectively). Note the acoustics shadows. Identification of plane debris in this type of environment is difficult.

Multi-scale seabed mapping

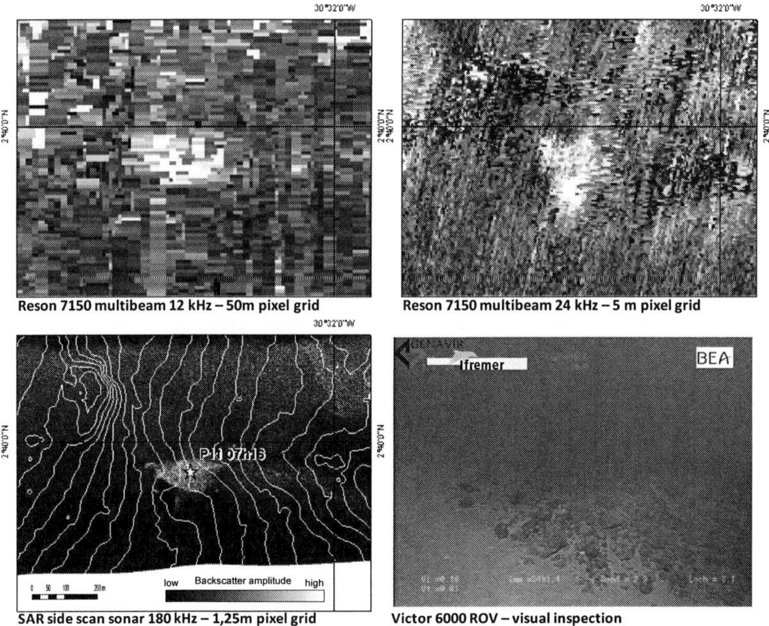

Figure 6: Multi-scale seabed mapping over a deep (2490 m water depth) area investigated with the VICTOR 6000 ROV.

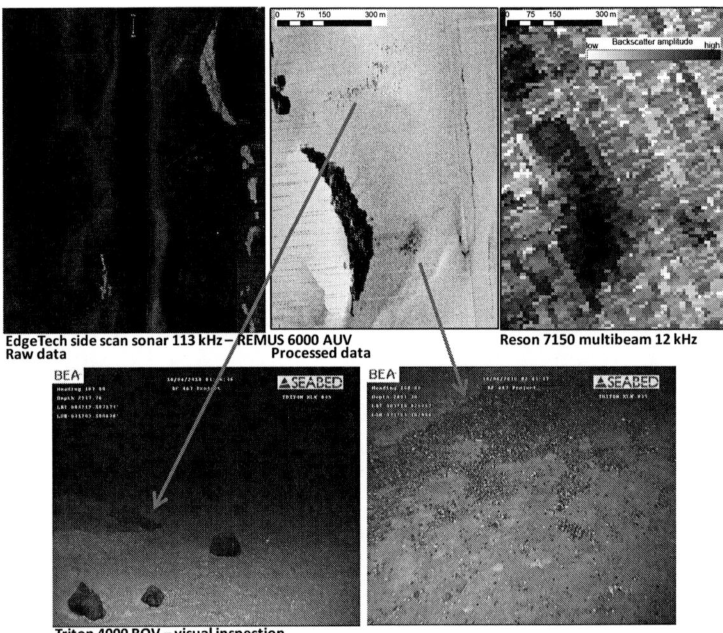

Figure 7: High backscatter amplitude targets surveyed with a REMUS 6000 AUV. These echoes are located in a flat area. The northern target is 400 m by 100 m. The second one is located 500 m further south at a water depth of 2876 m. The 12 kHz backscatter data shows a high amplitude return over these targets which are aligned with partially buried structures perpendicular to the ridge. These anomalies were interpreted as small-scale pieces of outcropping rocks. A TRITON ROV dive revealed a northern area associated with a relatively low density of small rock pieces at the seabed. The southern part is characterized by large fields of shell debris, highly bioturbated sediments and dark (reduced) sediments. *In situ* observations confirm the capability of the high-resolution sidescan sonar images to detect small features on the seabed.

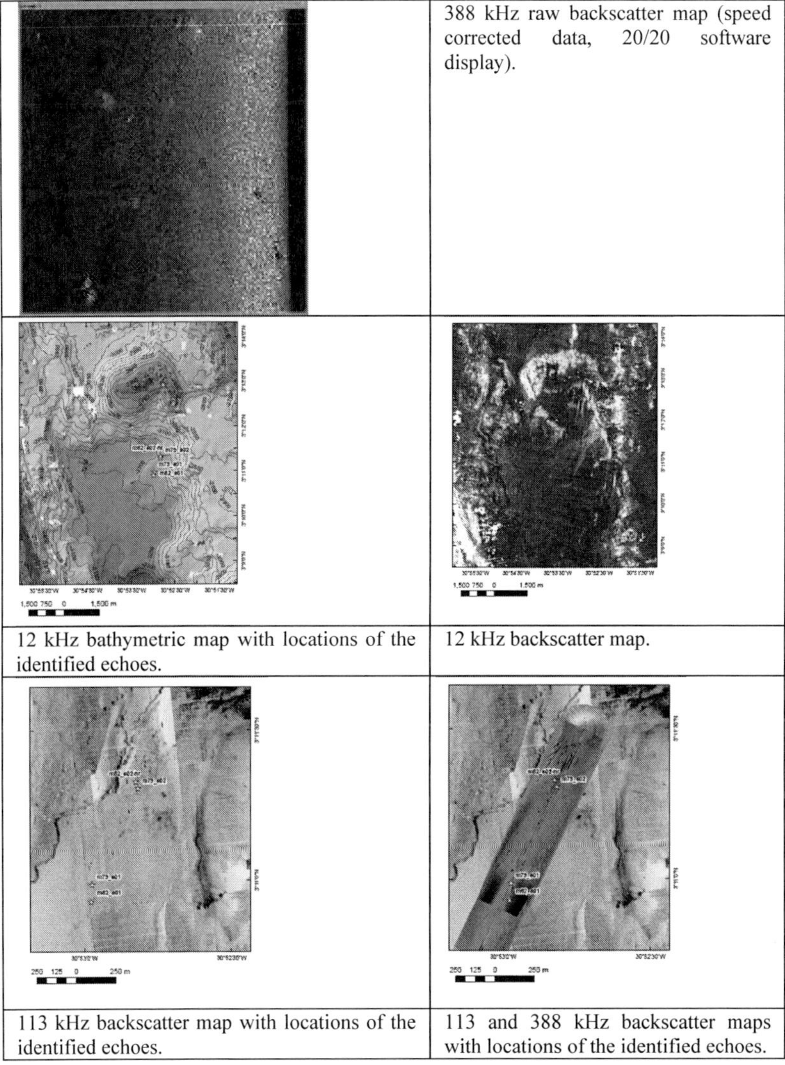

	388 kHz raw backscatter map (speed corrected data, 20/20 software display).
12 kHz bathymetric map with locations of the identified echoes.	12 kHz backscatter map.
113 kHz backscatter map with locations of the identified echoes.	113 and 388 kHz backscatter maps with locations of the identified echoes.

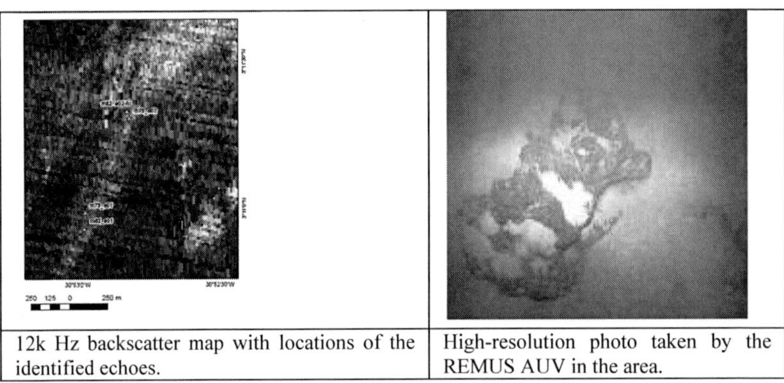

| 12k Hz backscatter map with locations of the identified echoes. | High-resolution photo taken by the REMUS AUV in the area. |

Figure 8: Numerous small high backscatter patches identified at the seafloor along a ~1500 m long band in a sedimented area. Some are slightly larger than 1 m, however most of them are <1 m in size. Their height produces small shadows. Some appear located in pockmarks and/or around disturbed sediment areas. The analysis of all available geophysical data pointed towards a geological origin. The high-resolution photos taken with the REMUS 6000 AUV confirmed this interpretation.

Examples of intriguing targets

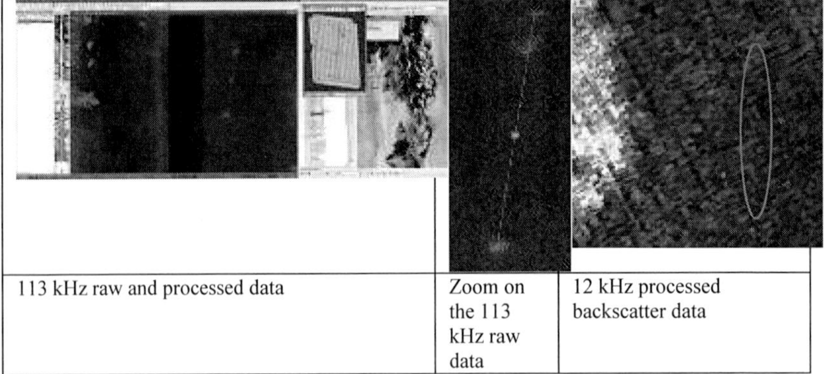

| 113 kHz raw and processed data | Zoom on the 113 kHz raw data | 12 kHz processed backscatter data |

Figure 9: High backscatter patches visible in the sidescan data, 40 to 50 m in diameter each, 770 m distant from each other and located 500 m off the ridge. Nothing significant is visible on the 12 kHz data.

Figure 10: Intriguing target of 250 m in size (113 kHz raw and processed data).

Examples of man-made objects

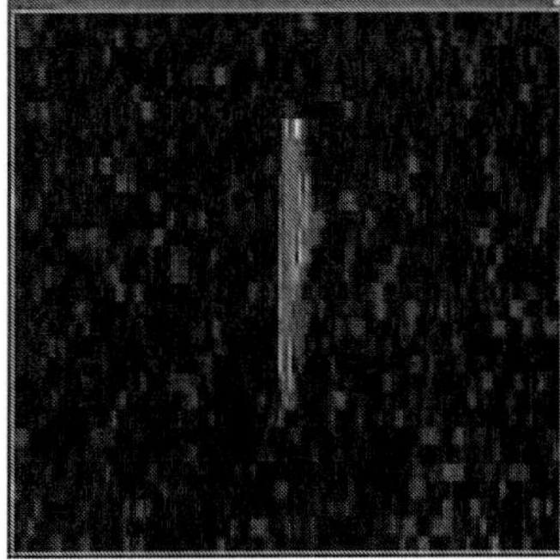

Figure 11: Backscatter map (113 kHz, speed corrected data, 20/20 software display) with four high backscatter patches having similar size and shape. The spatial distribution and the sharp acoustic outlines of these objects are striking. These patches are regularly spaced (20 m across track and 16 m along track).

Figure 12: Backscatter map (113 kHz, speed corrected data, 20/20 software display). It is very unlikely that this echo, isolated and single, is produced by a rock. Its elongated shape (1 m x 17 m) may be due to the speed correction and its far range position. The strong contrast in amplitude with the surroundings points to a possible man-made object on the seafloor.

4. Feedback for deep-sea wreckage search strategy

The search of the AF447 wreckage was unusual and difficult due to i) the little information that was available regarding the airplane trajectory and ii) the deep-water investigation associated with a rough terrain and a high backscatter seabed in many areas with rocky outcrops.

The acquisition of high-resolution data making use of the deep-water engines (deep-towed sidescans and AUVs) was crucial in this context. AUVs are, not surprisingly, very well suitable for wreckage investigation. The navigation is more flexible than for deep-towed systems and they may provide during a single dive not only acoustic seabed mapping but also visual inspection of the seafloor with a mounted camera. The amount of data and the quality of the backscatter mosaics at an excellent resolution helped to investigate large areas in a relatively short time with great accuracy.

Ship-borne multibeam data were also crucial, and not only for planning near-bottom surveys. Regarding the challenging context of the search and the wide investigated area, the multi-scale and multi-frequency data analysis provided key indicators for discriminating identified targets.

References

[1] S. Dupré, J. Woodside, I. Klaucke, J. Mascle, and J.-P. Foucher, "Widespread active seepage activity on the Nile Deep Sea Fan (offshore Egypt) revealed by high-definition geophysical imagery", *Marine Geology*, vol. 275, pp. 1-19, 2010.
[2] S. Dupré, J. Woodside, I. Klaucke, J. Mascle, J.-P. Foucher, and the NAUTINIL & MIMES Scientific Parties, "Multi-scale seafloor mapping of active seep-related structures, offshore Egypt", *CIESM Workshop Monograph*, vol. 29, pp. 65-71, 2006.

CHAPTER SEVENTEEN

ACOUSTIC RADIATION OF A SUBMERGED CYLINDRICAL SHELL IN LOW FREQUENCY

JULIEN VAN DE LOOCK,
DOMINIQUE DÉCULTOT, NICOLAS CITÉ,
FERNAND LEON, FARID CHATI,
RAPHAEL D. RAJAONA, GÉRARD MAZE
AND ALEKSANDER KLAUSON

Abstract

The assessment of sound pressure levels generated by submerged structures is part of regulations on underwater noise pollution. In particular, the fast growth of offshore wind farms and the fact that wind turbines have become larger have raised concerns about their impact on the marine environment. Studies have shown the effects of underwater noise on marine mammals and fish. The operating noise of offshore wind turbines is concentrated at low frequencies and as low frequency waves propagate well in water, it is crucial to evaluate the acoustic radiation resulting from the vibrations of these structures. The purpose of the present work is to characterize, at low frequencies, the acoustic radiation of a cylindrical shell submerged in water, which can represent, as a first approximation, a wind turbine tower. This paper focuses on the acoustic radiation of a 4.83 cm wide tube in a water-filled tank. Vibrations are measured using accelerometers and acoustic radiation is determined by a hydrophone. The experimental results are explained using predictions from elasticity theory. Relationships between the modes of the tube and the underwater noise are then discussed.

Keywords: Underwater Noise, Vibration Modes, Experimental Measurements, Wind Turbine, Acoustic Radiation.

1. Introduction

Assessment of sound pressure levels generated by submerged structures is part of the regulations on underwater noise pollution. In particular, the fast growth of offshore wind farms and the fact that wind turbines have become larger have raised concerns about their impact on the marine environment [1-4]. Studies have shown the effect of underwater noise on marine mammals and fish [5-6]. The operating noise of offshore wind turbines is concentrated at low frequencies, and as low frequency waves propagate well in water, it is crucial to evaluate the acoustic radiation resulting from the vibrations of these structures. Therefore, the purpose of the present work is to characterize at low frequencies the acoustic radiation of a cylindrical shell submerged in water, which can represent, as a first approximation, a wind turbine tower. This paper focuses on the acoustic radiation of a tube of 4.83 cm diameter in a water-filled tank. The tube is excited by means of an impact hammer and a vibration exciter. Vibrations and radiated acoustic pressure are measured, respectively, by using accelerometers and a hydrophone. Experimental results are compared to results from elasticity theory and the finite element method (FEM). Relationships between the modes of the tube and underwater noise are then discussed.

2. Experimental Study

Fig. 1 displays the experimental setup used for this work. The experiment is conducted with a stainless steel tube for which $\rho = 7900 \text{kg.m}^{-3}$. It has a diameter of 4.83 cm, a thickness of 2 mm and is 2.8 m long; the radius ratio is $b/a = 0.911$ with b the inner radius and a the outer radius. The shell is successively placed vertically in air and in water. The lower extremity is closed with a rubber stopper in order to keep the air inside. We have verified that it does not change the vibrational behaviour of the tube. A cube-shaped accelerometer (PCB Piezotronics W356A12) is fixed to the external wall of the tube. It measures the acceleration of the normal displacement due to the vibrations of the shell. The vibrations are produced thanks to an impact hammer (PCB Piezotronics 086C02) which hits the tube on the non-submerged part (<5%). The frequency content of the force impulse is 0-5000Hz (Fig. 2). A conditioner converts the signal of the accelerometer and provides time signals which are recorded by a digital oscilloscope (Lecroy Wave 64Xi). Acoustic pressure measurements are performed using a wide-band hydrophone (Bruel&Kjaer 8105), which is submerged at a depth of 1.5 m. The data acquisition system is the same as for the accelerometer. A preliminary vibration study is first made in air. The mode identification is performed by placing two accelerometers on a specific area (*i.e.* top, middle of the tube and other preferred positions) where we know which mode presents a node or an anti-node, and so on.

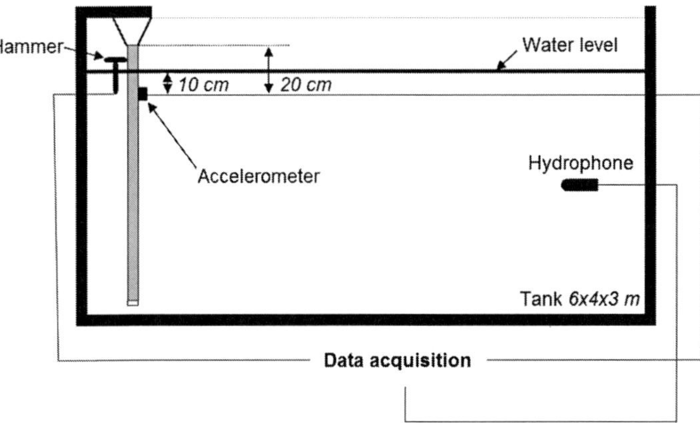

Figure 1: Diagram of the experimental setup.

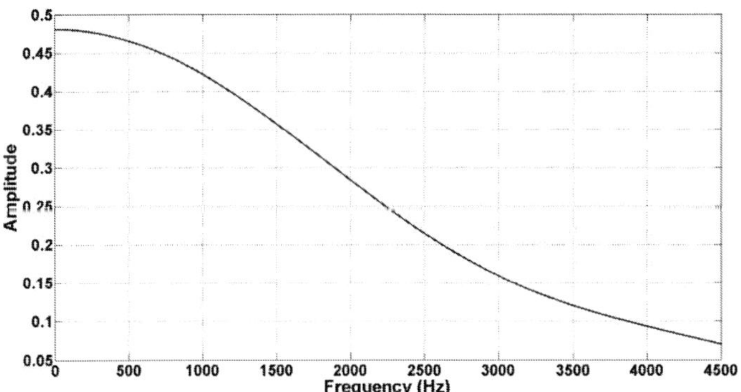

Figure 2: Spectrum of hammer force signal.

3. Theory of eigenmodes for a finite cylindrical shell

First, we need to identify the vibrational modes of the tube in air, as this will make it easier to do so in water. In order to determine the vibrational behaviour of the tube in air, a study based on elasticity theory is carried out. Some previous studies have investigated the case of acoustic radiation of the flexural vibration in air [7] as well as submerged [8, 9]. In the low frequency domain, flexural wave (A_0 wave) and extensional wave (S_0 wave) can propagate on cylindrical shell [10]. The calculation is made for a cylindrical shell placed in a vacuum, because the low density of the air has a very low impact on the calculation of the resonance frequencies. The acoustic waves only propagate in the stainless steel structure, so they can be formulated by a scalar potential φ and a vector potential ψ in cylindrical coordinates (r, θ, z). The scalar potential φ representing the longitudinal waves and the vector potential ψ corresponding to the transverse waves can be deduced from work of Leon et $al.$ [11] and Lecroq et $al.$ [12] in the case of the infinite length cylindrical shell. These potentials depend on the circumferential vibration mode n which is an integer. From the potentials and for the boundary conditions for $r = a$ and $r = b$, the radial, tangential, and shear stresses can be expressed as:

$$T_{rr} = T_{r\theta} = T_{rz} = 0$$

A linear homogeneous system of six equations with six unknown coefficients is obtained. The nullity of the determinant of the induced matrix enables us to determine the resonance frequencies and the axial phase velocity C_z corresponding to the different vibration modes n of the infinite length tube. For each value n, the values of the axial phase velocity C_z of the waves propagating along z axis can be plotted as function of the frequency f. This calculation is achieved for a cylindrical shell with the same characteristics as the experimental objet. The velocity values used for the longitudinal wave C_L and transversal wave C_T for stainless steel are 5790m.s^{-1} and 3100m.s^{-1}, respectively. In Fig. 3, the result of the calculation of C_z for the tube of 4.83 cm diameter, for the modes $n = 1$ and $n = 2$ are presented as a dashed curve and solid curve, respectively. For a finite length tube, a steady-state condition along the axis is considered. The longitudinal vibration modes are then noted by the integer m (1, 2, 3...). As the shell is free at both ends, m become $m* = \dfrac{2m+1}{2}$ (in fact, $m*$ corresponds to the number of half wavelengths in the length of the cylindrical shell). Therefore, the velocity C_z for each mode $m*$ is [12]:

$$C_z = \frac{2Lf}{m*}$$

For example, the velocity C_z deduced from the relation (2) is represented by dotted-straight lines in Fig. 3 for $m* = 7.5$, 10.5, 16.5. The intersection between a straight line (corresponding to a longitudinal mode

m^*) and a dispersion curve of C_z (corresponding to a circumferential mode n) gives the value of the resonance frequency of the mode (n, m^*). On this figure, the resonances measured are added. These resonances frequencies are determined from acceleration spectra of the normal displacement as shown in Fig. 4(a).

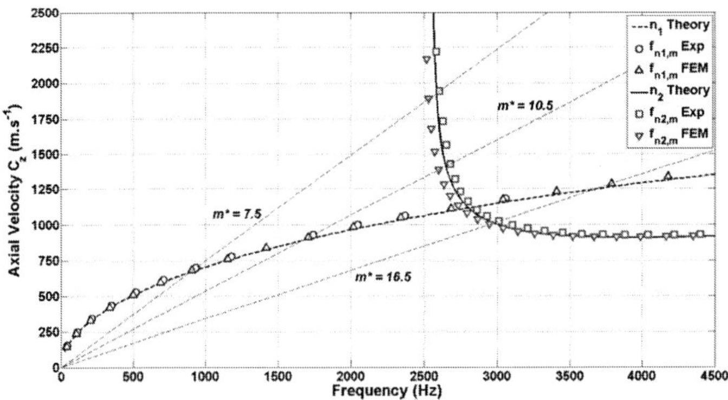

Figure 3: Dispersion curves of the A0 wave (dashed and solid curves) with the experimental resonances (upward and downward-pointing triangles) and numerical resonances (circles and squares). The three dotted-straight lines represent the stationary condition in the length of the tube for the modes m* = 7.5, 10.5, 16.5.

Each peak of these spectra is associated with a mode (n, m^*). In order to achieve this goal, we firstly identify with certainty the lowest longitudinal modes m^* in frequency of each circumferential mode n by finding where are the nodes and the anti-nodes of these modes. Then, the following peaks are associated with the right mode by comparing the evolution of the spacing between each mode with those from results of the elasticity theory. A numerical model of vibrations of the cylindrical shell based on the finite element method is realized using the ANSYS code [13]. The calculated resonances are also plotted on Fig. 3. The three approaches (experimental, FEM and elastic theory) are in a good agreement. The axial phase velocity C_z deduced from vibration modes established in the length and in the circumference of the cylindrical shell shows a similar evolution than the velocity C_z calculated from elasticity theory. For $n = 1$, the axial velocity C_z is growing with the increase in frequency. The circumferential vibration mode $n = 2$ appears with a cut-off frequency situated around 2500Hz. This cut-off frequency is clearly visible in Fig. 4(a). The spectrum presents a wide peak at 2500 Hz because of the concentration of many modes just behind 2500 Hz. The axial phase velocity drops until 800 m/s and represents a flat variation around this value which explains the regular spacing of the resonances after the cut-off frequency between 3000 and 4500Hz on Fig. 4(a).

4. Results in water

Hydrophone away from the tube

Once the modes are identified in air, the tube is immersed into water (Fig. 1). The measured acceleration spectrum of normal displacement is shown in Fig. 4(b). In order to measure the acoustic radiation in water, the tube is almost completely submerged (96%). The spectrum of acceleration of normal displacement is shown in Fig. 4(b). Regularly spaced resonances which correspond to the mode $n = 1$ are clearly observed below 2 kHz. Above 2 kHz, in addition to the mode $n = 1$, the influence of $n = 2$ is observable, similar to the results obtained in air. The cut-off frequency is shifted towards a lower frequency because of the surrounding water (2.5 kHz in air and 2 kHz in water).

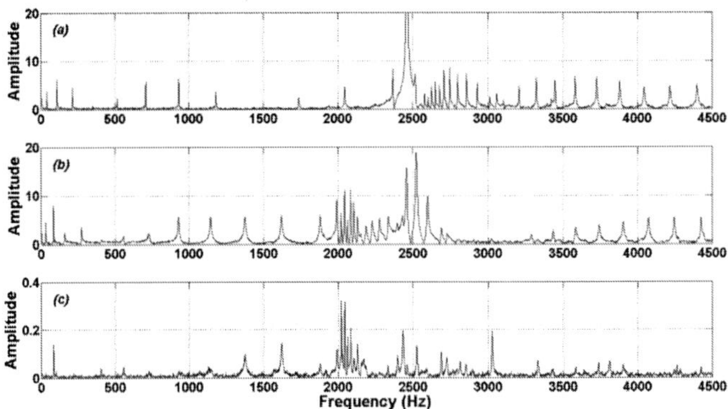

Figure 4: Spectrum of the normal acceleration in air (a) and in water (b), and the pressure measured by the hydrophone in water at a distance of 4.5 m from the tube (c).

An acoustic scattering calculation [10-12] shows that this cut-off frequency corresponds to the $n = 2$ mode related to the A wave. It confirms the frequency shift related to the external fluid which corresponds to the increase of the effective mass of the cylindrical shell. In Fig. 4(c), the spectrum of the acoustic pressure measured at a distance of 4.5 m from the cylindrical shell is shown. Pressure maxima are obtained for frequencies that correspond to vibrational mode frequencies obtained on acceleration of the normal displacement signal. The most important acoustic radiation level is observed for the circumferential vibration mode $n = 2$ at around the cut-off frequency.

Mode identification with a hydrophone

In order to match the resonances in water with the corresponding modes (n, m^*), the experimental setup was modified a little (Fig. 5). The tube is still almost completely sumberged in water (only 10 cm remains out of the water). Now, it is hit by a vibration exciter (Bruel&Kjaer 4809). The input signal is a single period of a sinusoid generated by a function generator and amplified by a power amplifier (Bruel&Kjaer 2718). The hydrophone is mounted on a sliding rod which moves up and down automatically thanks to a motion controller. It is at 5 cm from the tube.

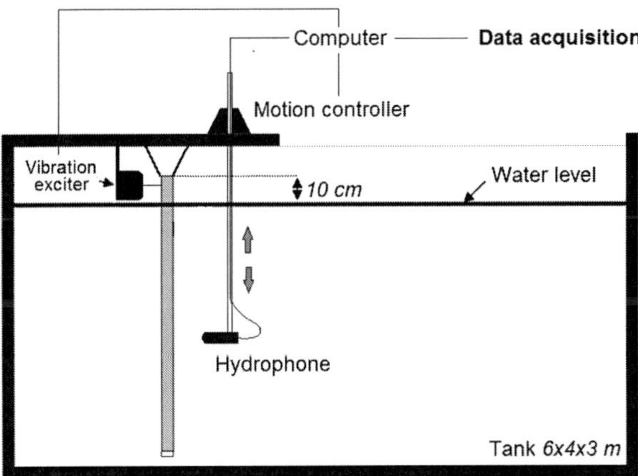

Figure 5: Diagram of the second experimental setup.

The hydrophone measures the acoustic pressure generated by the shock for each position, in steps of 5 mm, from the water level to 275 cm under the surface, such that measurements stop 5 cm after the end of the tube. Fig. 6 presents the Fast Fourier Transform calculated at each vertical position. In fact, this figure shows a "map" of the tube modes in water. It allows us to identify the length mode m^* for each resonance by determining the half wavelength, *i.e.* the distance between two successive nodes or two anti-nodes. These "estimated length modes" are stored in the second column of the Table 1 and 2 which summarize the modes for $n = 1$ and for $n = 2$, respectively.

Table 1: Experimental and numerical vibration modes for $n = 1$ with their identification in length of the cylindrical shell.

	WATER			AIR	
Length Mode	Estimated Length Mode in Water	Experimental Frequencies	Numerical Frequencies	Experimental Frequencies	Numerical Frequencies
1,5	-	32	30	41	38,4
2,5	2,69	84	84	111	105,4
3,5	3,81	174	164	214	205,5
4,5	4,65	266	268	350	337,3
5,5	5,47	397	398	518	499,5
6,5	6,38	565	552	712	690,5
7,5	7,85	738	728	934	908,7
8,5	8,48	943	924	1181	1152,2
9,5	9,58	1151	1142	1400	1419,2
10,5	10,59	1381	1378	1741	1707,6
11,5	11,64	1630	1632	2048	2015,8
12,5	12,57	1886	1904	2372	2341,8
13,5	13,63	2167	2188	2775	2683,9
14,5	14,53	2435	2488	3060	3040,4
15,5	15,63	2730	2800	3455	3409,9
16,5	16,80	3032	3122	3832	3790,8
17,5	17,53	3330	3456	4239	4181,9
18,5	18,56	3640	3794	-	-

On Fig. 6, from 0 Hz to 2000 Hz, we can clearly follow the increase in the number of nodes for modes $n = 1$. The first visible $n = 2$ mode appears at 2232Hz and corresponds with $m^* = 13.5$. The very low amplitude of the previous length modes for $n = 2$ do not allow us to find the value of m^*. A FEM approach has been carried out using the ANSYS code. Results are compared with the experimental values in Table 1 and 2. For $n = 1$, the error is less than 5% for the resonance frequencies for both air and water. In addtition, the length modes found match well with the relation $m^* = \dfrac{2m+1}{2}$, where m is an integer. For $n = 2$, the results move away from theory from $m^* = 17.5$. The error made in the estimation of the half wavelength is likely to be the reason.

Table 2: Experimental and numerical vibration modes for $n = 2$ with their identification in length of the cylindrical shell.

Length Mode	Estimated Length Mode in Water	WATER		AIR	
		Experimental Frequencies	Numerical Frequencies	Experimental Frequencies	Numerical Frequencies
7,5	-	2062	2114	2604	2532
8,5	-	2084	2134	2628	2549
9,5	-	2104	2154	2653	2572
10,5	-	2130	2176	2680	2601
11,5	-	2155	2214	2711	2637
12,5	-	2190	2252	2749	2680
13,5	13,69	2232	2298	2800	2733
14,5	14,50	2278	2350	2859	2794
15,5	15,56	2338	2408	2930	2866
16,5	16,60	2404	2466	3013	2948
17,5	17,58	2472	2528	3106	3041
18,5	18,18	2542	2606	3210	3145
19,5	18,92	2611	2696	3325	3260
20,5	20,28	2699	2804	3450	3386
21,5	20,79	2799	2918	3582	3522
22,5	21,76	2909	3046	3727	3669
23,5	-	3018	3180	3881	3825
24,5	23,65	3158	3330	4043	3992
25,5	24,78	3293	3486	4219	4167

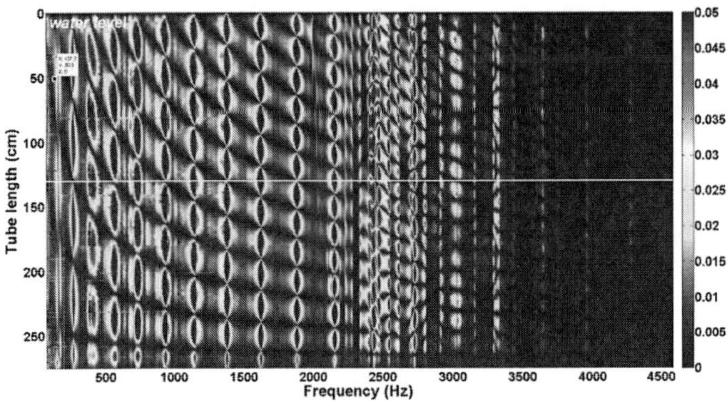

Figure 6: Spectrum of the pressure measured by the hydrophone along the tube of 4.83 cm diameter. The white line materializes the middle of the tube.

The spectra of the measured pressure and the pressure calculated by ANSYS for a depth of 1.4 m are plotted on Fig. 7 to illustrate that the prediction of the resonance frequencies by ANSYS is quite accurate.

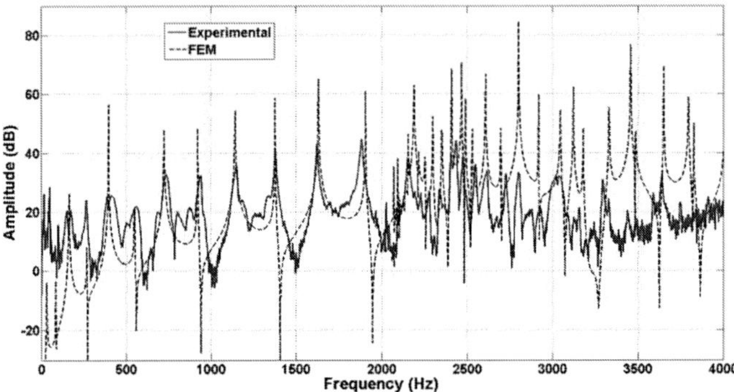

Figure 7: Spectra of the pressure measured by the hydrophone (blue solid line) and calculated by ANSYS (black dashed line).

5. Conclusion

This paper has presented experimental work on the vibrations of a submerged cylindrical shell of 4.83 cm diameter at low frequencies. The experiments are performed in a large, water-filled tank. The shell is excited by an impact hammer in order to determine its natural frequencies. Signals of the acceleration of the normal displacement and the acoustic radiation are measured. The results show a strong link between the resonances of the tube and the signal of the acoustic pressure measured in water. A preliminary study which consists in measuring the vibrational modes in air was carried out. These results are very close for the three approaches used (experimental, elastic theory and FEM) and allow us to identify precisely the different modes in air. In water, an identification of the length modes was achieved. The length modes identified are in a good agreement with those calculated by a FEM approach.

Acknowledgements

The authors would like to acknowledge the Agglomeration Community of Le Havre (CODAH) and the Normandy Hydrodynamics Network (RHYNO) for their supports to this work.

References

[1] K. Betke, M. Schultz-von Glhan, R. Matuscheck, "Underwater noise emissions from offshore wind turbines," *CFA/DGA'04*, Strasbourg France, March 22-25, 591-592, (2004).

[2] T Neumann, J. Gabriel, W.-J. Gerash, K.-H. Elmer, M.Schultz-von Glhan, K. Betke, "Standards for the assessment of Acoustic Emissions of Offshore wind Farms," *DEWI Magazin* 26, 49-53, (2005).

[3] C.A.F. De Jong and M. A. Ainslie, "Underwater radiated noise due to the pilling for the Q7 Offshore Wind Park," *Acoustic'08 Paris Conference*, June 29th - July 4th 2008, 118-122, (2008).

[4] H. Moller and C. S. Pedrersen "Low-frequency noise from large wind turbines," *J. Acoust. Soc. Am.* 129, 3727-3244, (2011).

[5] P. T. Madsen, M. Wahlberg, J. Tougaard, K. Lucke, P. Tyack, "Wind turbine underwater noise and marine mammals: implications of current knowledge and data needs," *Mar. Ecol. Prog. Ser.* 309, 279-295, (2006).

[6] R. Kikuchi, "Risk formulation for the sonic effects of offshore wind farms on fish in the EU region," *Marine Pollution Bulletin* 60 172-177, (2010).

[7] L. Shuyu, "Study on the radiation acoustic field of rectangular radiators in flexural vibration," *Journal of Sound and Vibration* 254, 469-479, (2002).

[8] D. Décultot, R. Lietard, F. Chati, G. Maze, A. Klauson, "Acoustic radiation of low frequency flexural vibration modes in submerged plate," *Acoustics'08 Paris Conference*, June 29th -July 4th 2008, pp. 441-446, (2008).

[9] Z. Cheng, J. Fan, B.Wang, W. Tang, "Radiation efficient of submerged rectangular plates," *Applied Acoustics* 73 150-157, (2012).

[10] G. Maze, F. Léon, J. Ripoche, H. Überall "Repulsion phenomena in the phase-velocity dispersion curves of circumferential waves on elastic cylindrical shells," *J. Acoust. Soc. Am.* 105, 1695–1701, (1999).

[11] F. Leon, F. Lecroq, D. Décultot, and G. Maze, "Scattering of an obliquely incident acoustic wave by an infinite hollow cylindrical shell," *J. Acoust. Soc. Am.* 91, 1388 1397, (1992).

[12] F. Lecroq, G. Maze, D. Décultot, and J. Ripoche, "Acoustic scattering from an air-filled cylindrical shell with welded flat plate endcaps: Experimental and theoretical study," *J. Acoust. Soc. Am.* 95, 762–769, (1994).

[13] ANSYS User's Manual.

Chapter Eighteen

Robust Vision-Based Detection and Tracking of Underwater Pipelines

Devendra Goyal, Karan R. Shetti and Timo Bretschneider

Abstract

Traditionally, the inspection of undersea pipelines was performed by underwater Remotely Operated Vehicles (ROVs), which are equipped with cameras and controlled by human operators on the surface. Autonomous Underwater Vehicles (AUVs) are now increasingly being used to detect and track underwater pipelines without direct human intervention. In this paper, we present the entire processing chain of a robust and self-adaptive system to autonomously perform this task. An optimised version of the Randomised Hough Transform is used to detect the edges of the pipeline. We describe a separate module that self-evaluates the detection results and provides feedback to the algorithm in order to adapt when there is a change in the environmental conditions. The system was rigorously tested using simulated data, an artificial test bed constructed in dry lab conditions, and finally in a water tank. In the conclusion, we discuss the results and compare it with manually generated ground truth to demonstrate the robustness and accuracy of the system with modest computational requirements.

Keywords: Pipeline Detection and Tracking, Randomised Hough Transform, Automatic Parameter Generation, Real-Time System.

1. Introduction

Undersea pipelines have been used extensively to transport natural resources such as oil and natural gas. As the technology to manufacture and deploy these pipelines is progressing, it is now possible to lay longer pipelines at even greater depths. For example, one of the longest pipelines that is used to transport natural gas is the Langeled Pipeline that extends for 1,200 km under the North Sea from the Ormen Lange field in Norway to the Easington Gas Terminal in the United Kingdom [1]. Apart from transporting oil and gas, underwater pipelines are also used for cross-continental telecommunication cables [1, 2]. These pipeline projects are considered important infrastructure and need to be constantly monitored and maintained against potentially hazardous damage from corrosion, the mobility of the seabed, marine traffic and fishing.

Inshore pipelines can be maintained by divers, however for offshore pipelines, unmanned underwater vehicles (UUV) are preferred [1]. Traditionally, video cameras attached to Remotely Operated Vehicles (ROVs) have been used to track and inspect the state of these pipelines by an operator. The process is complicated by the peculiar characteristics of underwater images like blurring, low contrast, non-uniform illumination and lack of stability due to the motion of the vehicle [2–4]. This makes the entire process of human-in-the-loop inspecting and tracking of the pipeline very tedious and prone to errors.

Another disadvantage associated with an ROV is that it requires an "umbilical cord" to provide the communication link for high-speed data rates and power between the underwater vehicle and the operating platform. As a result, the ROV needs to be operated at slow speeds in order to reduce the physical stress on the connection. This leads to longer mission times and hence an increase in operational costs. Therefore, automation of any section of this process can drastically reduce the number of errors as well as cost. One of the solutions is to use an Autonomous Underwater Vehicle (AUV) to track the pipelines without any direct human intervention. With an improved and faster acquisition of the video data, the inspection of the pipeline can then be carried out offline.

In this work, a deterministic approach for detecting and tracking underwater pipelines is described. The system provides guidance information to the AUV such that the target pipeline is within the field of view of a set of forward looking cameras. The algorithm proposed is hardware efficient and takes into account the temporal requirements of maintaining a speed of 4 knots by the AUV. The acquired video streams are processed in real-time.

2. Related work

Several approaches exist to solve the problem of tracking underwater pipelines and cables. Apart from vision-based sensors [5], other sensing devices that are used are sonar and magnetometers. Extensive research has been done [6–8] to employ these sensors for tracking. While the size and power requirements of the latter sensors are diminishing, vision cameras are better suited as they are cost-efficient, consume less power, and are more easily integratable in an AUV due to their smaller form factor. Moreover, optical sensors provide a higher resolution for shorter ranges and enjoy a higher degree of user acceptance due to their perceptually familiar data. However, one of the drawbacks of a vision-based solution is the additional requirement of lighting infrastructure. The power requirements of the lights are quite high but can be mitigated by using LED based dimmable lights [2].

Within the optical image processing domain, there are two approaches that have been explored, namely the stochastic and deterministic approaches. Zingaretti and Zanoli [4] proposed a robust system to detect pipelines using a stochastic approach, modelling a pipeline as two straight parallel lines. The system uses an image processing module in combination with a Kalman filter which compensates for the inaccuracies in detection due to poor image quality. They also overcame the variation in the pipeline model due to the different motion of the AUV (pitch, roll, heave and yaw) using the same.

Ortiz, Simo and Oliver [9] suggested a system based on image segmentation to extract the pipeline from the environment, followed by a Kalman filter to predict its position in subsequent images. In a similar approach, Antich and Ortiz [10] split the image to be analysed into a grid of cells that are processed separately in order to reinforce evidence of the cable in areas where it is clearly defined. A Kalman filter was also used to increase accuracy of the detection in subsequent frames. However, both of these approaches involve deciding the number of segments the image must be partitioned into manually. Due to the constantly changing environment and nature of the obstacles, such a static parameter might lead to false results.

In the deterministic approach, the goal is to determine the exact pose of the pipeline. Owing to the line-like appearance of pipelines, previous work has focused on extracting the edges and using the Hough transform to detect the outline of the pipeline. Matsumo and Ito [3] proposed a method that models undersea cables as a straight line. They process the image sequences by using edge detectors and the Hough transform to detect candidate edges. The final line is then selected from these candidates based on its likelihood of representing a line and closeness to the line detected in the previous frame. Hallset [11] suggested a similar method to track pipelines in a network of pipelines. Balasuriya and Ura [12] described a system for tracking telecommunication cables. The main contribution from this work is the ability to track pipelines that are partially buried under the seabed. They propose the use of dead reckoning position uncertainty to define a region of interest for the detection. With this reduced problem space and a 2D model of cables, they are able to detect cables more efficiently.

However, one of the major issues associated with the Hough transform is its time-consuming complexity. Matsumoto and Ito [3] as well as Balasuriya and Ura [12] attempt to solve this problem by limiting the boundaries of the Hough Space based on the previous computation results. However, the resolution of the Hough space still has to be set, which involves a trade-off between complexity and accuracy.

3. System architecture

The artificial nature of the pipeline presents many features that render it distinguishable from the rest of the underwater environment. Due to the rigidity and shape of the pipeline, the edges of the pipeline can be modelled as continuous straight lines running through the entire length of the image. Although the pipeline is expected to be covered with algae that possess similar characteristics to the ocean floor, a slight difference in colour and the difference in planes help distinguish it from the rest of the environment. This is the base strategy that is exploited in order to detect the pipeline. Two PAL RGB cameras along with dimmable LED focus lights are used for the purpose of detection. The layout of the system is shown in Fig. 1(a).

System Overview

Image frames acquired from the camera are first processed to compensate for poor illumination and low contrast to improve the quality of the edge detection. The Canny edge detector is then used to obtain the edges in the image, the parameters for which are selected automatically and adaptively. Finally, a modification of the Randomised Hough Transform (RHT) is applied to extract the pipeline's edges. The evaluation module then performs a quantitative evaluation of the detection results based on some pre-set standards that define a satisfactory detection. Fig. 1(b) shows the workflow of the different modules used in the proposed solution.

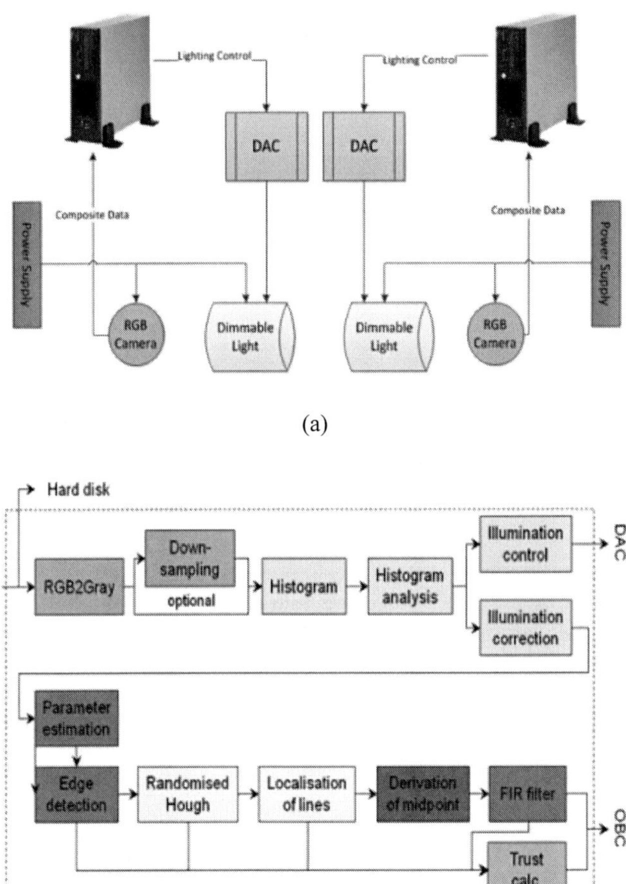

Figure 1: System design: (a) architecture setup, (b) software architecture.

Pre-Processing

In order to reduce the amount of data to be processed, every image acquired from the camera is converted into greyscale and then spatially down-sampled by a factor of two. Due to the insufficient natural illumination underwater, the AUV is equipped with dimmable onboard lights to improve visibility of the pipeline. It is advisable to operate the onboard lights at minimum intensity in order to reduce disturbing scattering effects and also to conserve power, which enables longer mission times. As the proposed tracking procedure distinguishes the pipeline from the surroundings, it is desirable to increase the contrast in the image. The image histogram is analysed and appropriately stretched to increase the contrast as shown in Fig. 2. However, there is a limit up to which this operation improves the quality of the image. If the image is categorised as too dark in the histogram analysis, the onboard lights are manipulated via the DAC in discrete intervals over many frames.

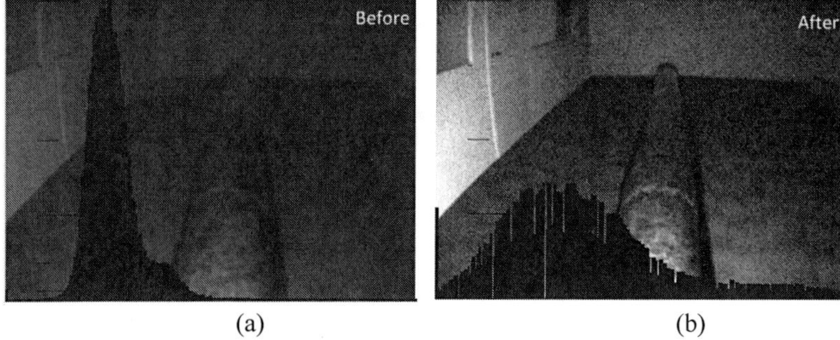

(a)   (b)

Figure 2: Histogram analysis for improved scene illumination: (a) acquired scene and (b) stretched histogram.

Edge Detection Process

After a survey of various edge detection methods [13], namely Roberts, Prewitt, Sobel and LoG, the Canny edge detector was found to be most suitable for our purpose [14]. The hysteresis thresholding helps suppress non-maximal edges and the noise reduction step is desirable to filter out unwanted details. Although the computational complexity of the Canny method is higher than that of the Sobel or Prewitt method, the non-maximal edge suppression greatly reduces errors by creating thin, linked edges.

It can be observed that the performance of the edge detector is greatly dependent on the parameters selected as its thresholds. While a very low threshold produces a very detailed edge map, it greatly increases the complexity while including undesirable features in the image. Moreover, the selection of the parameter for the Gaussian filter involves a trade-off between accuracy and noisiness in the image. As different depths produce images of a non-similar nature, they require different thresholds for optimal results. Thus the process of the parameter selection is automated to make the system adaptable. This is achieved by implementing a statistical objective performance analysis method proposed by Yitzhaky and Peli [15] and consists of two main steps. An example of edge maps derived using different parameters is shown in Fig. 3.

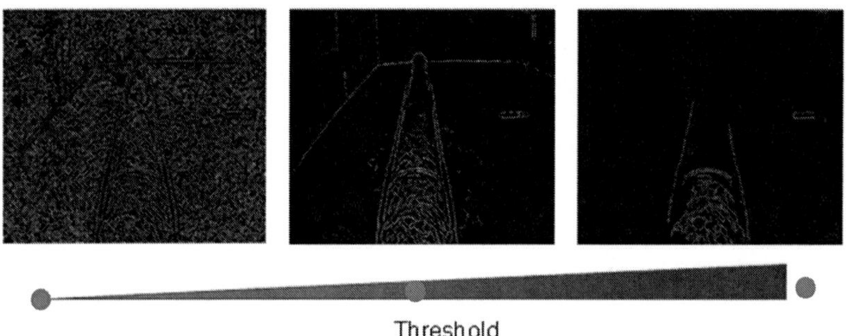

Figure 3: Edge maps for different parameters.

Generation of Ground Truth

A statistical analysis is first performed to produce an Estimated Ground Truth (EGT), which is then used to select the detector parameter values for an image namely sigma and the hysteresis threshold [15]. N edge maps are first computed using a range of values for each of the parameters. The range of the values is manually selected and is dependent on the nature of the sensor used. The low threshold for the hysteresis threshold is set to one third of the high [15]. The correspondence of N edge maps is then computed. The EGT is selected from this sample space by ROC and Chi-square measures. The higher Correspondence Threshold (CT) is selected from amongst the two measures, as a higher measure generally implies lower noise [15].

Selection of Parameters

Once the EGT is selected, ROC curve and Chi-square tests are used to select an edge image with the highest correspondence to the EGT. The parameters used to derive this result are considered the optimum parameters. The method of parameter selection is computationally intensive, but its contribution toward the adaptability of the system justifies such expense. Moreover, after an initial selection of parameters, this routine is run only at preset periodic intervals or when there is a considerable decrease in the detection accuracy as asserted by a separate evaluation module.

Randomised Hough Transform

After an edge image is obtained, the Randomised Hough Transform (RHT) [16] is applied to extract straight lines from the image. The RHT offers various advantages over the Standard Hough Transform (SHT) [17], such as lesser storage requirements, faster computation and an infinite parameter (rho, theta) space. The general approach for line detection using RHT is to randomly select two points from the edge image and store their parameters in an accumulator array. After a certain number of iterations (chosen by the user), each entry in the accumulator array is analysed and only the entries for which straight lines exist in the image are retained. The process can be further optimised to fit our chosen model of contiguous straight lines. A two stage approach is used in this paper. First, instead of randomly selecting points from the entire image space, they are selected from a Region of Interest (ROI) defined by where the pipe was located in the previous image. Obviously, such a filtering is possible only after the first frame has been processed. Next, the rho and theta parameters for the selected points are computed as in the RHT. However, instead of adding these parameters to the accumulator array, they are investigated for a possible edge and rejected or accepted in the same iteration. As the points are selected from a fairly narrow Region of Interest, it is likely that a match is found in the initial iterations. In order for a line to qualify as an edge, it is first tested for trivial constraints of inclination, length and proximity to edges from previous frames.

If a line passes such constraints, it is then evaluated in detail as described in the next section after which it is accepted or rejected as an edge. Such a two-step process ensures that trivial possibilities are not tested by the evaluation module and saves computational time. The RHT procedure for a frame is iterated until two such edges representing the two sides of the pipeline are found. The fact that our requirement is only of two lines rather than all of the lines in the image makes it practical to not have an accumulator array that stores all possible edges and also reduces storage requirements.

Evaluation Module

The evaluation of the detection is a separate module which provides a 'trust' value: this indicates the confidence of the edge detection. It is based on the following features:

- Length of the detected edge.
- Number of segments (contiguity) present in the detected edge.
- Average length per segment of the detected edge.

The length of the edges is an obvious choice as a factor in evaluating the edges, as the pipe is expected to run through the entire vertical length of the image and thus, be considerably longer than any other objects or patterns in the image. Therefore, for each edge in an image, the length of the longest possible line having the same parameters (rho, theta) as the edge is calculated. The percentage of the detected line over the maximum length is used for the trust calculation. In the edge detection step, the hysteresis thresholding and non-maximal edge suppression ensures that most prominent edges are linked to each other. Therefore another feature used in evaluating the trust is the number of segments present in the detected line. Finally, the average length of each segment is evaluated.

Detected edges that are short and fragmented indicate a poor detection. The above features are averaged into a single value, which is then compared to a minimum trust value required for acceptance of an edge. This value is an empirically determined value, selected so as to filter out any false positives while maintaining reasonable tolerance for detected edges.

4. Experiments and results

In order to evaluate the performance of the entire system, various tests were carried out using simulated data, dry lab tests and finally underwater tests in a water tank. The simulated video was generated using Virtual Battlespace 2 [18] software to mimic the pipeline and other underwater artefacts. Various scenarios including partially and fully covered pipeline were used to test the initial prototype of the system. The detection result of this test is shown in Fig. 4(a).

Dry Lab Experimental Setup

The system used in the dry lab tests include

- RGB camera with size 752 × 528 (PAL).
- Fully dimmable focus light with $30°$ beam angle.
- 10 m of PVC pipe ($\varnothing$ 40 cm) with mock up colour pattern.
- Test installation was mounted on a roll-able table to simulate AUV motion.

The main goal of these tests was to verify the basic setup required for underwater acquisition and obtain test data. It was also intended to test the performance of the system under different conditions of AUV motion (pitch, sway and yaw). The response of the algorithm to varying light conditions was also studied. The results of this test are shown in Figs.4(b) and 4(c).

Water Tank Test Setup

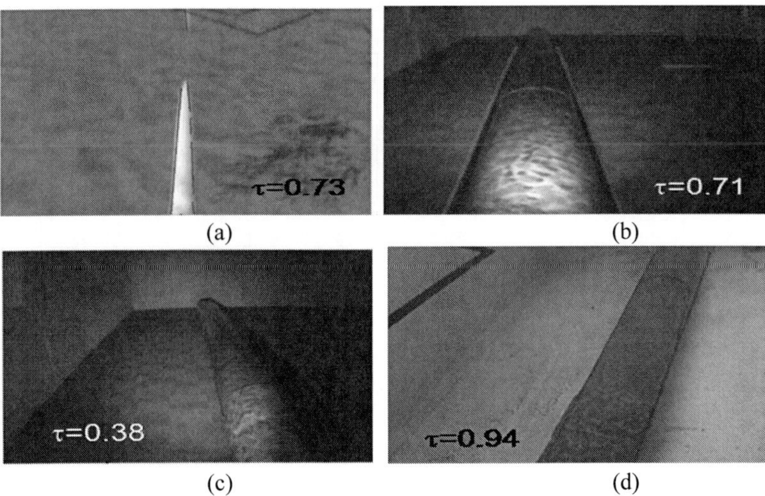

Figure 4: Pipeline detection results with trust values (τ): (a) partially buried pipeline in synthetic image, (b) pipeline mock-up with strong glare in the dry lab, (c) pipeline mock-up off-track, (d) pipeline mock-up in the water tank

With satisfactory results obtained from dry lab tests, the system was tested in a water-filled tank. The main aim of this test was to generate more test data and investigate the use of a two-camera setup. The cameras and lights used were the same as the dry lab test. The setup used consisted of

- 7.5m of PVC pipe ($\varnothing$ 40cm) with colour mock-up pattern
- Manual light intensity control
- 3m water depth

The result of this test is shown in Fig. 4(d).

Quantitative Results

Detection Accuracy

Fig. 5, shows the results of a water tank test. The pipes were placed at a depth of 3 m and the camera was glided over them underwater. The blue line represents the midpoint of the pipe over successive frames as judged by the human eye (ground truth). In order to test the robustness of the system, the camera setup was swayed first to the starboard side and then to the port side of the pipe. The unfiltered and filtered midpoints as detected by the algorithm are represented in red and green respectively.

As can be seen, the algorithm was able to seamlessly adjust to the erratic movement of the cameras and closely follows the ground truth. The mean deviation from the ground truth is 5.63 pixels. The actual deviation in distance can be calculated using the geometry of the setup.

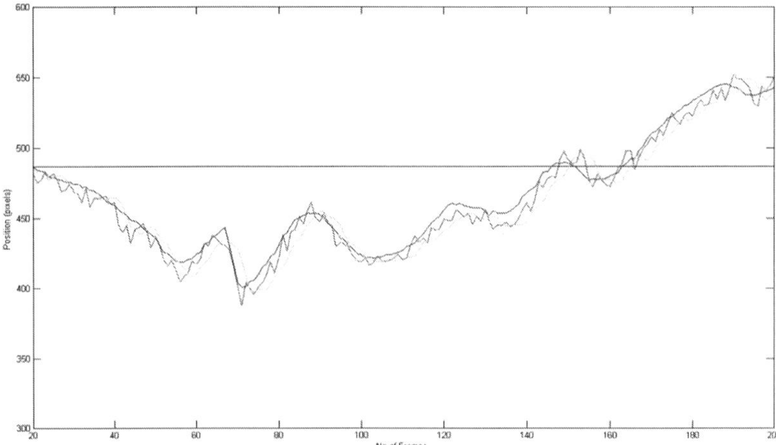

Figure 5. Detection results with ground truth.

Execution Time

The entire procession chain as described in Section 3 was implemented on a test bed with 1.84 GHz Intel dual core processor. The OpenCV library was used for most of the image processing functions. The mean execution time recorded is 94.02 ms for each frame (ignoring peaks for ground truth generation). This meets the system requirements of providing guidance information at 10 Hz. Fig. 6 shows the execution time of the dry lab test video (350 frames).

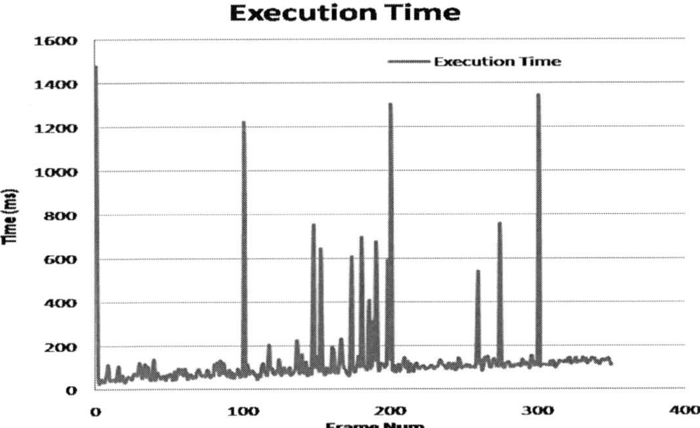

Figure 6: Execution time (dry lab test).

It can be observed that some frames require more time to select the correct point due to the element of randomness in RHT. This is due to the deteriorating image quality of the video, thereby making it harder to extract the edges and classify them correctly. The peaks (frame 100,200,300) that can be observed are due the computation to generate the estimated ground truth and derive new parameters for the edge detection module. If we observe the performance from frame 160 to 180, we can infer that it is harder to extract straight lines from the edge map (poor lighting conditions). However, the performance improves greatly after the new ground truth and parameters are generated, thereby justifying the use of this algorithm.

5. Conclusions and future work

In conclusion, a robust, real-time system to detect and track pipelines for an AUV has been presented in this work. Apart from the improvement in the detection algorithm, an overall processing chain is discussed. It takes into account real-world AUV constraints of processing speed, detection accuracy, storage limitations and optimum power consumption. From an algorithmic perspective, a simple geometric model (straight lines) is used to describe the pipelines. By exploiting the use of automatic generation of parameters for edge detection [15], the system is capable of adapting to different underwater conditions autonomously. A modified Random Hough Transform optimised for high throughput and lower storage is used to detect the edges of the pipelines. Detection results from previous frames are used to increase the accuracy of detection. Finally an independent evaluation module is added to provide feedback for the detection. The system has been thoroughly tested using different experimental setups and shown to perform well both in terms of accuracy and execution time.

Considerable work can be done to further improve the performance of this system. One of major drawbacks is still the presence of many empirically defined parameters for the RHT. These parameters can be dynamically adjusted through the use of a learning algorithm. The RHT algorithm can then be further streamlined to reduce the irregularity of the execution time. With acquisition of more data from the real underwater environment, the trust module also can be improved to improve the reliability of feedback to the AUV. Finally, the use of Kalman Filters can be studied to handle noise more effectively and increase the accuracy of detection [9].

References

[1] N. Mohamed, I. Jawhar, J. Al-Jaroodi and L. Zhang, "Sensor network architectures for monitoring underwater pipelines", *Sensors*, vol. 11, 10738-10764, 2011.

[2] A. Ortiz, J. Antich and G. Oliver, "A particle filter-based approach for tracking undersea narrow telecommunication cables", *Machine Vision and Applications*, vol. 22, pp. 283-302, 2011.

[3] S. Matsumoto and Y. Ito, "Real-time vision-based tracking of submarine cables for AUV/ROV", *MTS/IEEE Oceans*, vol. 3, pp. 1997-2002, 1995.

[4] P. Zingaretti and S. Zanoli, "Robust real-time detection of an underwater pipeline", *Engineering Applications of Artificial Intelligence*, vol. 11, pp. 257-268, 1998.

[5] J. Horgan and D.Toal, "Review of machine vision applications in unmanned underwater vehicles", *Proceedings of the International Conference on Control, Automation, Robotics and Vision*, pp. 1-6, 2006.

[6] P. Egeskov, M. Bech, R. Bowley and C. Aage, "Pipeline inspection using an autonomous underwater vehicle", *Proceedings of the International Conference on Offshore Mechanics and Arctic Engineering*, vol. 5, pp. 539-546, 1995.

[7] K. Asawaka, J. Kojima, Y. Kato, S. Matsumoto, N. Kato, T. Asai and T. Iso, "Design concept and experimental results of the autonomous underwater vehicle AQUA EXPLORER 2 for the inspection of underwater cables", *Advanced Robotics*, vol. 16, pp. 27-42, 2002.

[8] A.V. Inzartsev, "AUV Behavior Algorithm While Inspecting of Partly Visible Pipeline", *Oceans 2006*, pp. 1-5, 2006.

[9] Ortiz, M. Simo and G. Oliver, "A vision system for an underwater cable tracker", *Machine Vision and Applications*, vol. 13, pp. 129-140, 2002.

[10] J. Antich and A. Ortiz, "Underwater cable tracking by visual feedback", *Pattern Recognition and Image Analysis*, vol. 2652, pp. 53-61, 2003.

[11] J. O. Hallset, "Testing the robustness of an underwater vision system", *Real-time Imaging: Theory, Techniques and Applications*, IEEE Press, pp. 225-260, 1996.

[12] Balasuriya and T. Ura, "Vision-based underwater cable detection and following using AUVs", *MTS/IEEE Oceans*, vol. 3, pp. 1582-1587, 2002.

[13] M. Heath, S. Sarkar, T. Sanocki and K.W. Bowyer, "Comparison of edge detectors: A methodology and initial study", *Computer Vision and Image Understanding*, vol. 69, no. 1, pp. 38-54, 1998.

[14] A. Ortiz, G. Oliver and J. Frau, "A vision system for underwater real-time control tasks", *MTS/IEEE Oceans*, vol. 2, pp. 1425-1430, 1997.

[15] Y. Yitzhaky and E. Peli, "A method for objective edge detection evaluation and detector Parameter selection", *IEEE Transactions on Pattern Recognition and Machine Intelligence*, vol. 25, pp. 1027-1033, 2003.

[16] L. Xu, E. Oja and P. Kultanen, "A new curve detection method: Randomized Hough Transform (RHT)", *Pattern Recognition Letters*, vol. 11, pp. 331-338, 1990.

[17] R.O. Duda and P.E. Hart, "Use of the Hough transformation to detect lines and curves in pictures", *Communications of the ACM*, vol. 15, pp. 11-15, 1972.

[18] Bohemia Interactive Simulations, http://www.vbs2.com, last access: June 2012.

CHAPTER NINETEEN

SITAR:
A MODULAR SYSTEM FOR AUTOMATIC TARGET RECOGNITION IN SIDE-LOOKING SONAR IMAGERY

ØIVIND MIDTGAARD
AND HERMAN MIDELFART

Extended abstract

FFI has developed the SITAR (Sonar Image TArget Recognition) system over the last decade. The system recognizes bottom mines in high-resolution side-looking sonar imagery. It is primarily designed for HISAS 1030, but also supports other selected sonar models, *e.g.* Klein 5000 sidescan sonar (SSS). The motivation for this development is two-fold: Firstly, it may ease the burden of the sonar operator, which has to look through vast amounts of sonar data during mine hunting operations. Secondly, it will allow autonomous underwater vehicles (AUV) to adapt their behavior within a mission independent of an operator. Examples of adaptive behaviour based on ATR results are selective transmission of sensor data over narrow-band links and adaptive measurement strategies involving alterations of vehicle path and sensor operation.

SITAR has a modular design. Each module is a separate executable program written in C/C++. The main modules are:

- The **main control** module calls the other modules in sequence for each sonar data file.
- The **detection module** runs several detectors over the full data set and reports mine-sized objects (contacts). Each detected contact is assigned an initial confidence score (degree of mine-likeness) by a pre-classifier.

- The **detection fusion module** merges contacts from the detectors so that a seafloor object is reported only once for each time it is observed by the sonar. A fused contact is discarded if it's merged confidence score is below a user defined threshold.
- The **classification module** is based on template matching of the contacts from the fusion module. The sonar response of each contact is compared to a set of reference images covering all relevant targets types and orientations at the given sonar range and altitude. The match values and other extracted feature values of the contact are input to a classifier that assigns confidence scores for each target class, including a non-target (clutter) class.
- The **multi-view fusion module** merges the classification results from multiple sonar observations (different survey lines) of the same object.

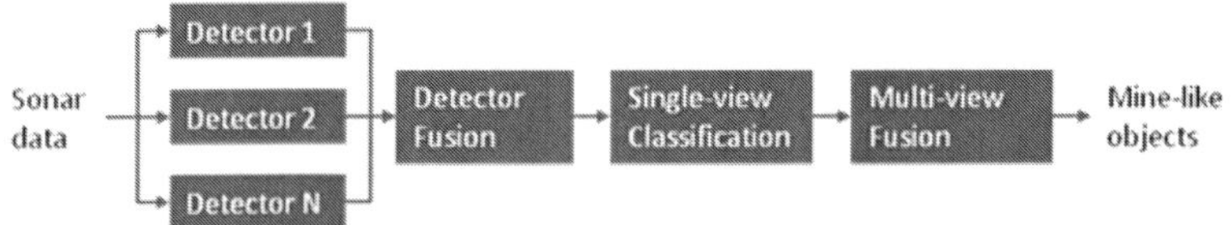

Figure 1: SITAR processing flow.

SITAR outputs a text file with the positions and confidence scores for the detected and classified objects. Mug shot files of the objects' sonar response can optionally be exported. The same text file format is also used to transfer results between the various SITAR modules. This provides well-defined and simple module interfaces and makes it simple to replace one module with another module based on a different algorithm. The configuration parameters of the detectors, fusion and classifier are specified in a set of text files.

SITAR can be operated in different modes, either in-mission or post-mission. The post-mission version is implemented both integrated into the HUGIN post-mission analysis system and as a stand-alone system. The processing is configured and monitored through a graphical user interface (Fig. 2). The in-mission version is implemented on the HUGIN payload processor and operates in delayed real-time. This allows the AUV to adapt its behavior based on the recorded sonar data (Fig. 3). The AUV may for example use SITAR to detect and classify mine-like objects in sonar data being collected from an area and then re-plan the last part of the mission to pass above these objects for identification at low altitude with optical camera. Contact positions and classification confidences can also be transmitted to the host vessel over acoustical or radio (when surfacing) links.

Figure 2: Graphical user interface for post-mission SITAR processing.

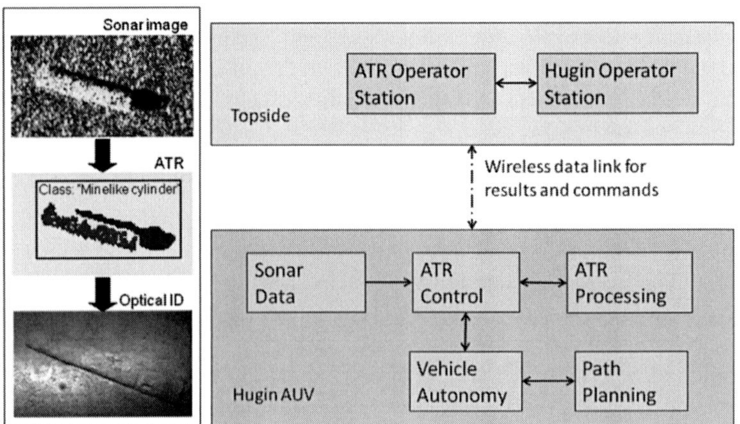

Figure 3: Left: In-mission ATR and identification concept. Right: ATR implementation on HUGIN AUV.

CONTRIBUTORS

Andreja Abina	Jožef Stefan International Postgraduate School, Jamova 39, SI-1000, Ljubljana, Slovenia	andreja.abina@mps.si
Ivan Aleksi	Faculty of Electrical Engineering, Josip Juraj Strossmayer, University of Osijek, Kneza Trpimira 2b, HR-31000, Osijek, Croatia	ivan.aleksi@etfos.hr
Ayman Alfalou	Département Vision L@bISEN, ISE, 20 rue Cuirassé Bretagne, 29228 Brest Cedex 2, France	ayman.al-falou@isen.fr
Stuart Anstee	Defence Science & Technology Organisation, PO Box 44, Pyrmont NSW 2009, Australia	stuart.anstee@dsto.defence.gov.au
Andreas Arnold-Bos	General Sonar Studies, Thales Underwater Systems, Route de Sainte Anne du Portzic, CS 43814, 29238 Brest Cedex, France	andreas.arnold-bos@fr.thalesgroup.com
Brian Bourgeois	Naval Research Laboratory, 1005 Balch Boulevard, Stennis Space Center, MS 39529, USA	brian.bourgeois@nrlssc.navy.mil

Timo Bretschneider	Real Time Embedded Systems, EADS Innovation Works, 110 Seletar Aerospace View, Singapore 797562, Republic of Singapore	timo.bretschneider@eads.net
Pavel Cevc	Department of Condensed Matter Physics, Jožef Stefan Institute, Jamova 39, SI-1000, Ljubljana, Slovenia	pavel.cevc@ijs.si
Philip Chapple	Defence Science & Technology Organisation, PO Box 44, Pyrmont NSW 2009, Australia	philip.chapple@dsto.defence.gov.au
Farid Chati	Laboratoire Ondes et Milieux Complexes, LOMC UMR CNRS 6294, Normandie Université, Université Le Havre, Place Robert Schuman, 76610 Le Havre, France	farid.chati@univ-lehavre.fr
Nicolas Cité	Normandie Université, ULH, LOMC UMR 6294 CNRS, Le Havre, France	
Michel Couillard	Centre for Maritime Research and Experimentation, Viale San Bartolomeo 400, La Spezia 19126 (SP), Italy	couillard@cmre.nato.int

Oliver Daniell	Ocean Systems Laboratory, Heriot-Watt University, Edinburgh Campus, EH14 4AS, Edinburgh, Scotland, UK SeeByte Ltd, Orchard Brae House, 30 Queensferry Road, EH4 2HS, Edinburgh, Scotland, UK	ojd5@hw.ac.uk
Dominique Décultot	Laboratoire Ondes et Milieux Complexes, LOMC UMR CNRS 6294, Normandie Université, Université Le Havre, Place Robert Schuman, 76610 Le Havre, France	dominique.decultot@univ-lehavre.fr
Fabrice Druaux	Groupe de Recherche en Électronique et Automatique du Havre, Normandie Université, Université Le Havre, 26 Rue Ph. Lebon 76600, Le Havre, France	fabrice.druaux@univ-lehavre.fr
John Dubberley	Naval Research Laboratory, 1005 Balch Boulevard, Stennis Space Center, MS 39529, USA	john.dubberley@nrlssc.navy.mil
Stéphanie Dupré	IFREMER Institut Français de Recherche pour l'Exploitation de la MER, Technopôle Brest-Iroise, 29280, Plouzané, France	stephanie.dupre@ifremer.fr

John A. Fawcett	Mine Warfare Group, Defence R&D Canada, PO Box 1012, Dartmouth, Nova Scotia, B2Y 3Z7, Canada	john.fawcett@drdc-rddc.gc.ca
Tai Fei	IWSS, University of Applied Sciences Bremen, Neustadtstadtswall 30, 28199, Bremen, Germany	tai.fei@hs-bremen.de
Julien Ferrand	Thales Underwater Systems, Route de Sainte Anne du Portzic, Site Amiral Nomy, CS 43814, 29238, Brest Cedex 3, France	julien.ferrand@fr.thalesgroup.com
Olivier Ferrante	BEA Bureau d'Enquête et d'Analyses, France	
Andrew Gong	Faculty of Engineering & Information Technologies, University of Sydney, NSW 2006, Australia	agon6326@uni.sydney.edu.au
Devendra Goyal	Mechanical Engineering, National University of Singapore, 21 Lower Kent Ridge Road, Singapore 11907, Republic of Singapore	devendra@nus.edu.sg
Raymond Guillou	SHOM Service Hydrographique et Océanographique de la Marine France	guillou@shom.fr
Roy E. Hansen	Norwegian Defence Research Establishment (FFI), P.O. Box 25, N-2027 Kjeller, Norway	roy-edgar.hansen@ffi.no

Anton Jeglič	Faculty of Electrical Engineering, University of Ljubljana, Tržaška cesta 25, SI-1000, Ljubljana, Slovenia	anton.jeglic@fe.uni-lj.si
Aleksander Klauson	Department of Mechanics, Tallinn University of Technology, Ehitajate tee 5, 19086, Tallinn, Estonia	aleksander.klauson@ttu.ee
Dieter Kraus	IWSS, University of Applied Sciences Bremen, Neustadtstadtswall 30, 28199, Bremen, Germany	dieter.kraus@hs-bremen.de
Dimitri Lefebvre	Groupe de Recherche en Électronique et Automatique du Havre, Normandie Université, Université Le Havre, 26 Rue Ph. Lebon 76600, Le Havre, France	dimitri.lefebvre@univ-lehavre.fr
Fernand Leon	Laboratoire Ondes et Milieux Complexes, LOMC UMR CNRS 6294, Normandie Université, Université Le Havre, Place Robert Schuman, 76610 Le Havre, France	fernand.leon@univ-lehavre.fr
Pierre Léon	IFREMER Institut Français de Recherche pour l'Exploitation de la MER, Technopôle Brest-Iroise, 29280, Plouzané, France	pierre.leon@ifremer.fr

Isabelle Leonard	Département Vision L@bISEN, ISE, 20 rue Cuirassé Bretagne, 29228 Brest Cedex 2, France	isabelle.leonard@isen.fr
Benoit Loubrieu	IFREMER Institut Français de Recherche pour l'Exploitation de la MER, Technopôle Brest-Iroise, 29280, Plouzané, France	benoit.loubrieu@ifremer.fr
Nicolas Mandelert	Thales Underwater Systems, Route de Sainte Anne du Portzic, Site Amiral Nomy, CS 43814, 29238, Brest Cedex 3, France	nicolas.mandelert@fr.thalesgroup.com
Gérard Maze	Laboratoire Ondes et Milieux Complexes, LOMC UMR CNRS 6294, Normandie Université, Université Le Havre, Place Robert Schuman, 76610 Le Havre, France	gerard.maze@univ-lehavre.fr
Herman Midelfart	Norwegian Defence Research Establishment (FFI), P.O. Box 25, N-2027, Kjeller, Norway	herman.midelfart@ffi.no
Øivind Midtgaard	Norwegian Defence Research Establishment (FFI), P.O. Box 25, N-2027, Kjeller, Norway	oivind.midtgaard@ffi.no
Vincent Myers	Mine Warfare Group, Defence R&D Canada, PO BOX 1012, Dartmouth, Nova Scotia, B2Y 3Z7, Canada	vincent.myers@drdc-rddc.gc.ca

Gregory Packard	WHOI Woods Hole Oceanographic Institution, USA	gjpackard@whoi.edu
Pedro Patron	SeeByte Ltd, Orchard Brae House, 30 Queensferry Road, EH4 2HS, Edinburgh, Scotland, UK	pedro.patron@seebyte.com
Yvan Petillot	Heriot-Watt University School of Engineering and Physical Sciences, Riccarton Campus EH144AS Edinburgh, United Kingdom	y.r.petillot@hw.ac.uk
Delphine Pierre	IFREMER Institut Français de Recherche pour l'Exploitation de la MER, Technopôle Brest-Iroise, 29280, Plouzané, France	delphine.pierre@ifremer.fr
Uroš Puc	Jožef Stefan International Postgraduate School, Jamova 39, SI-1000, Ljubljana, Slovenia	uros.puc@mps.si
Michael Purcell	WHOI Woods Hole Oceanographic Institution, USA	mpurcell@whoi.edu
Isabelle Quidu	ENSTA Bretagne, Ocean Sensing and Mapping Team, Lab-STICC UMR CNRS 6285, 2 rue François Verny, 29806 Brest Cedex 9, France	isabelle.quidu@ensta-bretagne.fr
Raphael D. Rajaona	Normandie Université, ULH, LOMC UMR 6294 CNRS, Le Havre, France	raphael.rajaona@univ-lehavre.fr

Scott Reed	SeeByte Ltd, Orchard Brae House, 30 Queensferry Road, EH4 2HS, Edinburgh, Scotland, UK	scott.reed@seebyte.com
Jamil Sawas	Heriot-Watt University School of Engineering and Physical Sciences, Riccarton Campus EH144AS Edinburgh, United Kingdom	jamil.sawas@hw.ac.uk
Andrew Sherrell	WHOI Woods Hole Oceanographic Institution, USA	
Karan R. Shetti	Real Time Embedded Systems, EADS Innovation Works, 110 Seletar Aerospace View, Singapore 797562, Republic of Singapore	karan-rajendra.shetti@eads.net
Yaya Sidibé	Groupe de Recherche en Électronique et Automatique du Havre, Normandie Université, Université Le Havre, 26 Rue Ph. Lebon 76600, Le Havre, France	yaya.sidibe@univ-lehavre.fr
Nicolas Valeyrie	Ocean Systems Laboratory, Heriot-Watt University, Edinburgh Campus, EH14 4AS, Edinburgh, Scotland	
Julien Van de Loock	Normandie Université, ULH, LOMC UMR 6294 CNRS, Le Havre, France	julien.van-de-loock@univ-lehavre.fr

José Vasquez	SeeByte Ltd, Orchard Brae House, 30 Queensferry Road, EH4 2HS, Edinburgh, Scotland, UK	jose.vasquez@seebyte.com
David P. Williams	Centre for Maritime Research and Experimentation, Viale San Bartolomeo 400, La Spezia 19126 (SP), Italy	williams@cmre.nato.int
Weizhen Zhou	Defence Science & Technology Organisation, PO Box 44, Pyrmont NSW 2009, Australia	weizhen.zhou@dsto.defence.gov.au
Aleksander Zidanšek	Jožef Stefan International Postgraduate School, Jamova 39, SI-1000, Ljubljana, Slovenia Department of Condensed Matter Physics, Jožef Stefan Institute, Jamova 39, SI-1000, Ljubljana, Slovenia Faculty of Natural Sciences and Mathematics, University of Maribor, Koroška cesta 160, SI-2000, Maribor, Slovenia	aleksander.zidansek@mps.si